DANTE'S AMERICAN PILGRIMAGE

PUBLISHED ON THE SOPHIE HART FUND

OF WELLESLEY COLLEGE

DANTE'S
AMERICAN PILGRIMAGE

A Historical Survey of
Dante Studies in the United States
1800 - 1944

By

ANGELINA LA PIANA, Litt.D.

NEW HAVEN

PUBLISHED FOR WELLESLEY COLLEGE BY

YALE UNIVERSITY PRESS

LONDON · GEOFFREY CUMBERLEGE · OXFORD UNIVERSITY PRESS

1948

PREFACE

IN A book written for Italian readers (*La Cultura americana e l'Italia* [Torino, 1938]), I sketched the history of the growth of a knowledge of Italy and Italian literature in America during the nineteenth century. Dante and American studies on his life and his works were omitted from that picture because they could be more adequately treated in a separate monograph.

The great vogue enjoyed by Dante after the eighteenth century in the two English-speaking countries, England and America, was described by James Bryce as an almost unique "literary phenomenon." This phenomenon is more striking in America than in England, for American cultural history is more recent and American intellectual life, spiritual experience, and social ideals are far removed from those of the Middle Ages, of which Dante is the most genuine exponent. The question why and how Dante, in spite of his medievalism, has appealed so strongly to the modern American mind and has awakened so much interest among American scholars has been raised again and again by students and lovers of Dante in this country. Various explanations have been offered; we shall let American Dantists speak for themselves.

As its title suggests, this book is intended to be a historical survey of the rise and growth of Dante studies—whether of a popular or of a scholarly nature—in this country. It is not an attempt to trace and analyze the influence, if any, that Dante the poet and the thinker may have exerted on American poets and thinkers, or on American literature in general. Such a task must be undertaken by some scholar more competent in American literary history than the present writer can claim to be.

In tracing the origins of Dante studies in this country, more space has been given to the first American essays on this subject than their merits would seem to justify. It is true that they possess no scholarly merit and have no place in Dante literature as a whole. They do, however, represent the first grafting of a new intellectual element upon American cultural life, and as such they deserve some attention. Moreover, the fact that these essays are scattered through the pages of many old and forgotten periodicals published in the various sections of the United States, adds something to their relative value as an index of the gradual geographical expansion of new cultural interests and traditions in nineteenth-century America.

The transition from the amateur to the scholarly stage of Dante studies began in the last decades of that century, a period that marked a turning-point in the political, social, economic, and cultural history of America. Dante studies form an integral part of the history of the rise and growth of modern American scholarship and reflect the ideas, methods, and tendencies of the new American cultural development.

In a survey of this new literature on Dante it seemed essential not to overlook the judgments passed by American literary critics upon books and essays on his life and works as well as upon American translations of his poetry. Book reviews written by competent scholars are a very valuable index to the level of scholarship of a given period, while those written by professional literary critics who cater to the general public reflect the tastes and cultural interests of the country at large. Occasionally reviews of American books by foreign critics have been quoted, thus providing material for useful comparisons.

American translations of Dante's works, especially of the *Divine Comedy* and the *Vita Nuova,* hold a conspicuous place in this survey, not only because of the intrinsic value of some of them as works of art, but also because of the significance of the fact that so many translators have vied with one another to make Dante's poetry—its artistic charm, its peculiar rhythmic structure, and its medieval vision of life—more accessible to the large American reading public. One more reason for a detailed survey of these translations was suggested by the fact that, during the debates and controversies concerning the best method of rendering Dante into English, the fundamental problems of Dante criticism came under consideration, first by implication, and then more directly.

In current histories of American intellectual life Dante studies, when mentioned at all, are usually identified still with the names of the Cantabrigian triad, Longfellow, Lowell, and Norton, giving the impression that theirs was the "classical age" of Dante in America, and that little or nothing worth mentioning has been accomplished in this field in more recent times. Few in this country and still fewer abroad seem to be aware that more and better translations of the *Divine Comedy* and more and better scholarly works on Dante than those of the preceding period have seen the light in America during the first decades of the present century. Historical and spiritual biographies of Dante, new researches on his symbolism, new philological and exegetical studies on special aspects and problems of his works, even new ventures in Dante criticism, and, last but not least, new and original explorations in the subject of Dante iconography now form a body of American Danteana that stands well the comparison with those of the same period in other countries.

In writing this book it has been my purpose to give a more adequate and, as far as possible, a complete picture of Dante studies in America which, without disparaging in any way the pioneer work done in the nineteenth century, should do justice also to the work done by more recent American Dantists. A second and more ambitious aim has been that of providing American historians with the material for a new and, in my opinion, interesting chapter in the history of American culture. With this purpose in mind I have tried to set this survey of Dante studies in the United States against the historical background of certain aspects of American cultural life.

I wish to express my deep gratitude to those who have given so generously of their time and labor to assist me while working on this book, and first of all to my brother, Professor George La Piana of Harvard University, who with unfailing kindness has discussed with me many of my problems and has been my constant adviser and most severe critic throughout the preparation and the extension of these pages. Without his assistance, which at times in dealing with historical-religious points of detail became almost a collaboration, this book could not have attempted to achieve such completeness at it may have. To Professor Kenneth McKenzie, now the dean of Dante scholars in America, who read the whole manuscript, I am heavily indebted for corrections, constructive criticisms, and valuable suggestions which helped me greatly in the last revision of my work. Mrs. Josephine M. Setton was my faithful assistant and my patient critic in the painstaking revision of these pages from the point of view of language and style. My thanks go also to Professor Arthur M. Schlesinger of Harvard University, to Professor Elizabeth Manwaring of Wellesley College, and to my Wellesley colleagues, members of the Committee on Publications, for their many helpful suggestions and criticism, to Mrs. Charles S. Singleton and Professor Kenneth M. Setton for their assistance in going over the proofs, and to Miss Kathleen Elliott of Wellesley College for her valuable help in the compilation and the revision of the Index.

I owe a debt of deep gratitude to the Trustees of Wellesley College for making this publication financially possible, to President Mildred McA. Horton of Wellesley College and to the members of the Committee on Research for the grant of a subsidy to meet the expenses incurred in collecting the material and in preparing the manuscript for the press, and to Dean Ella Keats Whiting, who has done so much to make possible the appearance of this book in the series of publications of Wellesley College. Lastly, I wish to express my appreciation and my thanks to the Librarian and members of the staff of the Wellesley College Library, and to the Librarians and the staff of Widener Library and of the Hutton Library in Harvard University, for their kindness in assisting me in my bibliographical research.

ANGELINA LA PIANA

Wellesley, Massachusetts,
November 1, 1946.

BIBLIOGRAPHICAL NOTE

THE existence of excellent old and new American bibliographies concerned with Dante and his works makes it unnecessary to burden this book with complete bibliographical lists merely for the sake of unessential completeness. It is hoped, however, that no work worth mentioning has been overlooked. The only general treatment of the subject to almost the end of the nineteenth century is the now fifty-year-old work of Theodore W. Koch, *Dante in America,* published in the *Annual Report of the Dante Society,* Cambridge, Mass., for the year 1896, and reprinted as a separate volume (Boston, 1896). In a long introduction Koch made a survey of the writings on Dante and of the activities in behalf of Dante studies in America by Lorenzo da Ponte, George Ticknor, Richard H. Wilde, Henry W. Longfellow, Thomas W. Parsons, James Russell Lowell, and Charles Eliot Norton. In dealing with them Koch, as he says in his preface, seldom ventured "beyond the limits of simple narration," because "so much has been said by others, and some of it so admirably said," that he had nothing to add. Hence he referred those who were seeking further criticism to the works listed in his bibliography.

Koch's bibliography is arranged chronologically (1807–96), giving the titles of books and articles with the usual indications as to the date and place of publication. Often he listed also book reviews which appeared in periodicals, but with no further indication of their content. In general, he refrained from expressing any opinion as to the value of books and essays included in his bibliography. A continuation of it to the year 1908 was compiled by Ethel Dane Roberts ("American Dante Bibliography, May 1896–May 1908") and published in the *Report of the Dante Society* for 1909 (Boston, 1910).

The sources of these bibliographies were primarily the Indexes of the *North American Review* (Bostonian period, 1815–78), the *Atlantic Monthly* (from 1857), the *Nation* (from 1867), and several other old American periodicals of the nineteenth century which not only published articles, essays, and notes on and translations from Dante, but in their book reviews and summaries of current literary events kept the American public informed on all publications on this subject which appeared in America.

In the following period they were superseded as sources of Dante bibliography by the new learned American periodicals of philological and literary studies, such as the *Publications of the Modern Language Association, Modern Language Notes,* the *Romanic Review,* and several others, as well as the many collections of studies in modern languages and literatures published in series by American universities and colleges. Since 1924, *Italica: Quarterly Bulletin of the American Association of Teachers of Italian,* has published regularly in each issue bibliographies of new publications in the field of Italian studies in America, compiled for many years by J. E. Shaw, continued by J. C. Fucilla, C. S. Singleton, and now by V. Luciani. In these bibliographical lists all the American publications on Dante of these last decades are not only mentioned, but often summarized and occasionally reviewed.

The *Annual Report of the Dante Society* (since 1882) published for several years general Dante bibliographies compiled by William C. Lane, and lists of additions to the Dante Collection in the Harvard Library. These general bibliographies were later discontinued because of the appearance of new and more complete current bibliographical lists and surveys in such periodicals as the *Bullettino della Società Dantesca Italiana* and other journals dedicated exclusively to Dante studies. An interesting list of "Forgotten Danteana" was published by J. C. Fucilla (*Publications of the Dante Society,* 1938).

The catalogues of the various Dante collections in American libraries, such as T. W. Koch's *Catalogue of the Dante Collection presented to Cornell University by Willard Fiske* (2 vols. Ithaca, N. Y., 1898–1900), and its *Additions* (1898–1920), by Mary Fowler (Ithaca, N. Y., 1921); *The Dante Collection of Harvard College Library and the Boston Public Library,* by W. C. Lane (Boston, 1890), and the additional lists in the periodical issues of *Library Notes* of the Harvard Library; as well as the catalogues of other valuable collections acquired during these years by several universities, colleges, and public libraries in America, show how large and exhaustive is the bibliographical material on Dante now available in this country.

On the subject of Dante in America in general, apart from Koch's book, there are only a few articles, lectures, or chapters in books— mostly mere summaries—providing now and then some useful information. Such are: Giacomo Boni, "Studi danteschi in America," *Rivista d'Italia,* January, 1898; a review of Koch's book, reprinted with additions in *Nuova Antologia,* July, 1921; Charles Grandgent, "Il Contributo americano agli studi danteschi," *Lectura Dantis* given before the Società Dantesca Italiana in Florence, *Giornale dantesco,* XVIII (1910); Emilio Goggio, "Dante Interest in 19th Century in America," *Philological Quarterly,* I (1922); "The Teaching of Dante in America," *Modern Language Journal,* VIII (1924); Howard Marraro, "Pioneer Italian Teachers in the United States," *Modern Language Journal,* XXIII (1944); Alice Galimberti, *Dante nel pensiero inglese* (Florence, 1921), chap. xv, "Gli americani," pp. 251–268; Michele Renzulli, *Dante nella letteratura inglese* (Florence, 1925), chap. xxvi, "Dante in America," pp. 141 ff. and a few other summaries of the same general character published in England and Germany.

The special bibliography on individual Dante scholars and on the various aspects and problems of Dante studies in America will be found in the notes.

ABBREVIATIONS

Atl. Mo.	*Atlantic Monthly*
BSDI	*Bullettino della Società Dantesca Italiana*
CAI	A. La Piana, *La Cultura americana e l'Italia* (1938)
Cambridge Hist. of Am. Lit.	*Cambridge History of American Literature*
DA	T. W. Koch, *Dante in America* (1896)
DEL	Paget Toynbee, *Dante in English Literature from Chaucer to Cary* (1909)
Dict. of Am. Biography	*Dictionary of American Biography*
GSLI	*Giornale storico della letteratura italiana*
Italica	*Italica: Quarterly Bulletin of the American Association of Teachers of Italian*
Mod. Lang. J.	*Modern Language Journal*
Mod. Lang. N.	*Modern Language Notes*
Mod. Lang. Rev.	*Modern Language Review*
Mod. Phil.	*Modern Philology*
NAR	*North American Review*
Phil. Quart.	*Philology Quarterly*
PMLA	*Publications of the Modern Language Association of America*
Rep. Dante Soc.	*Annual Report of the Dante Society,* Cambridge, Mass.
Rom. Rev.	*Romanic Review*
Speculum	*Speculum, A Journal of Mediaeval Studies*
Stud. in Phil.	*Studies in Philology*

NOTE TO THE READER

The English form *Divine Comedy* which is so familiar to all American readers is used throughout this book in preference to the Italian form *Divina Commedia*. Vice versa, the Italian *Vita Nuova* which now seems to be preferred by American and English writers, perhaps because the English *New Life* does not convey to many the exact shade of meaning of the Italian, has been preferred here too. In quotations from books and articles the form, either English or Italian, used in the source has been preserved. *Convivio* is now the accepted title of Dante's *Banquet* and is used here, but the form *Convito,* common to the writers of the nineteenth century, has not been changed in quotations from their works. The simplified English spelling adopted by Charles H. Grandgent ("rime" for "rhyme," "cherisht" for "cherished") has been respected in quotations from his books.

I am grateful to the following publishers for permission to quote passages from books edited by them as follows:

Harvard University Press:

Charles H. Grandgent. *The Ladies of Dante's Lyrics.* 1917.

George Santayana. *Three Philosophical Poets.* 1910.

Yale University Press:

Helen F. Dunbar. *Symbolism in Medieval Thought and Its Consummation in the Divine Comedy.* 1929.

Angelo Lipari. *The Dolce Stil Novo According to Lorenzo de' Medici.* 1936.

Princeton University Press:

James Shaw. *Essays on the Vita Nuova.* 1929.

F. J. Mather. *The Portraits of Dante, Compared with the Measurements of His Skull and Reclassified.* 1921.

Houghton and Mifflin Co., Boston:

Charles A. Dinsmore. *The Life of Dante Alighieri.* 1919.

John J. Chapman. *Dante.* 1927.

The Macmillan Co., New York:

Jefferson B. Fletcher. *The Divine Comedy of Dante Alighieri.* 1931.

CONTENTS

DANTE'S AMERICAN PILGRIMAGE

INTRODUCTION

THE AMERICAN BACKGROUND

IN A famous episode in the *Divine Comedy* (*Inferno*, XXVI, 70–143), Dante makes Ulysses tell how he met his death when in his old age, yielding once more to wanderlust, he set out with a few companions as old as himself on a last voyage of discovery. On a small ship they reached the Pillars of Hercules. Reminding his companions that men are made not to live as brutes, "but to seek after virtue and knowledge," Ulysses spurred them to dare and sail beyond the Pillars into the vast unknown ocean in search "of the unpeopled world behind the sun." They "made of their oars wings to the mad flight," and for five months ploughed the endless waters, bearing always to the left.

Finally they came within sight of a mountain which rose sharply out of the ocean. It was, according to Dante's geography, the mountain of Purgatory, at the antipodes of Jerusalem and the only land that emerged from the sea in the other hemisphere. They rejoiced, but were soon brought to grief when a sudden whirling blast swooped down upon their boat:

> Three times it made the boat and water spin,
> and at the fourth, lifted our stern amain,
> at Someone's beck, our stem went plunging in,
> Till over us the ocean closed again.[1]

Dante could not know that, following the direction he had chosen for them in their imaginary voyage, Ulysses and his companions would have landed eventually somewhere on the coast of South America. Nor could he dream that after the passage of centuries his *Divine Comedy* would be studied and translated in a

---

[1].   Tre volte il fe' girar con tutte l'acque
         alla quarta levar le poppe in suso,
         e la prora ire in giu', com' altrui piacque,
     Infin che il mar fu sopra noi richiuso.
                    (*Inferno*, XXVI, 139–142)
English version by C. H. Grandgent in his volume *Dante* (New York, 1916), p. 216.

new continent far beyond the Pillars of Hercules, or that his name would become a part of the cultural tradition of a new nation which was there to flourish in the distant future.

Unlike Ulysses, Dante did not come to America by way of the Pillars of Hercules. The keen interest in the Italian language and literature which had been so widespread in England at the time of the Renaissance but had died out at the end of the Elizabethan period flared up again during the last years of the eighteenth and the first decades of the nineteenth century. In this revival, however, Dante and his poetry, so much neglected and almost ignored in the English Renaissance, held the central place. The whole *Divine Comedy* was then translated for the first time into the English language. In this new dress it crossed the ocean and met its first American readers.

His was not a case of "come, see and conquer": Dante, like all immigrants from the Old World, had to wait patiently many years before winning slowly a place for himself in the new land. In 1843 Thomas W. Parsons published in Boston the first translation made in America of any considerable part of the *Divine Comedy: The First Ten Cantos of the Inferno*. Today there are over a dozen translations of the whole *Divine Comedy* or of one of its three parts made by Americans chiefly during these last decades. All that had been written in the United States about Dante a century ago were a few commonplace essays patterned after English models. Now America has a considerable Dante literature of its own. Books of a scholarly and general character, suggestive and at times brilliant essays, learned articles, and notes on Dante and his works have appeared steadily during the last two generations of American life. Dante studies have become an integral part of the American world of culture.

During the first decades of the nineteenth century the few readers and admirers of Dante's poetry were mostly gentlemen of culture or young people with cultural ambitions in Boston, New York, and occasionally Philadelphia. But after the 'thirties, in the "Flowering of New England," Dante found his chief devotees in the literary circles of Boston and then in the academic ranks of Harvard College. The *Divine Comedy* became a favorite with the

Brahmins, who did much to introduce the Italian poet to discriminating American readers.

A modern American school of literary criticism has turned rather bitterly against those old Bostonians as short-sighted, obstinate champions of a hollow romanticism, who, unresponsive to the life pulsating around them, made a fetish of antiquarian learning. In their scavenging among the ruins of a dead world they found Dante and the Middle Ages to toy with: "Translations and mediaeval scholarship were no better than remainder biscuits after a voyage"; "Lowell had nothing to say about Dante and said it with a great deal of verbal exertion." With their romantic clichés, far removed from the realities of life, with their Dante and their futile antiquarianism, they ended by being "a nation-wide nuisance." [2]

Other critics admit that such men as Longfellow, Lowell, and Norton performed a useful service to American culture by introducing the knowledge and study of several European languages and literatures, but in their opinion whatever was achieved in this activity does not concern the history of literature. According to one, Lowell's essays "have no structure," and

> He tells us nothing . . . on Dante which cannot be found better organized if not as warmly written in a dozen text books. Not in Lowell's day, it may be truly objected. Then these essays have a place in the technical history of education with which I have here nothing to do. They are in brief, able professorial exercises for undergraduates. [3]

Since essays and lectures on Dante's poetry are not "literature" but mere pedagogy, we are apparently to pity Lowell who, when made professor at Harvard, "turned bookman and for twenty-one years wandered with Norton and Longfellow in the Sahara of mediaeval scholarship." [4] These critics have been sharply rebuked by Bernard De Voto, who traces back their distorted vision of American cultural growth to the fact that they are victims of a deluding "literary fallacy." This fallacy consists in assuming that

---

2. Vernon L. Parrington, *Main Currents of American Thought;* I, *The Colonial Mind, 1620–1800* (New York, 1927); II, *The Romantic Revolution in America, 1800–1860* (New York, 1927); III, *The Beginning of Critical Realism in America, 1860–1920* (New York, 1930). These quotations are in order from III, 52; II, 466; III, 53.

3. Ludwig Lewisohn, *Expression in American Literature* (New York, 1932), p. 76.

4. Parrington, *op. cit.,* II, 465.

"a culture may be understood and judged solely by means of its literature, that literature embodies truly and completely both the values and the content of a culture, that literature is the highest expression of a culture, and that literature is the measure of life." [5]

Longfellow's translations and Lowell's essays, whether they are classified as literature or merely as professorial exercises, mark an important advance in the history of American culture. The "cosmopolitanism" of Longfellow and of other American writers, especially the New Englanders of his generation, can be appreciated at its full value only if we are aware "of the provincial quality of cultured America in those decades." [6]

At the beginning the new American interest in Italian literature, art and history in general, and in Dante in particular, was largely a reflection of the revival of Italian studies in England; but soon it became an expression of the urge felt by the American spirit to emerge from the relative intellectual isolationism of the past and, by plunging into the mid-stream of world culture, to enrich with new knowledge the cultural tradition derived from racial and historical connections with England.

To be seen in the right perspective, Dante's introduction to and his subsequent fortunes in America must be viewed in relation to the history of this American cultural evolution. The broadening of the cultural horizon which had taken place in eighteenth-century America under the influences of British philosophy and Deism and French Encyclopedism had much affected political and social thinking in this country and had found its highest expression in the spirit of the institutions of the new free America. The forces resulting in the establishment of political independence, the rise of a new consciousness of autonomy and self-sufficiency, as well as a widespread optimism concerning American material, moral, and intellectual resources, could not fail to strive for expression also in those forms of cultural life which are represented by literature and art. A proclamation of independence even in the fields of imagination and aesthetic creation was in order. Not a few Americans

5. Bernard De Voto, *The Literary Fallacy* (New York, 1944), p. 43.
6. Howard M. Jones, "Longfellow," *American Writers on American Literature,* John Macy, ed. (New York, 1931), p. 114.

thought that a new and original American literature and American art could be born simply by letting native American genius express its creative powers, untrammeled by any established models or by any influence from foreign sources. In their opinion American artists and writers, if they wished to attain originality of thought and expression, must shun any contact with the cultural traditions of the Old World and seek inspiration exclusively in the American scene and American life.

Had such theories prevailed over the antiquarianism and cosmopolitanism of many Boston literati to the point of excluding from the American educational system the study of foreign literatures and arts, American cultural growth would have been crippled from the very beginning. The counter-forces, however, were strong. Dante reached America in the midst of these controversies. The prospect of ever gaining a foothold in American cultural life appeared very slim for a poet whose massive thought was thoroughly medieval and whose art was heavily encumbered with allegory and with a strange mixture of pagan mythology and Christian theology. In fact, however, all the discordances and hesitations which then seemed so irksome to the American determination to find new channels of expression in literature and art were the signs of an exuberant vitality eager to experiment in all directions. There was plenty of room in that new America for both the old and the new.

The manifold aspects of American intellectual history in the first half of the nineteenth century have been described and analyzed in detail and from many points of view by American historians of literature and art and of social and political institutions.[7] For our purpose we need only mention certain features of that cultural life which may serve as a historical background to the introduction of Dante studies in America: the American periodicals, British influence on and criticism of American literary publications, the American reaction to and objections raised against foreign influences in literature and art, the rediscovery of Italian literature and history, and the new romantic interest in the Middle Ages.

7. For general guidance in the sea of American historiography, we have made extensive use of the volumes and bibliographies of the series *A History of American Life,* Arthur M. Schlesinger and Dixon R. Fox, eds. (12 vols. New York, 1929–44).

The great magazine era, in the modern sense, had not yet begun in America; but if we turn to the ponderous quarterlies of the first half of the nineteenth century, such as the *North American Review* of Boston (1815), the *American Quarterly Review* of Philadelphia (1827), the *Southern Review* of Charleston (1832), we cannot fail to be impressed by the variety of literary, historical, geographical, and scientific subjects dealing with foreign countries treated by their American contributors. Although most of these articles and essays are either simple expositions of the content of recent books or general descriptions of the life and cultural achievements of the past and of the present in many countries, they reveal the American eagerness to explore regions outside and beyond the British world. These periodicals are a valuable source of information for the history of the evolution of American culture in that period, for certain subjects the only source of information. This is the case with Dante studies. What those early American lovers of Dante appreciated most in his poetry, and why, can be learned primarily from the articles of these periodicals, especially from the *North American Review*. Apart from translations, no books on Dante were published in America before the second half of the century.

The reason for the importance of American periodicals in that period was well expressed by William H. Prescott, who remarked that periodical writing was more suitable to America's intellectual condition than it was to that of any country in Europe, because "although up to a certain point there is a more diffused and equal civilization here, yet here does not exist, as there, the depth of scholarship which leads men to take an interest in more laborious and erudite researches." [8] In addition, Prescott thought that "the more thoughtful periodicals," such as the *North American Review*, performed a distinct service to the nation not only "as invigorators of the patriotic principle," but also as a much-needed protection "against the blasts of foreign criticism, which swept too rudely over our young nurseries of literature."

This foreign criticism which blasted the young American literature came from England. Although the "more thoughtful" Ameri-

---

8. William H. Prescott, "English Literature of the Nineteenth Century," *North American Review*, XXXV (1832), 181 ff.

can periodicals were modeled after the English journals and although such literary traditions as America possessed and revered were British in origin and character,[9] the British critics had no good word to say for the new American literary products. The old-fashioned British periodicals, legitimate progeny of the *Tatler* and the *Spectator,* had degenerated, according to Prescott, into journals which "were devoted to analysis of modern publications but on the most frigid and spiritless principle, unenlivened by a single spark of philosophy or liberal speculation." [10] They looked down with scorn upon the new American literary upstarts, while other periodicals that championed more progressive ideas, such as the *Edinburgh Review,* belabored American writers for being old-fashioned and devoid of a truly American spirit.[11]

"The *Quarterly* reviles us, the *Edinburgh Review* sneers at us, *Blackwood* bullies us," wrote Alexander Hill Everett.[12] The *Edinburgh Review* summarized its opinion of American literature by saying that there were only two American writers: Irving, who was "deficient in nerve and originality," and whose best writings "were copies of our favorite English authors," and Cooper, who "labors under an epilepsy of the fancy." [13] The American periodicals in general and the *North American Review* in particular were denounced by the weekly *Edinburgh Scotsman* as being "woefully deficient in intellectual courage, in profound and original views, in lofty aims and in that love of truth and of mankind which atones for many errors and sanctifies the best efforts of the understand-

9. At that time young Prescott considered American literature as an integral part of the British: "Nourished as we are, from similar sources and subjected to a common discipline with English writers, our literature can only be a new variety of theirs." (*Ibid.*)

10. *Idem*, p. 185.

11. *The Edinburgh Review,* established in 1805 as a reaction to the existing stagnation, assumed from the beginning such an iconoclastic attitude as to shock all respectable Englishmen. "They stood aghast at the intrepidity with which these adventurers waged indiscriminate hostility, not merely against the smaller craft that infest the sea of literature, but those of the heaviest metal. Byron, Wordsworth, and Madame de Staël were denounced as literary misfits." (*Ibid.*)

12. "Tone of British Criticism. American Literature: An Article in the 99th Number of the *Edinburgh Review*," *NAR,* XXXI (1830), 22–66. "We are daily, weekly, monthly, and quarterly, from one year's end to the other, accused before these self-created courts of sundry high crimes, and misdemeanors, and to all these indictments we are regularly expected to plead guilty."

13. *The Edinburgh Review,* December, 1829; quoted in *ibid.*

ing." [14] The *Scotsman* deplored very much the fact that the Americans still believed in "the utility of classical literature as part of general education," taking upon their shoulders, from choice, "the load of prejudice and sophistry which is forcibly entailed upon us by our old establishment, and the feelings and interests which have grown out of them." [15]

This hostile British criticism, from both the right and the left, to which American writers were then as well as in later periods very sensitive, caused much pain and irritation to the editors of the *North American Review,* who thought that they were pilloried on flimsy pretexts. The long rebuttal of the British critics penned for the *North American Review* by Alexander H. Everett was filled with sarcastic professions of humility and guilt followed by sharp counterattacks, and concluded by asking whether the British derision of America was not "more like the petty spite of a faded beauty, who would gladly, if she dared, tear out the eyes of a younger rival, because she feels that their lustre eclipses that of her own." [16]

The irritation of the Bostonians of the *North American Review* can be easily understood. On the one hand the British critics were unnecessarily brutal and spiteful in their sweeping condemnation of new American literary efforts, and on the other hand the Americans were well aware that much of the British criticism was not wholly undeserved. They were not blind to the fact that newspapers, periodicals, and lecturers all over the country referred in glowing terms to a national American literature as if it were full grown or could be improvised at will after the fashion of the Hartford Wits. Meanwhile, the periodicals were but pale imitations when not outright copies of the British reviews; essay writers strove to become Addisons; poets followed in the footsteps of Pope and Gray when they were not trying to assume Miltonic proportions.

14. *The Scotsman;* quoted in *ibid.*
15. *Ibid.*
16. *Ibid.* Speaking of the British attack against the *North American Review,* Prescott, with raised eyebrows, remarked dryly: "The course pursued by our periodicals has generally, we may say indeed uniformly, been decorous and dignified, unstained by the vulgar party squabbles and brutal personalities, that disfigure the best of those in the mother country." (*Op. cit.,* p. 184.)

Only a few years before, in 1816, William Ellery Channing had published in the *North American Review* an article "On Models in Literature" in which, by way of reaction against the existing conditions, he advocated the intellectual isolationism of America as the only way to achieve originality in literature and art.[17] Channing was uncompromising. He condemned the training of young Americans in the classical or foreign literatures because such training had the result of destroying "the whole work and character of their genius." It made "man look at creation and society through another man's eyes"; it forced "all minds to one taste and pursuit" and it made "the difference of country, of habits, and institutions wholly ineffectual as to literature." Channing seems to scoff at learning:

Knowledge must now be drawn from libraries and collections. The difficulties of acquiring which were once encountered, are now done away, and with them the wholesome and invigorating labour . . . We have masters and schools at our very doors, to teach us everything . . . Here then is the very mischief of learning, the way to turn great men into confectioners and secondhand caterers.

Indeed, he goes so far as to say that it would have been better if the barbarians had destroyed all "the fair fabrics of Greece and Rome," rather than cause us "to grow tender among ruins and fragments." The remnants of the classical world are now but "a grave-yard . . . where the living from every land may come together." The charm of American literature must be "its nativeness"; "it should have nothing to do with strangers" unable to feel "the American pride in the splendid barbarism of the country, the hoarse and wild music of its forests and sea-shore." These should be the source of inspiration of American literature, "no matter for rudeness"; and Americans should be "unconcerned at the world's admiration or contempt."

Actually Channing, who was not a precursor of futurism, either did not mean to go as far as his rhetorical exaggerations implied or on maturer consideration of the problem, changed his views, for in his other essay, "Remarks on National Literature" (1823), he was

17. "On Models in Literature," *NAR*, III (1816), 202–209.

no longer the champion of isolationism.[18] He defined literature as "all the writings of superior minds, be the subjects what they may," and felt that the hour had struck for the emergence of "great minds among us." A national literature, while it is "the expression of a nation's mind in great writings," has a much wider sphere of action than the nation, because "literature is the concentration of intellect for the purpose of spreading itself abroad and multiplying its energies."

Channing then explains how all literatures have a universal and not merely a national value and are a common possession of all men. Mindful of his rash statements of 1816, he now tries to explain what he really meant: "Let us not be misunderstood. We have no desire to rear in our country a race of pedants, but we would have men explore antiquity . . . to learn its spirit as to accumulate on the present age the influences of whatever was great and wise in former times."[19] He also affirms: "We want the literary apparatus of Europe; her libraries, her universities, her learned institutions, her race of professed scholars." Still further: "We have no thought of speaking contemptuously of the literature of the old world. It is our daily nutriment. We feel our debt to be immense to the glorious company of pure and wise minds which in foreign lands have bequeathed us their choicest thoughts and holiest feelings."[20] And last but by no means least: "We earnestly recommend to our educated men a more extensive acquaintance with the intellectual labors of continental Europe. Our reading is too much confined to English books. In this we err . . . Nothing can favor more our own independence and vitality"[21] than to open new fields to American cultural life. This last sentence is of capital importance: it expresses clearly the psychological attitude of the best representatives of American intellectual life of the time and especially of the younger generation of New England, Edward Everett, George

18. W. E. Channing, *Works* (1st complete Amer. ed. Boston, 1841), I, 243–280: Address delivered before the American Philosophical Society in Philadelphia, October 18, 1823.

19. *Idem*, p. 259.
20. *Idem*, p. 269.
21. *Idem*, p. 276.

Ticknor, Jared Sparks, William H. Prescott, Henry W. Longfellow, and others.

Against the ultranationalists who clamored, like Channing in 1816, for a literature even rude and wild like the coasts of Maine, but virgin, like the American forests, of all contacts with strangers, they stressed the value of wide learning and comprehensive scholarship for the growth of a vigorous cultural life in America.[22] Against the blasting criticism of the British periodicals which, as we have seen above, continued to sweep over American literary efforts throughout the 'thirties and still later, they urged rebellion against the exclusive British domination of American culture by bringing in new currents of thought and art from the literatures of the European continent.[23]

There were, of course, other and more general reasons that spurred Americans to free themselves of all remnants of the old British tutelage; but as far as the realm of culture was concerned, the unfriendly and patronizing attitude of British literary circles contributed no little to quickening the American reaction and making many American scholars and men of letters turn eagerly to the treasures of other literatures. And there in the front line, towering above the others, stood Dante, whom the English themselves were

22. In a review of the *Memoirs* of the Italian orientalist Giovanni B. de Rossi (*NAR*, XXXV [1832], 194 ff.), Edward Everett warned American youth that "the sure path to learning and fame is best found out by looking into the lives of those who have travelled it farthest." Everett scorned "the Cleons of the day" who thought "that America could withdraw from the great literary games of the nations." The political freedom enjoyed by the Americans "gives us no immunity from those intellectual laws, which have made great effort necessary for great attainment. The forefathers and the heroes have done nothing to emancipate us from the burden of centuries of bookmaking; and not a constitution or charter from Maine to Florida has unlocked one of the dead languages."

23. Pierre du Ponceau in his pamphlet *On the Necessity and Means of Making Our National Literature Independent of That of Great Britain* (Philadelphia, 1834) urged Americans to rid themselves of their provincialism if they wished to create a national literature. They could not attain their goal by encouraging isolationism, a worse form of provincialism than could be laid at the door of the English, but by assimilating the great cultural traditions of the past and present and rethinking them in a new spirit. Du Ponceau had been a French officer in Lafayette's army and then a successful lawyer in Washington and a student of the languages of the American Indians. Most of his essays were published in the *Proceedings of the American Philosophical Society of Philadelphia,* of which he was president in 1828, and were reprinted in pamphlet form. See *Cambridge History of American Literature,* III, 448; *Dictionary of American Biography,* V (1930), 525–526 (contains no mention of his essay on American literature).

then glorifying as a great and universal poet. To Dante such Americans turned to discover new worlds of beauty and new horizons of thought and art. The New Englanders set his shrine next to those of Shakespeare and Milton, and to them Dante became almost a symbol of a new cultural cosmopolitanism cherished as the ideal to be attained by all America in the not distant future.

Meanwhile the movement which led so many American students to seek sound philological, philosophical, or historical training in European—especially German—universities had already begun. Other eager young Americans with artistic aspirations were already flocking to Florence, Rome, Venice, and Paris. The teaching of foreign languages and literatures was gaining ground as a normal part of a good education, and European travel, for those who could afford it, was considered indispensable to put the final polish on the training of those called to a life of literary or scientific activities.

The rediscovery of Italian literature by Americans, though it got its first impulse from England, was part of this general movement, which was strongest in New England but was not lacking in some other sections of the country. Some Bostonians were so favorably impressed by the new discovery as to rank Italian literature higher than the French. As early as March, 1817, Jared Sparks could write in the *North American Review:*

The passion for French, which many causes have concurred in exciting and keeping alive, seems to have excluded Italian from the catalogue of requirements necessary for an accomplished scholar. The few, whom inclination or accident has led to form an intimate acquaintance with the writers of Italy, have uniformly spoken of them in terms of admiration, and been struck with astonishment at the preference, which has been given by tacit consent, if not by direct avowal, to the French. It is generally allowed, by all adequate judges, that the Italian language is vastly better adapted to every species of composition, than the French; that it has more dignity and strength, a greater facility of expression, and infinitely more sweetness and harmony.[24]

The *North American Review* from the year it was founded (1815) to 1850 and the *American Quarterly Review* during the ten years of its existence (1827–37) published more essays, articles, and

24. "The Augustan Age in Italian Literature," *NAR*, IV, 309–327.

notes on Italian literature, art, and history than on those of France, Germany, or any other European country except England.[25] At a time when the extent of American interest in foreign literatures can be gauged only from the periodicals, the fact that the two reviews representing ambitious centers of American intellectual life, Boston and Philadelphia, assigned such an important place to Italian literature is very significant. By 1822 English translations of Dante, Petrarch, Ariosto, and Tasso had been reprinted in American editions. By 1850 English versions of one hundred and three Italian books, some of them reprints of translations already published in England, and others new versions made in this country, had come from the American presses.[26]

The *Divine Comedy* found favor with American men of letters not only as the great masterpiece of Italian literature and as great poetry having a spiritual and artistic value of universal significance, but also because it revealed to them the medieval world and its highest achievements in thought and art.

The Protestant Reformation had dismissed the Middle Ages as a long period of institutional and doctrinal deformity and decline in Christian history. By identifying its new religious experience with that of the early Church, Protestantism linked itself directly with ancient Christianity and dropped the intermediary period from the chain of history. In Europe, however, where monuments of the past rose on every side, where the Catholic Church stood rooted in centuries of unbroken medieval tradition, a complete obliteration of the Middle Ages could not take place as it did in America. Self-consciously Protestant, America as a nation was not then affected by the presence of small Catholic groups having neither social nor political importance.

The Puritan divines were usually isolated from all intellectual

25. William Cushing, *Index to NAR, I–CXXV (1815–1877)* (Boston, 1878). See under Italy, Italian Literature, Poetry, Fiction, Drama, Dante, Petrarch, and other names of Italian authors. It appears from this index that between 1815 and 1850 more than sixty articles dealing with Italian subjects were published in the *Review*, besides short notes and incidental discussions of Italian history and literature in essays dealing with other literatures or other countries. A partial list of these essays, together with those on Italian literature which appeared in the *American Quarterly Review*, may be found in A. La Piana, *La Cultura americana e l'Italia* (Torino, 1938), pp. 168 ff.

26. N. C. Shields, *Italian Translations in America* (New York, 1931).

contact with continental (especially Catholic) Europe, and in their contact with England usually confined their attentions to those theological and religious currents which coincided with their own thinking. Their interest in history, when they had any, was strictly local and was pursued with highly ecclesiastical prejudices and predilections. To them the most important event since New Testament times was the founding of New England, the new Canaan to which God had guided His people. In such a country it was possible to be unaware that a historical period called the Middle Ages had ever existed.

America of the eighteenth century was more occupied with making history than with writing it. Its political and social ideas found expression first in political revolutionary action, then in the establishment of institutions consistent with its faith in progress under a regime of liberty. Its thoughts were absorbed in the future. It was only with the advent of Romanticism that America made its first acquaintance with the Middle Ages.[27]

The picture of the medieval world which captured American attention was that set forth in English literature, in the sensational "Gothic" romances and in Walter Scott's novels, which "enchanted America after 1805." [28] This romantic picture of the Middle Ages took America by storm: "The inexperienced American imagination, starved at home of all traces of antique splendour, found itself most strongly stimulated by the most brilliant pageant of the romantic European past." [29]

The pageant was, however, more brilliant in color than firm in substance. It was more conspicuous for its sensationalism than for its historical reality. A more reliable guide than historical fiction was needed for a knowledge of the true medieval world. Americans found this guide in Dante, for his *Divine Comedy* was a striking

27. "The older America of Colonial days had been static, rationalistic, inclined to pessimism, fearful of innovation, tenacious of the customary . . . The America that succeeded was a shifting, restless world, youthfully optimistic, eager to better itself. . . . From it emerged, as naturally as the cock from the mother egg, the spirit of romance, gross and tawdry in vulgar minds, dainty and refined in the more cultivated. The days of realism were past, and it was quickly laid away with the wig and the small clothes of an outgrown generation." (Parrington, *op. cit.*, II, Introduction, iv.)

28. Van Wyck Brooks, *The World of Washington Irving* (New York, 1944).

29. Barrett Wendell, *A Literary History of America* (3d ed. New York, 1901), p. 271.

picture of medieval life, a key to medieval poetry and art, philosophy and theology, religious and political thought, and historical
and scientific lore. But Dante and his medieval world do not yield
easily to unprepared minds. *Lungo studio e grande amore* [30] are
the price that one must pay who wishes to penetrate the secret of
Dante's art and the essence of the medieval spirit, of which the
Divine Comedy is the highest expression. Many years of toil and
persevering effort had to pass before Dante and the Middle Ages
could gain the position which they now hold in American culture.

30. *Inferno,* I, 83.

CHAPTER I

DANTE COMES TO AMERICA

THE history of the fortunes of the *Divine Comedy,* marked as it is by alternating periods of great popularity and utter oblivion, is a significant index of the changes in philosophical, religious, and literary trends which have taken place from the late Middle Ages down to our time. Even in Italy, where Dante was always recognized as a great national poet, and where the *Divine Comedy* was always cherished, studied, and written about by faithful devotees, his works suffered long periods of general neglect.[1]

The *Divine Comedy,* so much admired by Dante's contemporaries and by the following generation for its poetry, as well as for its philosophical, theological, and scientific content, found little favor with most humanists of the fifteenth and sixteenth centuries. They were not blind to its poetic beauties and to its classical reminiscences, but the medieval world, of which the poem was the most elaborate synthesis, was no longer their own. Like the Gothic cathedrals, Dante's *Comedy* appeared to them to be tainted by a barbaric spirit, far distant from that of the classical tradition which they worshiped.

Literary criticism in the sixteenth century sneered at all poetic forms which did not fall within Aristotle's classifications. Critics and compilers of treatises on the art of poetry admired Dante's episodic poetical grandeur, but they reserved all their enthusiasm for the elegant rhymes of Petrarch and, later, for the smooth, transparent stanzas of Ariosto. As a whole, Dante was scholastic, obscure, "Gothic."

In the circles of the Counter-Reformation, Dante's memory was stained by his Ghibellinism, his invectives against the Papacy, and

1. Giosuè Carducci, "Della Varia Fortuna di Dante" (14th cent.), in *Opere,* VIII (Bologna, 1893). Also the essays of V. Rossi, "Dante nel trecento e nel quattrocento"; F. Flamini, "Dante nel cinquecento e nell'età della decadenza"; and others, in the volume *Dante e l'Italia* (Rome, 1921). Also M. Barbi, *Della Fortuna di Dante nel Sec. XVI* (Pisa, 1890).

his political theories expounded in *De Monarchia*. It was not until the late eighteenth century that the *Divine Comedy* emerged from its relative obscurity to take its place by universal consent among the great masterpieces of all literatures. Formerly, the eighteenth century was disparaged by Italian historians as an age of frivolous poets and ridiculous academicians, the century of Metastasio's *ariette*. Recent historians have come to regard it as a period of intense intellectual activity in all fields of learning, marking progress in thought and leading to the literary revival of its last decades, when Italy's cultural life began to be dominated more and more by a newly awakened national consciousness:

With the revival of patriotic pride arose the desire to emulate our great writers of old: this emulation became national and the Italians went back to the ancient models, to the models of the time when Italy was the teacher of the world.[2]

The Romantic Movement which followed swept gradually over the whole intellectual life of Europe, carrying in the wake of its new aestheticism a keen interest in the Middle Ages and consequently in Dante, the greatest exponent of medieval thought and poetry:

Pre-Romanticism and Romanticism advocated the canonization of Dante along two main directions of thought and taste. There was the curiosity for mediaeval lore and Christian poetry, which made of Dante worship a chapter of romantic historiography. There was also the enthusiasm for the individualist and genius, for Dante as pathfinder and hero of poetry.[3]

The irrepressible aspirations toward independence and political unity of the nation inspired and dominated the whole Italian literature of the Risorgimento. The cult of Dante assumed a patriotic, nationalistic character; he was made to appear as the prophet of a free, united Italy, the nation which in its turn was destined to lead the other countries of Europe in the path of freedom. According to Mazzini, "Dante's great soul foresaw that Italy should be the per-

2. Giosuè Carducci, "Del Rinnovamento letterario in Italia," in his volume *Prose*, a collection of studies and essays in a final revised edition (Bologna, 1904), p. 742.

3. G. A. Borgese, "On Dante Criticism," *Annual Report of the Dante Society* (Cambridge, Mass.), 1936, p. 19.

ennial initiator of the religious and social unification of Europe and the angel of civilization to the nations." [4] Thus Dante was proclaimed the prophet of Italian nationalism and at the same time the universal poet of European civilization.

With more respect for historical reality, Giosuè Carducci traced back to the early period the reason why the appeal of the *Divine Comedy* was not restricted to Italy and the Italians alone:

The poetry of the other peoples of Europe, who developed a national spirit much earlier than the Italian people did, was national in both form and content. The Nibelungen is a picture of the Germans of the migrations; the French romances sing the glories of Charlemagne's empire; the Spanish ones sing the struggle against the Arabs. Italian literature, as the nation itself, did not have any national content. The *Divine Comedy*, the *Canzoniere*, and the *Decameron* are in their content European, Christian, and universal, rather than only Italian . . . Mediaeval Italy lacked the consciousness of being a new nation; she considered herself the continuation of Rome, the capital of Europe. Hence, our poets were the poets of Christian Europe, of the whole Latin West . . . Dante bestowed Christian and classical consecration upon all the visions of the other world which were current in the British Isles, in Germany and in France; Petrarch closed the cycle of the Provençal, French, and German love poetry; Boccaccio gathered the pebbles of the fables, stories, and legends of jongleurs and jesters, and made of them a great Roman mosaic. What other nations had produced in fragments, in Italy became one harmonious living thing. The land of the Communes could not restrict itself within national exclusivism. Like her Roman ancestors with their arms, Italy and her art conquered all countries; like the Empire and the Church which bestowed Roman citizenship upon all bodies and souls, so Italy bestowed it upon all traditions and ideas, and clothed them with artistic form, and with a new social spirit, thus creating the universal literature of the Renaissance.[5]

Even so, while Petrarch's influence as the great model of lyric love poetry was felt immediately and continued for several centuries in all European literature, and Boccaccio's *Decameron* and his poems also found imitators and disciples everywhere, the *Divine Comedy,* though usually mentioned as a great poem, does not seem

---

4. Quoted in "Dante," article in *Enciclopedia italiana*, XII (Milan, Treccani, 1931), 345.
5. Carducci, "Dello Svolgimento della letteratura nazionale," *Prose*, pp. 344–345.

to have stirred literary circles in and outside Italy deeply enough to produce a school of Dantean poetry.[6]

The manner in which Dante fared in England is typical of the treatment he received throughout Europe.[7] Chaucer was well acquainted with the *Divine Comedy,* quoted passages from it, and made the first condensed paraphrase in English of the Conte Ugolino episode. But the English humanists who studied in Padua, Florence, and Rome, and imported the New Learning into England, do not seem to have taken any interest in Dante and his works.[8] During the Elizabethan period, when Italian literature and art were still exerting a great influence on English men of letters, and when even mediocre Italian writers were read and imitated by them, Dante was ignored. It would seem that his works were unknown to Shakespeare.

The name of Dante occurs here and there in English writings of that period, but no English author before Milton seems to have acquired any familiarity with his works. Milton read the *Divine Comedy,* the *Convivio* and *De Monarchia* even before his travels in Italy, and quoted passages from them in his treatise "Of the Reformation Touching Church Discipline in England" (1641).[9] Whether there are in the *Paradise Lost* imitations or reminiscences of the *Divine Comedy* may be questioned. At any rate, it is admitted

6. No translations of the *Divine Comedy* were made in European languages before the eighteenth century, with the exception of three Spanish versions and an insignificant French one in the fourteenth and fifteenth centuries. (*Idem,* p. 343.) For the course of Dante's fortunes outside Italy see the following: M. Besso, *La Fortuna di Dante fuori d'Italia* (Florence, 1912); A. Farinelli, *Dante in Spagna, Francia, Inghilterra, Germania* (Turin, 1922); G. A. Scartazzini, *Dante in Germania* (Milan, 1881–83); T. Ostermann, *Dante in Deutschland; Bibliographie der Deutschen Dante-Literatur, 1416–1927* (Heidelberg, 1929); Paget Toynbee, *Dante in English Literature from Chaucer to Cary (c. 1300–1844)* (London, 1909), and *Britain's Tribute to Dante in Literature and Art, 1380–1920* (Oxford, 1920); A. Counson, *Dante en France* (Erlangen, 1906); F. L. Cohen, *Dante in de Nederlandische Letterkunde* (Haarlem, 1929); G. Kaposy, *Bibliografia dantesca ungherese* (Budapest, 1921); S. P. Koczorowski, *Dante in Poland* (in Polish) (Cracow, 1921); Jukiki Oga, *Bibliografia dantesca giapponese* (in Italian) (Florence, 1930).

7. Paget Toynbee, *Dante in English Literature from Chaucer to Cary (c. 1300–1844)* (2 vols. London, 1909); exhaustive collection of all the passages of English writers and all references to Dante and his works in five centuries of English literature.

8. *Idem,* I, xix ff.; Lewis Einstein, *The Italian Renaissance in England* (New York, 1903), especially chap. iii, "The Traveller," and chap. viii, "The Italian Influence."

9. Toynbee, *DEL,* I, 124 ff.

that in a general way the *Divine Comedy* was one of the sources of Milton's inspiration.

From the middle of the seventeenth century on, interest in Italian literature waned in England altogether. In France, beginning with Boileau and reaching its height in Voltaire, literary criticism consigned all the great Italian poets, Dante particularly, to the limbo of mediocrity. British criticism followed eagerly the French leadership. According to the great Addison of the *Spectator,* all the literary works of "modern Italians" (by which he meant the whole literature in the Italian language from the very beginning) were such as only pedants could write: "They fill their writings with such poor imagination and conceit, as our youths are ashamed of before they have been two years at the University." Moreover, "if we look into the writings of the old Italians, such as Cicero and Virgil, we shall find that the English writers, in their way of thinking and expressing themselves, resemble those authors much more than the modern Italians pretend to do." [10] No wonder that most of the famous British authors of the eighteenth century—Fielding, Swift, Hume, Sterne, Johnson, and even Gibbon—either ignored Dante altogether or mentioned his name with disdain. The only exception was Thomas Gray, who turned the episode of the Conte Ugolino into English blank verse.[11]

The first signs of a reaction against the total proscription of Italian literature in England began to appear in the second half of the century. The former Elizabethan favorites, Ariosto and Tasso, were translated anew into English by John Hoole. William Huggins, who translated once more the *Orlando Furioso,* seems to have undertaken the task of rendering the *Divine Comedy* into English

10. The *Spectator,* No. 5 (Tuesday, 6 March), 1711. R. Marshall remarks: "In Addison's day Englishmen seem to have become more painfully aware than ever before, that they themselves, compared with most Europeans, were uniquely rich, uniquely enlightened, uniquely moral and uniquely free." (*Italy in English Literature* [New York, 1934], p. 12.)

11. Toynbee, *DEL,* I, xxxvii–xxxviii; Marshall, *op. cit.,* pp. 109 ff. Gray's translation was a juvenile and not very successful exercise done in Cambridge, probably in 1737, while he was studying Italian with Hieronimo Piazza, a teacher at the University. (Toynbee, *DEL,* I, 231.) According to Toynbee (I, 192), Pope had only an imperfect knowledge of the *Divine Comedy.*

for the first time; but his translation never appeared in print and does not exist in manuscript form.[12] In 1782 Charles Rogers (1711–84) issued anonymously a blank-verse translation of the *Inferno,* the first complete printed English version of a whole canticle of the *Divine Comedy.* Unfortunately this translation was neither faithful nor poetical.[13]

Henry Boyd (1750–1832), an Irish curate, was the author of the first English version of the whole *Divine Comedy* (*Inferno* [Dublin, 1785]; *Purgatorio* and *Paradiso* [1802]). Boyd's is really not a translation but a paraphrase in rhymed stanzas of six lines in which it is rather difficult to recognize Dante at all. Nonetheless, it was praised by the critics of the day, one of whom admired Boyd's method of "dilating the scanty expressions of Dante into perspicuous and flowing diction" (*Monthly Review,* March, 1805). Another observed that "the dullness of Dante is often enlivened by Boyd with profuse ornaments of his own, by which he is rather elevated than degraded" (*Critical Review,* March, 1803).[14] Even the *Edinburgh Review,* which was well known at that time for its severe handling of authors and books, bestowed lavish praise on the translation: "Boyd has done as much for Dante as can well be done in English rhyme; and is justly entitled to praise for the diligence and perseverance with which he has executed his laborious task" (January, 1803, pp. 207–313).[15]

12. Of Huggins' version only the short paraphrase of the *Pater Noster* (*Paradiso,* XL) was published in the *British Magazine.* (Toynbee, *DEL,* I, 307–308.)

13. Rogers was an art collector. In making this translation "he chiefly attended to giving the sense of his author with fidelity; the character of a poet not seeming to have been the object of his ambition." (Quoted by Toynbee, *DEL,* I, 383.)

Strange as it may seem at first, a new interest in Dante was awakened in England more by painters than by literary men. In 1719, Jonathan Richardson (1665–1792), portrait painter and author, published the first English translation of the Conte Ugolino episode. In 1773, Sir Joshua Reynolds (1723–92) exhibited at the Royal Academy in London his famous painting of Conte Ugolino and his children in the dungeon. This picture, as well as the drawings and paintings of Henry Fuseli, the illustrations of the *Divine Comedy* by John Flaxman, and Dante's portrait by William Blake, did more to familiarize·the English public with Dante's name than any literary work could have done. (See Paget Toynbee, "Dante in English Art," *Rep. Dante Soc.,* 1921.)

14. Toynbee, *DEL,* I, 410 ff.; Marshall, *op. cit.,* p. 316.

15. Years later, Charles Eliot Norton remarked that the more than favorable judgment of Boyd's translation on the part of the *Edinburgh Review* and its statement that no more could be done in English "affords a curious instance of the low state of English criticism at the period, for a more unsuccessful attempt at translation is hardly to be found." (*NAR,* CII [1866], 516.)

The famous biographies of William Roscoe (1753–1831), *The Life of Lorenzo dei Medici, Called the Magnificent* (1795), and *The Life and Pontificate of Leo the Tenth* (1805), had considerable influence in reviving interest in Italian history and literature: Roscoe's work pictured the Italian Renaissance so colorfully, thoroughly, and enthusiastically as to give it wide popularity first in England and then in America.

For the first time a large number of Englishmen were made to feel really at home in Italy's political, literary and artistic past. Four editions of his *Lorenzo* and two of his *Leo* were called for before 1815 and several of each afterwards. Once for all, Roscoe acclimatised Italy in England.[16]

From the standpoint of modern historical criticism, Roscoe's biographies, with their exaltation of the Medici as heroes of the republican spirit, and of Alexander VI, Julius II, and Leo X as Italian patriots who planned to free Italy from foreign domination, are a romantic travesty of history. Nevertheless, they did a great deal toward creating a strong current of sympathy for the political situation in Italy, a current which was to prove important during the Risorgimento. Of more interest to us here are the many pages which the author dedicated in both his books to the origins of Italian literature, to Dante, Petrarch, and Boccaccio. Some of his happy characterizations of Dante's poem, such as his assertion: "Compared with the Aeneid, the *Divine Comedy* is a piece of grand Gothic architecture at the side of a beautiful Roman temple," were constantly repeated and often elaborated upon by essayists and other writers on Dante.[17] Above all, Roscoe made Englishmen "want to learn still more about Italy and to lay down the lines along which such knowledge could be most effectively brought before the public." [18]

The best refutation of the *Edinburgh Review's* optimistic appraisal of Boyd's translation came when Henry F. Cary (1772–1844) published his blank-verse translation of the *Inferno* in 1805, and of the entire *Divine Comedy* in 1814. Cary's work attracted

16. Marshall, *op. cit.*, p. 272.
17. Tonybee, *DEL*, I, 527 ff.
18. Marshall, *op. cit.*, p. 285.

little attention at first. It was noted with contempt by the *Critical Review,*[19] and for several years lay dead and forgotten. But after Coleridge praised it in February, 1818, in his lecture "On the Meaning and the Importance of Dante's Works," it went rapidly through several editions.[20] England, which had welcomed Dante with such reluctance, became one of the countries contributing most to the study and understanding of the Florentine poet. With the exception of Scott, and in some measures Wordsworth, all the great English writers and poets of that and the following generation—Hazlitt, Byron, Shelley, Keats, Macaulay, Browning, Ruskin, Tennyson, and Carlyle—were great admirers and devoted students of Dante's works.

Cary's translation not only marked the turning-point of Dante's fortunes in England; it was also instrumental in introducing him to America. The oldest evidence that the *Divine Comedy,* or passages from it, were in the hands of American men of letters is a translation in heroic verse of part of the Conte Ugolino episode published in the *New York Magazine* in 1791 (II, 297–298) and signed W.D.[21] These were the initials of William Dunlap, the most versatile busybody in the intellectual and artistic life of New York in that period. A portrait painter, a playwright, a novelist and biographer, and a theater manager, he was known in after days as the "father of American drama" and also as the "American Vasari" because of his

19. "The study of the Italian language ranks so essentially among the accomplishments of the present day, that we apprehend those possessing the advantage of reading Dante in the original language, would never barter his chaste beauties, for the fanciful portrait of an English artist. The subject is sublime—not so the prevailing language of his translator." (*Critical Review,* 4th series, V [1814], 647; quoted by Toynbee, *DEL,* II, 157.)

20. Samuel Rogers in his *Recollections of the Table-Talks* stated that it was not so much Coleridge's lecture that established Cary's reputation as the "Essays on Dante" by Ugo Foscolo published in the *Edinburgh Review* the same year, 1818, in which Cary's version was very highly praised. This part of the essay, however, was not written by Foscolo, whose knowledge of the English language never progressed very far, but by Sir James Mackintosh, who translated into English Foscolo's Italian original, taking many liberties with it. Rogers also made further additions to it and claimed for himself the credit of having thus secured the fortune of Cary's version. (Toynbee, *DEL,* I, 466; II, 161; also Margaret C. W. Wicks, *Italian Exiles in London* [*1818–1848*] [London, 1937], p. 20.) Foscolo's essays on Dante and others on Italian literature were collected by Giuseppe Mazzini and edited in the four volumes of Foscolo's *Works* (London, 1842–43). These essays were widely read and much appreciated by American lovers of Dante.

21. Joseph G. Fucilla (*Italica,* VIII [1931], 40–41) was the first to note this passage and to identify the translator.

Lives of American Artists whom he had known intimately.[22] To all these laurels he added that of being the first to make and to publish in America a translation into English of a passage from the *Divine Comedy*.

In 1803 a group of literary-minded Boston gentlemen organized the Boston Anthology Club and issued a new periodical under the title *The Monthly Anthology and Boston Review, Containing Sketches and Reports of Philosophy, Religion, Art and Manners*. It existed until 1811. As its motto the review adopted the Latin verse: *Omnes undique flosculos carpam atque delibem*. Disgusted with "the democratic vulgarity" of American life and letters, the anthologists of Beacon Hill followed closely the English literary trends of the day. At the same time they "picked flowers" from other gardens and disclosed to their readers new lands of beauty, hoping thereby to raise the standards of American literary products.[23] The revival of Italian studies in England and especially Roscoe's biographies and their enchanting picture of Italy's artistic traditions did not escape their attention.[24]

One of those who took up the challenge was Benjamin Welles, a frequent contributor to the *Anthology*. His articles, dealing mostly with literary subjects, appeared under the general heading "Silva." He seems to have had some acquaintance with Italian and to have read the *Divine Comedy* in Boyd's translation. In the May issue of the *Anthology* for 1807, his "Silva" consisted of a four-column sketch of Dante's life together with a summary of the *Divine Comedy* containing three quotations from the *Inferno*, both in the original Italian and in Boyd's version.

William Tudor (1779–1830) may have acquired some knowledge of Italian while contributing to the *Anthology* essays which he later collected in his *Miscellanies* (1821). His prose sketch "The Prince

22. Brooks, *The World of Washington Irving*, chap. vii, "William Dunlap and His Circle," pp. 152 ff.

23. "The magazine, though somewhat staid in manner, decidedly starched and impersonal, was yet an enterprise that promised much. . . . In style it resembled the British reviews. . . . It abounded in Addisonian bric-a-brac, playful bits on toast, and cranberry sauce . . . The magazine was well informed." (Van Wyck Brooks, *The Flowering of New England* [New York, 1935].)

24. These biographies were in the hands of all the early American students of Italian, as we shall see when dealing with their articles in the *North American Review*.

of Power of the Air, A Vision," inspired both by Milton and by a passage in the *Purgatorio* (III, 28–97), bears witness to his study of the *Divine Comedy*.[25] Besides its articles on Italian subjects, the *Anthology* published for several years a series of letters from Europe, many of which came from Italy. Those dated from Florence are filled with reminiscences of Dante's life and of the *Divine Comedy*.

Translations, even good ones such as Cary's, were useful when they finally reached America only as a first step in the appreciation of a masterpiece of literature like the *Divine Comedy*. No true understanding of the art of a great poet is possible without a knowledge of the language in which he wrote. At the beginning of the nineteenth century, knowledge of Italian was rare in America. During the eighteenth century, there had been a few Italians who gave lessons, but they were generally musicians and seldom did more than teach young ladies to understand and pronounce correctly the words of songs and *ariette*.[26]

The first regular teacher of Italian of whom we have any knowledge was Carlo Bellini, who in 1779, through the good offices of his friend Filippo Mazzei, and on the recommendation of Thomas Jefferson, was appointed teacher of foreign languages at William and Mary. Bellini does not seem to have had much opportunity to further the study of Italian, however, and confined himself chiefly to French. After his resignation in 1803, his chair was left vacant.[27]

Lorenzo da Ponte (1749–1838) was the first to open a private school in which Italian was taught by a competent and effective teacher. Da Ponte came to New York in 1805, but it was not until late in 1807, after some unfortunate business ventures, that he established his "Manhattan Academy for Young Ladies and Gentle-

25. William Tudor was one of the founders and editors of the *Anthology*, the story of which he told in his *Miscellanies* (Boston, 1821), pp. 1–7. In 1815 he became the first editor of the *North American Review*. (*Infra*, Chapter II.)

26. On the scanty knowledge of Italy and the paucity of Italian books during the Colonial period and the early decades after the Revolution, see La Piana, *CAI*, pp. 20–40.

27. Howard H. Marraro, "Pioneer Italian Teachers of Italian in the United States," *Mod. Lang. J.*, XXXIII (1944), 555–582; On Mazzei see his biography by Richard C. Garlick, *Philip Mazzei, Friend of Jefferson, His Life and Letters* (Baltimore, Johns Hopkins Univ. Press, 1933); *Memoirs of the Life and Peregrinations of the Florentine Philip Mazzei*, trans. from the Italian by H. H. Marraro (New York, Columbia Univ. Press, 1942); also La Piana, *CAI*, pp. 54–64.

men" where he and his wife taught Latin, French, and Italian. That same year, he published in New York a short autobiography in Italian to which he appended the episode of Conte Ugolino from the *Inferno* and selections in prose and verse, together with English translations of them made, he said, by some of his pupils. This book, intended as a reader for Da Ponte's Italian classes, has the distinction of being the first in Italian to come from an American press.

Besides teaching, Da Ponte carried on a little business importing and selling Italian books; but in 1811 his affairs were in such bad shape that he gave up teaching, left New York, and settled in the village of Sunbury, Pennsylvania, where he opened a grocery store. As was usual with him, he became involved in debts and lawsuits. Finally he went bankrupt, and in 1819 he returned to New York to resume his teaching.[28]

Da Ponte, who had been reared in the humanistic tradition of Italian scholarship and was himself a poet of the Arcadian-Metastasian fold, worshiped Dante. He belonged to the generation which fought a long, hard battle against the denigration of Italian literature still surviving in some literary circles of France and England. Having spent most of his life outside Italy, in Austria, Germany, England, and finally in the United States, he felt strongly that it was his duty to defend Italian literature against all attack. And defend it he did, with the zeal of a crusader and the unbounded devotion of a knight-errant for the lady of his heart.

Da Ponte made his pupils, mostly girls from well-to-do families, read the *Divine Comedy* and memorize passages from it as soon as they were able to stumble through the nouns and verbs in their Italian grammar. For the rest of his long life he was very proud to have been, as he often said, the one who first introduced the study of Italian and Italian literature, especially Dante, into the New World. Yet, while Da Ponte was starting his school in New York, the Boston gentlemen of the *Anthology* were reading Dante with

28. The *Memoirs* of Da Ponte published in installments during his long residence in New York were reëdited and annotated by G. Gambarin and F. Nicolini in the series *Scrittori d'Italia* (2 vols. Bari, 1918). Two English translations of them appeared in 1929: one by L. A. Sheppard (Boston and New York); the other by Elizabeth Abbott (Philadelphia), with introduction and notes by A. Livingston, who wrote an excellent monograph on Da Ponte's American period (*Lorenzo Da Ponte, Poet and Adventurer* [Columbia Univ. Press, 1922]). See La Piana, *CAI*, pp. 87–96.

the help of Boyd's translation on Beacon Hill. And when Da Ponte was wasting his time in Sunbury, a young Sicilian, Pietro D'Alessandro, a political exile and romantic poet, settled in Boston and made a living by giving private lessons in his native tongue.[29] Shortly afterward he was joined by another Sicilian, Pietro Bachi, a man with an excellent cultural background, whom we shall meet again as the first instructor in Italian at Harvard College.

Thus, in the early decades of the nineteenth century, Dante had already found some American devotees on Beacon Hill and was about to cross the Charles River on his way to Harvard. In New York, then little more than a noisy, glorified village, the busy merchants who passed under the windows of the Manhattan Academy could hear the fresh, ringing voices of Da Ponte's girls declaim with zest: *"La bocca sollevò dal fiero pasto,"* and the voice of their teacher utter ecstatically his refrain: "Oh! Dante! Dante! *Il più gran poeta del mondo!"*

29. Antonio Gallenga (his real name was Filippo Mariotti), another political refugee, who later came to Boston and met D'Alessandro in 1836, in his *Episodes of My Second Life: English and American Experiences* (London, 1884, and Philadelphia, 1885), describes D'Alessandro as "a romantic poet author of tragedies and elegies. Exiled for political reasons, went in business and became vice-consul of a South American republic in Boston. He spent all the time that he could spare from his office in the teaching of languages. But he never divorced the Muses and published a poem in Italian blank verse under the title 'Mount Auburn' [Cambridge, 1835], a pathetic illustration of a garden-cemetery which forms the pride of the citizens of Boston. It is a poem modelled on the 'Sepolcri' of Ugo Foscolo, with some reminiscences from Gray's Elegy.' In his private conversation as in his writings he was much inclined to pessimism. He was always in love, and always without hope, but very eloquent in describing the beauties of New England's girls." (Philadelphia ed., p. 41.) See La Piana, *CAI*, p. 98 ff.

CHAPTER II

THE FIRST STEPS

Not long after the *Anthology* ceased publication in 1811, a new, more ambitious periodical took its place. This was the *North American Review,* the first issue of which appeared in May, 1815. Its first editor was William Tudor. The many articles published on Italian subjects, on literature in particular, during the first decades of the *Review's* existence indicate the remarkable progress in the knowledge of the Italian language and in the appreciation of Italy's literary history made by these Bostonians. The extreme dearth of Italian books and of books on Italy so lamented by George Ticknor, who in 1814 had been unable to find an Italian grammar in Boston, was no longer a problem. England was now supplying America with reprints of old translations and with new ones of the Italian classics, with English books dealing with Italian literary and artistic history, and with poetry, drama, and fiction based on Italian history. In addition, new editions of the Italian classics in their original tongue were being published in London. These editions in leather-bound, dainty, small volumes, correctly printed in handsome types, had a great vogue and are still much appreciated by book collectors.

London also made available several manuals of literary history and criticism translated from the Italian, such as the works of Menzini, Gravina, and Crescimbeni. The most important of all was the three-volume work *Storia della poesia italiana* (London, 1805), culled from Tiraboschi's monumental *Storia della letteratura italiana*. New, improved editions of the English-Italian dictionaries of Baretti, Bottarelli, and Graglia were now provided, together with Italian grammars and readers which were being printed and reprinted in London to fill the demands of increasing numbers of students in England, where Italian had become "a recognized branch of what was called 'polite education,' ranking beside, and in some cases superseding, French itself." [1] From the articles and essays which were appearing in the *North American Review,* it is evident that this literature was gradually becoming available to Bostonians. Furthermore, they were able to secure other literary and historical works, either directly from Italy or perhaps through the bookstore reëstablished by Da Ponte in New York sometime after 1820. [2]

It is not without significance that in its first issue (May, 1815) the *North American Review* undertook a strong defense of the merits of the Italian language in an article written as a comment upon an essay by Abbé Prévost which had appeared in the *Journal étranger.* The French Abbé held the view that no known tongue is more distant from the sublime or less suited to expressing the great movements of the soul "than the Italian language." The anonymous contributor to the *Review* rebuked the French critic sharply for not having either read or understood a page of the great Italian poets Dante, Tasso, and Ariosto. If he had, he would have been filled "with admiration of the genius of the Italian language, which can express everything with simplicity, a grace, a force, in fine, that cannot be approached by any other living language." [3]

Jared Sparks's "The Augustan Age of Italian Literature," [4] a survey of Italian literature from Dante to Tasso, was a compilation drawn chiefly from Roscoe's biographies, and revealing the youthful enthusiasm of the Boston literati for the newly discovered beauty of Italian poetry. [5] More elaborate was Francis Calley Gray's essay on Niccolò Machiavelli, published the same year (V [1817],

1. Marshall, *Italy in English Literature,* p. 304.

2. The Harvard College Library had already begun to buy Italian books. In his article on the *Memoirs* of De Rossi, quoted above, Everett concluded by saying: "We are happy to learn that copies of the greater part of his works have recently been imported for the University Library at Cambridge."

3. Following the British practice, articles appearing in the *NAR* and other similar periodicals of the time were not signed; but William Cushing, who compiled (1878) a general Index for the *NAR* from Vol. I to Vol. CXXV, traced the names of the authors of the articles contributed to the *Review.* Unfortunately, either this article on the Italian language escaped his attention, or, more likely, he found no clue to the author's identity.

4. *NAR,* IV (1817), 309–327.

5. Jared Sparks (1789–1866) was a frequent contributor to the *NAR* from the time of its inception to Vol. LVI. This essay on the Augustan Age is the only one by him dealing with Italian literature.

344-365).[6] Gray rose to the defense of Machiavelli, whose bad reputation as the teacher of tyranny he felt was the result of misunderstanding and "pitiless calumnies." The *Principe* was not a cynical guide for tyrants. On the contrary, as Foscolo had said in his *Sepolcri,* Machiavelli "snatched the dagger from the hands of tyrants" so that the people could see "of whose tears and blood it is stained" (*di che lagrime gronda e di che sangue*). Gray not only shows an accurate knowledge of the Machiavellian problem as it was debated at that time, and a considerable first-hand knowledge of Machiavelli's works, from which he quotes long and pertinent passages, but also an unusual familiarity with fifteenth-century Italian history.

Coleridge's lecture on Dante (1818), which created such a stir in England, was also greatly appreciated by the Bostonians. In its March issue for 1819, the *North American Review* (VIII, 322-347) published a long essay on Dante written by John Chipman Gray, who had obviously been influenced by Coleridge's interpretation of the spirit of Dante's poetry.[7] This essay, written to introduce Cary's translation to the American public, far exceeded the scope of the few articles previously published in America on Dante. In it Gray sketches Dante's life against the background of the turbulent Florence of his times. Then he gives a summary of the three parts of the *Divine Comedy,* adding some general remarks on the significance of Dante's work in the history of Christian thought and culture. He includes also a brief comparison between Dante and Milton, a subject which almost invariably appears in essays on Dante written in America in the following years.

Commenting upon Johnson's criticism of Milton for "perplexing his poetry with his philosophy, and of making of his infernal and

6. Francis Calley Gray (1790-1856) was secretary to John Quincy Adams, U. S. Minister to Russia in 1813, and later an influential member of the Massachusetts legislature. He contributed a dozen articles to the *NAR* during the first eight years of its existence, among them one on the Catacombs of Naples. The others dealt mostly with American politics, especially foreign relations.

7. John Chipman Gray's contributions to the *NAR* were few and far between. In one of them he dealt with Tasso's *Gerusalemme Liberata* in connection with a reprint of Fairfax's English translation of the poem. (*NAR,* XIV [1822], 87 ff.) In other articles he exposed his views on the study of the classics, on American education, or discussed aspects of American history.

celestial powers sometimes pure spirit and sometimes animated matter," Gray sought to show that Dante almost always avoided this pitfall. He observed also that Dante's Lucifer, although very briefly described, is a more impressive and real figure than Milton's Lucifer, who sometimes appears to emerge as a hero.

Gray wished to persuade his readers to approach Dante without being repelled by the current notion that Dante is very difficult to understand. He explains that "this idea of the extreme obscurity of Dante is indeed founded, in some measure, in truth, but principally on the representations of the Italians themselves. The Divine Comedy, as Dante informs us more than once, is an allegory, and his commentators, as might be expected from the nature of the subject, have busied themselves partly in explaining, and partly in creating mysteries." According to Gray, the two aspects of Dante's work that must be considered are, on the one hand, its narrative structure and its greatness as poetry, and, on the other, its mystical and doctrinal character. To understand the former no very great effort is necessary if one is well acquainted with Italian. He compares this with the problem presented by Bunyan's *Pilgrim's Progress,* "which everyone reads, even children, with great delight," although the meaning of Bunyan's dreams escapes even men of depth and learning. The narrative of the *Divine Comedy* may likewise be easily understood and its poetry may be a source of great pleasure to the reader, whether the reader is interested or not in its background of medieval dogma and theology. In conclusion, Gray states:

Dante is the poet of our hours of sober contemplation. When we would escape for a season from the vexations of life, when we would relinquish awhile its pleasures and labours that we may resume them with renovated interest and unclouded judgment, we may accompany Dante through regions far beyond the sphere of all earthly objects and feelings.

We have dealt at some length with this article not only because it was the first well-rounded essay on Dante to appear in America, but also because it may be considered as a typical example of several articles on Dante, patterned after English models, which from that time on continued to appear in American periodicals.

Gray's point of view that Dante's poetry can be enjoyed and appreciated by itself, even though the reader may not have any background for understanding the involved allegorical, theological, and mystical framework of the *Divine Comedy,* was a view commonly held in England and elsewhere. This approach to Dante was not, then, based on aesthetic theories concerning the essence of poetry or the unity of a work of art, such as have inspired more modern critics. It was the practical method of approach, by which a poem can be enjoyed, though in a fragmentary way, by those who are unable to penetrate its inner meaning and its true spirit, and who are thus prevented from seeing the great structure of the whole in the right perspective. From the sixteenth century and with the decline of Scholasticism, this was, after all, the usual approach to the *Divine Comedy,* especially outside Italy. Early in the nineteenth century a romantic infatuation for the Middle Ages served to bring about a thorough exploration of the history and the intellectual and spiritual life of that period. Great scholars of the eighteenth century, men like Ludovico A. Muratori in Italy, had paved the way for modern historians by collecting and making available an immense amount of source material. Years were to pass, however, before the thought and institutions, the literature and art, the changing life, and the multiform spirit of that long period of history revealed themselves in their genuine light through the painstaking scholarship which has not yet completed its task.

These early American lovers of Dante, brought up as they were in a strict Protestant tradition, had no great interest in the medieval theological thought which permeated the *Divine Comedy;* but the universal moral lesson of the poem was not lost on them and contributed much to their appreciation of Dante's poetry. The human drama of sin, expiation, and retribution was a familiar element in their religious and moral ideas, and, as presented in action in the *Comedy,* it stirred their imagination and appealed not only to their conscience but also to their taste. To extend its allegorical meaning was not necessary. Down almost to the end of the nineteenth century, this was the spiritual attitude with which American readers and students approached the *Divine Comedy* and sought to appreciate its poetical beauties.

The year 1819, in which Gray's article was published in the *North American Review,* marked also the beginning of George Ticknor's teaching of modern languages and literatures at Harvard and Lorenzo da Ponte's return to New York for a fresh start as a teacher and man of letters. Spurred by the keen competition of rival Italian teachers—most of them political refugees who had come over from Italy after the restoration of the old governments in 1815—Da Ponte was more steady and successful this time in his effort to create an interest in Italian literature among well-to-do New York families. The study of the *Divine Comedy* was an integral part of his courses and the results obtained filled him with pride. According to his *Memoirs,* his pupils became so proficient that one day he was able to invite a woman who visited one of his classes "to open the first volume of the Divine Comedy and ask my girls to interpret any passage she preferred. On the successful outcome of that experiment I asked her which of the first six cantos she would like to hear declaimed." [8]

In 1825, when Da Ponte was appointed teacher of Italian at Columbia College, he felt that the long-sought opportunity for teaching on a larger scale had finally arrived. In an address delivered in New York at the time of his appointment, he said that his love for Dante, on the one hand, and his gratitude toward the city of New York, which had encouraged him in his work, on the other, were the reasons why he "assumed the sweet and honorable charge to teach the language created by Dante to those who still ignored it or who did not know it enough to understand the beauties, the profound doctrines and the high mysteries dealt with by that great genius." [9] But, because Italian was an extracurricular subject, not included in the required program of studies, Da Ponte was not made a member of the faculty and received no fixed salary. He was entitled only to such small fees as should be paid by the students who took his course. The experiment failed; few students registered and fewer still attended his lessons, which, as he said, were often deserted. At the end of the academic year in June, 1826, Da Ponte

8. Lorenzo da Ponte, *Memoirs,* trans. Elizabeth Abbott, Arthur Livingston, ed. (Philadelphia, 1929), p. 462.

9. T. W. Koch, *Dante in America,* pp. 16–17.

resigned. He tried again in the year 1829–30, but again he found no students.[10]

Da Ponte made a more direct contribution to Dante studies in his "Notes on Dante," or "Critique on Certain Passages in Dante." [11] These notes suggested either a different reading or a new interpretation of three passages of the *Inferno*. It does not seem, however, that these suggestions were taken seriously by Dantists. In his *Memoirs* Da Ponte remarks that he sent a copy of his notes to Biagioli, the well-known commentator on Dante in Italy, but that Biagioli "never considered me worthy of a reply." [12] A reprint of Byron's poem "The Prophecy of Dante" with a translation in Italian verse by Da Ponte (New York, 1821 and 1822) was reviewed rather unfavorably by an unknown critic who was evidently familiar with Italian.[13]

As a contribution to America's cultural history, it must be admitted that Da Ponte's influence upon Italian studies, though considerable, was not far-reaching. His pupils were mostly young girls from the best New York families, who learned Italian and read the Italian poets with him but went no further. There were, of course, a few men of culture whom he inspired with an appreciation of literature and its beauties in the humanistic tradition of Italy.[14] Unfortunately, however, the New York of Da Ponte's day, a rapidly growing commercial center, was hardly the place for spiritual and intellectual undertakings to flourish. Unlike Boston, New York had few families who maintained a balance between cultural and commercial affairs. At that time, Philadelphia and Boston were undoubtedly the vital centers of American intellectual life. As Parrington remarks:

10. Da Ponte, *op. cit.*, p. 457 n.; H. R. Marraro, "Da Ponte and Foresti: The Introduction of Italian at Columbia," *Columbia Quarterly*, March, 1937, pp. 23–32.

11. "Critique on Certain Passages in Dante," *New York Review and Athenaeum Magazine,* I (1825), 156–158; 241–242; 325–327. Reprinted by Koch, *DA*, pp. 64–71.

12. Da Ponte, *op. cit.*, p. 464.

13. "La Profezia di Dante di Lord Byron," trans. into Italian in *terza rima* by L. da Ponte, *Literary and Scientific Repository*, IV (New York, 1822), 310–317.

14. Georges Perkins Marsh (1801–82), said to have been a pupil of Da Ponte, was certainly a good Italianist. He was U. S. Minister to Italy from 1860, and lived in Turin, then Florence, and then Rome, where he died in 1882. Most of his scholarly work, however, was on Icelandic and Anglo-Saxon glottology and philology. To the *NAR* he contributed an article on "The Origin of the Italian Language" (CV [1867], 1–41).

In sharp contrast with Boston, New York was wanting in intellectual background and intellectual stimulus. It had never gone to school to dogmatic theology and neither clergy nor laity had been disciplined by a severe Puritan regimen. Gentlemen were little given to metaphysical speculation and the subtleties of creed never provided the staple of talk in the farmer's kitchen. . . . No other stimulus supplied the want and in consequence ideas and books were held in low esteem and the things of the mind suffered. . . . The result was a low plane of intellectual life, which even in Cooper's time was remarked by him.[15]

Da Ponte's claim that he introduced Italian literature in general and Dante in particular into America had little basis in fact where Boston was concerned. He was never in Boston, and had he gone there his lack of a grasp of English literature, not to mention his vanity and his loquacity, make it difficult for one to believe that he would have been a success among the stately Brahmins. Neither his familiarity with the Latin classics nor his humanistic claims would have made much impression upon a group of intellectuals who had had, for the most part, considerable training in the classics, which were at that time a "required" subject in the program of Harvard College. These Bostonians could quote verses from Horace and Virgil, though perhaps not as easily as Da Ponte could. It is quite possible that he would have been looked down upon by such men as Edward Everett and George Ticknor, who had studied in Germany under the most famous philologists of the day, and who numbered among their friends the literary and artistic great of Europe.[16]

15. Parrington, *Main Currents of American Thought*, II, 195–196. The picture of New York in the early nineteenth century drawn by Brooks in his *World of Washington Irving* (chap. ii, pp. 27–55) is less discomforting than Parrington's. "Literature," says Brooks, "was represented in two or three clubs, the Drone, the Friendly Club, and the Calliopean, at which the members read papers and acclaimed their favourite compositions, passages from Addison, Shakespeare, and especially Poe. . . . They composed dissertations on wedlock and recited the speech of Coriolanus or Orlando Furioso, as translated by Hoole. . . . Men talked in the eighteenth century way. . . . The meetings were convivial, and many of the men sang hunting-songs between glasses of punch and Madeira, and played on their flutes; but the prevailing style was sententious and even excessively formal, for the Grandisonian manner was still in vogue. . . . There were no professional men of letters, nor had there ever been one in New York, save possibly Lindly Murray, who had gone to England" (pp. 39–41).

16. On the classical training at Harvard, see Samuel Morison, *The Tercentennial History of Harvard University* (Cambridge, 1936); for Virginia, see Brooks, *op. cit.,* chap. iii, "South of the Potomac," pp. 262 ff.

Da Ponte seems to have first learned of the existence of these Boston lovers of Italian culture through an article published by William H. Prescott in the *North American Review* of October, 1824 (XIX, 337–389). From its title, "Italian Narrative Poetry," to its conclusion, this article enraged Da Ponte. With his usual impetuosity he claimed the monopoly on Italian studies in America and rushed to attack these Bostonians who, without having attended his school, presumed to speak of Italian poetry. In an eighty-page pamphlet *Alcune osservazioni sull'articolo pubblicato nel North American Review il mese di Ottobre 1824* (New York, 1825), Da Ponte heaped his scorn on the youthful Prescott. Holding the strange notion that English literature, from beginning to end, owed its very existence to Italian influences, he reproached Prescott for stating that, after the Elizabethan period, Italian literature had been ignored by everyone in England except Milton. He was still more indignant at Prescott's reference to the "monotonous sweetness of Metastasio." One who spoke thus of Metastasio, said Da Ponte, was "wanting in respect to this famous man." To Da Ponte, Prescott's essay betrayed a willful determination to disparage Italian literature. And, of course, the American demonstrated his ignorance, for such a statement about Metastasio could only have been made by one completely unschooled in the works of so great a poet and ignorant of his life and his critics.

In reality, Prescott's article was far from hostile to Italian literature. The critical remarks which he had included in his outline were not his own. There was nothing original in the article; it was an excellent compilation made with good taste and discrimination, primarily from Italian sources—Tiraboschi, for example, and the various essays of Ugo Foscolo.

Prescott's answer to the attack (*North American Review,* XXI [July, 1825], 189–217) was calm and courteous, covering all the points raised by Da Ponte, who evidently "had not understood or had not been willing to understand many pages" of the essay. It was very strange, Prescott remarked, that Da Ponte should be so irritated because "an American writer availed himself of that freedom of criticism of which the Italian writers made such a large use in Italy." In conclusion, Prescott stated that there was nothing he desired more than to see Italian literature become popular in America, but that this end could not be achieved through indiscriminate panegyrics. After all, Italian literature needs no injudicious praise; "it shines with such a brilliant light that it may stand all just criticism without losing anything of its splendor." [17]

William Hickling Prescott (1796–1859), though almost blind throughout his career, made a name for himself as the historian of Ferdinand and Isabella of Spain, and of the Spanish conquest of Mexico and Peru. After his graduation from Harvard he spent two years abroad, where he fell under the spell of the Latin world. In the early period of his life he was greatly attracted to Italian literature and spent many hours reading and studying the great Italian poets, particularly Dante. In a letter to George Ticknor he wrote: "I have finished the Paradiso of Dante, and feel as if I had made a most important addition to the small store of my acquisitions. To have read the Inferno is not to have read Dante: his genius shows itself under so different aspects in each of his three poems." In Prescott's opinion Dante's devils and bad spirits, with few exceptions, "are much inferior in moral grandeur to Milton's. How inferior that stupendous overgrown Satan of his, to the sublime spirit of Milton, not yet stripped of all its original brightness!" [18]

Prescott's interest in Italian literature was still keen when he published his essay on the "Poetry and Romance of the Italians" in the *North American Review* for July, 1831 (XXXIII, 29–81). The main purpose of this essay was to introduce to the American public three recently published histories of Italian literature by Camillo Ugoni (1820), Giuseppe Maffei (1825), and Antonio Lombardi (1827–29). He assumes in his brief exposition of the *Divine Comedy* that his readers are already familiar with the works of Dante and repeats the statement made previously in his letter to Ticknor that one cannot know Dante from reading the *Inferno* alone; one must

17. In his *Memoirs* Da Ponte boasts that he taught the presumptuous Bostonian a lesson and adds that his only reason for mentioning Prescott's article was to show the latter's ignorance of Italian literature. Recent biographers of Da Ponte, who evidently have not taken the trouble to read Prescott's article, or who have read it without considering the sources from which Prescott derived his material, have summarily dismissed the matter by accepting Da Ponte's boasts. In fact, Da Ponte was wrong and his attack was unjustified.

18. George Ticknor, *Life of W. H. Prescott* (Boston, 1864). The letter from which the above passage is quoted was reprinted by Koch, *DA*, pp. 71–74.

familiarize oneself with the *Purgatorio* and the *Paradiso* as well, both of which Prescott considered more beautiful than the first canticle.

In 1833 a more ambitious essay appeared in the *North American Review* (XXXVII [October], 506–536), written by Frances Inglis, a young woman with literary aspirations who shortly became the wife of Calderon de la Barca, the Spanish minister to Washington. The article, entitled "Dante," contains the usual biographical sketch of Dante and the usual summary of the *Divine Comedy*. It contains also some original translations of passages from the poem which reveal that the author was well acquainted with both Italian and the *Comedy*. In history she was not as well versed. During the course of her comments, she states naïvely that in Dante's time "the Jesuits amused the credulity of the public," a slip pardonable in an American Protestant lady, but rather disastrous for a student of Dante and perhaps embarrassing to the future wife of the Spanish envoy of His Most Catholic Majesty.[19]

To the men who formed the nucleus, first of the Anthology Club, then of the Athenaeum, and finally of the *North American Review*, credit must be given for having contributed much toward introducing Italian literature and Dante into America. Most of these men, especially those of the earlier generation, were not professional men of letters. The early nineteenth century produced a class of American intellectuals, particularly in Boston, whose main calling in life was either business or a profession. As A. M. Schlesinger points out: "The most casual scrutiny of the Dictionary of American Biography discloses countless instances of great versatility." [20]

To most of these men knowledge of Italian and other literatures

19. Later, as Madame Calderon de la Barca, she spent several years in Mexico, where her husband was the first Spanish envoy to the new republic. While there, she published a two-volume work, *Life in Mexico* (1841), which was reviewed more favorably than it deserved by Prescott in the *NAR* for January, 1843.

20. Arthur M. Schlesinger, "What Then Is the American, This New Man?" *American Historical Review*, XLVIII (1943), 234. "Necessity had forced the early American colonists to be jacks-of-all-trades, and their cultural interest had done the rest. As a result of this exercise of ingenuity in all quarters, versatility became an outstanding American attribute. Besides engendering versatility, necessity also ingrained the habit of work, which entered so deeply into the national psychology that, when a wealthy class emerged, it did not become a leisured class such as was to be found in European society. The rich man has no more right to repose than the poor." (*Idem*, p. 232.)

was merely a cultural accomplishment, since their main work lay in other fields. Obviously there was not much to be expected of them by way of important contributions to Dante studies or to the history of European literatures. Their articles and essays, written for the general public, were chiefly informative. They consisted largely in summaries of books, old and new, condensed discussions of opinions and theories expounded by literary historians and critics, and comparisons of tendencies and literary forms of one period with those of another period or of another literature. In general, their purpose was to inform the American reader of the existence, the content, and the artistic value of Italian literature, as well as of its history, its influence over other literatures, and its contributions to European culture. They were eager to enlarge the basis of American cultural life, and the best way to do it seemed to be by fostering a knowledge of all the great European achievements in literature and art. Since Italy had been the cradle of the New Learning and of the new European culture, it was natural that she should receive close attention.

It has been noted that both in England and in America translations of the *Divine Comedy* came later than those of the other great Italian poetical works. Likewise American reprints of English translations of Petrarch (1809), Tasso (1810), and Ariosto (1816) preceded the reprinting of Cary's version of the *Divine Comedy,* which did not appear until 1822 (Philadelphia). "This antedating of Dante in America by the other three great Italian poets," Koch remarks, "is but another indication of the source of our first introduction to Italian literature. Both in England and America Dante came last, but he was destined to stay longest." [21] Not only did Dante stay longest, he remained and became part of the American cultural tradition. Since his arrival, he has been the chief reason why many American students of the humanities have been, and continue to be, eager to learn Italian.

Harvard College was destined to be the first to make instruction in modern languages part of the curriculum. While still in Europe,

21. Koch, *DA,* p. 10. "From England we inherited many of our traditions and tastes; when Dante came to be widely read in England, we welcomed him here, read him and began to study him for ourselves."

where he spent three years traveling, studying, and making illustrious acquaintances, George Ticknor (1791–1871) was appointed by Harvard to the newly established Abiel Smith Professorship of French and Spanish Languages and Literatures.[22] When he returned in 1819 to take over his new duties, Ticknor brought with him a strong enthusiasm for German scholarship, a determination to raise Harvard's standards to university level, and many books acquired in Europe not only for himself but also for the college library.[23] The books were welcome in a country where books—especially those on Italy and on foreign literatures in general—were still too few, but Ticknor was to find very soon that his plans for scholarly reforms were looked upon by his older colleagues as undesirable novelties.

In the early 1820's, American colleges were going through a crisis to which Harvard was no exception. The old programs and methods of teaching were not meeting the needs of the time. The curriculum needed broadening; the rigidity of the old schedule needed modifying. The general level of teaching was not high, and the disciplinary system was too lax to be effective. Furthermore the old guard, firmly rooted in tradition, eyed all innovations with distrust, and Ticknor was forced to relinquish his hopes of bringing about a general reform. He was able, however, to obtain a certain amount of freedom in the organization of the new Department of Foreign Languages. Originally the Smith Professorship included only the teaching of the French and Spanish languages and literatures, but an additional appointment as professor of belles-lettres enabled Ticknor to extend his teaching to other modern literatures, although the classicists who controlled the Department of Belles Lettres never allowed him to gain a real foothold in their domain.[24]

22. In the *Life, Letters and Journals* of George Ticknor (2 vols., Boston, 1876 [13th ed., 1909]), there is a complete account of Ticknor's travels in Europe and his experiences with princes, diplomats, and men of letters; on his visits to and studies in Italy, see also La Piana, *CAI*, pp. 138–153.

23. *Life of Ticknor*, I, 353 ff. The administration had sent him one thousand dollars to buy books on modern languages and literatures for the college. The same amount was given to Longfellow for the same purpose during his trip to Europe in 1835.

24. They made it so difficult for students to take the new language courses, and cramped Ticknor in such a way that on February 28, 1825, he wrote to President Kirkland: "My lectures have been made so entirely a farce, that I have of late, thought little of them and expressed no opinion or desire as to the time of delivering them. . . . I know not what

Soon, however, the two appointments held by Ticknor were merged and his successor became Smith Professor of Modern Languages and Literatures.

In 1825 instruction in foreign languages was extended to include German and Italian. Believing that the purpose of instruction in languages should be to give the students a sound speaking and reading knowledge of modern tongues in preparation for further work in the fields of philology and literature, Ticknor engaged native instructors to teach the four languages under his direct supervision and confined his own teaching to literature.[25] His choice of instructors was good in general, but his best appointment was Pietro Bachi, who taught Italian so effectively that he attracted an increasing number of students and contributed not a little to the establishment of a sound tradition of Italian studies at Harvard.

At first Ticknor limited his teaching to general surveys of European literatures, but by 1831 Italian had gained some ground, and he found it possible to lecture to a special class in Dante. Thus he inaugurated a practice which in time spread to other American colleges and made Dante an accepted part of the American academic tradition. There is no published work by Ticknor on Dante. As a matter of fact, he published little besides his *History of Spanish Literature* [26] and the biography of his friend William H. Prescott. There are among his manuscripts, however, three volumes of notes on the *Divine Comedy,* the result partly of his course at Harvard and partly of his subsequent studies. Of these notes Koch writes as follows:

The first pages are concerned with such introductory topics as the political state of Italy, the state of religious power and opinion, and of

---

is wanted of me, or by what authority it is required." (Quoted from the Harvard Archives by Carl L. Johnson, *Professor Longfellow of Harvard* [Univ. of Oregon Press, 1944], p. 88.) On Ticknor's teaching career, see Henry Grattan Doyle, "George Ticknor," *Mod. Lang. J.,* XXVI (October, 1937).

25. In an address on the best method of teaching living languages, he remarked that "the great masters in all ages and in all nations have built on the same foundations, and can be successfully approached only in one way." He thought also that to understand and appreciate Dante one should know the condition of the Italian language before his time: "Who can be aware either of the sublimity or the tenderness of Dante unless he studies that unwritten language from which alone this first and greatest master of Italian poetry could draw his material and inspiration." (Koch, *DA,* p. 19.)

26. In 3 vols. (Boston, 1849). A final revision came out in 1872.

poetry and language in the time of Dante, together with a sketch of his life in which he questions some of Boccaccio's statements. Then comes a brief account of Dante's works. In his analysis of the *Divina Commedia* he puts the question, "What kind of a poem?" and makes answer that it is "no more an epic than a comedy. It is essentially historical . . ."[27]

There is, however, no evidence that Ticknor's teaching of Italian literature, of Dante in particular, left a very deep impression at Harvard. His coldness of manner, the fact that his main interest in Dante was linguistic, as his notes show, the short time in which he taught Dante—only four years, from 1831 to his resignation in 1835—all these factors may explain why neither his students nor his colleagues responded to his efforts with much enthusiasm. His resignation did not cause great regret. He was never popular in the college life. He was often accused of "putting on airs," and his aristocratic tastes, intensified by his European travels, together with his condescending ways, seem to have been resented by his associates.

While Ticknor was conducting his classes at Harvard, a young man at Bowdoin College, Henry Wadsworth Longfellow, was considering seriously whether or not to study Italian under him and his instructors after graduation.[28] Upon being promised the chair of modern languages which was to be established at Bowdoin, Longfellow decided that the wisest plan was to go to Europe and study firsthand both the languages and the literatures of France, Spain,

27. Koch, *DA*, p. 22. Koch also writes: "From the fly-leaves of the three manuscript volumes we learn that the notes on the *Inferno* were prepared at Blue Hills, July and August, 1832; those on cantos I–XXIX of the *Purgatorio* at Rome, January and February, 1837; while the remainder of the work was done at Woods Hole in July and August, 1840." He had drawn heavily upon the early commentaries of the *Divine Comedy* and upon other sources still unpublished at that time. Since all this ancient Dante literature soon afterward was made available in print, Ticknor's notes lost their usefulness.

28. *Life of Henry Wadsworth Longfellow with Extracts from His Journals and Correspondence,* Samuel Longfellow, ed. (2 vols. Boston, 1886), and a third volume under the title *Final Memorials of H. W. L.,* S. Longfellow, ed. (Boston, 1887). Letter to his father, December 5, 1824 (I, 53): "I want to spend one year at Cambridge for the purpose of reading history, and of becoming familiar with the best authors in polite literature; whilst at the same time I can be acquiring a knowledge of the Italian language, without an acquaintance with which I shall be shut out from one of the most beautiful departments of letters." For the early period of his life a more complete biography is now available in Lawrence Thompson's *Young Longfellow* (New York, 1937), who has shown that the biography of the poet by his brother Samuel is often inaccurate, the author having taken great liberties with Longfellow's journals and letters.

and Italy. During the winter of 1826–27 he studied Italian in Paris with one Ferranti, primarily a teacher of music.[29] He spent the next year, 1828, in Italy. There he deepened his acquaintance with Dante and often quoted verses from the *Comedy* in letters to his friends.[30]

At Bowdoin College, where he began his teaching in September, 1829, Longfellow did not have the assistance of instructors for the teaching of languages. At first he offered elementary courses in French and Spanish and gradually added courses in German and Italian, compiling for the use of his classes a series of textbooks, elementary grammars, exercises and small anthologies.[31] His idea of writing in French rather than in English a *Syllabus de la grammaire italienne* (Boston, 1832) may have been suggested by practical reasons, but we do not know whether this experiment met with any success. Also for his classes in Italian he compiled a little volume of samples from the Italian novelists.[32]

At the beginning of his second year of teaching (September 2, 1830) Longfellow delivered an address on the "Origin and Growth of the Languages of Southern Europe and Their Literatures," [33] a subject which he developed on a larger scale in a series of essays for the *North American Review*.[34] In one of them, a long and elaborate article on the "History of the Italian Language and Its Dialects," [35] he discussed the various theories on this motley question, showing an excellent knowledge of the sources and of the literature of the subject, and giving his American readers the first summary and analysis of Dante's *De Vulgari Eloquentia* to appear

29. Longfellow, ed., *Life of H. W. Longfellow*, I, 19.
30. *Idem*, I, 153. Letter to George W. Greene from Venice, December, 1828.
31. Longfellow's Bibliography in Longfellow, ed., *Final Memorials*, pp. 421 ff.
32. *Saggi de'novellieri italiani d'ogni secolo: Tratti dai più celebri scrittori, con brevi notizie intorno alla vita di ciascheduno* (Boston, 1832), with preface in Italian by the editor.
33. This inaugural address which Longfellow never thought worthy of publication was printed in 1907 by G. T. Little (Bowdoin College Library, Brunswick, Maine). In his prefatory note the editor states that at that period courses in modern languages were already "required" at Bowdoin: French for Sophomores, Spanish for Juniors, and either German or Italian for Seniors.
34. Longfellow, ed., *Final Memorials*, Bibliography, p. 422.
35. *NAR*, XXXV (October, 1832), 285–342.

in this country. Of the various Italian dialects (Longfellow placed them at seventeen) he described the chief characteristics and gave examples, mostly short lyrics or passages from longer poems, accompanied by his own translations into English.[36]

In December, 1834, President Josiah Quincy of Harvard, acting upon the suggestion of Ticknor, who wished to resign his chair, offered the Smith Professorship to Longfellow with the condition that before entering upon his duties he should spend a year or a year and a half in Europe "for the purpose of a more perfect attainment of the German."[37] His formal appointment to the Harvard chair was made on November 12, 1836. The sharp opposition of the faculty to the new department encountered by Ticknor had not yet abated. Longfellow too had to struggle against rules and regulations passed by the faculty which directly or indirectly imposed harmful restrictions upon the teaching of modern languages and literatures. It was not until 1845 that he succeeded in obtaining the abolition of those regulations and in blocking further trespasses in his field.[38]

From the beginning he lectured extensively on Dante and even conceived the idea of widening the circle of his audience by offering public lectures on this subject. In a letter of February 8, 1838, he wrote to his father:

I am now upon Dante, as you know, unwritten lectures: but I have petitioned the Corporation for the use of the chapel next summer for a course of written public lectures. By public I mean free to any and every one who chooses to attend, whether in college or out of col-

36. Among Longfellow's translations is that of a famous little poem by the eighteenth-century Sicilian poet Giovanni Meli, entitled "Apuzza nica" ("Little Bee"). This lyric had already been translated into English by George Bancroft, who included it in an essay on Johann G. von Herder's book *Sämmtliche Werke zur schönen Literatur und Kunst*, which contained samples of popular lyrics from all literatures. This essay had been published in the *NAR*, XX (1825), 146 ff. Longfellow either missed this translation or did not think much of it. Actually, though more literal, Longfellow's version does not seem preferable to that of his predecessor. For both versions, see La Piana, *CAI*, pp. 182 ff.

37. For details concerning Longfellow's appointment at Harvard and the letters of Ticknor and others about him, see Carl L. Johnson, *Professor Longfellow of Harvard* (Univ. of Oregon Press, 1944), pp. 4 ff.

38. *Idem.,* pp. 28–30, 34–42, 56–59, 71.

lege. . . . In the meantime, I am preparing; and devote the whole day to it.[39]

This proposal, which would have revived in Cambridge the *Lecturae Dantis* begun by Boccaccio in fourteenth-century Florence, did not meet with the approval of the Harvard Corporation, and the idea was dismissed, never to be reconsidered. "They do not approve my plan," he wrote to his father. "So it ends. Human life is made up mostly of a series of little disappointments and little pleasures." [40]

One of the most irksome duties of the Smith Professor was that of visiting every week the classes taught by the four foreign instructors in modern languages. "This four-in-hand of outlandish animals, all pulling the wrong way, except one," he wrote to his father on October 20, 1837, "this gives me more trouble than anything else. I have more anxiety about their doing well than about my own. I think I should be more satisfied if I did the work all myself. Nevertheless, I take things very easily, not expecting perfection and making the best of all things." [41]

The exception among the four "outlandish animals" was Pietro Bachi, the Italian instructor, of whom Longfellow always spoke well and affectionately, calling him on one occasion: "Bachi the Italian with his charming accent . . . who has a cloud of mystery in his life." [42] Indeed, Bachi was a competent teacher, not only of

39. Longfellow, ed., *Life of H. W. Longfellow*, I, 275.
40. *Idem*, I, 282; Johnson, *op. cit.*, p. 29.
41. Longfellow, ed., *Life of H. W. Longfellow*, I, 267; Johnson, *op. cit.*, pp. 30 ff.
42. Koch, *DA*, p. 38. Edward E. Hale (letter to Koch, *ibid.*) also mentions the "mystery" in Bachi's life, and the impression that he gave of "being wretched here." We learn from Antonio Gallenga (*Episodes of My Second Life*, p. 38) that Bachi was not a political refugee, but had left Sicily after an unfortunate love affair. Gallenga does not say, however, that his real family name was not Bachi, but Batolo, and that his father Salvatore Batolo was Chief Justice of the Supreme Court of the Kingdom of Sicily. Bachi's change of name was obviously suggested by consideration for the high status of his family. He had studied law at Padua and was a man of broad culture and considerable learning. In America, Gallenga tells us, he had the further misfortune of marrying an Irish girl of low extraction who deserted him, but not without first having communicated to him an unhealthful passion for strong drink. "This fact, however," Gallenga remarks, "did not affect his professional activities. He kept his position at Harvard, and though he preferred to spend his evenings at home in the company of a good bottle, in day time he was very careful never to forget himself and hence those few who knew of it preferred to ignore this weakness of which after all, few Americans were then altogether free." On Bachi's true name and other details see La Piana, *CAI*, pp. 99 ff.

language, but of literary history and philology as well. The text-books which he compiled for his classes compare favorably with those published in England during the same period.[43] His two essays, "A Comparative View of the Italian and Portuguese Languages" (1831), and "A Comparative View of the Italian and Spanish Languages" (1832), were the first publications in the field of romance philology to appear at Harvard. In his advanced linguistic courses, Bachi read extensively from the *Divine Comedy,* thus preparing his students for the special course on Dante given by Longfellow. In a letter to T. W. Koch, Edward Everett Hale, author of *The Man Without a Country,* wrote:

Longfellow read the whole of Dante with us and we were well prepared for this by what we had read with Bachi. . . . We all had a great regard for Bachi, and his work in the Italian Department was excellent. As a critic of Dante, he had exactly the gift which a good teacher ought to have in interesting wide-awake young men in this study. And I can say that when we came to hear Longfellow lecture, we were more than prepared for his lectures by the very thorough work which Bachi had done in this same subject with us.[44]

Thus it seems that no little credit for the success of Longfellow's courses on Dante should be given to Bachi, whose preliminary instruction in Dante's linguistic problems not only provided the students with that essential background, but left Longfellow free to dedicate his lectures to interpretation and aesthetic comments. Bachi's dismissal from the university in September, 1846, deprived Longfellow of this valuable help and the students of one of their best teachers. Bachi, whose salary was only five hundred dollars a year, got in financial difficulties and in 1844 was forced into bankruptcy. President Quincy took no action, but two years later his successor, Edward Everett, decided that it was time to wash away

43. *Anthology of Italian Prose-writers* (1828); *A Grammar of the Italian Language* (1829); selections from the Italian theater under the title *Teatro scelto italiano* (Boston, 1829); and *A Collection of Italian Fables in Prose and Verse,* with an interlinear English version for beginners in Italian (1836). In the preface of his *Teatro scelto italiano,* Bachi gave a considerable list of editions, old and new, of the plays he included in his book and a bibliography of the literary sources used in his notes and comments, with the remark: "All these books together with many others, adorn the remarkable collection of Italian books which is part of the very rich library of Harvard University."
44. Koch, *DA,* p. 38.

the blot on Harvard's escutcheon. Longfellow, who several times had pleaded with the Corporation for a raise of Bachi's salary, did his best to shield his worthy instructor, but President Everett was adamant: "The College must not be trifled with" was his answer.[45]

It seems also that after this unfortunate incident the Corporation objected to the appointment of any other Italian to the instructorship and as a result Longfellow had to take over the classes in Italian and carry on this work until Luigi Monti was appointed on his recommendation seven years later in January, 1854.

In his Dante course Longfellow read the whole of the *Divine Comedy* and explained whatever he thought needed comment.[46] This practical method proved more effective than that of giving professorial lectures, which usually require that the students have already a thorough knowledge of the Italian text. Longfellow's method served to bring his students into closer contact with Dante's thought, his manner of expression, and his poetic imagery.

More detailed information about Longfellow's course on Dante has been secured by Emilio Goggio from a manuscript record of his lectures:

Ordinarily his course would open with a discussion of the merits of the *Commedia* as a literary masterpiece, the vogue which it enjoyed and the peculiar influence which it exerted for generations past upon the greatest scholars from all over the world. . . . Longfellow read with his students all of the *Inferno* and discussed at length the scholarly contributions of such men as Schelling, Leigh Hunt, Carlyle, Macaulay, and a few others. One of the things by which he was most deeply impressed in reading Dante was the poet's character, his austere nature, his indomitable will and inflexibility of purpose, his honesty and magnanimity, his indestructible faith in right and justice . . . his wonderful knowledge of the human heart, his kindly attitude toward women and his strong and steadfast devotion to his beloved Beatrice "which flowed from the sunny clime of his youth like the Gulf Stream forever waving through the cold and stormy ocean of his life."[47]

45. Johnson, *op. cit.*, pp. 60–65. Everett could not bear to have it appear that Harvard instructors could not live on their salaries. Longfellow wrote in his Journal: "Poor Bachi! I am afraid it is a hard case with him: with his poverty and his pride." (*Idem*, p. 60.)

46. Letter of E. E. Hale to Koch, in *DA*, p. 39.

47. E. Goggio, "Longfellow and Dante," *Rep. Dante Soc.*, 1924, pp. 26 ff. From Hale's letter, as well as from passages in his diary, it is clear that Longfellow read the whole of

In expounding the *Divine Comedy* to his students, Longfellow paid but little attention to its allegory, which he considered rather a blemish than a beauty:

He realized that the poem contained figurative passages and allegorical references, but these, he thought, were not as common as some critics would lead us to believe and of no vital importance . . . It is evident, however, that by not giving due consideration to the allegory of the poem, Longfellow failed to bring out the full significance of Dante's work.[48]

It cannot be said, however, that Longfellow ignored Dante's theology and philosophy altogether. He seems to have made an effort to become acquainted with medieval speculative thought, which is so prominent in the *Divine Comedy,* especially in the *Purgatorio* and the *Paradiso.* In 1848 he translated into English Friedrich Schelling's essay on "Dante and the Divine Comedy," [49] read it to his Dante class, and then wrote in his diary: "It must have been darkness deep to them." And again: "Schelling's paper to students of Dante is interesting, though throwing much darkness visible upon the subject to minds not philosophical. It is like a dark cave with some gleaming stalactites hanging from the roof." From then on, Longfellow preferred to draw from the commentaries, old and new, of the *Divine Comedy* such elementary explanations of philosophical and theological problems discussed by Dante as were strictly necessary for the verbal understanding of the text.

Even with its limitations, Longfellow's course, faithfully given during his almost twenty years of teaching at Harvard, was, together with his translation of the *Divine Comedy,* one of the main

the *Divine Comedy* to his classes in different academic periods. Goggio gives several passages from the manuscript lectures which show that "his remarks were clothed with a sentimentalism which was quite characteristic of his romantic temperament." For instance: "I lay my hands upon it [the *Divine Comedy*] with reverence, indeed with so great reverence, that it amounts to unwillingness. The book is already disfigured by too much commentary scribbled all over it: it is a stately tree which lords it over the landscape, and no one is willing to sit still in its shadow, but all must need cut their names on the bark with pen-knives." (*Idem,* p. 26.)

48. *Idem,* pp. 27–28. On Longfellow's lack of interest in Dante's symbolism, see *infra.*

49. This version of Schelling's essay was published in the *Graham Magazine,* June, 1850, pp. 351–354. It was later included in Longfellow's volume of prose works, *Driftwood, A Collection of Essays* (Boston, 1857), and reprinted in 1866 with the lecture on Dante.

channels for spreading the knowledge and study of Dante in America. As Koch remarks:

Although the early American students of Dante were not without their influence in creating a local and limited interest in their author, yet they left but little lasting incitement to the study of him. They did not succeed in bringing Dante before the American reading public, or in giving him the audience he merited. To Longfellow this honor chiefly belongs.[50]

Interestingly enough, there were people in the higher spheres of New England culture who looked askance at this introduction of Dante's poem into the curriculum of American colleges and schools. Margaret Fuller (1810–50), the brilliant starlet of the Transcendentalist group gathered around Emerson, called the study of Dante in the schools "a pedantic folly."

Not only the tragedies of Alfieri and the Faust of Goethe, but the Divina Commedia of Dante—a work which it is not probable there are upon earth, at any one time, a hundred minds able to appreciate—, are turned into school books for little girls who have just left their hoops and dolls, and boys whose highest ambition it is to ride a horse that will run away, and brave the tutor in a college frolic. This is done from the idea that, in order to get acquainted with a foreign language, the student must read books that have attained the dignity of classics, and also which are "hard." Hard indeed, it must be for the Muses to see their lyres turned into gridirons for the preparation of a school-girl lunch; harder still for the younglings to be called to chew and digest thunderbolts, in lieu of their natural bread and butter.[51]

In her opinion, the Harvard boys to whom Longfellow was then lecturing on Dante and reading the *Divine Comedy* not only did not learn anything, because they remained "in perfect ignorance of its meaning," but, still worse, they left college "fancying to their life-long misfortune, that they had read Dante." This mistrust of young minds on the part of a woman who was proud to have been

50. Koch, *DA*, p. 36.
51. "Italy—Cary's Dante," reprinted in *Life Without and Life Within*, a collection of Margaret Fuller Ossoli's reviews, narratives, essays, and poems, Arthur B. Fuller, ed. (Boston, 1860), p. 103. The article was written as a review of the new American edition of Cary's version of the *Divine Comedy* (New York, 1845). At that time Margaret Fuller had left Boston and the editorship of the *Dial* (1840–42) and was on the staff of the *New York Tribune*, where she gained a wide reputation as a critic.

able to read Ovid in Latin at the age of eight years and to have begun the study of philosophy at the age of twelve is singular, to say the least. It may be explained in part, however, by the fact that she looked upon the *Divine Comedy* as being primarily a work of high philosophical speculation and profound spiritual experience. She felt it could be understood only by those who, like Dante, had been lost "in the forest of human passions," and then had passed "through the purgatory of speculation and struggling hopes," finally to see, with cleared vision, the stellar dance and to hear the spheral melody when "thought, with costly accelerated motion, raises itself a spiral which can only end in the heart of the Supreme."

This transcendental view of the *Divine Comedy* led Margaret Fuller to deplore and condemn not only the "piling upon a brain still soft the mountainous meanings of Dante," but also the "pedantic style in which the grown-up, in stature at least, undertake to become acquainted with his work." They get hold of the best Italian dictionary, of a long string of commentators, and they seek "with anxious attention to know who *Signor This* is, and who was the cousin of *Signor That,* and whether any deep papal or anti-papal meaning was couched by Dante under the remark that *Such-a-one* wore a great-coat." Shut your books and give up all this nonsense, because, although Dante

took the stuff that lay around him and wove it into a garment of light, it is not by ravelling that you will best appreciate its tissue or design. It is not by studying out the petty strifes or external relations of his time, that you can become acquainted with the thought of Dante . . . The difficulty is in the thoughts and this cannot be obviated by the most minute acquaintance with the history of the times.

This lack of appreciation of the historical approach to Dante and his works is not surprising in a young woman whose fine intellectual and spiritual powers were entirely absorbed in the search for and clarification of a universal philosophy of life and conduct in the Emersonian way.

But did the Harvard "boys" who took Longfellow's Dante course deserve to be so pilloried as Margaret thought they should? And who were those American students of Dante who labored so painfully with dictionaries and commentators to find out who was who in the kaleidoscopic procession of sinners and saints of the *Divine Comedy?* Longfellow could hardly be accused of overindulging in such pleasures; Ticknor, perhaps; but he was no longer a professor and was not publishing anything on Dante.

Fuller's remarks concerning young girls struggling with Dante seem to suggest that as far back as the 'forties Dante was a common subject of study in the curriculum of fashionable schools for girls in Boston and elsewhere. But since at that time Margaret had moved from Boston to New York, it is probable that her humorous description of girls in their teens playing with dolls and with Dante at the same time was a caricature of Da Ponte's Manhattan Academy, the memory of which was then still very fresh in the "polite" circles of the city.

At any rate, Margaret's indignation against what she thought was tantamount to casting pearls before swine does not seem to have caused the abolition of the Dante course at Harvard or elsewhere. Neither did it turn away any serious student of Dante from trying to understand better Dante's thought and art by setting his personality and his works against their native medieval background.

CHAPTER III

THE ESSAYISTS. RICHARD H. WILDE,
JAMES RUSSELL LOWELL

RUSKIN once said that he could not live in a country which had no castles and no cathedrals. English and European men of letters, poets, and artists were born in an atmosphere of unbroken continuity with a long past, and they wrote for a public familiar with that vision of the Middle Ages so greatly cherished by the Romanticists. Castles and cathedrals, ancient streets and houses, monuments and legends were part of their heritage. Even among the unlearned, stories were handed down from generation to generation, stories of great poets, artists, and popular heroes, real and legendary, who had taken part in the drama of religious and political events. The American Romanticists had no such inheritance. They had to acquire it from books and occasional travels in Europe. Furthermore, they wrote for a public which had little idea of castles and cathedrals.

When James Russell Lowell sighted the shores of Spain on his first visit to Europe in 1854, he wrote in his journal:

The first sight of a shore so historical as that of Europe gives an American a strange thrill. What we always feel the artistic want of at home is background. It is all idle to say we are Englishmen, and English history is ours too. It is precisely in this that we are *not* Englishmen, inasmuch as we only possess their history through our minds, and not by life-long association with a spot and an idea we call England. History without the soil it grew in is more instructive than inspiring—an acquisition, and not an inheritance. It is laid away in our memories, and does not run in our veins.[1]

What our American men of letters sought chiefly in their European travels was this past which they lacked, a past with which they

1. James Russell Lowell, "Leaves from My Journal," in *Works of J. R. L.* (Boston, 1890–1915), I, 113.

could connect their intellectual background, their cultural aspirations, and their aesthetic emotions.

America had first been inspired to learn something of Italy, of its art and literature, by England, but now direct connections were being established. Americans began to discover Italy by themselves. From the third decade of the century on, a growing stream of American travelers crossed the ocean to England, then to France, and finally to Italy. Many of them, especially those with literary ambitions, penned their impressions in travel-books, letters, diaries, journals, and memoirs—all of which were much relished by the American public and formed a considerable section of the American literature of that period.[2] In the newly established American consular offices in the largest Italian cities, the consuls (who usually had little official business to transact) spent their time studying Italian literature, art, history, and often writing books and memoirs which, like the travel-books, were widely read by the American public at home.[3]

On the reverse side, the political reaction of the post-Napoleonic period and the failure of successive Italian revolutionary movements forced many Italians of the educated classes to seek refuge in foreign countries. Several of them came to the United States, where usually they tried to make a living by teaching the Italian language and literature.[4] It was through these channels that a knowledge of Italy,

2. For a list of American travelers in Italy and a bibliography of their publications, see Giuseppe Prezzolini, *Come gli Americani scoprirono l'Italia* (Milan, 1933). Also La Piana, *CAI*, pp. 109–161. This vogue of travel books and journals was viewed with favor by Alexander H. Everett, who felt that such books, even when mediocre, helped to deepen America's knowledge of foreign countries. (Review of A. Bigelow's *Travels in Malta and Sicily*, *NAR*, XXXV [1832], 228.) The *American Quarterly Review* of Philadelphia was more exacting, especially where books on Italy were concerned. In a long essay on this type of literature published in 1834 (XVI, 324–358), as a review of G. Hume Weatherhead's *The Philosophical Ramble; a Pedestrian Tour Through France and Italy* (1834), the critic stated that such books were to be written only by those who spent sufficient time in Italy, were free from prejudice and bias, and had a spark of poetical enthusiasm enriched by the treasure of classical erudition. "How can it be possible to expect satisfactory information by those travellers who make or rather murder Italy in a few weeks?" The author of the *Philosophical Ramble* is then taken to task very severely for his lurid description of the character of the Italian people, judged from the political condition of the time.

3. La Piana, *CAI*, pp. 111 ff.

4. G. Schiavo, *The Italians in America Before the Civil War* (New York, 1934), pp. 254–262; E. Goggio, "Italian Educators in Early American Days," *Italica*, VIII (1931), 5 ff.; H. Marraro, "Pioneer Italian Teachers in the United States," *Mod. Lang. J.*, XXIII

of her natural and artistic beauty, and of her achievements in history filtered gradually through to a widening section of the American people.

Florence, more than any other Italian city except, perhaps, Rome, had an irresistible attraction for the Americans of that generation. What they had read in Roscoe's biographies about her past and what they had read in travel-books about her artistic treasures stirred their imaginations and warmed their hearts. Young American artists flocked there, often settling for life. The name of Florence always evoked the name of Dante. The two appeared to be so identified the one with the other that no serious student of the *Divine Comedy* thought he could understand the great poem unless he paid a visit to Florence and set Dante's personality against the screen of Florentine medieval monuments.

Throughout the nineteenth century essays on Dante appeared constantly in American periodicals. Most if not all of them were of indifferent value or had no value at all. All of them tried, however, to set Dante's figure in relief against his Florentine background. The allegory and the symbolism of his poem could be ignored, its theological structure could be overlooked; but a historical or pseudo-historical reconstruction of his Florentine environment, of the romantic story of his love, of his political adventures and fateful exile—these were indispensable to any American essay on Dante.

The *North American Review,* the oldest and the first periodical to give much space to Italian literature, did not remain alone in the field for long. Neither did Boston possess the monopoly on a keen interest in Dante. By the 1830's a similar interest was to be found among men of letters outside New England.[5] American periodicals

---

(1944). Goggio and Marraro have published also several articles on individual Italian teachers in America. See La Piana, *CAI,* pp. 78 ff. On Italian travelers in America and their writings, see G. Torrielli's *Italian Opinions of the United States as Revealed in Italian Travellers* (Harvard Univ. Press, 1941).

5. In 1830 George W. Featherstonhaugh, an English geologist in the employment of the U. S. Government, published *The Death of Ugolino* (Philadelphia), a dramatization of the *Inferno* episode. The author explains in the preface to his tragedy that he had been working for a long time on a translation of the *Divine Comedy* in blank verse, but gave up the task when Cary's translation appeared. Wishing, however, to preserve some of the better passages of his rendering, he conceived the idea of "raising a tragedy out of the ruins of his translation," and chose for that purpose the story of Conte Ugolino, "so preg-

from other parts of the country began to offer to their readers articles on aspects or periods of Italian literature and occasionally essays on Dante.

In the ten years of its short life (1827–37), the *American Quarterly Review* of Philadelphia vied with the *North American* in its efforts to acquaint the public with the intellectual and artistic history of Italy. In one essay on "The Great Italian Poets" (VII [1830], 1–23) the lion's share fell to Dante and the *Divine Comedy*. The *Southern Literary Messenger* of Richmond, Virginia (1834–64), took no notice of Dante during the editorship of Edgar Allan Poe (1835–37). Poe's ideas on poetry in general and epic poetry in particular, as exemplified in his disparagement of Milton's *Paradise Lost,* were certainly obstacles to his appreciation of the *Divine Comedy,* if he ever read the whole of it.[6] A decade later, however, the *Messenger* (XII [September, 1846], 545–552) published a rather eccentric review of the reprint of Cary's translation in New York in 1845. The unknown writer roams without a compass through the medieval jungle, now glancing at monks copying manuscripts in their scriptoria, now making an excursion through the England of Geoffrey of Monmouth, and now wandering about the Courts of Love so dear to the Troubadours. From the mists of darkness and frivolity Dante emerges as a miracle. He forged the Italian language, a language very strange and difficult, which resembles "a capricious beauty who accords her smiles to all, her favors to few." After explaining that the loss of political liberty caused the decline in importance of the Italian language in European cultural life from the end of the sixteenth century, the writer remarks in a jocular vein:

We may easily conclude then, that—despising Italy as the world does—difficult of acquisition as her "sweet tongue" is, our young ladies, who

nant with terrible images." It cannot be said that the result of this salvage was very impressive, either in structure or in dramatic coherence. In 1834 Featherstonhaugh published a translation of Manzoni's *I Promessi Sposi* (Washington, D. C.). (See N. C. Shields, *Italian Translations in America* [New York, 1931], p. 27.)

6. J. C. Mathews, "Did Poe Read Dante?" *University of Texas Studies in English,* 1938, pp. 123–236. Poe mentions Dante several times and shows some knowledge of the first canto of the *Inferno* and of the episode of Conte Ugolino. He may have read some parts of the *Divine Comedy* in a translation. There is no evidence that he knew the other works of Dante.

sing Italian love songs, are pretty nearly alone in an accurate and profound knowledge of the Italian language. Perhaps we ought to lament
that their unusual learning in this department should seldom survive
matrimony. . . .

Seemingly confident that he was one of the few to whom the
"capricious beauty" was ready to accord her favor, the writer ended
his casual ramble through Dante's world with his own English
translation of the episode of Conte Ugolino. Alas, he received only
a faint smile.[7]

Farther south, William Gilmore Simms, "this Scott and Cooper
of South Carolina, poet, prolific novelist, playwright, biographer
and editor," [8] did more than glance at the *Divine Comedy,* influenced perhaps by his northern friend the poet Bryant, who was a
devotee of Dante. Like many other American poets, Simms could
not resist the temptation of putting into English verse, and into
terza rima, the episode of Francesca da Rimini. He thought well
enough of his exercise in translation to publish it in the *Southern
and Western Monthly Magazine* of Charleston (1845), of which he
was the founder and editor.[9]

Still farther south, in Georgia, lived one of the outstanding
American students of Dante of that period, Richard Henry Wilde
(1789–1847). Born in Ireland but reared in Georgia, Wilde became
a successful lawyer and member of Congress. By inclination, however, he was a poet and a man of letters.[10] His interest in Italian
literature was first awakened when, beginning with Dante and

7. Another translation of the Conte Ugolino episode was made by Edward Dorr Griffin
as part of a lecture delivered at Columbia College in 1830. It was published the same year,
after the author's death, in a volume entitled *Remains,* and was reviewed rather favorably
by the poet William Cullen Bryant (*NAR,* XXXIV [January, 1832], 119 ff.), who quoted
several passages from it.

8. Brooks, *The World of Washington Irving,* pp. 298 ff.; Koch, *DA,* p. 87.

9. This translation was reprinted in his collected *Poems: Descriptive Dramatic, Legendary and Contemplative* (New York, 1853), II, 356–360.

10. Aubrey H. Starke, "Richard Henry Wilde: Some Notes and a Check-list" in *The
American Book Collector,* IV (November, December, 1933), 226–232, 285–288; V (January, 1934), 7–10, with bibliography. Koch, *DA,* app. 23–26. In 1819 Wilde published
anonymously his lyric "The Lament of the Captive," which was to be part of a projected
epic poem on the Seminole War. The lyric "stirred a tempest of speculation, being variously
claimed as the work of another, or as a translation from the Greek." It was set to music
by Lanier and others under the popular title "My Life is Like the Summer Rose." Twenty
years later, Wilde avowed his authorship of it. (Brooks, *op. cit.,* pp. 268, 326.)

Petrarch, he read the Italian lyric poets. He started to translate some of them into English with the intention of publishing an anthology that would give the American public some idea of the development of lyric poetry in Italian literature.

His interest then shifted to Tasso, the romantic and strange vicissitudes of whose life fascinated him. In 1835, Wilde went to Italy where he spent about four years, chiefly in Florence studying Italian literature and writing his *Conjectures and Researches Concerning the Love and Madness of Torquato Tasso* (2 vols. New York, 1842). In connection with these researches, he obtained access to the Medicean archives. Having completed his work on Tasso, he returned to the lyric poets. He says of this period of his activities:

> I was then engaged in translating specimens of the Italian lyric poets, and composing short biographical notices of each author; and, being much puzzled with the obscurities and contradictions abounding in the ordinary lives of Dante, it occurred to me to seek in the archives thus fortunately opened to my curiosity whatever explanations they might afford.[11]

This was the origin of his ambitious plan of writing a large book on the life and times of Dante. In spite of his best efforts, however, Wilde's lack of training in the scholarly method of research set him adrift in that sea of archival documents and charts, and he steered his course haphazardly, reading everything that came into his hands, but making now and then by chance some valuable discovery. Upon his return to the States he was made a professor of law at the newly established University of Louisiana, where he met an untimely death by yellow fever in 1847. Both his *Anthology of Italian Lyrics* and *Life of Dante* remained unfinished.

Wilde summarized his findings on Dante as follows:

> The fortunate discovery of a record establishing Dante's services as one of the secret council, and his vote against furnishing troops to Boniface VIII, which had escaped all my predecessors . . . Various other discoveries enabling me to arrange and elucidate the order of events during a short but most perplexing period of Florentine history, whose con-

11. Quoted from the manuscript of Wilde's work on Dante by Koch, *DA,* p. 26.

fusion all had admitted and despaired of correcting. A vindication in many points of the old biographers and commentators, most unjustly censored. The identification of one of the young men poisoned during the faction of 1300,—Pigello Portinari, as a brother of Beatrice and a friend of Dante. The satisfactory solution of that hitherto unsettled question,—the Poet's Roman virtue in recommending the banishment of his best friend, Guido Cavalcanti, and the full conviction of his own innocence, and the iniquity of the sentence passed upon him by his enemies.[12]

T. W. Koch, who examined the manuscripts, has this to say about Wilde's Dante:

The Life and Times of Dante was planned to consist of two volumes but no more than the first was ever written. The manuscript consists of about eight hundred closely written quarto sheets, the last of which is dated October 10, 1842. As it stands it deals more with the times in which Dante lived than with his life. A score of appendices to which references are made throughout the volume, are lost or were never written.

It was unfortunate for the progress of Dante studies in this country that Wilde was unable to complete and publish his work.[13] His interest in Italian poetry became a passion which extended to include history and led him to long and exacting erudite researches. Meanwhile he was fully conquered by the charm of old Florence and of Italy's cultural traditions:

> My Italy! although of thine not born
> Nor worthy mine own lands' maternal breast,
> Thy child in heart I am. . . .[14]

---

12. *Idem*, p. 29.

13. A short note in the *Southern and Western Monthly Magazine* (August, 1845, p. 144) announced that "the life of Dante by R. H. Wilde is in rapid preparation for the press. . . . We have had the pleasure of hearing portions of the work read by the accomplished writer himself. . . . We look anxiously for this work as an honorable addition to American and particularly to Southern literature." Wilde's manuscripts are now in the Library of Congress. In 1867 his son William Cummings Wilde, sometime professor of ancient languages in the University of Louisiana, tried to secure a publisher for them, but, as was to be expected, without success.

14. These lines are to be found in *Hesperia, a Poem*, by R. H. Wilde, in four cantos in *ottava rima*, edited by his son (Boston, 1867), p. 173. Canto IV opens with a translation of *Purgatorio*, VIII, 1–6. I owe this information to the courtesy of Professor Kenneth McKenzie.

A life of Dante written by an American who, in spite of his limitations, had steeped himself in Florentine history and wrung new evidence from the archives, and who was, moreover, a gentle poet and a gifted writer, would have introduced Dante to a large circle of readers and aroused a new interest in the history and literature of Italy. As it was, many years passed before the subject approached by Wilde with such enthusiasm, though with little sense of method, was taken up again, more successfully, in America by trained scholars who had the advantage of the new material on the Florence of Dante's time which has been gathered by historians able to use more profitably the archives consulted by Wilde.

Wilde is most often remembered for the important part he played in the rediscovery of the Dante portrait attributed to Giotto in the Bargello. Although accounts of this incident differ, since so many were eager to claim the credit for the find, there seems to be little doubt that Wilde contributed much to it. But, as he says, being "a foreigner from a new world," and not liking to appear as an intruder, he did not add his name to such official documents as the memorial addressed to the Grand Duke to obtain permission to remove from the walls of the Bargello the whitewash under which the frescoes were hidden.[15]

By the middle of the nineteenth century, progress was clearly discernible in American appreciation of Dante. Thomas W. Parsons had already published, in 1843, his translation of the first ten cantos of the *Inferno,* and Longfellow his first samples of translation from

15. The account of Wilde's part in the discovery, which he had written or planned to write as an appendix to his book on Dante, has not been found, but Washington Irving's article "American Researches in Italy," published (under the pseudonym of Geoffrey Crayon) in the *Knickerbocker Magazine,* XVIII (October, 1841), 319–322, contains a detailed narrative of the affair which seems to have been written on information supplied by Wilde. It appears from Irving's article that Wilde was the first to seek permission from the government to remove the whitewash from the walls and to obtain financial aid. But in the account written by Seymour S. Kirkup, an English artist who had a part in the affair and claimed all the credit for the discovery (see Toynbee, "Dante in English Art," *Rep. Dante Soc.,* 1921, pp. 29–35), there is only a passing reference to an "American" who joined Kirkup in the enterprise. The whole affair is discussed with abundant references by R. T. Holbrook, *Portraits of Dante from Giotto to Raffael* (London and Boston, 1911), pp. 73–150; A. D'Ancona, *Scritti danteschi* (Firenze, 1912), pp. 533–568; Frank Jewett Mather, *The Portraits of Dante* (Princeton Univ. Press, 1921), pp. 6 ff.; and summed up by Kenneth McKenzie, *Antonio Pucci, Le Noie* (Princeton Univ. Press, 1931), pp. 59–68, in connection with Pucci's sonnet on Dante's portrait in the Bargello. On Holbrook's and Mather's works see below pp. 279 ff.

the *Comedy* and a sketch of Dante's life and works (1839 and 1845). In 1844 Samuel Gray Ward, reviewing Parsons' translations in the famous though short-lived Transcendentalist organ, the *Dial*, remarked:

Many of us must remember our introduction to the Prince of Tuscan Poets. We had formed perhaps the dim vision of a Miltonic hell, enveloped in smoke and flame, dusky, lurid, indistinct, out of which peered gaunt shapes of horror. The Italians told us how hard he was to read,—how impossible for any but an Italian to understand,—how obscure—enigmatical—allegorical. We heard that no one has ever yet fully and fairly explained him. All conspired to make us approach with awe this dim and tremendous shadow. With how different feelings do we now look back. We tell our good Italian friends that the beautiful explains itself, and may be found by Italians or English alike. The allegory he hides so deeply was temporary, and whether it means this or that, is of little importance to us,—but the poetry, in which it is enveloped, belongs to all time, and can be understood by all men. To his language, at first unusual, we discover in a few cantos the key. His rhyme, which impeded at first, soon seems to us the only medium that could adapt itself to his varied theme. The Terza Rima does not flow, but walks,—does not declaim, but converses, philosophizes, reasons,— above all, describes,—and, however difficult to us, in Dante, it seems to be the natural frame of sentences among his interlocutors. Instead of obscurity or vagueness, we find an unexampled clearness, rendered transparent by images that with a single word give the most forcible pictures. . . . So many reviews, books, and magazine articles have of late years been busy with the subject, that now-a-days it is to be hoped students are better prepared what to expect than chanced in our days. Everybody has read a few cantos, that has read Italian at all. Many have read the Inferno; but to almost all the Purgatorio and the Paradiso remain unsought mines. Still, from an Italian author, Dante is becoming a world-author; the knowledge of him is no longer confined to Italian scholars,—and it is a fair sign of the times that we have in Boston a new and good translation.[16]

Among the essays on Dante of that period there are a few worthy of special mention.[17] Longfellow's "Dante Alighieri," in his *Poets*

16. "Translation of Dante," *The Dial,* IV (January, 1844), 285–290.
17. B. G. Niebuhr, "The Allegory in the First Canto of Dante's Inferno," trans. from German by Francis Lieber in *Reminiscences of an Intercourse with Niebuhr* (Philadelphia,

and Poetry of Europe (Philadelphia, 1845, pp. 512–524), while little more than a commonplace summary for beginners and students, is a charmingly written introduction to the examples of Dante's poetry in English translation which Longfellow included in his book.[18] Samuel Gilman Brown's essay "Dante" (*NAR*, LXII [April, 1846], 323–350) is one of the best of the many American sketches of the Florentine poet made during that period. As was the case with many others, this essay was written on the occasion of the reprinting of Cary's translation in New York in 1845 (from the fourth and last edition revised by Cary). From such sources as were available to him,[19] Brown outlined the Italian and Florentine background of Dante's life and times. His description of Dante's death at Ravenna is a good sample of his romantic style:

Wrapped in the coarse garb of a friar, he lay down to die. From before his eyes this vain world was passing away. No requiems were sung; no crowds hurried through the streets to inquire how it fared with the great poet. . . . He was ushered into that world of whose mysteries he had sung. He went to take up his abode, if hope is a true prophet,

> "With those just spirits that wear victorious palms,
> Hymns devout and holy psalms
> Singing everlastingly."

Brown was very much concerned with Dante's "grossness," "vindictiveness," and similar sins which had been the stock in trade of all the poet's hostile critics since he had emerged again into the

---

1835), pp. 189–192; "Dante's Beatrice" (author unknown), a sketch in a book entitled *Token and Atlantic Souvenir* (Boston, 1836); "Homer, Dante, Rabelais and Shakespeare," *Corsaire*, I (New York, 1834), 609–611; "Carlyle on Dante," *Arcturus*, I (New York, 1841), 356 ff.; "Dante Alighieri," a fanciful sketch of Dante's life in the *Knickerbocker Magazine*, XVIII (October, 1841), 275–287, depicting Dante and Beatrice as "enjoying that passionate intercourse which had been so long denied them"; "Dante," *American Review, A Whig Journal*, III (April, 1846), 453 ff. Phillip Schaff, "The Life and Genius of Dante Alighieri," *Am. Review*, VIII (August, 1848), 125–141; A. S. Hyde, "Dante," *Methodist Quarterly Review*, IV (1852), 49–66; *Idem*, VIII (1856), 381, 404; "The Divine Comedy," *National Magazine*, VII (1855), 28–30; E. V. Scherb, "Dante's Beatrice as a Type of Womanhood," *Christian Examiner*, LXIV (1858), 39–56. For others, see Koch, *DA*, pp. 80–87.

18. In the volume were included two translations by Francis C. Gray, one of *Paradiso*, XXII, 1–34, the other of Boccaccio's sonnet "Dante Alighieri son, Minerva oscura," which was later republished several times. (Koch, *DA*, p. 84.)

19. His main historical source seems to have been Sismondi's *Histoire des républiques italiennes du moyen age* (Paris, 1809–15).

limelight. Boston lovers of Dante, who valued highly the moral lesson of the *Divine Comedy,* were eager, if not to erase, at least to minimize the importance and implications of these faults. The arguments for the defense had been rehearsed again and again. The task lay in presenting them effectively by stressing the fact that in Dante's age, and in the society in which he lived, a certain "grossness" in manners went along with the greatest intellectual refinement, and that, furthermore, these examples of "grossness" occur in the *Inferno* where a measure of realism fits the character of the place. All in all, however:

The moral tone of the poem is as remarkable as any part of it. The immoralities of the age have no reflection here. Some of the scenes may be incongruous, but, as a whole, it is decidedly Christian. There are a few, comparatively very few, examples of grossness; but no sentence or verse, we believe not one, which offends the strictest moral purity. . . . We fear as much cannot be said for Chaucer, or Spenser, or our old dramatists, much as we love them, while in grossness they exceed the great Italian a thousand-fold.

The accusation of vindictiveness is likewise a distortion of the truth:

Dante was a stern, just man. One cannot but admire the intrepidity, the audacity even, with which he attacks the reigning vices and crimes of the day. Neither power, nor rank, nor the church itself, shielded the criminal. . . . Some of his own kith and kin are found in the dreary rounds . . . Dante was no coarse, vulgar, selfish man, pitifully to obtrude his private animosities into such a solemn and grand subject.

Dante's theology, his abstruse scholasticism, and his Catholic, doctrinal orthodoxy were certainly repellent to the Boston literati, raised as they had been in the Deism of the Unitarians or in the Calvinistic traditions of the Congregationalists. Nevertheless, the moral significance and universal value of Dante's poem appeared to them so overwhelming as to obscure all else:

What is the pervading idea of the Divine Comedy, but that the future, the limitless future, is determined by the fleeting present . . . that time is enveloped by eternity—the idea of man's destiny as extending infinitely beyond the present life—of the utter impossibility of his fulfilling the purposes of his being in his threescore years and ten? This idea binds together in vigorous unity the three parts of the poem. . . . Though false in theology, it had a lesson in it which would touch every heart . . . .

Finally, Brown, who seems to have been acquainted with Hegel's *Philosophy,* digresses briefly in order to touch upon the notion and essence of poetry and of art in general as the work of pure imagination:

The broad light of actual fact shall not dispel the splendid illusions of our poetic dreams . . . . The power of the imagination is none the less real because we know that the scenes portrayed by it are fictitious. . . . the power of the narration does not depend upon its truth or falsity, but on the heartiness of the assent which we yield to the demand of our sensibilities. The imagination requires congruity, and not absolute fact; and we demand of the poet that he should be an artist, a *poet*, and not a historian. . . . This mighty power of the imagination Dante brought to bear upon the most solemn realities. We know the strong tendency of the mind to form some picture of the future state,—to render definite those dim and vague phantoms which oppress a guilty soul, as well as the visions of joy which comfort the penitent. The poet satisfied those strong yearnings of the common heart. He interpreted its feelings; its dumb voice spake; its blind eye saw. [20]

Previously, American essays on Dante had never failed to devote several more or less rhetorical pages to the most famous episodes of the *Divine Comedy,* often presenting new translations of them. Brown's essay is a notable exception. What Brown admired most in the poem was not so much the impressiveness of certain episodes as the greatness—intellectual, moral, and emotional—of the poet's experience, which was reflected in the structural unity and poetic beauty of the *Divine Comedy.*

After reading a French article by Charles Labitte, "La Divine Comédie avant Dante" (*Revue des deux mondes,* Paris, September, 1842), and A. J. Ozanam's book *Étude sur les sources poétiques de la Divine Comédie* (Paris, 1845), Robert Wheaton was also moved to depart from the usual pattern of essays on Dante in his article

20. Brown quoted a long passage from Hegel on the "aim of art" and came to the conclusion that Dante had fully realized this aim.

"The Sources of the Divina Commedia" (*NAR*, LXIV [1847], 97–117). To search for Dante's sources, said Wheaton, would formerly have been considered as "wishing to depreciate the genius of the great Florentine poet." No such feeling need be entertained now. "We are all convinced that to subject the works of men of genius to such an analysis is not to diminish their glory, but rather to add to it, inasmuch as it shows their superiority to their predecessors."

It would not be just either to disregard completely these early efforts to explain Dante to the American public, or to look at them disdainfully. The work of the pioneer has its uses in preparing the ground for future developments. James Russell Lowell's famous essay on Dante, which marked a step forward of considerable importance, bears witness to the progress made in the study and understanding of Dante in those few decades of endeavor.

James Russell Lowell (1819–91) is usually associated with Longfellow and Norton, forming the great Cantabrigian triad upon which the older generation of American Dantists that is passing away looked with reverential awe. Unlike his colleagues, Lowell translated neither the *Divine Comedy* nor the *Vita Nuova*. His only important contribution in print to Dante studies was this one essay. His popularity with Dante students was due primarily to his Harvard course, which he inherited from Longfellow in 1855 upon the latter's resignation, and which he in his turn passed on to Norton in 1877 after his appointment as United States Minister to Spain.

Like Longfellow's, his reputation, which was great with his friends and immediate pupils, declined in the eyes of the following generation, and was reduced still more by the modern school of American literary criticism. Formerly, as Koch states, he was reputed to be above Longfellow and even above scholars of other countries as an interpreter of Dante:

It is no exaggeration to say that, in the understanding of Dante few of any time or country have surpassed our own genuinely American Lowell. His appreciation was of the keenest, and his ability, as a critic, of the highest order. Poet and scholar, he combined happily the insight of the one with the trained judgment of the other.[21]

21. Koch, *DA*, p. 53.

His essay, which according to Norton "makes other writing about the poet and the poem seem ineffectual and superfluous," [22] is now looked upon by some as an elegant tapestry of empty phrases. Although this is far from true, there is little doubt that his reputation and influence as a Dantist rest more upon his teaching than his writings.

From what can be gleaned from his addresses, letters, and other writings, and, much more, from what his friends and former pupils have said of him, it is clear that Dante had a great deal to do with Lowell's intellectual development:

It was my own profound admiration for the *Divina Comedia* of Dante that lured me into what little learning I possess. . . . The moment you have an object and a center, attention is quickened; and whatever you acquire groups and arranges itself in an order which is lucid because it is everywhere in an intelligent relation to an object of constant and growing interest. Thus, as respects Dante, I asked myself, what are his points of likeness or unlikeness with the authors of classical antiquity? In how far is either of these an advantage or a defect? What and how much modern literature had preceded him? How much was he indebted to it? How far had the Italian language been subdued and suppled to the uses of poetry or prose before him? How much did he color the style or thought of the authors who followed him? Is it a fault or a merit that he is so thoroughly impregnated with the opinions, passions, and even prejudices, not only of his own age, but of his country? To what extent is a certain freedom of opinion, which he shows sometimes on points of religious doctrines to be attributed to the humanizing influences of the Crusades in enlarging the horizon of the Western mind by bringing it in contact with other races, religions, and social arrangements? These, and a hundred other questions were constant stimulants to thought and inquiry, stimulants such as no merely objectless and, so to speak, impersonal study could have suggested.[23]

This array of questions suggested to Lowell by his reading of Dante points most significantly to the growing intellectual interest in the Middle Ages among American scholars. Lowell's approach to Dante was not merely aesthetic but also historical, and he, unlike

22. Quoted in *idem,* p. 54.
23. Quoted in *idem,* p. 55, from a lecture given at Harvard.

Longfellow, did not overlook Dante's allegory and symbolism; at least, he realized its importance for setting the *Divine Comedy* against its historical background. On the other hand, he had no patience with Dante commentators who analyzed all allusions to figures or historical events in the *Comedy,* or with those who debated the exact meaning of his philosophical and theological expositions. Then, too, he resented very much "the Italians forever twitching at Dante's sleeves and trying to make him say he is of their way of thinking."

The method he followed in his Dante course was far from orthodox. One of his students, Barrett Wendell, described it thus:

Mr. Lowell never gave us less than a canto to read; and often gave us two or three. He never, from the beginning, bothered us with a particle of linguistic irrelevance. Here before us was a great poem—a lasting expression of what human life had meant to a human being, dead and gone these five centuries. Let us try, as best we might, to see what life had meant to this man; let us see what relation his experience, great and small, bore to ours; and, now and then, let us pause for a moment to notice how wonderfully beautiful his expression of this experience was. Let us read, as sympathetically as we could make ourselves read, the words of one who was as much a man as we, only vastly greater in his knowledge of wisdom and beauty. That was the spirit of Mr. Lowell's teaching. . . . Now and again, some word or some passage would suggest to him a line of thought—sometimes very earnest, sometimes paradoxically comical. . . . I remember too, that one tremendous passage in the "Inferno" started him off in a disquisition concerning canker-worms, and other less mentionable . . . vermin. And then, all of a sudden, he soared up into the clouds, and pounced down on the text again. . . . In a single college year, we read through the *Divine Comedy* and the *Vita Nuova;* and dipped into the *Convito* and the lesser writings of Dante.[24]

How successful Lowell was in bridging the gulf which stood between the world of Dante's experience and that of his Harvard boys is a matter of conjecture. All seem to agree, however, that one—perhaps the best—result of his teaching was, as Barrett Wen-

24. Barrett Wendell, "Mr. Lowell as a Teacher," *Scribner's Magazine,* X (1891), 645–649.

dell said, that of awakening in his students a keen interest in learning "This love of learning was also the temperamental quality which made the best feature of his literary essays." [25]

According to some critics his essays "lack general views and the structure that is dependent on them; they are desultory and appreciative rather than profound and interpretative." But in detail "Lowell's scholarship and wit shows to excellent advantage. . . . The chief example is his essay on Dante." [26]

In a more sympathetic vein, A. H. Thorndike remarked:

The personal essay as a literary form seems to require maturity of mind, breadth of experience and reading, a responsive humor, and intensity and discrimination in taste. These qualities Lowell brought to his essay writing, whether the subject be drawn from nature, or society, or the world of books. . . . His essays on Chaucer and Dante are among his best, and have done their part in stimulating among thoughtful Americans a study and appreciation of the great centuries of human progress that preceded Columbus' discovery. . . .[27]

While the many other essays on Dante lay buried and forgotten in old American periodicals, Lowell's "Dante" remained for more than a generation the most inspiring brief survey on the subject that American students were expected to read in their general courses in literature.[28] Although it has been superseded by other scholarly American works on a larger scale, it still makes good reading. He wrote eloquently of Florence, the city where "the past is so contemporary with us in unchanged buildings and undisturbed monuments," the home of Dante. The Florentine atmosphere appealed strongly to his own deep sense of tradition:

25. R. M. Lovett, in John Macy. ed., *American Writers on American Literature*, p. 185.
26. *Idem*, p. 186.
27. *Cambridge Hist. of Am. Lit.*, II, 254.
28. In 1859 Lowell wrote a biographical sketch of Dante for the *Appleton New American Encyclopedia*. In 1872 he wrote an article apropos of Maria F. Rossetti's "The Shadow of Dante, an Essay Towards Studying Himself, His World and His Pilgrimage," which had been reprinted in Boston the same year. In his *Letters* (II, 84), Lowell writes: "The article on Dante was written in all the distraction of getting away [to Europe], with the thermometer at 95, and keeping abreast of the printers, so that I could not arrange and revise properly." Both the biographical sketch of 1859 and the article of 1872 were fused together in the final form of the well-known Dante essay as published in *Among My Books* (2d series [Boston, 1876], pp. 1–124), and then reprinted in later editions of Lowell's *Works*.

To an American, there is something supremely impressive in this cumulative influence of the past full of inspiration and rebuke, something saddening in this repeated proof that moral supremacy is the only one that leaves monuments and not ruins behind it. Time, who with us obliterates the labor and often the names of yesterday, seems here to have spared almost the prints of the *care piante* that shunned the sordid path of worldly honor.

The tone of the essay is both reverent and enthusiastic. With an emotion akin to awe, Lowell marvels at the "cumulative influence" of the great Italian:

Dante penetrates to the moral core of those who once fairly come within his sphere, and possesses them wholly. His readers turn students, his students zealots, and what was a taste becomes a religion. The homeless exile finds a home in thousands of grateful hearts.

Objections raised against the *Divine Comedy,* says Lowell, are the result of ignorance and prejudice, or of wrong ideas about the distinction between the artist and the moralist:

But where, as in Dante, the religious sentiment and the imagination are both organic, something interfused with the whole being of the man, so that they work in kindly sympathy, the moral will insensibly suffuse itself with beauty as a cloud with light.

Dante is often misinterpreted; the temptation to find subtler meanings in his verses is irresistible:

Italians in exile . . . made Dante the stalking-horse from behind which they could take a long shot at Church and State, or at obscurer foes. Infinitely touching and sacred to us is the instinct of intense sympathy which draws these latter towards their great forerunner, *exul immeritus* like themselves. But they have too often wrung a meaning from Dante which is injurious to the man and out of keeping with the ideas of his age.[29]

In expounding the *Divine Comedy* one should seek to bring out the great and perennial issues contained in it and relegate "minute exegesis" to a secondary position. In analyzing the plan of it, its

29. Lowell refers to Italian political exiles like Vincenzo Botta, who in 1865 had published a book on Dante (New York). On this book see below, pp. 135–136.

actual unfolding in three parts and the unity of Dante's conception, Lowell stresses the universality of the poem, not only as a great poetical work, but from the point of view of its philosophical and moral content.

Dante's Other World is not in its first conception a place of *departed spirits*. It is the Spiritual World, whereof we become denizens by birth and citizens by adoption. It is true that for artistic purposes he makes it conform, so far as possible, with vulgar preconceptions, but he himself has told us again and again what his real meaning was. . . . To give his vision reality, he has adapted it to the vulgar mythology, but to understand it as the author meant, it must be taken in the larger sense. To confine it to Florence or to Italy is to banish it from the sympathies of mankind. It was not from the campanile of the Badia that Dante got his view of life and man.

Dante was not only the founder of modern literature; he was the first Christian poet in any proper sense of the word, the first who so subdued dogma to the use of plastic imagination, as to make of it poetry of the highest order. To be sure, Christianity had infiltrated into European literature before Dante's time, but as a mythological concept. The Christian idea had not previously been incorporated into a literary work. It was to make its first appearance in Dante. The *Divine Comedy*, like the Gothic cathedral, typifies the Christian idea.[30] In addition, Lowell analyzes Dante's concept of the Church, his attitude toward the hierarchy and its political interests, his emphasis on the unity of the human race, his solution to the problem of the salvation of infidels, his orthodoxy in matters of faith, and shows that in Dante's mind the structure of the poem gave a concrete form to the message of Christianity.

In conclusion. Lowell thus summed up the significance of the poet:

Dante was the first poet who ever made a poem wholly out of himself. . . . He discovered that not only the story of some heroic person,

---

30. This comparison of the architectural structure of the *Divine Comedy* to a Gothic cathedral was first used in the eighteenth century to disparage Dante's work, which was considered to be uncouth, extravagant, and barbaric. Later, during the periods of Romanticism and Medievalism, the comparison came to be used as highest praise. See Croce, *La Poesia di Dante* (Bari, 1921); Eng. trans. by Douglas Ainslie, *The Poetry of Dante* (New York, 1922), p. 92.

but that of any man might be epical; that the way to heaven was not outside the world, but through it. . . . Dante is the highest spiritual nature that has expressed itself in rhythmical form . . . he has shown us the way by which that country far beyond the stars may be reached, may become the habitual dwelling place and fortress of our nature, instead of being the object of its vague aspirations in moments of indolence.

The universal value of Dante's own human experience, which inspired his great poem and provided his artistic genius with soaring wings, seems to have been the dominant note in Lowell's Dante course. Longfellow's lectures on Dante dealt chiefly with the literary merits of his poetry and were delivered in the rather vaporous rhetorical vein dear to the Romantic literary critics. Lowell was by no means unaware of the linguistic and literary problems raised by Dante's works; his strictures on Parsons' version reveal his critical sense in matters of language as well as his care in details. Unlike Longfellow, Lowell realized that "in the allegory lies the profound meaning and the permanent force of the *Divine Comedy*," and that Dante's personality, thought, and art should be set against a broader horizon than that envisaged by his predecessor in the Harvard chair. His lectures seem to have been learned and suggestive, though sometimes erratic. Rather than directing his students in a methodical analysis of Dante's works, and in a painstaking consideration of philological, historical, and doctrinal problems, Lowell seems to have delighted more often in using his wit and imagination to make Dante, the man, the poet, and his world intelligible in the light of mankind's everyday intellectual, physical, and moral experience.

Ticknor had been cool and perhaps dull; Longfellow, a glowing but at times only verbal flame. Lowell added to his brilliancy a broader vision and a deeper insight into the life reflected in the *Divine Comedy*.

CHAPTER IV

THE FIRST AMERICAN TRANSLATORS OF DANTE. THOMAS W. PARSONS, RALPH W. EMERSON

IN NO other language are there so many translations of the *Divine Comedy* as there are in English, and it is safe to say that no other poet, ancient or modern, save perhaps Horace, has been rendered into English as many times as Dante. Although the majority of these translations have been made in England, America has contributed a considerable group of them.

The advance of Dante studies and a growing acquaintance with the original text made English Dantists aware that Cary's translation, despite its merits, did not always convey faithfully Dante's thought and poetic beauty. Cary's use of blank verse with its marked Miltonian ring seemed to many of them a poor substitute for the *terza rima* of the original. The main criticism of Cary's version was its not infrequent dilution of Dante's imagery and its general polite varnishing of Dante's language and style. Those who are familiar with the Italian text and know how Dante forged anew the rude linguistic material inherited from his predecessors in Italian poetry are struck by the incongruity of clothing his poem in Miltonian dress, thereby altering its tone and dimming its artistic originality.

However that may be, Cary's version remained without competitors for almost twenty years, until 1833, when Charles Ichabod Wright (1795–1871) published his new version of the *Inferno,* and followed it with the *Purgatorio* in 1836 and the *Paradiso* in 1840.[1] Wishing to retain something of the original rhythmic structure in his English rendering of Dante, Wright adopted a modified form of the *terzina,* omitting the middle rhyme. As one of his critics remarked:

1. Toynbee, *DEL,* II, 568 ff.; "Wright's translation is an unequal performance, but at times it reaches a high level of excellence."

Wright's measure is the Dantesque one to the eye, but not to the ear. It is printed exactly like the Italian verse, but the writer has not grappled with the difficulties, and he missed the chief grace, of the *Terza Rima*: he has few triple rhymes at all—and none in the right places; and the subtle link by which Dante binds every section of his measure into the succeeding one is thus wholly lost.[2]

The same reviewer also noted that Wright had taken from Cary's version not only many lines but "in innumerable instances had obviously and incontestably drawn his words not directly from the Italian fountain-head, but from the previous English of his predecessor."

The *Edinburgh Review,* on the contrary, praised Wright's version for the same reason for which the *Quarterly* condemned it:

Wright has very luckily solved the problem of the English *Terza Rima*. In preserving the triplet, he has secured the entire effect of an analogous versification; while, by throwing off one of the rhymes—which nobody will miss—he has made it possible to reproduce the sense and freedom of his original, within an equal compass.[3]

Ten years later (1843), John Dayman's (1802–71) version of the *Inferno* presented Dante to the English reader for the first time in the *terza rima* of the original.[4] It was very favorably reviewed in the *Spectator,* which remarked that "of all the Italian poets Dante would seem susceptible of being most finely translated into English." This is because "Dante's manner is English: it is more direct, more concise, graver, than that of his countrymen in general." A translation of Dante "should as nearly as possible let the English reader know what Dante *is;* not what the poet might have been had he been our own contemporary." From this point of view, Dayman's translation "gives the English reader a better idea of Dante than any previous translation. . . . Upon the whole, if Cary's ver-

2. *Quarterly Review,* July, 1833; quoted in *idem,* II, 576.

3. *Edinburgh Review,* July, 1833; quoted in *idem,* II, 578.

4. Dayman stated in his preface that he had "rigidly abstained from making any acquaintance with the English translations which have preceded this"; but Wright accused him of having borrowed from his: "[Dayman] pretends ignorance of my translation, though it has been published ten years." Furthermore, Wright called Dayman's version "a burlesque upon Dante: rhyme without either sense or poetry, a mere verbal translation." (See *idem,* II, 680.)

sion is the more even composition as a piece of English writing . . . Dayman conveys to the English reader a more spirited copy of the poet's images and a more vivid representation of his manner." [5]

In 1849 John Aitken Carlyle came forth with his literal prose translation of the *Inferno*. Thus, within a few decades all possible methods of rendering Dante into English had been tried. Instead of precluding other new attempts, however, these versions seem to have opened the field for a most lively competition, since from that day to this new versions of the *Divine Comedy* have appeared at frequent intervals in England.

Parallel with the appearance of new translations, endless discussions as to their merits and defects arose and resolved into analytical surveys of how Dante could or should be translated best into English. The substantial differences between the Italian and English languages, the peculiar traditions of the English rhythmical systems in poetry, the paucity of English feminine rhymes in comparison with the wealth of them in Italian, and other pertinent problems concerning translations of poetical works—all were debated at great length.

The American periodicals of the first decades of the century contributed little to these discussions. Although most of the articles and essays mentioned above were written on the occasion of the appearance of Cary's translation, or of American reprints of it, a real interest in this problem was awakened by the first attempt in this country to produce a new and different version of the *Divine Comedy*. The attempt was made by Thomas W. Parsons, whose *First Ten Cantos of the Inferno* was published in Boston in 1843.[6]

5. *Spectator*, August 19, 1843; quoted in *idem*, II, 682.

6. There is no extensive biography of Parsons. A few facts of his life were given first in Charles Eliot Norton's Preface and Louise Imogen Guiney's sketch at the beginning of the volume *The Divine Comedy of Dante* (Boston, 1893), which contained all Parsons' translations from the poem, and in the preface of its companion volume of original *Poems* (Boston, 1893). Little more was added by George R. Carpenter in "A Poet's Dante," *Atl. Mo.*, LXXIII (1894), 843–846. Joseph Chamberlin collected more biographical data in *Thomas W. Parsons, Poet and Gentleman,* a brochure privately printed by the Chile Club (Boston, 1923). A brief account of his life and of his poetry was given by Kenneth McKenzie in his article "Parsons" for the second edition of the *Dict. of Am. Biography*. More recently an essay on Parsons and excerpts from his Letters which appeared first in *More Books,* bulletin of the Boston Public Library (September–December, 1938, January, 1939) were reprinted with some additions in the volume *Letters of Thomas William Parsons,* Zoltan Haraszti, ed., with an essay by Austin Warren (Boston, 1940). In this vol-

Thomas William Parsons (1819–92) was the son of an Englishman who had emigrated to New England, studied medicine at
Harvard, and practiced medicine and dentistry in Boston. The boy
attended the Boston Latin School but did not go to Harvard
College. Instead, in 1836, his father took him to Europe, where they
spent the winter in Italy, chiefly in Florence, and then proceeded to
Paris and London, returning to Boston at the end of 1837. He then
studied medicine at Harvard but did not complete his course, and,
following his father's profession, he too practiced dentistry. He
spent another year (1847) in Italy, and later on (1871–72) he
lived for fourteen months in London. He returned to Boston again,
but lived more often in the country, in Wayland or in Scituate,
where he died in 1892.

Well grounded in the classics (occasionally he wrote passable
Latin verses), Parsons gained a considerable reputation as a poet
and was friendly, if not intimate, with the Boston and Cambridge
literati, Emerson, Andrews Norton and his son Charles Eliot
Norton, Holmes, Lowell, Longfellow, and others, smaller stars of
that constellation. In Longfellow's *Tales of a Wayside Inn,* Parsons
is the poet

> whose verse
> Was tender, musical, and terse,
> The inspiration, the delight,
> The gleam, the glory, the swift flight
> Of thought so sudden that may seem
> The revelation of a dream.

In modern histories of American literature Parsons is given little
space and chiefly remembered as the author of the "Ode on a Bust
of Dante" (1841), which is considered a good example of the
American lyric. As for the rest of his work, he is disposed of summarily as one "who wrote poems of small merit." [7] One historian

---

ume Warren draws an attractive picture of Parsons' personality and gives a valuable critical
analysis of his poetical works, while Haraszti reconstructs from correspondence still extant
in the Harvard Library, in the Boston Public Library, and in private hands, episodes in
Parsons' life, and his relations with the Boston and Cambridge literati. Our quotations are
from this volume.

7. *Cambridge Hist. of Am. Lit.,* II, 280.

mistakenly remembers him as "having translated the *Inferno* admirably in *terza rima!*" [8]

More balanced is Austin Warren's appreciation of Parsons:

His inaugurals belong to New England's Golden Days, his latter years to the Gilded, that age when the didactic impulse of Cambridge and Concord had yielded to the separation of art and religion from the conduct of business and politics; when, from being a prophetic passion, poetry had become a craft. By virtue of his Anglophilism and Anglo-Catholicism, Parsons was an alien to the place in which he lived; and his absorbed and single devotion to Dante symbolized his withdrawal from his time. His own poetry, too, had its affiliation with vanished or vanishing idioms: in his satires, his theory of translation and his lyric style, he was a conscientious survivor of an earlier day . . . . [9]

Parsons' interest in Dante began at the time of his first visit to Florence in 1836, when he was only seventeen years old: "There in the venerable Borgo Sant'Apostoli, consecrated, in my imagination by a verse of Dante's, in the ancient house of the Acciaiuoli, and in the home of a learned lady who bore the name of the poet, I became enamoured of the *Divina Commedia.*" [10] The lady was Giuseppa Danti. Under her guidance Parsons began to read the *Divine Comedy.*[11] From those early days in Florence, where

> carried by the spell
> Of that Florentine whose native streets
> . . . . where he used to dwell
> My father made me pace with reverent feet,[12]

Parsons was taken by the idea of making a good English translation of the entire *Divine Comedy.* As was the case with many others before and after him, his first impulse was to keep the *terza rima* of the original, but after experimenting he gave up the task: "I found, in looking over my detached fragments, that the difficulty of the work was too plainly discernible under a partial only and

8. *Idem*, III, 38.
9. A. Warren, essay in Haraszti, ed., *Letters of T. W. Parsons*, p. 9.
10. Quoted in *idem*, p. 10.
11. According to Chamberlin (*op. cit.*), Parsons' *First Ten Cantos* were dedicated to this Florentine lady; but the printed edition contains no such dedication.
12. T. W. Parsons, "La Pineta Distrutta," *Poems* (Boston, 1893).

inelegant success." It became clear to him that "the more exactly the measure of Dante was imitated, the ruder the verse; and the more this fault was avoided, the greater the deviation from the true sense." [13]

After all, a strict adherence to "the triple jingle" was, in his opinion, just as futile as the care taken by other translators to tie themselves to the same number of lines as the original and to "show by marginal figures that they are mathematically faithful." According to Parsons, the English meter most likely to permit a close rendering of Dante was "the stately and solemn quatrain, the stanza of Gray and Dryden. This is the nearest approach to the lengthened harmony of the Italian *terza rima* which is recognized by English ears. It is more than a resemblance—as far as it is carried, it is the same." [14]

The 1843 edition of the *First Ten Cantos of the Inferno* was prefaced by Parsons' "Ode on a Bust of Dante," and was followed by a few notes and an essay, "A Word More with the Reader," on Dante's character and the greatness of his poem. This essay, though vigorous and effective in language and style, is little more than commonplace, and refers the reader to Foscolo, Macaulay, and Carlyle, who "have already expressed whatever the world was waiting to have uttered on this head." It is interesting to note that in this essay young Parsons took the view that Dante was an enemy of the Papacy and a rebel to the Church. He quotes approvingly a long passage "from an eloquent Lecture by one of our best Italian scholars," in which it is stated that "Dante was the Father of the Reformation," and "nothing in this particular can equal the boldness of his muse." Dante not only "disputes the temporal power of the pope," but "denounces also his spiritual usurpations, denies his infallibility, denies him the power of absolution and excommunication." [15] Further on—this time expressing his own opinion—Parsons says that Dante "in his earnestness and truly Christian zeal,

---

13. T. W. Parsons, *First Ten Cantos of the Inferno* (Boston, 1843). At the end of the volume, in "A Word More with the Reader" (p. 73), Parsons says first that he rendered "a good portion of the *Divine Comedy*" in *terza rima;* but then he goes on to speak only of "detached fragments."

14. *Idem*, p. 74.

15. *Idem*, p. 80.

in tone and sentiment at least, is indeed an earlier Luther." Above all, this essay shows Parsons' youthful enthusiasm and the almost religious fervor with which he had undertaken his task. "To render Dante properly," he wrote, "requires somewhat of Dante's own moods; it needs time and toil—fasting and solitude might not be amiss." [16]

Notwithstanding Longfellow's compliment about the poet's "swift flight of thought so sudden," Parsons professed to be a slow and painstaking worker, waiting for the right mood and inspiration to come spontaneously and with no effort, because

> if then subdued
> To serve a master, my own goddess flies
> And inspiration cometh not if sought. [17]

He worked all his life on his translation of the *Divine Comedy,* his periods of industry varying with the tide of his inspiration. But, although he lived to be over seventy years old, he never completed the task undertaken in his early youth.

Twenty-three years after the publication of his *First Ten Cantos,* Parsons issued a revised edition of them which included seven more cantos (1865) as "a humble tribute from New England" to the coming celebration in Florence of Dante's six hundredth birthday.[18] His entire version of the *Inferno* appeared two years later, in 1867. His translation of the *Purgatorio* was published canto by canto in the periodical *The Catholic World* between 1870 and 1882, but it was never completed.[19] Of the version of the *Paradiso* only a few fragments were found at the time of his death.

---

16. *Idem,* p. 83.

17. Quoted by Koch, *DA,* p. 50. The lyric to which these lines belong is not included in Parsons' collected *Poems.*

18. Parsons had finished his translation of the entire *Inferno* many years before. In a letter to Charles Norton in late 1857 or early 1858, he wrote: "The Inferno has been lying by me for many years, as complete, I suppose, as I shall ever be able to make it." Lack of time, he adds, had prevented him from going through "the wearisome and thankless task-work of getting out sheets for the press." Furthermore, he was studying the *Paradiso* and was "so spellbound by the splendours of it," and "so much occupied by its theology and the grave allegory," that he could not go back to the *Inferno.* (Haraszti, ed., *op. cit.,* p. 52.)

19. The version of the *Purgatorio* is complete to the end of Canto XXI. Of the remaining cantos, XXIV, XXVII, and XXX are also complete; XXII, XXV, XXVI, XXVIII,

The *First Ten Cantos* were received with delight, although not without some reservation, by the Boston literati. Parsons, who was then only twenty-four years old, had not been a student at Harvard College and did not belong to the inner circle of the Brahmins. It would seem that he never made any effort to identify himself closely with that group. Inclined to aloofness by temperament, he had no love for Boston or for American life in general, feeling that it lacked the intellectual and cultural refinement of the Old World. As Warren says, "There can be little doubt that, had family responsibilities permitted, he would permanently have lived abroad—in Italy like W. W. Story, or, like Henry James, in England." [20]

In later years he established a warm friendship with Lowell and Charles Eliot Norton, but even then, living as he did mostly in the country rather than in the city, his personal contacts with them were not frequent.[21] He never joined the famous Saturday Club, and was not of the group that gathered in Longfellow's Cambridge mansion to discuss his Dante translation. In fact, Parsons' views concerning the best method of rendering Dante into English were different from those of Longfellow and his friends. Parsons followed the old method of free translation which enabled the translator to paraphrase his author and thus to make his version read like an original English poem; while the Boston group, in general, had been won by the method of literal translation, which attempted to give in English not only the thought and the images but also the modes of expression of the original.

Cornelius Conway Felton (1807–62), a classicist and later presi-

---

XXXI, and XXXIII are translated in part only; and XXIII, XXIX, and XXXII are missing altogether.

20. Warren, *op. cit.,* p. 11. In his epistles in verse he ridiculed the "barbarities of America," the "tap-room statesmen's never ending rant," the effrontery of Cockney journalists and lecturers, Puritan morals, Boston's aversion to the drama, and the Yankees, "this bargain-making tribe." He was not blind, however, to American cultural growth and its future possibilities. The Charles River might become as famous as the Isis to England's Oxford:

> In Harvard's names, that now so humbly sound,
> St. John's and Pembroke may by then be found
> And what old England is to you and me,
> Such may New England to Nebraska be.

> *(Idem,* p. 17)

21. These relations are minutely described from his letters by Haraszti (*op. cit., passim*).

dent of Harvard, felt that, although Parsons showed "considerable skill and metrical power," his selection of the quatrain of Gray's *Elegy* as the nearest approach to Dante's *terzina* was not a wise one (*NAR*, LVII [1843], 496–498): "Parsons' versification is generally easy, fluent and expressive, but in too many passages his translation departs from the expression, if not the sense of the Italian." Nor did Felton approve of the liberties taken by the translator in inserting under the stress of rhyme "epithets and clauses not found in the text, which invariably weaken or falsify the original," even when the addition may seem to be an improvement.

Samuel Gray Ward (*The Dial,* IV [1844], 285 ff.) confessed that he had taken up his task of criticism "not a little prejudiced; for who with the deep music of the original ringing in his ears, but must view the best translation with some aversion?" Comparing Parsons' version to Cary's, Ward remarked that, in general,

Cary is faithful, and literal, and has been a very useful translator . . . but seems to possess quite a faculty of giving a prosaic translation of a poetical passage. Parsons is spirited, often poetical; not always literal enough. A translator is bound to clip nothing, above all, in an author who like Dante, has never an unnecessary word or line.

In conclusion, Ward, as a good old Bostonian who never overlooked the glory of his city, remarked: "We have no little pride, that our city should produce a mark of such devotion to the highest walks of pure literature."

Somewhat similar was the judgment passed on Parsons' cantos by Cary in England. In a letter addressed "from an old Brother Translator" to young Parsons, Cary said that the translation "appears to me to possess, in a remarkable degree, the fluency, vivacity and harmony of original composition. This, unavoidably, is effected at the expense of some departure from Dante's grave and sedate character, though his general meaning is faithfully given." [22]

The most useful criticism came from Andrews Norton, at that time professor of Biblical literature at Harvard, who was a lover of Italian literature and a good Dante student. In a long private letter

22. Toynbee, *DEL,* I, 499.

to young Parsons, Norton made many remarks on various points of
The Ten Cantos; and in a second, longer letter he submitted to
searching criticism Parsons' version of the second canto of the
Inferno, listing some fifty phrases or words which did not convey
the exact meaning of the original, or failed to bring out nuances of
thought or intentional emphasis found in the text. Thus, Dante's
passage:

> ed io sol uno
> M'apparecchiavo a sostener la guerra
> Sì del cammino, e sì della pietate,

was rendered by Parsons:

> I only rose and girt myself to fight
> The struggle with compassion and my road.

Norton rightly remarked that "I only rose" was a mistranslation of
ed io sol uno, m'apparecchiavo, and that reversing the objects of
the struggle by putting the *pietate* before *il cammino,* while in the
original the former is subordinated to the latter, and obliterating the
emphasis on their distinction connoted by *sì* and *sì* had made harsh
and obscure a passage which in the original was clear and effective.

In other instances, Norton objected to the use of "modern"
phrases, as in the passage:

> Me degno a ciò nè io nè altri 'l crede,
> Perchè se del venire io m'abbandono
> Temo che la venuta non sia folle.

This had been paraphrased by Parsons:

> Me worthy! no; I cherish no such dream;
> Should I resign me to thy charge, I fear
> Th' attempt would prove but madness in the extreme.

Norton objected:

"Me worthy! no"—this is a modern, not an antique fashion of expression.
To speak of "cherishing a dream" is more modern still. . . . "madness
in the extreme"— the last words detract, instead of adding to the force

of the expression. They are supernumeraries, introduced for the sake of rhyme.[23]

In general, Norton's criticism was for less freedom and more literality, and close adherence to the text.

Parsons was not indifferent to these criticisms, and during the many years which elapsed between his first youthful experiment and the new edition of the ten cantos with seven more added in 1865, he revised his former version again and again, following many, though not all, of Norton's suggestions.

Meanwhile the competition among English Dante translators had become very keen. Since 1843 nine new translations of the whole *Divine Comedy* plus seven of the *Inferno* alone had appeared in England. In America, a New England clergyman from Newburyport, the Reverend J. C. Peabody, had published *Dante's Hell, Cantos I to X: A Literal Metrical Translation with Notes* (Boston, 1857). In a caustic review of this book (*Atl. Mo.,* I [1858], 382 ff.), Charles Eliot Norton rightly denounced Peabody's version as "nothing more than a poor versification of Carlyle's prose translation of 1849, from which Peabody had also copied the notes." Denouncing the "presumption and ignorance" of this "faker," Norton remarked that from the absurd mistakes made in several quotations from the original, it was evident that the Reverend Mr. Peabody was entirely unfamiliar with the Italian language.

Parsons' *Seventeen Cantos* and Longfellow's version of the *Inferno* appeared at the same time (1865). Both versions were sent to the committee for the celebration of Dante's six hundredth birthday in Florence, as homage from America to the great Italian poet. The president of the committee, Duke Caietani of Sermoneta, a good Dantist and a man of wide cultural interests, thanking Parsons for his homage to Dante, wrote the following appreciation:

Although I am no competent judge of the English language, I can feel all the vigor of your verses which, by your felicitous choice of the quatrain, have succeeded very well in rendering the peculiar force of the Dantesque tercet. Then happily I discovered many of your verses possess-

---

23. Haraszti (*op. cit.,* pp. 58–68) gives several examples of the corrections and suggestions made by Norton and Lowell.

ing even something of the nature of Milton, which is very suitable for the substance of Dante's Poem and its solemn resolute style.[24]

We wonder how Parsons took this compliment. The old Duke, an amiable and courteous gentleman, was not aware that the most serious criticism raised against Cary's translation was that it rendered Dante in Miltonic style, and that all the new translators were eager to avoid incurring the same censure. Another exalted personage, King John of Saxony, who had published a German translation of the *Divine Comedy* under the pseudonym of Philalete, praised Parsons' version highly for its "exactitude . . . and the true antique colorature of the verses and language," which had greatly excited his admiration.[25] Warm praise came also from the two American poets William Cullen Bryant and Fitz-Greene Halleck, in acknowledging copies of the version sent to them.

The authoritative opinion of the Boston Dantists was voiced by Charles Eliot Norton, who, in his article "Dante, and His Latest English Translators" (*NAR,* CII [1866], 509 ff.), summarized their feeling about Parsons' version in the following words: "The Divine Comedy in Parsons' translation remains at least a poem; but its tone is not that of Dante's poem; its merits are its own."

Parsons does not seem to have resented this criticism or to have thought it unfair. His translation was not considered to be very faithful, but at least it was good English poetry; this was much more than could be said of most other versions of the *Comedy.* He seems to have been convinced, however, that his translation could be made more literal without losing any of its poetical merits. Since his friendship with both Lowell and Norton had ripened, from the end of 1865 on, beginning with eighteenth canto of the *Inferno,* he sent either to the one or to the other—sometimes to both—the proofsheets of each canto which he had translated, asking for their corrections and suggestions. From his correspondence we gather that both his friends, Lowell especially, were very generous with their time and labor in calling his attention to mistranslations, inexact or too-free renderings, and in analyzing minutely each of the cantos which he submitted to them.

24. *Idem,* p. 61.
25. *Idem,* p. 61.

Parsons' complete translation of the *Inferno*, published in 1867, received more attention than his previous partial editions of it.[26] Since Longfellow's translation of the entire *Divine Comedy* came out the same year, however, most reviewers dealt with them together, comparing the one with the other, and, in general, blaming Longfellow for his extreme literalness and Parsons for his too-free rendering. Parsons' version was highly commended by all for its poetical merits and criticized by all for "his freedom in departing from the actual words and actual phrases of the original," thus weakening Dante's poetry and sacrificing "fidelity to rhyme."[27]

Both Norton (*The Nation*, V [October 3, 1867], 269) and Lowell (*NAR*, CVI [1868], 348) took this opportunity to praise Parsons' original poems, as well as his version of the *Inferno*, as excellent English poetry. Parsons' original poems, wrote Lowell, are conspicuous for their "naturalness of thought, a grace of sentiment, and purity of diction truly Horatian." His rhymed version of the *Inferno* has "all the charm of original production," and at its best is "real poetry, such as speaks the same meaning in all tongues." In Lowell's opinion no comparison between Longfellow's and Parsons' versions is really possible from the point of view of their fidelity to the original, because, without entering upon the vexed question of rhyme and blank verse, "the kind of fidelity attainable by each is different from that of the other, though it is not always safe to define this difference absolutely, as if it were inherent by the nature of the case, for surely blank verse is as capable of wings, as rhyme liable to jog wearily afoot." In conclusion Lowell states: "Parsons' translation should be welcomed by all who are interested in native genius and scholarship, not as the rival of Longfellow's, but as a *succedaneum* to it."

A long, warm eulogy of Parsons' *Inferno*, almost without reservation, was published in the *Catholic World*, the new review founded in 1865 and edited by Father Isaac Hecker. It was written by an Italian Catholic priest living in the United States, Joseph M. Finotti,

26. *The Nation*, V (1867), 269 ff. (by Charles Eliot Norton); *Athenaeum*, February 22, 1868; *The Living Age*, XCVIII (1868), 690 ff.; *Putnam Magazine*, February, 1868, pp. 155 ff. (by George Calvert); *The Catholic World*, VIII (1868), 213 ff. (by Joseph Finotti).

27. *The Living Age*, XCVIII (1868), 690 ff.

who said that "after a close and careful study we deem it to be the best of all translations of Dante." Parsons must have expressed his warm appreciation of the compliment to the editor and thus have established friendly relations with him, for, from 1870 on, the *Catholic World* published Parsons' version of the *Purgatorio* canto by canto at more or less regular intervals.[28]

Parsons was devoted to the Anglican Church and, in his later years at least, rather given to piety. He must have thought that the publication of his version of the *Purgatorio* in the pages of a Catholic periodical might mislead the public as to his religious convictions, and took the precaution of heading the first canto (*The Catholic World,* November, 1870) with a brief explanatory note. Mindful that the Thirty-Nine Articles of the Anglican Church reject the Catholic doctrine of Purgatory, Parsons stated:

In perusing our version of the *Purgatorio* of Dante, the Protestant reader of *The Catholic World* may profitably direct his attention less to any dogma of the Church, or any formula of a special creed, than to any allegorical sense of the poet, founded, as it must be acknowledged, by all Christian believers, upon the facts of our nature and the history of the human heart. The Romish doctrine of Purgatory may be combated as an article of faith, but it must be admitted as a true statement of the condition of mankind religiously considered. The wretched state of man living without God in the world, the self conviction of sin, the

28. In a letter dated October 4, 1872, to his brother-in-law, George Lunt, editor of the *Boston Courier,* from New York, where he stayed for a few days upon his return from England, Parsons stated that he had received fifty dollars from Father Hecker for the third canto of the *Purgatorio,* which the *Catholic World* had published the previous September, and added: "We saw Father Hecker last night and he read me a letter from Rome containing a very high compliment from Professor Ubaldi of the Propaganda upon this Canto in my version. . . . Father Hecker wishes me to go on with selected Cantos, not caring to publish in order so long a series—especially, as I think his readers would not find all of them equally interesting." (Haraszti, ed., *op. cit.,* p. 93.) In his youth, Parsons had shown a strong dislike of the Catholic Church, as may be seen in the essay appended to the *First Ten Cantos.* One of his most pungent satires, "St. Peray" (the name of a French wine), is a caricature of the cult of the saints. Gradually, however, he became "as nearly a Roman Catholic as he well could be without absolutely stepping over the dividing line" (Warren, *op. cit.,* p. 12). In a letter written in 1872, he stated that he felt "heartily ashamed to be recognized as the writer of 'St. Peray,' those rhymes copied from a wine bottle" (Haraszti, ed., *op. cit.,* p. 91). The study of Dante brought him to that of Aquinas, and in a sonnet "Turning from Darwin to Aquinas," he rejected modern science in favor of medieval theology. During the last years of his life, he versified "The Collects of the Holy Catholic Church as They Are Set Forth by the Church of England in Her Book of Common Prayer for Every Sunday of the Year."

possibility of attaining through contrition and penance to the *peace
which passeth understanding,* is the sum of the doctrine embodied in the
Divina Commedia.[29]

After Parsons' death in 1892, all his Dante translations were
collected in one volume (Boston, 1895) by Louise Imogen Guiney,
with a preface by Charles Eliot Norton, who summarized his own
and his friends' final opinion on Parsons' work as follows:

It is safe to assert that as a rhymed version in English of the *Divine
Comedy* it has no superior . . . It does not attempt to render verse for
verse, nor even to follow literally the words of the original without other
addition or subtraction than that which the genius of the language requires. The translator allows himself a certain freedom. He is a poet,
and his translation is to be an English poem. The substance is Dante's,
but the mode of expression is often changed from his. Without knowledge of the original, one may read it with ease and pleasure, and with
little sense of any hampering conformities to a foreign original. . . .
But the student of Dante's own verse feels throughout that the style and
tone were the translator's, not Dante's. It may be a fine style, it may be a
fine tone, but neither one nor the other is that of him who *sovra gli altri
come aquila vola.* . . . The difference is not a mere difference between
Italian and English; it is a difference of essence, a difference in poetic
nature.

Notwithstanding his worship and life-long study of Dante, Parsons, whose poetical taste and habits were those of eighteenth-
century English poetry,[30] could not "re-think" Dante, except in the
language, rhetoric, and imagery peculiar to that tradition. His
choice of the quatrain chained him, from the very beginning, to a
method of translation in which all the advantages were for the
translator's special habits, and none for the original text of Dante.
The efforts made by his Cambridge friends, the Nortons and

29. The first eight cantos of the *Purgatorio* were reprinted in one volume under the
title *The Ante-Purgatorio* (London, 1876). In thanking Parsons for a complimentary copy
of the book, Gladstone wrote: "The opening verses please me much. I am glad you do not
despair of or abandon the *terza rima.* . . ." Evidently the British statesman and scholar
had merely glanced at the first page but had not even recognized the quatrain. (Haraszti,
ed., *op. cit.,* p. 110.)

30. While in England in 1872, Parsons became very much disturbed by the enthusiasm
he found there for the poetry of Walt Whitman and was indignant that the English could
see any merit in it. (Warren, *op. cit.,* p. 17.)

Lowell, who in their criticisms and suggestions tried to lead him to a more literal rendering of Dante, impressed him and he often followed their advice. But no matter how often he yielded to their suggestions, he could not change radically his mental attitude, and much less the method to which he had bound himself with iron fetters.

Zoltán Haraszti, the most recent writer on Parsons and editor of some of his letters, expresses the opinion that the results "of Parsons' relationship with his later mentors," the Nortons and Lowell, did a great deal of harm to his translation:

Excellent scholars and writers though they were, they did not possess Parsons's gift for clear and strong expression; and their influence, with its academic aura, served to tame and intimidate the Boston poet. There can be hardly a question that the first ten Cantos of 1843 are the best part of Parsons's Dante; that in the seventeen Cantos of 1865 the new portions are inferior to the old; and finally that the second half of the completed translation is altogether beneath the first. All this is worth stating, because Parsons's *Inferno,* even as it is, is probably the best in the English language; and because his original Ten Cantos are a masterpiece of which any literature could be proud.[31]

This rather extravagant eulogy of Parsons' *Inferno* may have been suggested by some theory on the art of translation in which the text of the original author is left out of consideration. Lowell, too, had said that Parsons' *Inferno* was the best of those made up to that time, but Lowell had added prudently, "the best of its kind." [32] In other words, it was the best free version, or paraphrase, and, as Norton remarked, "the merits are its own and not Dante's." There is no evidence that the criticisms made by the Nortons and Lowell so intimidated Parsons as to spoil the good work done. From the passages that Zoltán Haraszti quotes from the correspondence between Parsons and his friends, it seems, on the contrary, that they saved him from many pitfalls.[33] Parsons was aware of the weak-

31. Haraszti, ed., *op. cit.,* p. 58.
32. More balanced is K. McKenzie's statement: "Among rhymed English renderings of Dante's poem, that of Parsons, incomplete though it is, takes high rank for its nobility of style and its verbal felicity." (Article on Parsons, *Dict. of Am. Biography.*)
33. It is rather strange that Haraszti (*op. cit.,* p. 31), transcribing one of his letters, should make Parsons quote a famous verse of Dante thus: "*La vocca mi vacio*

nesses of his method of translation, and the expressions of gratitude which occur in his letters to his friends—"I enjoy a friendly Aristarchos," he wrote to Lowell—are more than mere polite gestures.

As a poet, Parsons is very uneven, both in his translations and in his original work. Even when his wings were soaring with poetical vigor and expression, he would often end the flight in a rhetorical commonplace. As Austin Warren remarks: "Even in his best lyrics there are lines or stanzas in need of excision." Parsons "had no sure apprehension of idiom or aim, no sufficient care for the maintenance of tone . . . no precision in measuring the distance of departure from the platitudinous figure or phrase."

According to the same critic:

Parsons' own poetry suffered because of his early conversion to Dante. . . . One can imagine the consequence, to a talent, of living persistently under a colossal shadow. To be a great poet requires . . . invincible faith in oneself and one's uniqueness, but to be any kind of a poet stipulates . . . some presumption that one's personal vision has virtue. Yet how can any man of discernment avoid comparison of his talent . . . with the range and power of Dante? He must read the master and then forget him; for Dante, who enlarges the reader, may very well stifle the poet.[34]

Earlier critics of Parsons' poetry thought, on the contrary, that, although "never was a poet more under a noble spell than Parsons," and although "it is no exaggeration to say that to him Dante was heart blood and life-breath, and never absent from his meditations," nevertheless, this noble Dantean spell did not mar even slightly his originality and poetic power. "Nothing better proves the essential robustness of his intellect than the fact that while he walked so devoutly in the great Florentine's shadow, nowhere in his individual verses is there a single unconscious imitation of him, a single borrowed and unacknowledged excellence."[35]

The verdict of time has not been favorable to the claims of poetic greatness in Parsons. That "gentleman of breeding, cultivation and

---

motto tremante" (sic). Parsons not only knew his Italian well; he knew Dante by heart, and every schoolboy who knows Dante at all knows the line: *"La bocca mi baciò tutto tremante,"* in the Francesca da Rimini episode.

34. Warren, *op. cit.,* pp. 21–22.

35. Louise I. Guiney, Introduction to Parsons' *Divine Comedy,* p. xiv.

talent, and endearing amateur of the arts," is now considered only a minor star in the Old Boston constellation:

> O Time! whose verdict mocks our own
> The only righteous judge art thou.[36]

In 1867 Ralph Waldo Emerson (1803–82) received a presentation copy of Parsons' *Inferno,* and wrote a flattering report of his impressions to the author:

I find the book good beyond my expectation, and, in my opinion, excellent. I am by no means a good Dantean, as you know, but I am quite sensible of his prodigious force, and I find this fairly rendered, and with flowing elegance, from page to page, through all these cantos. In many places, the felicity is admirable . . . I read with the original at my elbow, and from time to time under my eye. I am proud of the work of my countryman, and give you joy in your success.[37]

Emerson had only a superficial knowledge of the Italian language and of Italian literature, but in time he became well acquainted with Dante.[38] It seems to have been Margaret Fuller (1810–50) who first urged him to read the *Vita Nuova,*[39] sometime in 1842 and since Emerson was not able to read it in the original, she volunteered to make him an English translation of it. In a letter to Emerson dated December, 1842, she says:

When you were here, you seemed to think I might perhaps have done something on the Vita Nuova; and the next day I opened the book, and considered how I could do it. But you shall not expect that, either, for your present occasion. When I first mentioned it to you, it was only as a piece of Sunday work, which I thought of doing for you alone; and because it has never seemed to me you entered enough into the genius of the Italian to apprehend the mind which has seemed so great to me, and a star unlike, if not higher than all the others in our sky. Else, I should

36. Parsons, "On a Bust of Dante."
37. Haraszti, ed., *op. cit.,* pp. 67–68.
38. Emilio Goggio, "Emerson's Interest in Italy and Italian Literature," *Italica,* XVII (1940), 97–103; Joseph C. Mathews, "Emerson's Knowledge of Dante," *The University of Texas Studies in English* (1942), pp. 171–198. Emerson had known something of Dante as early as 1818 and had read at least part of the *Divine Comedy* by 1825, but only after his trip to Italy in 1833 he acquired an abiding interest in his works.
39. *Memoirs,* of Margaret Fuller-Ossoli, edited by James F. Clark, Ralph W. Emerson and William H. Channing, Boston, 1852, I, 240.

have given you the original than any version of mine. I intended to translate the poems with which it is interspersed, into plain prose. Milnes and Longfellow have tried each their power at doing it in verse, and have done better, probably than I could, yet not well. But this would not satisfy me for the public. Besides translating Dante is a piece of literary presumption, and challenges a criticism to which I am not sure that I am, as the Germans say, *gewachsen*. Italian as well as German, I learned by myself, unassisted, except as to the pronunciation . . . my not going abroad is an insuperable defect in the technical part of my education.[40]

After confessing that in attempting to translate the *Vita Nuova* she had discovered that she did not know the language sufficiently to do it well, she concludes: "But Lord Brougham should not translate Greek orations, nor a maid-of-all-work attempt such a piece of delicate handling as to translate the Vita Nuova."

Emerson must have been disappointed. In 1842 no translation of the entire *Vita Nuova* into English was available in print, either in England or in America.[41] Spurred, perhaps, by Margaret's remark that he had never "entered enough into the genius of the Italian" to be able to read Dante, he decided to make an effort in that direction and to translate the *Vita Nuova* himself. Among his papers, now in the Harvard Library, there is a manuscript in Emerson's own handwriting containing this translation and dated with certainty as having been done early in 1843. There is no doubt of the fact that Emerson made this translation without any intention of publishing it, but only for his own use and partly as an exercise to improve his Italian.

By courtesy of the Emerson Associates in Cambridge, I received permission to inspect the manuscript of Emerson's translation of the *Vita Nuova* in the Houghton Library of Harvard University, and to copy from it the two following passages; one his version of the sonnet "A ciascun alma presa e gentil core," in Chapter III, and the other the prose of Chapter VII. These two passages were chosen as good examples of this rather unusual performance by Emerson,

40. *Idem*, I, 240–241.

41. The first complete English version of the *Vita Nuova* was Garrow's, printed in Italy in 1846.

who, in general, seems to have had no liking for this kind of work: [42]

> To each taken soul and gentle heart
> To whose sight comes the present word,
> To this end that they may write again their thought;
> Greetings in the name of their lord, that is, Love.
>
> Already was it the third hour
> Of the time when every star is most bright,
> When Love appeared to me suddenly
> Whose substance seen made me tremble.
>
> Glad seemed Love, holding
> My heart in his hand; in his arms had
> My Lady asleep, rolled in a garment;
>
> Then he waked her, and with that burning heart
> Fed he her lowly trembling
> Then bewailing it, he seemed to go away.

The gentlewoman through whom I had for some time concealed my inclination, happened to quit the above mentioned city and went into a distant country. I, as it were, frightened from my fine defense, greatly discomforted myself more than I should have believed beforehand, and thinking that if I should not speak somewhat dolorously of her departure, people would very soon become aware of my secret, I proposed to make a lament in a sonnet which I will copy, because my lady was the immediate cause of certain words which are in the sonnet as appears to whoever understands it, and then I wrote this sonnet.

Emerson's manuscript, with its many cancellations, changes, and corrections, betrays his effort to make a faithful verbal translation of the *Vita Nuova,* relying primarily on the help of a dictionary. But, as everyone who has had experience with translation knows well, no dictionary can register all the possible meanings, and shades of meaning, of which a word is capable in various contexts. The task is especially difficult when dealing with writers having a pe-

---

42. Goggio, *op. cit.,* p. 103. I have been informed that Emerson's entire version of the *Vita Nuova* is being prepared for publication by Dr. J. Chesley Mathews of the University of Texas.

culiar stylistic mannerism and a symbolic terminology proper to a poetical school, as is the case with the *Vita Nuova*.

It is small wonder, then, that Emerson was unable to discover the meaning of some phrases and misunderstood others. Thus, in the prose passage quoted above, the phrase *quasi sbigottito de la bella difesa che m'era venuta meno, assai me ne disconfortai* was not fully understood by Emerson, who translated it: "I, as it were frightened from my fine defense, greatly discomforted myself . . . ," omitting the clause *che m'era venuta meno* ("frightened by the loss of my defense"), which is so essential to Dante's thought.

The lines of the sonnet:

> In ciò che mi rescrivan suo parvente,
> Salute in lor segnor, cioè Amore,

proved at first to be an insoluble puzzle to Emerson. He tried translating them as follows:

> That they may write again their manifest
> Greetings to their lord, that is, Love.

But then he realized that the "greetings" were Dante's and addressed by him in the name of their Lord, Love, to his friends, the *fedeli d'amore*. Hence, he corrected his translation thus:

> That they may write again their thought;
> Greetings in the name of their Lord, that is, Love.

But the meaning of the verse *In ciò che mi rescrivan suo parvente,* which is "so that they—those who have a gentle heart, that is, the *fedeli d'amore*—may write back to me what they think about it," escaped Emerson entirely. No dictionary could have helped him unravel the problem of the word *parvente,* which does not mean "manifest" here, but *ciò che a lor pare,* literally, "what it seems to them," or "what their opinion is." Likewise, in translating the last two verses, Emerson believed at first that it was the lady who, after eating the heart of the lover (symbolic cannibalism), departed in tears:

> Then bewailing it, *she* seemed to go away.

This mistake, which changed the whole symbolism of the sonnet, and which could have been made only by one very little acquainted with the Italian language—since *lo* could not be mistaken for the feminine *la*—was then corrected by Emerson.

In spite of these mistakes, which became less frequent the more he advanced in his practice in Dante's language, his translation is remarkable for its literalness and verbal simplicity. A comparison of the passages quoted above with the version of them by Norton, who tried to preserve something of the rhetorical flavor of the original texts, shows how Emerson (sometimes, perhaps, by sympathetic guessing) expressed Dante's essential thought and emotions faithfully and forcibly.

However irksome the task may have been, Emerson completed his version, and he was so fascinated by the little book that he wrote in his *Journal* (June 22, 1843):

Dante's Vita Nuova reads like the Book of Genesis, as if written before literature, whilst truth yet existed. A few incidents are sufficient, and are displayed with oriental amplitude and leisure. It is the Bible of Love.[43]

Emerson read the *Inferno,* using the *Ten Cantos* of Parsons, which had just appeared, and Cary's version, though later on he preferred the prose translation of Carlyle (1849). He read also the *Purgatorio* and the *Paradiso,* using other translations, but keeping the original "at his elbow." Thus he acquired a certain familiarity with the entire *Divine Comedy,* as is shown by the references to passages and verses of it in his journals and other writings.[44]

After her experience with the *Vita Nuova,* Margaret Fuller had come to the conclusion that "translating Dante is a labor of love," but "one in which even a moderate degree of success is impossible." In the first place, no great poet can be well translated. "The form of thought is inseparable from his thought. The births of his genius are perfect beings; body and soul are in such perfect harmony that you cannot alter the one without veiling the other." In the second place, the difficulties of translation, always insuperable, are multi-

43. *Journal of R. W. Emerson,* eds. E. W. Emerson and W. E. Forbes (New York, 1910), VI (1841–44), 418.

44. Mathews (*op. cit.*) has found some one hundred seventy-five Dante references scattered through Emerson's published writings.

plied a hundredfold in Dante. Translations "come to us as a message to the lover from the lady of his love through the lips of a confidante or menial—we are obliged to imagine what was most vital in the utterance."

As a consequence, she believed that translations, "even such as Cary's, can never be to diffuse a knowledge of Dante." But thinking of Emerson struggling with the Italian of the *Vita Nuova* and of the *Divine Comedy,* and unable to read them well without the help of a translation, she made a concession:

Translations can be of use only to the translators, as a means of deliberate study of the original, or to others who are studying the original, and wish to compare their own version of doubtful passages with that of an elder disciple, highly qualified, both by devotion and mental development, for the study.[45]

Had she returned safely to America after her four years in Italy, spent chiefly in Rome, her greatly increased knowledge of the Italian language and Italian literature and her friendship with Mazzini in the days of the Roman Republic of 1848–49 Margaret Fuller might have been a powerful influence in America for advancing the knowledge of Italy's history and literature, for awakening a greater interest in the painful struggle which was then going on there for the freedom and independence of the country. Unfortunately her death in 1850, only a few miles from the shore of New Jersey, in the wreck of the ship on which she was returning from Europe, ended a life lived in a feverish intellectual activity during her youth and full of promise of greater things for a chastened maturity. Shortly before leaving Rome, she had written to Emerson:

I shall come home humbler. God grant it may be entirely humble! in future, while more than ever penetrated with principles, and the need of the martyr spirit to sustain them, I will ever own that there are few worthy, and that I am one of the least. A silken glove might be as good a gauntlet as one of steel, but I, infirm of mood, turn sick even now as I think of the past.[46]

45. Fuller, "Italy—Cary's Dante," *Life Without and Life Within,* pp. 102–107.
46. *Memoirs,* II, 268.

Like Ulysses, she had "gained experience of the world and of human vice and worth," and like Ulysses and his companions, Margaret Fuller and her little family were overcome by the tempest in sight of the land of promise,

In fin che il mar fu sopra *lor* richiuso.

CHAPTER V

HENRY WADSWORTH LONGFELLOW
(1807–82)

LONGFELLOW's first attempt to translate Italian poetry appeared in his article "The History of the Italian Language and Dialects." [1] At that time his ideas on translation were not dissimilar to those held by Parsons. In the preface to his version of the Spanish *Coplas de Manrique* (Boston, 1833), he stated:

As there are certain beauties of thought and expression in a good original which cannot be represented in the less flexible material of another language, he the translator too, at times may be permitted to transgress the rigid truth of language, and remedy the defect, as far as such defect can be remedied, by slight and judicious embellishments.

In the winter of 1838 Longfellow read the *Purgatorio* to his Harvard class and commented upon it. On March 21 he wrote in his diary: "Closed my lecture on Dante's *Purgatory* by an analysis of the whole. I breathe more freely, now that the appointed task is done." [2] In connection with this course he began to translate passages from the *Purgatorio* into English verse. His volume of poems *Voices of the Night* (Cambridge, 1839) included his versions of the "The Celestial Pilot" (*Purgatorio,* II, 13–51), "The Terrestrial Paradise" (*Purgatorio,* XXVIII, 1–33), "Beatrice" (*Purgatorio, XXX,* 13–33; 85–99), and lines 13–21 of Canto XXXI.[3]

According to Charles Eliot Norton, Longfellow, while making these translations, began to realize that the literal, unrhymed, verse-for-verse method was preferable. Always a devoted friend and admirer of Longfellow, Norton thought these early versions of Dante

---

1. *NAR*, XXXV (1832), 285–362.
2. Longfellow, ed., *Life of H. W. Longfellow*, I, 280.
3. The same passages, slightly revised, were published again in his volume *Poets and Poetry in Europe* (Philadelphia, 1845). In this book he included a *terza rima* translation of *Paradiso*, XXIII, 1–34, by Francis Calley Gray.

to be "of great beauty," but exhorted the reader to compare them with the final form in the complete translation of the *Divine Comedy,* and "to mark the signs it affords of increased simplicity, literalness, and perfected art." [4]

Longfellow began his translation of the *Purgatorio* in 1843, but made a slow progress because for the subsequent ten years he devoted himself primarily to original work. It was not until 1852 that he returned to translation. Upon the completion of the *Purgatorio,* he wrote in his diary (February 27, 1853): "Forty-six years old. Finished Dante XXXIII. . . . The college term begins. Farewell the rest, the ease of vacation. I have not been wholly idle; Let the completed *Purgatorio* answer for me." [5] After another long pause he went back to translating the *Divine Comedy* after the tragic death of his wife in 1861. As if to make up for lost time, he worked with unusual speed, and on April 16, 1863, he could write in his Journal: "Finished the translation of the *Inferno.* So the whole work is done; the *Purgatorio* and *Paradiso* having been finished before." [6]

During the following years he labored constantly at correcting and revising his work. "How I am weary of correcting and weighing, and criticising my translation!" he wrote in his Journal. "It takes more time than it did to make it." The burden of revision was somewhat lightened by the kindly aid of his friends, James Russell Lowell, Charles Eliot Norton, George W. Greene, James T. Fields, William Dean Howells, and others, who offered valuable suggestions. These men formed an informal Dante Club, which met at Longfellow's house on Wednesday evenings. [7]

The publication of the *Inferno* (1865) was hastened so as to coincide with the six hundredth anniversary of Dante's birth. In forwarding Longfellow's translation to the Centennial Committee in Florence headed by the Duke of Sermoneta, George P. Marsh, the

---

4. *Rep. Dante Soc.,* May 16, 1882, p. 19.

5. Longfellow, ed., *op. cit.,* II, 233. The following year, 1854, he resigned his professorship, delivered his last lecture at Harvard on April 19, and wrote in his Journal: ". . . the last lecture I shall ever deliver here or anywhere." (*Idem,* II, 243.)

6. *Idem,* II, 392. Samples of this new phase of his work—translations of Cantos XXIII, XXIV, and XXV of the *Paradiso* with explanatory notes—were given in the *Atlantic Monthly,* XIII (January, 1864), 47–55.

7. Longfellow, ed., *op. cit.,* II, 424.

American Minister to Italy and himself a distinguished man of letters and Italianist, wrote:

I am persuaded that the Committee will receive this first American reproduction of the great poem . . . as a contribution most fitting the solemnity of the Centenary, and at the same time as a worthy homage from the New World to one of the chief glories of the country of its discoverer.[8]

At this time Longfellow was at the peak of his reputation and his poetical works had been translated into other languages. He was hailed as the greatest poet that America had ever produced. It is little wonder, then, that his complete version of the *Divine Comedy* (Boston, 1867), so long awaited and so loudly heralded, should be greeted enthusiastically by Boston literary circles.

Charles Eliot Norton, as was to be expected, lauded it generously. To him the translation was not only "the best that has ever been made of the *Divine Comedy* into English, but also . . . hardly likely to be superseded or surpassed." [9] William Dean Howells, who had returned from his consulship in Venice (1862–65) and was making a place for himself in Cambridge literary circles, took a more reserved tone.[10] He agreed with Norton that it was the best of all translations made up to that time, but was not convinced that it could not be surpassed. Moreover, he complained that, in an effort to combine poetry with literalness of translation, Longfellow sometimes translated Dante's words "into the English dictionary rather than the English language." [11]

8. Koch, *DA*, p. 42.
9. *The Nation*, IV (May 9, 1867), 369 ff.
10. While in Venice, Howells had read the entire *Inferno* and most of the *Purgatorio* and *Paradiso* with the assistance of a priest. In *My Literary Passions* (New York, 1895), pp. 215 ff., he states that he was fired to enthusiasm by the poetical beauty of the poem and bored to death by its doctrinal disquisitions. What impressed him most was the fact that the *Divine Comedy* "had sprung from the very heart of Italian life" and was, therefore, a picture of that life with all its light and shadows, splendor and squalor. This notion spurred him in his youthful ambition to attempt to become America's Dante by writing a great poem in Dantean style and in *terza rima*, describing the history and life of America from its birth to the Civil War. He actually wrote the first cantos of it. Realizing, however, that the poem "was not so like Dante, as I would have liked to make it," and that "Dante is not so easy to imitate," he dismissed the idea, especially after samples of his poem sent for publication to American periodicals met with refusal from their editors. (La Piana, *CAI*, p. 328.)
11. *The Nation*, IV (June 20, 1867), 492 ff.

Norton, however, maintained his enthusiasm at a high pitch. In the *North American Review* for July, 1867 (CV, 124–148), he wrote a long treatise dealing with translation in general and with Dante translations in particular. Norton admits that no translation can do full justice to the original. Yet translations are necessary, and the problem is whether the literal or the free translation is the more desirable. It depends, he says, on the ability of the translator. Here he quotes various authoritative opinions, for and against literal translation. Arnold, for instance, held that the reader of a translation should be able to feel that he is reading an original work, while Newman declared that a translation "must retain every peculiarity of the original." As a golden mean, Norton suggests that we demand of the translator not variations on a theme but the "exact substance" of the work. "The good translator," he says, "is not he who sticks most closely to the letter, but he that gives the meaning of the letter most nearly." Measured by this standard, Norton judges Longfellow's *Divine Comedy* to be "the most faithful of Dante, that has ever been made."

As for the question of rhyme, Norton thinks with Carlyle that the essence and the material of a great poetical work are themselves rhythmic. This "deeper music" is what a translator must render and reproduce. But if he sticks to the external form, forgetting the substance, he runs the risk of producing a work of erudition rather than of poetry. The avoidance of this danger depends upon his own genius, judgment, and feeling. The directness and simplicity of Dante's diction requires of the translator a like directness and simplicity. Longfellow, he observes,

discarded the rhyme for the sake of preserving more important elements of language and style. The method he has chosen is free alike from the reproach of pedantic literalism and from unfaithful license. In freeing himself from the clog of rhyme, he secures the required ease of expression; and in selecting a verse of the same metre as that of the original, and keeping himself the number of verses, he binds himself to the pregnant conciseness of the poem, and to a close following of its varied tone.

To illustrate these points Norton compares passages of Longfellow's translation with those from several English versions, and finally condemns to the limbo of ignorance all dissenters, because it will be only "want of culture on the part of the English reader if he does not enjoy this translation."

George W. Greene, another lifelong friend of Longfellow, was convinced that Longfellow's translation is "true to the form as well as to the spirit of the text." [12] In his opinion, a good translator must conscientiously follow his text word for word, line for line. He must also have the power of forgetting himself in his author and must possess a thorough mastery of both languages. Finally, he must be a poet in the highest and truest sense of the word, not merely a skillful artificer of verse. Longfellow possessed all these qualities; his version was the best ever made and a great addition to American literature.

All voices were not lifted in unalloyed praise, however. For instance, John Fiske (1842–1901) did not consider the work a success and blamed for its partial failure the literal method of translation used, rather than the ability of the translator.[13] While appreciating the fact that Longfellow's chief aim was a faithful rendering of the original, and that he succeeded admirably in realizing it, Fiske nevertheless felt that the version had two serious defects: "first, the too frequent use of syntactic inversion, and, secondly, the too manifest preference extended to words of Romanic over words of Saxon origin."

These two defects Fiske illustrates by giving quotations from several passages of Longfellow's version and comparing them with the original and with the translations of Cary and Parsons. Then he concludes:

Does it not seem that in all those cases, Longfellow, by his strict adherence to the letter, transgresses more gravely the laws of English construction, and that Parsons by his comparative freedom of movement, produces

12. *Atl. Mo.,* XX (August, 1867), 188–198. Greene and Longfellow met on their first trip to Europe and became close friends. Greene, who lived many years in Italy and who was for a time American consul in Rome, was well versed in Italian literature and wrote many articles, chiefly for the *NAR,* on Italian literature. Longfellow's Journal and the correspondence which they kept up through the years show that a close bond of affection united these two lovers of Italian culture.

13. John Fiske, "Longfellow's Dante," *New York World,* May 31, June 22, July 29, 1867. This article was later reprinted in Fiske's *The Unseen World and Other Essays* (Boston, 1876).

better poetry as well as better English? . . . Does not this show clearly enough that the theory of literal translation where two languages so widely different as English and Italian are concerned, is not the true one? By Longfellow's work, as we think, this theory is crucially weighed and found wanting.

More severe was T. W. Hunter (*Philadelphia Press,* July 24, 1867), who found Longfellow's version merely "a quasi-perfect interlinear translation" from which all the poetical flavor of the original has vanished. There are hardly "thirty consecutive lines to be found in it, in which the rhythm is perfect and unbroken." Not only was the version disappointing, but the notes and illustrations were "deluding" and betrayed an "almost entire neglect of the great German scholars, of nearly all the modern Italian scholars and of some of the best French scholars."

Most devastating of all was the attack against Longfellow's translation by Edward J. Sears, the bellicose Irish founder and editor of the *National Quarterly Review* of New York. Sears, a facile and aggressive writer, a remarkable man of talent, but above all a past master in the art of improvising knowledge and of bluffing,[14] had come to New York in 1848, and founded his *Review* in 1860, with the ambitious program of making of it a periodical which should be to America "what the *Edinburgh Review* was to Scotland and the London *Quarterly* to England, a review that should embody and symbolize the scholarship of the nation." [15] In his opinion, not wholly unjustified, there was no periodical in the United States that

14. His biographer describes Sears as a man of encyclopedic learning: "He read and translated easily German, French, Italian, Spanish . . . but these languages did not afford him the delight which he derived from Latin and Greek. . . . He was quite in his element in the higher mathematics, and entirely at home in chemistry and microscopy. And in the collateral science of medicine his knowledge was far superior to that of the average practitioner. . . . History was his specialty . . . he had a large acquaintance with biography and belles-lettres. . . . His forte was interpreting the ideas and explaining the methods of other minds, rather than original thinking. . . . The subject was not material. Whether it were historic or pre-historic; modern customs or ancient civilizations . . . the literature of China, or the Tragedies of Sophocles . . . It was all the same." (From "Impressions and Reminiscences of Edward I. Sears," *National Quarterly Review,* XXXIV [March, 1877], 197 ff.) Such an extravagant eulogy cannot fail to raise doubts concerning Sears's real learning. A cursory glance at some of his articles in the *National Quarterly Review* shows that he could write on anything, but seldom with accuracy and true knowledge. Even his occasional quotations from the Latin classics are marred by grammatical mistakes.

15. Quoted by his biographer, *idem,* p. 201.

exactly fulfilled this need. The *North American Review,* which might have advanced such a claim, "was Bostonian rather than national and, although able and scholarly, it did not sustain the critical requisite of a thorough review." In fact, however, the *National Quarterly Review* was and remained a personal organ of Sears; it never gathered around its editorial table men of national reputation such as those of the Boston circle, and it died out with the passing away of its founder. In order to make room for his *Review* in the rather crowded field of American periodicals of the time, and to make its presence felt in the intellectual life of the country, Sears let no occasion for polemical thrusts go by; occasionally he went so far as to attack either openly or by innuendo the personal character of his victims.

Italian literature and history was a subject on which he claimed to speak with authority; nay, it seems that he had a special predilection for the great Italian poets and writers. The first issue of the *National Quarterly Review* carried a long article on "Dante" by Sears, interspersed with many quotations from the *Vita Nuova,* the *Convivio,* and the *Divine Comedy,* giving the impression of great familiarity with Dante's works and with Dante literature.[16] In fact, the article was little more than a conventional compilation with occasional attempts at a rather commonplace humor. For example, mentioning the fact that Beatrice was married, he added this comment:

Italian public opinion is ever lenient to such offenders. It was so in the time of Dante. The author of the *Divina Commedia* was not the only young man of his day who openly avowed a passion for a married woman; and no one save the husband of the beloved one seems to have taken any offense. Whether he would take the theory of Platonic love as a sufficient explanation or not, is another question. Experience shows us that he would be much more likely to act the part of Othello.

Sears saw in the publication of Longfellow's translation of the *Divine Comedy* a good opportunity to administer a sound thrash-

16. "Dante," *Nat. Quart. Review,* I (June, 1860), 1 ff. The following essays on Italian subjects also appeared in the same review: "Tasso," I (September, 1860), 375 ff.; "Modern Italian Literature," IV (December, 1861), 76 ff.; and "Alfieri," XIV (March, 1867), 209 ff.

ing to the great Boston Brahmins. Although Longfellow had already published all three parts of his version, Sears chose in his article "Dante and His New Translator" (*National Quarterly Review*, XV [September, 1867], 286–316) to review only the *Inferno*. He began by making a formidable, almost terrifying, list of the qualifications that any translator of Dante must possess. He must be not only master of both languages, English and Italian, and move at ease in the world of medieval allegorism; but he must be also "familiar with history, mythology, systems of philosophy, and general literature of Greece and Rome." All this knowledge is not enough:

It is equally essential to be acquainted with the peculiar characters of all the personages of the Bible; and with all the great events that are recorded by the sacred writers. Then he must know modern history down to the time of Dante; not alone the history of Italy, but that of all Christendom, and not alone the history of kings and emperors, but that of all those who rendered themselves illustrious or infamous in their reigns. He must know the characteristics of the Popes and their leading Cardinals; he must have some knowledge of the habits as well as the disposition of each. Nor can he overlook the political system of Europe during the Middle Ages. The Italian republics have to be studied in particular, but, above all the Florentine Republic, with its Guelphs and its Ghibellines, its Whites and Blacks.

Measured by these absolute standards, Longfellow fell short of the requirements. But he ranked high among American poets and, having been a Harvard Professor, he was supposed to be "something of a scholar." From such a man one would expect a superb English translation of Dante. Unfortunately, however, the Cambridge poet did not live up to expectations: his translation is much inferior to both Cary's and Wright's.

There is, Sears complains, no evidence that Longfellow made elaborate preparations for the task, and he "does not even give us a preface, no biographical sketch, no introduction of any kind, except we are to regard some pious verses in that light." Most of the notes appended to his translation are taken from Cary, Wright, and others, "omitting often the most valuable, and substituting in their stead the platitudes of friends." Such are the "Illustrations" added at the end, which consist of several "indifferent" passages from the writings of his friends Lowell and Norton, who have bestowed high eulogies on Longfellow's translation. The reader is reminded "very forcibly of the famous bargain 'you tickle me and I tickle you.' " Sears condemns as the greatest mistakes Longfellow's use of blank verse in a translation of the *Divine Comedy* and his method of turning every Italian line into an English line. This method is far too mechanical; "it is little in accordance with nature as it would be to chop off two or three inches of one's legs in order that he might be exactly the size of his neighbor." He then flays Longfellow for having overlooked Dante's allegorism in his notes and illustrations, and enlarges upon the criticism made by Fiske and Hunter concerning Longfellow's "grandiloquence and fondness for inversions."

Above all, Sears was indignant because he felt that the Cambridge poet had not devoted sufficient time and labor to his translation. Cary devoted seven years to the *Inferno* and sixteen years to the rest of the poem; John Carlyle, although he made only a prose translation of the *Inferno,* worked at it many years both in Italy and at home. But Longfellow "seems to have commenced the *Divina Commedia* as he would a Fourth of July oration or an appendix to the Song of Hiawatha." As a result, his translation makes it appear that "Dante is a dull poet and that Hiawatha is greatly superior to the *Divina Commedia.*"

As a precaution against those who may take these remarks as spiteful, Sears assures his readers that he has no grudge against Longfellow, and that his criticism stems from the fact that he cannot bear "bombastic" translations of great poets. Furthermore, he has no grudge against Boston or Boston men of letters. To prove this he compares Longfellow's version with that of the Bostonian Parsons to the latter's advantage. "It was not as a business speculation that Parsons made his translation," Sears writes; "he was actuated solely by his admiration of Dante. We should be sorry to accuse Mr. Longfellow of a less worthy motive; and yet we are constrained to say that his work looks very much like a hasty job." With the parting thrust that Longfellow has "degraded" the characters of the *Divine Comedy* Sears closes his diatribe.

We have given to Sears what may seem to be more space than he deserves because he was a typical though extreme example of the supercilious attitude assumed often by European intellectuals who settle in America. As a professor—at least for a time—in one of the colleges of New York, and as a conspicuous personality in Irish circles, Sears was not without followers and influence. His *Review* carried on for over fifteen years, as long as he lived, and fought many battles in which it was not always on the wrong side. In the history of the old and often impudent art of "debunking" in America, the name of Sears must not be omitted.

If Sears thought that the Boston *cénacle* was going to accept his challenge and give him a chance to use his sharp tongue and Irish wit in a long series of polemical attacks and counterattacks of great advertising value to himself and his *Review,* he was cruelly deceived. Literary Boston ignored entirely the *Review* and its editor.

But there were other critics who could not be ignored. Besides Fiske and Hunter, the English Dantist H. C. Barlow pointed out both the virtues and weaknesses of Longfellow's translation.[17] At that time the competition among translators of the *Divine Comedy* was very keen in England. The critics were getting weary of their task and accordingly more exacting in their judgments. Barlow welcomed Longfellow's translation as America's tribute "to the genius of the immortal Florentine . . . in the person of her most popular poet. . . ."

Concerning the translation itself, he states very gently:

The translation of the Divina Commedia by Longfellow, which may be called the *American Version* combines literality with poetical form. It is not prose—we can scarcely call it poetry—but it is rather poetic-prose in a tripartite arrangement. Our meaning will be better shown by a specimen, which we take, at hazard, from the fourteenth canto of the

---

17. *The Athenaeum,* May 18, 1867. Barlow, who had made the study of Dante his life work, had written extensively on the poet and was considered one of the most authoritative Dantists of the time. The Barlow Lectureship on Dante which he established in 1878 at University College, London, is witness to his love of the great Florentine.

Inferno. Compare these lines with the corresponding passage in Carlyle's prose version, and we cannot but observe how very nearly these faithful renderings agree.

Longfellow

Because the charity of my native place
Constrained me, gathered I the scattered leaves
And gave them back to him, who now was hoarse;
Then came we to the confine, where departed
The second round is from the third, and where
A horrible form of Justice is beheld.
Clearly to manifest those novel things,
I say that we arrived upon a plain,
Which from its bed rejected every plant;
The dolorous forest is a garland to it
All around about, as the sad moat to that;
There close upon the edge we stayed our feet.
The soil was of an arid and thick sand
Not of another fashion made than that
Which by the feet of Cato once was pressed.

Carlyle

The love of my native place constraining me, I gathered up the scattered leaves, and gave them back to him, who was already hoarse. Then we came to the limit, where the second round is separated from the third, and where is seen the fearful art of Justice. To make the new thing clear, I say we reached a plain which from its bed repels all plants. The dolorous road is a garland to it round about, as to the wood the dismal foss. Here we stayed our feet close to its very edge. The ground was a sand, dry and thick, not different in its fashion from that which once was trodden by the feet of Cato.

The implication of Barlow's remark and of his comparison of the two versions is clear: Longfellow had merely made a "poetic-prose" adaptation of Carlyle's prose translation. The chief difference between the two was Longfellow's substitution of Romance words for Carlyle's Anglo-Saxon words: "charity" for "love," "horrible" for "fearful," "forest" for "woods," "soil" for "ground," "arid" for "dry," "pressed" for "trodden." [18]

The task of answering these critics was undertaken by Charles Eliot Norton, who had become the champion of Longfellow's translation. In his third article within the year, "Longfellow and His Critics," [19] Norton freely admits that Longfellow's translation is not easy reading. But then, neither is Dante easy reading. To read the *Divine Comedy,* whether in translation or in its original Italian, requires a mind steeped in medieval cultural tradition; otherwise the reader cannot comprehend it. For this reason, says Norton, the remarks made by most of Longfellow's adverse critics are of little value, for these men lack the background necessary to judge such a work. Fiske, for instance, assumed that Longfellow failed as a translator because he had chosen the wrong method, that of literal translation. Norton, who, because of the strictures of the criticisms leveled at his beloved friend, had pondered over the problem and had gained a clearer perception of its essential points, aptly remarked that the case of literal versus free translation cannot be settled dogmatically; for "it has its origin not only in difference of taste, culture and sense of literary art, but in absolute difference of mental constitution." In the present century the literal method seems most popular, while in the last century free rendering was preferred. The critic, before passing judgment on a translation, must consider the purpose which the translator had in mind in making it. Longfellow sought

to make a translation which should give to the English reader the most exact acquaintance not only with the thought, but with the form of expression of his author, so far as it could be conveyed in another tongue. Of course, if Longfellow had chosen, he could have made a poem in English, and called it a translation of Dante.

18. Another English review (anonymous) of Longfellow's translation of the *Purgatorio* (*Atheneum,* June 29, 1867, pp. 845–846) was more complimentary. After some criticism concerning certain textual readings adopted by Longfellow, the critic concludes: "We know of no translation in English in which the beautiful and profound thoughts of Dante in his Purgatorio are rendered with a more conscientious, loving regard, and laudable desire to do him honor." Bibliography of other reviews of Longfellow's translation in Koch, *DA,* p. 98.

19. *The Nation,* V (September 19, 1867), 226–228.

Last but not least—and here Norton touched upon a most essential point of the whole problem—we must remember:

The quality and essential nature of every work of art is primarily dependent on its position in the long and continuous series of works of human thought and genius, that is, on its historical relations. These are expressed not only in its general sentiment, but in its special form. They can be but imperfectly preserved and rendered in any translation, and the best translation is that which preserves the most of them.

Judging Longfellow's translation by these standards, is it a success or a failure? This time Norton discards the wholly eulogistic attitude of his previous reviews and admits that Longfellow's translation "is not perfect"; that there are lines which might without loss of exactness be rendered more poetical; that there are some inversions which might have been avoided; and that some words are used of which the excellence may be questioned. Yet in spite of these imperfections, Longfellow's version is a success, "a surprising testimony to his skill, to his genius, to his sympathy with his author."

As for the criticism that the notes and illustrations added to the translation were "disappointing and deluding," and that Longfellow did not make use or mention of the great Dante scholars of Europe, Norton points out that translations of Dante are not made for Dante scholars, who are able, supposedly, to read the *Divine Comedy* and all its commentators in the original. Hunter's criticism would have been justified if Longfellow had been preparing a critical edition of the text.

What irked Norton most was the statement made by the critics to the effect that Longfellow's version "lacked rhythm" and was not poetical. He confesses to be nonplused by such criticism. To him it was preposterous to think that Longfellow could write something in verse which was not poetical. In his opinion, Parsons' free translation of the *Inferno,* though it was the most poetical free rendering of Dante ever made, was no more poetical than Longfellow's literal translation. In the end, Norton reiterated his boundless faith in the enduring value of the work: "Longfellow has made a translation which is not only the most faithful, but is the most poetic, and will be the most popular of all the versions of the *Divine Comedy."*

Norton's defense did not convince George H. Calvert, whose article "Dante and His Latest Translators" appeared a few months later.[20] Calvert believed that all English translations of the *Divine Comedy* made up to that time were worthless and Longfellow's was no better. Translations in prose are "an aesthetic impertinence"; those in *terza rima* are ludicrous because the *terza rima* is not admirable in any language:

It keeps the attention suspended too long, keeps it ever on the stretch for something that is to come, and never does come, until the end of the canto, namely, the last rhyme. The rhymes cannot be held down, but are ever escaping and running ahead. It looks somewhat like an artificial contrivance of the first rhymers of an uncultivated age.

Neither does Calvert approve of the blank-verse, line-by-line method adopted by Longfellow:

Longfellow sacrifices the spirit to the letter . . . he deprives himself of scope, only to give a billowy notion, a heightened color, a girded vigor to choice passages. . . . Loose poetic endings do a part in causing Longfellow's Dante to lack the clear outline, the tonic ring, the chiseled edge of the original, and in making his Cantos read as would sound a high passionate tune played on a harp whose strings are relaxed.

In conclusion, Calvert proposes a rhythmical scheme of his own as the most suitable for an English translation of the *Divine Comedy*. His suggestion is "to put into English lines of eight syllables the whole meaning of Dante's lines of eleven," keeping the rhyme if and when possible, and ignoring it whenever it would force to break the octosyllabic measure, or to add epithets, or to submit to awkward inversions. As a sample, Calvert gives his own translation of a few short passages, some with rhymes, some without. This suggestion has not found favor with American Dantists, and the samples of translation which he offered were neither long enough nor good enough to prove his theory.

The influence of Longfellow's version of the *Divine Comedy* upon Dante's fortunes in America cannot be overestimated. The

20. *Putnam's Magazine,* I (February, 1868), new series, 155 ff. George H. Calvert (1803–89) was educated at Harvard and Göttingen and was familiar with European literature. A writer of poetry, dramas, and essays, he did not achieve great distinction.

fact that the most famous and most popular of all the American poets of the time turned his talents to making a translation of the *Divine Comedy* was a potent factor in inducing American readers to strike up an acquaintance with the great poem. From a more general point of view, Longfellow's version of Dante brought forcibly before American scholars and men of letters the problem of what a translation should be. This problem, perennial in all literatures, had a special importance in the cultural life of America in that period, when new translations of the classics and of lesser poets and writers of the ancient and modern literatures were being steadily produced in this country. One is reminded of the Italian humanists of the fifteenth century, so busy putting into Ciceronian Latin all the newly rediscovered Greek works. At that time, too, the controversy about the various methods of translating from Greek into Latin waxed hot, especially where translations, or rather paraphrases, in Augustan Latin of the works of the Greek philosophers, notably Plato, were concerned. The rank and file of students of philosophy preferred still the older literal translations in crabbed and often barely intelligible scholastic Latin.[21]

In modern aesthetic theories the principle of the unity of the creative act of which the work of art is the product, and hence the absurdity of the distinction between content and form as two things which could be analyzed separately, have led to the conclusion that translation is a theoretical impossibility, if by translation is meant the transfer of one artistic expression into another, as we transfer a liquid from one container into another of a different shape. As Croce remarks, we cannot take something which has already received its aesthetic form, and transmute its essence into another aesthetic form. Every translation either lowers the tone of the original or destroys it entirely, or a translation may become in itself a new creation by the process of combining the expressions and ideas of the original author with those of the translator. In the case of the former, the mode of expression is always that of the original; the translator has no form of his own. In the case of the latter, two modes of expression are mingled, but the essence of the original has

21. Giovanni Gentile, *Storia dei generi letterari italiani, La Filosofia* (Milan, Vallardi, 1915), II, 238 ff.

gone. In other words, the translator is faced with the choice of being "either homely and faithful or beautiful and unfaithful," as the saying is.[22]

The notion that no translation could ever do full justice to the original was such a commonplace that neither Longfellow nor his friends and his critics had any illusions on this point. But they certainly would have denied that there was no way out of Croce's dilemma. Whatever may be said about the theoretical impossibility of translations of literary masterpieces—especially of poetry—one must admit that in practice they are necessary and that there are good and bad translations. The American translators had seen how Cary, by casting Dante in a Miltonian mold, had produced a readable translation, even though he had sacrificed what Norton called "the historical relations" of the original. They had seen how Parsons, by adopting the method of free translation, had produced a good English poetical work, even though it was no longer Dante but Parsons.

In their opinion, then, it was possible to make a translation of the *Divine Comedy* which would be faithful in rendering the thoughts, the images, the mood, and even the very words of the original, and they were confident that such a translation would approximate in some degree the beauty of the original. According to Norton the success of such a translation was dependent upon "the genius of the translator" and "his sympathy with his author," by which he probably meant the ability of the translator to identify himself as much as possible with his author and to re-create within himself the artistic experience of which the original poem was the product. This was a difficult task indeed.

Longfellow was criticized chiefly for his crude literalness, his method of line-by-line translation, his use of Latin-English rather than Anglo-Saxon words, his inversions, and his rhythmical irregularities—defects which, it was thought, deprived his translation of all, or almost all, its poetical character and value, and weakened and sometimes made more obscure the thought of the original. Even Norton, devoted as he was to his old friend, had to admit that these defects existed, although he felt that they were of little importance

22. Benedetto Croce, *Estetica* (Bari, Laterza, 1908), p. 78.

and did not mar the value, poetic or otherwise, of the translation.

From his own experience as a poet, Longfellow must have been fully aware that the modes of expression of Dante's poetry were not interchangeable with others of different periods or with those of different literary traditions. Dante's imagery could not be Miltonized or modernized without altering the essence of his art. A literal translation of the *Divine Comedy* appeared to him as the only safe way of not betraying the original. Nowhere in his Journal is there any mention that he ever thought, as Parsons and others did, of employing the *terza rima* and found it too difficult. But as a compensation for the inevitable loss of the charm of interlocked rhymes, he made his literal rendering more rigid by the method of line-by-line translation.

In his studies of the history of the Italian language and of Dante's great contribution to it, Longfellow had learned how the Florentine poet, with superb daring and skill, had taken into his hands the rude, stiff linguistic material of the *volgare,* and had forged out of it a wonderful instrument for poetic expression. Latinisms, archaisms, neologisms, words taken from dialects and words coined by himself—these Dante had thrown into the alembic of his creative art, and had distilled from them a poetic language as docile and responsive to his thought and his taste as soft clay to the fingers of the artist. Longfellow and other translators of the *Divine Comedy* have found out that English, though a rich and artistic language indeed, stubbornly resists the Dantean form. Did the Cambridge poet think that, following Dante's steps, he too should dare to try overcoming the resistance of English and forcibly bring it nearer to Dante by giving preference to words of Latin-Romance origin, no matter how unusual and obsolete, and by using syntactical inversions alien to the English stylistic tradition and taste? Dante attracted Longfellow primarily, if not solely, as the creator of unrivaled poetical visions. The Cambridge poet could not resist the challenge of matching his own linguistic and poetic skill with that of the master.

On the other hand, the method of word-by-word translation had its advantages, in that it relieved the translator of the necessity of digging deep into Dante's allegorical and symbolical phrases and images, a necessity which the free translator must face. To be sure, the general moral significance of the structure of the *Divine Comedy* was not lost on Longfellow, but he shrank from the idea of being inveigled into the maze of Dante's allegorism and preferred to ignore, even to deny, its existence. It seemed to him that the search for allegorical and symbolic meanings was not only a useless task but one which cast annoying shadows over the transparent beauty of Dante's poetry. He could not persuade himself that there was an allegorical structure in the *Divine Comedy* from beginning to end, a sort of scaffold on which Dante's poetry was hanging as an ornamental feature.

Longfellow's translation of the *Divine Comedy* is faithful, to be sure; but its verbal faithfulness often becomes mechanical and pedantic; indeed at times the English equivalent which Longfellow has chosen does not convey the true meaning or suggest the implications of the original text. Thus, for instance, Dante's lines (*Purgatorio,* XVIII, 13–15):

> Però ti prego, dolce padre caro,
> che mi dimostri amore, a cui riduci
> ogni buono operare e il suo contraro,

are rendered by Longfellow thus:

> Therefore I thee entreat, sweet Father dear,
> to teach me love, to which thou dost refer
> every good action and its contrary.

This is a word-by-word translation with no additions and no omissions, and using the obvious English equivalents of the Italian words as found in the dictionary. But no reader of the English rendering could ever guess that what Dante asks Virgil for is not "to teach him love," but to explain to him the psychological process of attraction and desire which causes all human actions, good or bad.[23]

Norton's faith in the high destiny reserved for Longfellow's translation in the future was ill-founded. There are now many other translations of the *Divine Comedy* in English which surpass Long-

---

23. Parsons never expressed his opinion of Longfellow's translation in public, but in a private letter to his sister, the wife of Luigi Monti (August, 1882), he stated that "Longfellow was himself in many passages wholly astray." (Haraszti, ed., *op. cit.,* p. 112.)

fellow's in fidelity to the original as well as in rhythmic structure and poetical feeling. Nevertheless, his version, his tribute of love to the great Florentine, has not lost its usefulness. Above all, it has not lost its place and much less its significance in the history of American culture. Its literal dullness is now and then relieved by lines wrought with impeccable craftsmanship, and occasionally there are passages which effectively reflect the precision of Dante's thought, the poetic terseness of his images and descriptions, and the emotional depth of his passions.

It is not difficult to understand why Longfellow's friends, charmed as they were by his poetical gifts and attractive personality, were greatly impressed by his translation of the *Divine Comedy*. He was held, moreover, in high esteem as a poet and a scholar by almost everybody in America. That there were sober critics even within his circle who could discern the essential defects of his translation and point out the causes of his failure is clear evidence of the progress achieved not only in the restricted field of Dante studies, but in literary taste and aesthetic discrimination in general, by the generation which was just emerging from the tragic experience of the Civil War.

CHAPTER VI

CHARLES ELIOT NORTON
(1827–1908)

WHEN Lowell resigned his chair at Harvard in 1877 to accept the appointment of United States Minister to Spain, his Dante course was entrusted to Charles Eliot Norton, professor of the history of art since 1875.[1] A keen interest in Italian literature, especially in Dante, was traditional in the Norton family. His father, Andrews Norton, was somewhat of a Dante scholar, as shown by his friendly criticisms of Parsons' *Inferno*.[2] Charles Eliot Norton visited Italy for the first time in 1850 during a two-year trip which had taken him first to India and then to Europe. In 1856–57 he spent a whole winter in Rome.[3]

Besides his spirited defense of Longfellow's translation of the *Divine Comedy* and many other articles and book reviews on Dante literature, Norton's chief contributions to Dante studies were his versions of the *Vita Nuova* and the *Divine Comedy*. His *New Life of Dante, An Essay with Translations,* which appeared first in three consecutive issues of the *Atlantic Monthly* (January, February, March, 1859), was reprinted the same year in one volume, "con-

1. No extensive biography of Charles Eliot Norton has been written. His *Letters* (2 vols. Boston, 1913), with biographical comments by his daughter, Sara Norton, and M. A. De Wolfe Howe, are an important source for the history of the American culture of that period. His correspondence with Lord Vernon was published by William C. Lane in *Rep. Dante Soc.*, 1930, pp. 17–48.

2. His interest extended to contemporary Italian literature, and he translated into English the great Italian novel of the nineteenth century, Manzoni's *I Promessi Sposi* (2 vols. New York, G. Dearborn, 1834). (See N. C. Shields, *Italian Translations in America* [New York, 1931], pp. 27–28.) Andrews Norton's wife was also familiar with Italian and with Italian literature. With the assistance of P. Maroncelli, then a political exile in America, she made an English translation of Silvio Pellico's *Le Mie Prigioni* (2 vols. Cambridge, Mass., 1836). The second volume contained "Additions to Pellico's My Prisons" by the same Maroncelli. The volumes were edited with notes by Andrews Norton. (Shields, *op. cit.*, pp. 29–30.) A. Lo Grasso, "Maroncelli in America," *Rom. Rev.*, October–December, 1933.

3. C. E. Norton, *Travel and Study in Italy* (Boston, 1860). In this volume there is a chapter on "Rome in the Times of Dante." Norton revisited Italy several times in the years that followed.

siderably enlarged with additional translations and original matter." [4] By way of introduction to the narrative, Norton wrote a brief sketch of Dante's youth and of Florentine life during the period when the lyrics were composed. He also added some considerations on the poetry of the *dolce stil nuovo* and on the general character of the *Vita Nuova,* "the first book in which modern sentiment finds free expression." The narrative of the *Vita Nuova* is given partly in summaries made by Norton, and partly in translations from the text, including verse translations of the lyrics also by Norton, with the exception of the canzone "Donna Pietosa," translated by Charles T. Brooks. The entire narrative is accompanied by comments, explanations, and even digressions—all intermingled with the text. The appendices contain three short essays on the "Date of the *Vita Nuova,*" the "Structure of the *Vita Nuova,*" and the "Inconsistency of Statements in the *Convito* with those of the *Vita Nuova.*" To these is appended an English translation of Guido Cavalcanti's canzone "Donna mi priega" made also by Brooks. [5]

In the second edition, published in 1867, Norton gave his translation of the whole text of the *Vita Nuova* and relegated his comments and explanations to the notes. The former introduction was remade into an essay and appended to the translation, together with

4. Translations of individual sonnets and canzoni, or of groups of them from the *Vita Nuova,* had been numerous in England, fewer in America, where they were generally inserted into essays on Dante. The earliest English version of all the poems of the *Vita Nuova* was published by Charles Lyell: *The Canzoniere of Dante Alighieri including the Poems of the Vita Nuova and Convito* (London, 1835), and several times reprinted. Lyell's version kept the original meter of the poems, but without rhyme. Lyell also translated the prose part of the *Vita Nuova,* but never published it. (See Paget Toynbee, *Britain's Tribute to Dante* [London, 1921], p. 76.) As we have mentioned above (p. 90, Note 41), the oldest printed version into English of the *Vita Nuova* was Joseph Garrow's *The Early Life of Dante Alighieri,* published in Florence in 1846. Garrow was an Irishman (not an American as stated by some), who spent several years of his life in Italy.

5. The translation of "Donna Pietosa" had been published by Brooks in the *Crayon* (February, 1858), from which Norton reprinted it. The translation of Cavalcanti's "Donna mi priega" was made at the request of Norton, who remarked that Brooks had succeeded "in performing the difficult task of rendering the meaning while preserving the involved rhyme of the original. Even the *rimal-mezzo* has been secured without sacrificing sense or sound" (p. 98). But in the 1867 edition Norton substituted for Brooks's version of "Donna Pietosa" a new and better one which he himself had made, and omitted Cavalcanti's canzone. Charles T. Brooks (1813–83), a Unitarian clergyman and poet, was known for his verse translations of Goethe's *Faust,* Schiller's *William Tell,* and other German poetical works. (See W. P. Andrews, *Poems Original and Translated, by C. T. Brooks,* with a Memoir by C. W. Wendte [Boston, 1885].)

the two essays on the "Date" and the "Structure of the *Vita Nuova*." The essay on the "Inconsistency" was omitted. In the third, much revised edition, which appeared twenty-five years later (Boston, 1892), Norton corrected his translation, using the new critical editions of the Italian text which had been published meanwhile, and made further changes in both the essays and the notes. The essays on the *Vita Nuova* and on the "Structure" were reprinted with some additions. The essay on the "Inconsistency," omitted in 1867, was included again under the title "The *Convito* and the *Vita Nuova*," but entirely rewritten and with a new conclusion. Norton's prose translation of the *Inferno* was published in 1891, of the *Purgatorio* and *Paradiso* in 1892. The whole poem, with further revisions, was reprinted during Norton's lifetime and again after his death.

As with the other two members of the Cambridge triad, Longfellow and Lowell, Norton's great reputation as an eminent Dantist appears out of proportion to his scholarly production in this field. Longfellow was not given to the writing of scholarly books and essays. The few pages on Dante which he published in his early period are little more than summaries made for his students. Lowell's essay, brilliant as it may be as a suggestive expression of his own spiritual reaction to Dante's art, can claim but a modest place in Dante literature next to the famous English essays of Carlyle, Macaulay, Church, and others. Neither are Norton's three short essays appended to the *Vita Nuova* very impressive, but they have the distinction of being the first contribution made by an American scholar to the discussion and eventual solution of some specific problems concerning Dante's life and work. Norton's essays marked the beginning of a new tradition of Dantean scholarly research in America.

The first draft of his translation of the *Vita Nuova* was made in Rome during his visit there in the winter of 1856–57. At that time scholarly research on the text of this work of Dante had not progressed very far. The best edition available, which Norton used, that of Fraticelli, was notoriously defective.[6] When, two years later,

6. Florence, 1834 (many times reprinted). In his 1859 edition Norton remarked that a critical edition of Dante's lyrics was badly needed, "but there is little hope of this from Italy; for the race of Italian commentators on Dante is, as a whole, more frivolous, more

he prepared the manuscript of his version for publication, first in the *Atlantic Monthly* and then in a little volume, Norton, misguided on the one hand by his inexperience in the matter of literary texts, and on the other hand by doubts about the capacity of his American readers to understand Dante's intimate confessions, made a very strange decision. Instead of giving the public an integral translation of the entire text of the *Vita Nuova,* he concocted a mixture of passages, some literally translated, some rewritten, some paraphrased, and some merely summarized by him and accompanied by remarks, explanations, and comments woven into the narrative of the text.

Thus the reader was led by the hand through the little labyrinth of Dante's love story by a loquacious but vigilant guide, who let him see only what Norton thought was good for him to see. In the short preface he admitted that there were omissions in his work: "I have left unsaid many things which are suggested to one who reads carefully the *Vita Nuova.*" Being aware that his method was open to question, Norton gave his reason for the choice he had made:

I have done so because this volume is only for those *che sanno con prudenza amor seguire.* They will feel that a certain reserve is appropriate in treating of a book so full of tenderest sentiment veiled often under formal expressions, and that a respectful deference is required in dealing with the intimate revelations of a character so great and so peculiar as that of Dante.

It seems that Norton had some misgivings about the American reader, who, being unfamiliar with the poetical love-making of the *dolce stil nuovo,* might have interpreted too realistically Dante's love for Beatrice and, much more, for the other women, such as the Lady of the Screen and the Lady of the Window. Dante was pictured by the American essayists as the highest embodiment of human intellectual and moral greatness, and it is quite likely that

---

impertinent, and duller than that of English commentators on Shakespeare" (*Notes,* p. 101). This remark was omitted in the 1867 edition. Italian Dantists contributed a large share in producing critical editions of the *Vita Nuova,* beginning with A. D'Ancona's edition (1872)—the first to mark an important advance both in text and in notes—to M. Barbi's (1907), which, in its new editions (1921 and 1932), is now accepted as the standard text.

Norton did not want to risk casting a shadow on that picture.

In 1859 neither Dante Gabriel Rossetti's nor Theodore Martin's English version of the *Vita Nuova* had yet been published, and Joseph Garrow's crabbed translation of 1846 had passed unnoticed. Norton could very well consider his version the first to introduce the story of Dante's youth to American readers. As such, he felt that it should be presented with appropriate reserve and "respectful deference" to Dante's emotional life. From the very beginning he stresses the "tenderness and purity" of Dante's love for Beatrice and reminds the reader that "the fact of Beatrice's marriage changed in no degree the feeling with which Dante regarded her. . . . His love was of no low quality . . . it was a love of the soul" (p. 33). The affair with the Lady of the Window was only "a short faintness of the heart," a kind of "sweet romantic sentiment which affords new insight into the recesses of Dante's heart, and exhibits the permanence of the gracious qualities of his youth" (p. 67).

Norton always believed firmly in the historical reality of Beatrice, who "was no allegorical piece of humanity, no impersonation of attributes, but an actual woman." In that early stage of his study of Dante, and for some time afterward, he believed also no less firmly in the reality of all the episodes of the *Vita Nuova* and of the various women mentioned therein. He accepted then as fully historical Boccaccio's *Life of Dante*. At the very beginning of his introduction to the first edition of his translation, he quoted at length from Boccaccio's description of the feast offered to his neighbors by Folco Portinari, Beatrice's father, which marked the beginning of Dante's love for her. The opinions, "from that of Canonico Biscioni . . . to that of the mystic Rossetti," of those who regarded the *Vita Nuova* and the women appearing in it—Beatrice included—as merely allegorical, Norton did not think worth considering.[7]

In his essay on the "Date of the *Vita Nuova*," then a highly controversial question, Norton, through a new analysis of the internal evidence, sided with those who advocated an early date, not later

7. A. M. Biscioni, Preface to his *Prose di Dante Alighieri e di Giovanni Boccacci* (Florence, 1723); G. Rossetti, *Commento Analitico della Divina Commedia*, II (London, 1827); *Il Mistero dell'Amor Platonico nel Medio Evo* (London, 1842); *Saggio Critico sulla Beatrice di Dante* (1842). See N. Zingarelli, *La Vita, le Opere e i Tempi di Dante* (Milan, 1931), I, 307.

than 1292. At the same time, however, he held the theory that the *Vita Nuova* in its early form ended with the sonnet "Lasso per forza di molti sospiri," and that the last three chapters, together with the last two sonnets, were added by Dante in 1300, "after the conception of the *Divina Commedia* had taken form in his imagination, in order to connect the work of his youth more directly and in indissoluble relation, with the work of his maturer years" (p. 83).

In the second essay, "The Structure of the *Vita Nuova*," Norton discovered that its thirty-one poems, while ostensibly arranged chronologically, fall into groups of ten and form a symmetrical design which Dante may have intended to be symbolic.[8] Rossetti had already noticed this fact in 1836; but Norton found it independently of Rossetti, whose discovery seems to have passed unremarked up to that time.[9] It was through Norton's essay that this question of the symmetrical structure of the *Vita Nuova* came to be included among the long list of problems raised by this work of Dante.

More important was the subject of the third essay on the contradictory statements made by Dante in the *Via Nuova* and the *Convivio,* a problem which has challenged for so long the ingenuity of Dante scholars. In 1859 Norton was sure that the narrative concerning Dante's "thoughts of love," which lasted only "for some

8. According to Norton the symmetrical arrangement of the poems is as follows:
    a) Ten minor poems, all sonnets but one,
    b) Canzone I,
    c) Four sonnets,
    d) Canzone II,
    c) Four sonnets,
    b) Canzone III,
    a) Ten minor poems, all sonnets but one.
Canzone II is thus at the center of the scheme having four sonnets, one canzone and ten minor poems to the right, and an equal number of each to the left, forming thus three groups of ten poems each with the second canzone at the center.

9. For the story of this discovery see K. McKenzie's "The Symmetrical Structure of the Vita Nuova," *PMLA*, XVIII (1903), 341–385. Rossetti first described this symmetrical arrangement in a letter to Charles Lyell, dated January 13, 1836; but this letter was not printed until 1901. Rossetti, however, published a statement of his discovery in his work *Il Mistero dell'Amor Platonico*, II (London, 1842), 637. The only writer on Dante who seems to have noticed Rossetti's discovery was E. Aroux, in his rather bizarre book *Dante Hérétique, révolutionnaire et socialiste* (Paris, 1854); nobody else seems to have noted the arrangement of the poems until Norton's independent rediscovery of it. Norton's scheme was not the same as that of Rossetti, who counted the poems of the *Vita Nuova* as thirty-three, while in reality there are only thirty-one.

few days" toward the Lady of the Window in the *Vita Nuova,* "bears on its face the marks of truth," and there is not in that narrative "a single expression which could suggest that it was to be taken in any other way than as a statement of actual facts." But in the *Convivio* (II, 12) Dante regards this episode as having an allegorical meaning and states that the gentle lady of whom he was enamored was Lady Philosophy. In the *Vita Nuova* the struggle between his love for Beatrice's memory and the new love is represented as terminating in favor of the former, while in the *Convivio* it is Lady Philosophy who triumphs.

According to Norton, there is really no irreconcilable contradiction, but only a difference in representing the same fact. The *Vita Nuova,* which was written only a short time after the occurrence of the events it recorded, is to be taken literally. "The events connected with the lady who for a time disputed Beatrice's sovereignty over Dante's heart, passed, leaving but slight trace either on his memory or on his life." When, at a later period, he was writing the *Convivio,* he "found in the book of his youth this account of the power which another feeling had for a time exerted over him, and unmindful of the fact that it had been a real feeling, and led by the allegorizing tendencies of his intellect, he treated it as simply a type of his first entrance into . . . the acquaintance with philosophy." The statement of the *Convivio* was "ideally true though literally false" (p. 98). Thus the contradictions of the two books may "perhaps be accounted for. But whether they be so or not, we see that in exalting Philosophy Dante was also exalting Beatrice who had become to him the type of the highest Philosophy." [10]

In this essay Norton does not mention the famous passage in the

---

10. Norton overstressed Dante's tendency to transmute dreams into reality and reality into dreams. In his introduction to the 1859 edition, he wrote: "With Dante, external impressions and internal experiences—sights, actions, thoughts, emotions, sufferings—were all fused into poetry as they passed through his soul. Practical life and imaginative life were with him one and indissoluble. Not only was the life of the imagination as real to him as the life of fact, but the life of fact was clothed upon by that of imagination; so that, on the one hand, daily events and common circumstances became a part of his spiritual experience in a far more intimate sense than is the case with other men, while on the other, his fancies and his visions assumed the absoluteness and the literal existence of positive external facts" (p. 4). By 1867 Norton had realized that medieval conventionalism in poetical language and imagery explained those points better than his far-fetched psychological analysis; hence in the second edition he omitted this passage.

Purgatorio (XXX, 118 ff.) in which Beatrice addresses to Dante words of stern rebuke for his fickleness and his infidelity to her memory. He had already quoted that passage, however, in his running commentary intermingled with the narrative of the *Vita Nuova* and had remarked that, while it shows that Dante's "grief and shame are real, and there is no element of feigning in them," at the same time it stresses the fact that he had "fully atoned for the transient unfaithfulness of his heart" (p. 69).

One wonders whether at this stage of his studies Norton was fully aware of the implications of the problem which he tried to solve by assuming that Dante had forgotten that the Lady of the Window had been a real woman of flesh and blood whom he had loved with a burning passion. In reality, the question implied much more than a passing episode in Dante's biography. It involved the whole question of Dante's allegorism and symbolism, which has its starting point in the *Vita Nuova*.

The articles in the *Atlantic Monthly* were gathered in a handsome little volume in a limited edition dedicated to James Russell Lowell, and distributed mostly among friends and acquaintances. One of the recipients was Ruskin, with whom Norton had entered upon a lasting friendship while on his second trip to Europe. Ruskin published a short note on Norton's volume (*London Christian Examiner,* January, 1861), remarking that the new version of the *Vita Nuova* was "tender and just."

Meanwhile, Dante Gabriel Rossetti published in England his translation of the *Vita Nuova* (1861). This was followed shortly by the new translation of Theodore Martin (1862).[11] It was natural that they should be compared with the American version. A Boston critic was firmly convinced that Norton's version, though partly translation and partly paraphrase of Dante's text, was far superior to the complete English versions of Rossetti and Martin. The reviewer had no doubts that

11. D. G. Rossetti, *The Early Italian Poets* (London, 1861). The part of this book containing the *Vita Nuova* and other poems of Dante, in a revised edition under the title *Dante and His Circle* (London, 1874), was reprinted several times both in England and America. T. Martin, *The Vita Nuova of Dante* with Introduction and Notes (London, 1862). Years before, Martin had published his translation of the poems of the *Vita Nuova* in the *Edinburgh Review,* XII (1843).

Norton's treatment is in closer sympathy with the poet's passion and its varying moods. The shifting phases of that vital experience, the motive of so much that he was and did afterwards, are noted with a more delicate sense of their intellectual and spiritual bearing. There is a charm of style besides, which reflects the matchless refinement of style of the *Vita Nuova* itself. And, throughout, the work shows a delicacy of comprehensive kindred with the white celestial thought which it illustrates.[12]

What Norton himself came to think of his work was made clear by the fact that he now decided to publish his complete version of the *Vita Nuova*. This appeared in 1867, as a companion volume to Longfellow's *Divine Comedy*.[13] In a long note at the end of the first essay, Norton remarked that Rossetti's version of the *Vita Nuova* was

so excellent, and made in so poetic and sympathetic a spirit, that my own might well seem a work of supererogation. But my translation was made before I knew that Mr. Rossetti was engaged in the same labor of love, and the methods we respectively followed are so different, that perhaps it is well that both translations should be published [p. 109].

Rossetti had adopted "a freer style of version," while Norton had sought to be literal "in the belief that thus its [the *Vita Nuova's*] essential spirit could be best rendered." At this point, Norton inserted a modified version of the passage from his 1859 preface (omitted in the new edition) concerning the "respectful deference" with which Dante must be treated. This time deference is invoked not to veil Dante's sentimental life, but to justify Norton's own method of literal translation, for he says:

In dealing with the intimate revelations of a character so great and so peculiar as that of Dante, a respectful deference is required for the very words in which they are contained. Dante has a right to demand this homage of his translator [p. 109].

12. Loami Goodenow Ware, "New Translations of the Vita Nuova," *Christian Examiner,* LXIII (Boston, 1867), 363–381.

13. The Wednesday evening meetings of Longfellow, Lowell, Norton, and other friends, which started in 1863 for the purpose of revising Longfellow's translation of the *Divine Comedy,* continued after the translation was completed. "We continued for a time to meet once a week, but now in my study, to revise in the same manner my version of the 'New Life.' " (Norton, in *Rep. Dante Soc.,* 1882, p. 24.)

His interpretation of the *Vita Nuova* remained essentially the same as before; he still relied on Boccaccio and on the historical character of Dante's narrative. But Norton was no longer so sure of his own explanation of Dante's contradictions, and hence he eliminated in this new edition of his work the essay on the "Inconsistency Between the *Convito* and the *Vita Nuova*." Part of it was incorporated into the essay on the "Date of the *Vita Nuova*" with his former statement that Dante's allegorical interpretation of the Lady of the Window in the *Convivio* was "ideally true, though literally false" (p. 114).

Proud of its Cantabrigian triade, literary Boston lavishly praised Norton's work, though a discordant voice was not lacking even in Boston. Eldridge J. Cutler (*Boston Daily Advertiser,* November 5, 1867), after duly remarking that Norton "as acting editor of the North American Review holds the highest position in American criticism," and that his theory on translation is the same as Longfellow's, expressed disapproval of Norton's choice for his version of "an English style as old as Milton in preference to one still older, or one more modern." To be consistent, said the critic, Norton should have chosen the language of the century before Chaucer, rather than deriving his vocabulary in great measure from King James's version of the Bible. It must be granted that his imitation of that style is remarkable, and since after all the *Vita Nuova* "is not sufficiently important to merit the effort of reading it in the original language," Norton's translation is adequate. Only the poems of the *Vita Nuova* which "bear the impress of Dante's mind, deserve to be studied in the original for their intrinsic beauty." Norton had translated them, now keeping the rhymes as in the original, and now omitting them. According to Cutler, the rhymed versions were preferable to the others.

William Dean Howells, on the other hand (*Atl. Mo.,* XX [1867], 638 ff.), highly approved Norton's choice of archaic English as well as his adoption of Longfellow's literal method of translation. But Norton "is literal with a difference," thus proving "that within his proper limits the literal translator can always find room for the play of individual feeling." Howells, like Cutler, regretted that Norton "sacrificed rhyme to literality" in his rendering of some of the poems; and, in fact, those passages where the rhyme is kept "are the better for his having done so."

These and similar reviews dealt almost exclusively with the question of how good and how preferable to others Norton's version was, but no critical analysis of his theories as presented in his essays was attempted. American reviewers of books on Dante were not yet familiar enough with such problems to undertake a thorough re-examination of the evidence for or against Norton's conclusions.

During the twenty-five years which elapsed between the 1867 and the 1892 edition of Norton's *Vita Nuova,* a large new Dante litera-ture had come into being in Europe, and much light had been shed over Dante's historical and spiritual biography. Reconstruc-tions of the original texts of the *Vita Nuova* and the *Divine Comedy* had made great progress, and new versions of both had been pub-lished in many languages. Following this progress in Dante scholar-ship, Norton not only revised his translation thoroughly, but also changed his mind considerably about some of the problems which he had discussed in his essays.

His faith in the historical reality of Beatrice was never shaken, but that she was the Portinari girl and all that was said about her by Boccaccio and other old and new commentators he now considered untrustworthy. He writes in the 1892 edition: "I am, on many grounds, disposed to reject Boccaccio's statement in regard to Bea-trice, and, consequently, to believe that nothing is known of her but what Dante tells" (p. 149).

In the revised essays, instead of stressing the historical, autobi-ographical character of the *Vita Nuova* according to the literal interpretation, he gave more importance to the allegorical meaning. His essay on "the *Convito* and the *Vita Nuova,*" omitted in the 1867 edition, was now rewritten along new lines of thought. The reader, says Norton, gradually discovers that the charm of apparent sim-plicity and sincerity in the *Vita Nuova* is misleading. While profess-edly the record of actual experience, it is a work of poetic art, of elaborate and highly artificial structure, in which the story is ordered not in literal conformity with fact, but according to an ideal of the imagination; and its reality does not consist in the exactness of its report of fact, but in the truth of the imaginative conception.

Underneath the narrative lies a studied allegory. "The record of professed fact is in part a fiction invented for the garb of an inner meaning, of which the text gives no hint" (pp. 106–107), but which was revealed by Dante in the *Convivio*.

The essay is then devoted to a minute analysis of that part of the *Convivio* in which Dante, explaining his canzone "Voi che intendendo il terzo ciel movete," states in the most elaborate fashion that the Lady of the Window who won his affection was Lady Philosophy. Norton's conclusion is no longer that Dante's explanation was "ideally true, though literally false," but that both the narrative of the *Vita Nuova* and the explanation of the *Convivio* were true and that the apparent difference is due only to the fact that "in the *New Life* the same doctrine lies concealed under a poetic garb" (p. 127). In other words, Norton implies that the episode of the Lady of the Window was only an allegorial fiction and not a real event. Dante's "apparent faithlessness to Beatrice's memory had not been such in reality; to no other earthly love had he turned, but he had given himself to the love of that wisdom" represented by Lady Philosophy (pp. 128–129).

This revised edition of the *Vita Nuova* appeared at the same time as Norton's prose translation of the *Divine Comedy* (*Hell* [Boston, 1891]; *Purgatory* and *Paradise* [1892]).[14] Norton averred that he used the translations of the *Divine Comedy* of his predecessors, and that he "had not hesitated to borrow a felicitous word or phrase wherever he had found it." In the introduction he expressed his firm conviction that no translation of a poem can transfer from one language to another "the perfection of which the life of poetry consists," and that "to preserve in its integrity what may be transferred, prose is a better medium than verse." On this point, too, Norton had considerably changed his mind since the days of his passionate defense of Longfellow's poetical translation.

He stated also that his reason for adding yet another translation to the many already in existence in the English language was be-

---

14. Before Norton's version of the *Divine Comedy*, other prose translations of the poem had been made in England. Besides John Carlyle's prose translation of the *Inferno* (1849), there was E. O'Donnell's complete translation—the first—of all three parts of the *Comedy* (1852). The task was taken up again by A. J. Butler (*Purgatorio*, 1880; *Paradiso*, 1885; *Inferno*, 1892) and by W. S. Dugdale (*Purgatorio*, 1883).

cause those made in verse had sacrificed substance to form, giving a very imperfect reflection of the original. He did not exclude Longfellow's version from this class, and its value seems to have suffered in his eyes with the passing of years. His devotion to the memory of his friend had not diminished, however, for he dedicated his translation to his memory as well as to Lowell's. Of the existing prose translations, Norton acknowledged that Carlyle's was excellent, but included only the *Inferno*. Butler's version was "unnecessarily crabbed through an excess of literality."

The notes added to the translation were short and explanatory in character, usually avoiding discussion of controverted questions.

Needless to say, the translation was amply reviewed in a dozen American periodicals as a welcome addition to American Dante literature, and more briefly by English and Italian Dantists. William Roscoe Thayer took the lead with a long article in two sections (*The Nation*, LIII [1891], 356 ff.; 377 ff.). Formerly a student of both Lowell and Norton at Harvard, Thayer seems to have been as interested in Italian literature as he was in Italian history, the field in which he later made his reputation. His review dealt with the translation of the *Inferno,* which was the first part to appear (1891). Thayer shared Norton's view that no satisfactory poetical translation of a poem can be made, because "form is individual, peculiar to the race and to the given poet." Neither is a compromise possible by the use of so-called rhythmic prose, which, according to those who advocate it, would preserve the charm and flavor of the original. Such mixtures of prose and poetry "are mongrels wanting the best qualities of both parents." Rhythm in prose "is often a source of annoyance rather than of pleasure." He then states dogmatically—as he was inclined to do—that "prose . . . honest, flexible prose, with no poetical embellishments bound like the wings of Icarus upon it, we believe to be the vehicle by which Dante's epic can best be conveyed to the English reader."

In Thayer's opinion, Norton's prose version was the best in English, excelling even the poetical versions of Cary and Longfellow. By comparing the episode of Francesca da Rimini in these three versions it becomes clear that Cary's circumlocutions and additions spoil the effect: "Cary is like a musical conductor who, after transposing a score to another key, plays it in a different time from that the composer intended." Longfellow was not wholly successful either, chiefly because his version lacks flexibility and true rhythm.[15] Norton, on the contrary, has managed to retain the straightforward simplicity of Dante's style, "and though we necessarily miss the charm of Dante's verses, we have in its stead the charm which belongs to excellent prose." Furthermore, Norton's version compares favorably with that of Carlyle, because, excellent as Carlyle's was generally considered to be, Norton's was "invariably more concise, more exact, and no less lucid." [16]

Of even greater satisfaction to Norton must have been the favorable review of his *Inferno* by Paget Toynbee (*The Academy*, London, XLI [February 13, 1892], 156 ff.), who declared that his version was superior to that of A. J. Butler.[17] Concerning Carlyle's version, Toynbee remarked that Norton had borrowed freely from it, but that, on the other hand, Norton's was superior to Carlyle's in many passages in which the latter's rendering was "strangely inadequate." [18] In addition, Norton had had the advantage of using a better Italian text, that published by Karl Witte and corrected by Edward Moore. "This consideration is quite sufficient justification for Norton's present undertaking."

15. By lack of flexibility, Thayer seems to have meant primarily Longfellow's predilection for words which exaggerated the color of Dante's expressions. For instance, *cotanto amante*, which means simply "such a lover," is amplified by Longfellow into "such a noble lover"; the famous verse *la bocca mi baciò tutto tremante* is translated: "kissed me upon the mouth all palpitating." The original "trembling" was not enough for Longfellow; he had to amplify it into "all palpitating," "a word proper to the libretto of an Italian opera."

16. Norton, moreover, "has style and an extraordinary felicity of expression." Take, for example, the verse *Ellera abbarbicata mai non fue—ad albero*, which Norton translated: "Ivy was never so bearded to a tree"; Longfellow diluted it into "Ivy was never fastened by its barbs"; and Carlyle weakened it still more by using the word "rooted," whereas "bearded" gives the exact picture intended in the original.

17. Toynbee remarked that Butler, in the preface to his translation, "had declared that his object was not to attempt an addition to English literature, but merely to aid beginners in understanding that of Italy, by the production of a *crib*, pure and simple. There was ample room, therefore, for another version."

18. For instance, in the episode of Francesca da Rimini, Dante's *il disiato riso* is rendered tamely by Carlyle as "the fond smile"; more literal and forceful is Norton's "the longed-for smile." A passage from the Conte Ugolino episode is also quoted by Toynbee to show that Carlyle's version is not always so accurate as was commonly supposed, and again a comparison with Norton's version of the same passage proves the superiority of the latter. Toynbee does not hesitate to say that, both as to accuracy and to English, Norton's version is decidedly better than Carlyle's.

In his review of Norton's version of the *Purgatorio,* however (*The Academy,* London, XLII [July 23, 1892], 64 ff.), Toynbee reversed his judgment altogether. This version he considered

to be lacking in ease and rhythm, and to err, strangely enough, not infrequently in being too literal, and hence awkward. . . . Indeed we are bound to say, since Mr. Norton challenges the comparison, that we find Butler's crib taken as a whole, at least as readable as Norton's present volume.

In fact, Toynbee was of the opinion that W. S. Dugdale's prose version of the *Purgatorio* (1883) was also preferable to Norton's and should receive the recognition which it merited.[19]

The translation of the *Paradiso* did not create much of a stir. William Morton Payne,[20] who in reviewing the *Purgatorio* (*The Dial,* XIII [June, 1892], 56 ff.) had preferred Butler's "more literal" to Norton's "more graceful" version, reiterated the same opinion in his review of the complete translation in three volumes. According to Payne, although Norton's rendering of the *Divine Comedy* is "at once accurate and elegant," yet "he who knows something of Italian—if ever so little—will find Butler more useful than Norton" (*The Dial,* XIII [September, 1892], 190).

More severe was the English critic of the *Saturday Review* (London, March 19, 1892, p. 336), who thought that Butler "succeeded, like his English predecessor, Carlyle, but unlike the American Professor, in giving a rendering which while it does not evade difficulty, does not unnecessarily suggest it." Even this critic felt, however, that Norton's version could be useful both to Englishmen who did not wish to be bothered with the Italian text, and to Americans who, "with not improper patriotism, wish not to be indebted to an Englishman, but to have an exact prose version, worthy to rank with the verse one which they already possess from the hand of Longfellow."

19. To show that Norton's rendering is inferior to Dugdale's, Toynbee compares both translations of the apostrophe to Italy in the sixth canto to the advantage of the latter.
20. In his review of the *Inferno* (*The Dial,* XII [November, 1891], 219), Payne stated that Norton had "measurably escaped the crabbedness that attends the over-literality of Butler's prose and of Longfellow's blank verse. He is, on the other hand, slightly more literal than Carlyle."

American Dante scholars of today going over Norton's Danteana
and over his theories and views, which we have summarized here,
find his essays obsolete but his translations still very useful. Obviously Norton does not stand on a high and conspicuous place in
the general picture of Dante literature.[21] But his importance in the
more restricted field of American Dante studies must not be overlooked, because Norton was the spiritual father of the new generation of American Dantists. Many of them walked in his footsteps, or
at least held his views at the beginning and were deeply affected by
his influence. As a matter of fact, Norton's great reputation as a
Dantist was primarily dependent upon his wide range of learning,
which he was always ready to put at the disposal of those with
whom he had personal contact, especially of the many students who
took his Dante course at Harvard. Very often they carried away
with them not only the memory of his kindness but also his ideas
and theories, and the picture of Dante which he impressed upon
their minds. Yet now all these memories are gradually vanishing
with the generation that knew him.

When he first took over the Dante course from Lowell, he found
a small class, and its meetings were rather informal.[22] In a letter to
Lowell he described it as "a class of young graduates and of Seniors,
eight in all, with whom on Tuesday evenings I read Dante. It is
interesting work, for they are a picked set, and all full of fresh
interest and zeal in the study. By the end of the year we shall have
read the whole *Divine Comedy,* and there will be eight more lovers
of Dante in the land. In the ideal University I should like to be
professor of Dante." [23]

William Roscoe Thayer, speaking out of his own experience,
stated that Lowell "was never the minute and indefatigable searcher
of texts Norton was; and Lowell never felt Dante as Norton felt

21. Norton did not think worthy of publication the lectures on Dante which he gave
at Johns Hopkins in Baltimore in 1894, and again at Harvard in 1895. Only a short, six-
page syllabus of them in the Johns Hopkins *Bulletin,* of which mention was made in the
Bolletino delle pubblicazioni italiane, May 31, 1894, appeared in print. He did contribute,
however, a monograph to *Warner's Library* on Dante's career and genius. This was compiled in part from the lectures delivered in Baltimore.

22. H. H. Yeames, "Charles Eliot Norton and the Study of Dante," *Harvard Graduate
Magazine,* XXXVI (March, 1928), 343–351.

23. Norton, *Letters,* II, 87.

him." Norton did not confine himself to expressing his aesthetic appreciation of Dante's poetry, but trained his students in Dantean research:

To read Dante with Norton was almost an act of worship. There was in his voice something wonderfully stirring and wholly incommunicable. As he reached a favorite passage his face became radiant and his tones more tender. He explained fully from every side,—verbal, textual, literary, spiritual. . . . In his interpretation of Dante Norton had one immense advantage which neither Lowell nor any other English-speaking Dantist has possessed: he had a specialist's knowledge of mediaeval art. So the thirteenth century lived for him not merely in its poetry, theology, and chronicles, but in paintings and statues in its churches and town halls, and its palaces and dwellings . . . he could compass the whole circle of the experience and the ideals of that world of which the Divine Comedy is the supreme expression in language.[24]

Norton's influence as a teacher seems to have been more widespread and more lasting than either Longfellow's or Lowell's. Although he did not possess the creative imagination and the poetical talent of his two warm friends, Norton was more intimate with Dante and Dante's world than either of them. Endowed with an exquisite sensibility to artistic beauty, Norton had also the gift of communicating his enthusiasm to others. He had many friends and admirers, not only in America but also in England and Italy, and his name became familiar to European Dantists.

The establishment of the Dante Society in Cambridge was primarily the work of Norton. In 1878 the first Dante Society was organized in Oxford, England, and was soon followed by the Dante Society of London in 1881. As early as December, 1880, however, a circular letter signed by Longfellow, Lowell, and Norton proposed the formation of "a society for the promotion of the study of Dante's life and works," in Cambridge. In February, 1881, a meeting was held at Longfellow's house at which he was designated first president of the Society. At that and subsequent meetings at Norton's house the organization of the Society was planned in detail, but its actual inauguration did not take place until May 16, 1882, two

24. *Rep. Dante Soc.*, 1909; Norton, *Letters*, II, 105–106.

months after Longfellow's death, when the first meeting of the forty-eight members was held and elected Lowell president. In 1891, after Lowell's death, the presidency of the Society passed to Norton, who held it until his death in 1908. During those sixteen years the development of the Dante Society was due largely to Norton.[25]

The annual meeting of the Society held in his house was attended by members who often came from great distances to share in the intellectual pleasure of the discussions and to greet with affection their former teacher and guide in Dante studies. There are still many who remember him in his declining years, a little old gentleman with impeccable manners and unfailing kindness, whose home on Shady Hill—a name that somehow reminds one of the slopes of the *Purgatorio* where Dante met Casella—had become a kind of shrine to his old friends and former pupils. Climbing the gentle slope, they still could hear ringing in their memories Norton's voice reading with solemn tenderness:

> Love is but one thing with the gentle heart
> As in the saying of the sage we find.[26]

25. The first bulletin, published the same year, contained the by-laws of the Society, a report, and a commemoration of Longfellow by Norton. In the report it was stated that the Society had thought of undertaking the task of printing the hitherto unpublished *Comment* on the *Divine Comedy* by Benvenuto da Imola, and had therefore arranged to secure an exact copy of the manuscript of the *Laurenziana*. Part of it, made at Longfellow's expense, had already been received. But at this point it had been learned that Lord Vernon's son had already given the printer the copy of the manuscript prepared by his father, and hence the Society regretted that it was to be deprived of the credit for the first complete publication of the important *Comment*. A second and more practical decision was to establish "a library of Dantesque literature." Norton had already arranged to have part of his Dante collection deposited in the Harvard Library, where the books were now available to students. The Society was to supplement and continue this collection. Furthermore, the Society would "keep record of what is being done in America on Dantesque subjects."

26. Norton, *New Life,* sonnet in chap. xx.

CHAPTER VII

THE LAST DECADES
OF THE NINETEENTH CENTURY

In 1854 Luigi Monti, a political refugee from Sicily, where as a boy of eighteen he had taken part in the revolution of 1848, was appointed instructor of Italian at Harvard. Monti seems to have been greatly liked by Longfellow, who often invited him to the Craigie house to play on the piano airs from Italian operas, and introduced him as the "Young Sicilian," great lover of music, in the *Tales of a Wayside Inn:*

> Much too of music was his thought;
> The melodies and measures fraught
> With sunshine and the open air,
> Of vineyards and the singing sea
> Of his beloved Sicily.

How successful he was in his teaching and whether he continued Bachi's tradition in preparing the students for the Dante course is a matter of conjecture. In 1859 he was not reappointed at Harvard, but continued to enjoy the friendship and protection of Longfellow and Lowell. Meanwhile he had married Fanny Parsons, the poet's sister, and had become an American citizen. Through the good offices of Longfellow and especially of Parsons, who again and again used all his influence and mobilized all his friends and acquaintances in behalf of his brother-in-law, Monti was appointed American Consul in Palermo, where he spent several years.[1] Upon

1. Monti was appointed consul in Palermo in 1861. With the advent of Grant's administration in 1869, he was recalled, but Parsons solicited the assistance of Lowell, who obtained his reappointment through Senator Sumner of Massachusetts. Two years later Monti was again recalled, this time for good. His book *Adventures of a Consul Abroad* appeared in 1878 (New York). In a letter to his sister Parsons remarked (August, 1882): "Monti in making himself a literary man has in some degree unmade himself for an official position. Uncle Sam does not want 'literati' to contend with mutinous crews and ignorant sea captains. A scholar like Hawthorne might indeed be sent to Liverpool in remuneration for electioneering services to the Democratic President; a lofty compliment from a genius like

his return to Boston he gave, in the winter of 1876–77, a series of public lectures at the Lowell Institute on the subject of "Modern Italian Literature," and another series in 1880 on "Dante, His Times and Works," the summaries of which were published, as usual, by the *Boston Evening Transcript*. It seems that Monti cherished the hope of obtaining a professorship at Harvard, but his expectation was never fulfilled. Parsons himself does not seem to have thought very highly of Monti as a Dante scholar. In a letter to his sister, who had urged him to use his influence at Harvard in Monti's favor, Parsons told her frankly that although her husband had become "a down-right, double-distilled Cape Cod Yankee," and although he had given the Lowell Lectures, he was not "reckoned among the sacred band whom the vulgar designate as 'literary fellows.'" While he could be a good tutor in the Italian language, he was not qualified for a professorship:

> I dwell on this distinction because you so frequently have spoken of a professorship at Cambridge and ignorant people often talk to me of Professor Monti. . . . It is more than Luigi Monti can do to understand fully a single canto of the Paradiso. Is he then qualified to succeed Mr. Longfellow who was himself in many passages astray? A higher tone of scholarship is now exacted in New England than that which might content Palermo. I will not speak of Chicago, or any of these newly sprung and pretentious places.[2]

More conspicuous was the contribution made to increasing the knowledge of Dante in America by another Italian refugee, Vincenzo Botta, who had settled in New York and married into a wealthy family. His wife, Anne Charlotte Lynch, a poetess, was

---

Hawthorne to a boon companion and so forth. But Hawthorne was not a good consul like Luigi Monti: in fact, he appeared on most occasions of business the booby that he really was, out of his own department, which was surely of imaginative literature." (Haraszti, ed., *Letters of T. W. Parsons.*) Monti died in Cambridge in 1914.

2. *Idem*, p. 112. Parsons' disparaging remark about the "tone of scholarship" in Palermo as compared to that of New England reflects his lack of knowledge of the intellectual life of Sicily in that period. While Monti was there as consul and not as a professor, an eminent Dantist, Francesco Perez, was teaching in Palermo where he published his book *La Beatrice Svelata* (Palermo, 1865), a "most learned and most interesting work" (Zingarelli, *La Vita, i Tempi e le Opere di Dante*, I, 307), which still ranks high in literature on Dante's symbolism.

popular with the New York world of letters as a gracious hostess whose salon was frequented by poets, literary critics, and writers.[3]

The sixth centennial (1865) of Dante's birth was celebrated with solemn commemorations in Italy, especially in Florence, which was then the governmental seat of the new kingdom of Italy. America's homage to the great Florentine poet on this occasion was represented not only by Parsons' and Longfellow's versions of the *Inferno,* but also by other books and many essays, articles, lyrics, and sonnets, which were published during that period. The most impressive contribution—at least as far as bulk was concerned—was Botta's volume *Dante as Philosopher, Patriot and Poet* (New York, 1865).

Since Wilde's plan to publish a life of Dante never came to fruition, Botta's was the first book of some length to be published on this subject in America. The merit of Botta's work, chiefly a compilation, consists mainly in this chronological distinction. In the first hundred or so pages, he deals with the events of Dante's life, interrupting his narrative with chapters on Dante as a philosopher, a naturalist, and a political thinker. The second part of his book (about three hundred pages) Botta devotes to analyzing the *Divine Comedy.* His analysis consists in quoting long passages from Cary's English translation (he quotes more than one third of the whole poem), and filling in the gaps between the quotations with brief summaries of the omitted parts and occasional explanations of the allegories.

Although Botta appears to have been a man of broad culture, and certainly familiar with Dante, the only Italian works he quotes are Foscolo's *Discorso sul testo del poema di Dante,* and Rossetti's *Sullo spirito antipapale che produsse la Riforma.* In his chapters on Dante as a philosopher and a naturalist, Botta depends chiefly upon H. C. Barlow's *Critical, Historical and Philosophical Contributions to the Study of Dante.* He also quotes once Renan's *Averroès et l'Averroïsme.*

3. Botta taught Italian for a while at the College of the City of New York. He was also the author of *Discourses on the Life, Character and Policy of Cavour,* and *An Historical Account of Modern Philosophy in Italy.* He died in New York in 1894.

Though merely an outline, this was the first description of Dante's philosophy as a whole to be published in America. Unfortunately, in Botta's hands, medieval Aristotelianism as reinterpreted by Aquinas and then reshaped by Dante in poetical form became a hodge-podge, and the reader is left to wonder whether Dante is to be admired or pitied for having embraced such a philosophy.

More instructive is Botta's treatment of Dante as a scientist thoroughly acquainted with the scientific learning of the time and a keen observer of natural phenomena. Great though Dante's talents were in this direction, however, it does not follow that he was omniscient, or that by some kind of mysterious intuition he foresaw and described in advance later scientific discoveries, as Botta and other overenthusiastic commentators on the *Divine Comedy* seem to hold. In his exposition of Dante's political ideas, Botta likewise followed the current exegesis of the Risorgimento, which made Dante a precursor of liberalism and Italian nationalism and the prophet of Italy's political unity and independence. Having become a good American, Botta went so far as to suggest that in *De Monarchia* Dante "anticipates in some measure the plan adopted by Washington and his companions in the Constitution of the United States," [4] and that therefore Dante was a true democrat in the modern sense of the word.

Botta's Ghibellinism is more prominent in his chapter on the Papacy, which Dante is made to oppose and condemn not only as a political power, but also as a spiritual sovereignty. It must be said in Botta's favor that he refused to follow Rossetti in presenting Dante as a precursor of the Reformation, or the youthful Parsons of the *Ten Cantos,* who maintained that "Dante was indeed an earlier Luther." [5] Botta contents himself with declaring that, while Dante was a good Christian and in general accepted the theology of the Church, he rejected the claim that the Church personified Christianity, was infallible, and the exclusive possessor of the whole truth. Dante, says Botta, "believes in a Church, but his Church is as wide as humanity; it embraces all creeds and doctrines, the good and the great of all ages, the illustrious pagans as well as the martyrs

4. Botta, *Dante,* p. 57.
5. Parsons, *First Ten Cantos of the Inferno,* p. 82.

and apostles." [6] With Botta, Dante escaped becoming "an earlier Luther," only to become an earlier Mazzini.

Whatever its shortcomings, Botta's book did not pass unnoticed. Henry Tuckerman believed that it would do a great deal toward popularizing Dante's great poem, and complimented the author on his command of English.[7] Equally if not more appreciative were notices of the book published in several periodicals, organs of the Protestant churches. In these the antipapal Dante, as pictured by Botta, gave the reviewers an opportunity to enlarge upon a subject at that time still very much in the fore among religious controversialists.[8] The substance of their comments was that, whatever Dante's philosophy and theology might have been, he was one of the first to cry "No Popery!" before Luther and Calvin, and this was something which could not fail to endear his memory to the militant Protestantism of America.

A few years before, Gordon W. McCabe, writing on Dante in the *Southern Literary Messenger* (XXXIV [1862], 136 ff.), had taken his cue from an article published by Mazzini in the *Foreign Quarterly Review* (XXXIII [London, 1844], 13 ff.). McCabe displays a considerable familiarity not only with the *Divine Comedy,* but also with Dante's minor works, with the exception of *De Monarchia,* of which he says he had read only a few excerpts in translation. How far this familiarity was genuine and firsthand is rather doubtful, since his article is for the most part dependent upon that of Mazzini, whose name, by the way, McCabe does not mention. In discussing the *Vita Nuova* (Florentine edition of 1859), he remarks: "It seems to us that this book can only be translated by a gentle, womanly woman." This was taken almost verbatim from Mazzini's "At present we think that the task of translating the *Vita Nuova* can be confided only to the soul of a woman." But the

---

6. Botta, *op. cit.,* p. 75.

7. *The Nation,* I (October, 1865), 440.

8. Two articles were published in *The Christian Examiner* by William Alger: LXXIX (November, 1865), 429 ff.; and LXXXI (July, 1866), 37 ff. The article of July, 1866, "The Character of Dante," was published again in a revised and enlarged form as a chapter of Alger's book *Solitudes of Nature and of Man, of the Loneliness of Human Life* (Boston, 1867), pp. 213–223. Articles also appeared in *The American Presbyterian and Theological Review,* III, new series (1865), 645; and in *The Boston Review,* VI (January, 1866), 138 ff.

rhetorical question which McCabe appended to this remark was entirely his own: "Is it not the first book we see in the boudoir of a good and clever woman, a worn copy of this *Vita Nuova?*" Did McCabe really mean that Dante was so popular with the gentle ladies of the South that they kept a copy of the *Vita Nuova* at their elbow to read and reread to the great delight of their husbands or their friends? If so, we should revise our opinion about the intellectual interests of the elegant feminine society of the Old South.

On the subject of Dante's religion, McCabe expresses agreement with "a writer in the *Foreign Quarterly Review*" (that is Mazzini): "Dante was neither a Catholic, nor a Guelph, nor a Ghibelline; he was a Christian and an Italian." This opinion could not have been shared by American Catholics who chanced to have some knowledge of and interest in Dante. By the 'sixties, Catholicism had already gained much ground in America. Father Isaac Hecker, a convert from Protestantism, had established his new religious congregation of the Paulist Fathers and was busy promoting the "Apostolate of the Press" among the heretics and infidels of this country. To this end he organized the "Catholic Publication Society" and founded the *Catholic World,* the first Catholic periodical in America with a broad cultural program. Its first issue appeared in April, 1865.[9] This being the year of the commemoration of Dante's birth, an article on Dante was in order. But Father Hecker must have found it impossible to secure what he wanted from an American Catholic writer, for he reprinted in the second issue of his magazine an essay,[10] in English translation, which had appeared in Germany in the periodical *Der Katholik.* The writer of the article was intensely German. He drew an extravagant picture of the Middle Ages as a period in which "the Roman and the Germanic races had become a spiritual community under the hier-

9. The *Catholic World* dealt chiefly with literature and education. At first it relied a great deal on translations of articles from European periodicals. In its first issue (April, 1865) there appeared in English an article from the French *Correspondant* written by a French priest, Rameur, who had paid a short visit to the United States and found out to his satisfaction that "The Colleges and boarding-schools founded under the direction of the Catholic Clergy though inferior to those of France, are yet vastly superior to all other American establishments in their methods, their discipline and the attainments of their professors."

10. *Catholic World,* I (1865), 268 ff.

archy of the popes . . . and were bound together under the government of one worldly empire, the German empire." The great voice of that unity and that civilization was Dante, poet, theologian, philosopher.

Turning from the Middle Ages to contemporary events, the German writer grows indignant because "the great Catholic poet has now become the sainted protector of the Italian revolution." In Italy, those who seek to establish a single republic or monarchy and find the Papacy a hindrance to their plans, now employ the *Divine Comedy* to disseminate their propaganda. He is still more indignant at the "politicians" who have made Dante anti-German:

We have lived to see the day, when Dante, the fanatical Ghibelline adherent of the German Empire, has become the herald of a party whose watchword is "Death to the German and foreign rulers."

His final shaft against the Risorgimento is no less rabid:

What folly it is to imagine Dante, the haughty aristocrat, a partisan of a faction, the Italian liberal faction, which like the faction that governed Florence during the Middle Ages, is made up of rabble and of levelers, haters of all nobility!

It was very unfortunate that Father Hecker, who was accused during his lifetime of harboring liberal ideas and consequently held in suspicion by some Irish prelates, and who was denounced after his death as a forerunner of the heresy of "Americanism," should have so blundered as to choose this rank effusion of aristocratic German bile as representing the Catholic interpretation of Dante.

A happier choice was an article in the November, 1868, issue of the *Catholic World*. Its primary purpose—as we have noted above in dealing with Parsons—was to review the latter's translation of the *Inferno,* but it dealt also with the problem of Dante and the Papacy in a restrained tone. The author, Joseph Finotti, an Italian priest in the United States, was more concerned with Dante than with hurling thunderbolts at the Italian patriots.[11]

11. Finotti spent the last part of his life in Boston, where he was for a time editor of the Catholic weekly, *The Pilot.* He prepared a modest index of Catholic publications in America under the title *Bibliographia catholica americana,* and wrote books of devotion. (Schiavo,

During the years from 1880 to 1900, Dante's popularity in America reached a high level. The large number of books, articles, essays, and lectures on his life, thought, and poetry, and the long list of sonnets and other poems written by American devotees of the Muses on Dante or on subjects from his poetry, form a bulky dossier of this amazing episode in the history of American culture. During this period neither the great poets of classical antiquity nor those of modern literatures—outside the English—appealed as much to the American mind as the great Florentine did. The essential Christian and moral content of the *Divine Comedy,* in spite of its symbolism and its medieval theology, seems to have been more attractive and more appreciated than either the mythological splendor of Homer or the cloudy, philosophical myth of Faust.

Only a small part of this American literature on Dante may be classified as scholarly research; the rest—books, essays and articles— were written and published chiefly for that class of omnivorous readers which has always been so numerous in this country, and especially for those cultivated people who, without claiming to belong to the ranks of the literati, are lovers of literature, some of them even trying their hand occasionally at writing prose or verse.

The old and new American periodicals, whose editors kept a keen eye on the weather vane of public taste, gave to Dante as much space and publicity as they were asked for. The *Century Monthly Magazine* in 1884 (XXVII, 626) acknowledged that there was an increasing demand for Dante literature among its readers. To comply with it, the *Century,* in the February issue of the same year, 1884, published a long article on "The Portraits of Dante" by Sarah Free-

---

Italians in America, p. 325.) During that period the *Catholic World* also published an English translation of Eugenio Bianchi's "The Tomb of Dante and His Portrait in Ravenna" (XXXVI [1882], 352 ff.), from the Italian periodical *La Rassegna nazionale* (1881); "The Legend of Pia dei Tolomei," by T. H. Child (XLIII [May, 1886], 206); and an analysis of Ozanam's "Dante et la philosophie catholique au treizième siècle" (XLIII [September, 1886], 790 ff.), by Louise Duncan Pychowska, who later, in two issues (LI and LII [September and October, 1890]), published a partial translation of the same book under the title "The Student Life of Dante." *The American Catholic Quarterly Review* (XI [July, 1886], 418 ff.) published a long essay by Patrick F. Mullany (Brother Azarias) on "The Spiritual Idea of Dante's Divine Comedy." Other articles: Reuben Parsons, "The Charge of Heresy Against Dante," XII (October, 1887), 714 ff.; Conde B. Pallen, "The Time That Led up to Dante," XV (October, 1890), 681 ff.; and "Beatrice and Other Allegorical Characters," XVI (May, 1892), 253 ff.

man Clarke (XXVII, 574 ff.). This was followed in the issues for March (pp. 734–752) and April (pp. 833–858) by a long study in two parts, "Notes on the Exile of Dante," by the same writer. The same year, the *Atlantic Monthly* also published two papers on Dante, one of which was a well-written and well-informed essay on "The Underworld in Homer, Virgil and Dante," by William C. Lawton (LIV [July, 1884], 99–110). For several decades the *Nation,* established in 1865 by E. L. Godkin, published steadily articles, notes, and controversial papers on Dante, as well as a stream of reviews of Dante literature, especially of books from England and continental Europe.[12]

This widespread interest in Dante coincided with and was part of a general cultural revival that marked that period of American history. As Arthur M. Schlesinger has stated, the educational advance of America during the 1880's and 1890's was astonishing: "All parts of the country and all classes of society were affected. Through the spread of schools, bookstores, libraries, magazines and newspapers America had become, in Freeman's phrase, 'the land of the general reader,' the home of the greatest reading public hitherto known in the history of the world."[13]

A glance at the mixed collection of writings on Dante which this decade produced reveals two salient facts: first, that much of it came from new centers—Chicago, St. Louis, St. Paul, and Denver—as well as from the South, and even from the Far West; second, that the contributions made by women were equal to, if not greater than, those made by men. It is well known that women writers have held a conspicuous place in American cultural history, but that they contributed so much to the fortunes of Dante has been passed over in spite of the fact that this is a peculiar feature of

12. *The Critic* and *The Dial* also published frequently notes and reviews of books on Dante. In Arthur M. Schlesinger's opinion (*The Rise of the City, 1878–1898* [New York, 1933], p. 269), "never before in America had the art of book reviewing reached so high a plane" as in *The Nation, The Dial,* and *The Critic.* Norton and other devotees of Dante in Cambridge and Boston were frequent contributors, especially to *The Nation,* of such book reviews.

13. *Idem,* p. 201. The three chapters of this book dealing with "The Educational Revival" (vi), "Increasing the World's Knowledge" (vii), and "Renaissance in Letters and Arts" (viii), together with the selected bibliography in footnotes and at the end (pp. 458–488), are the most complete and suggestive general survey for that period of the cultural life of America in all its aspects.

American culture and in a lesser degree of English culture, but without parallel in other countries, Italy included.

Botta's biography of Dante, hitherto the only extensive one written in America, was superseded by May Allen Ward's *Dante* (Boston, 1887), an unpretentious but adequate general presentation of the subject for all who wished an easy and readable approach to the *Divine Comedy*. According to a review in the *Nation* (XLIV [1887], 537), the book "filled very acceptably a desideratum of our libraries," for it was an "unconfused outline biography of Dante, one sufficient for the ordinary student at the start, and capable of indefinite filling in."

As a general introduction to Dante, this little book, so graceful in its simplicity and so warm in its appreciation of the beauty of Dante's poetry, performed a very useful service to a generation of young Americans in colleges and to general readers who hardly could have been expected to read either Botta's high-flown treatise or the later loose compilation of William Clark, *Dante and His Age* (Akron, Ohio, 1898, with original translation of five poems from the *Vita Nuova*), or Epiphanius Wilson's more elaborate *Dante Interpreted* ("A brief summary of the life, times, and character of Dante with an analysis of the Divine Comedy and original translations in the Spenserian stanza," New York, 1898). More restricted in purpose and reflecting to a large extent Norton's ideas on the emotional and moral aspects of Dante's life was Lucy Allen Paton's "The Personal Character of Dante as Revealed in His Writings," published in the *Report of the Dante Society* for 1892.

Women were also among the first to approach directly the involved subject of Dante's philosophy. Susan E. Blow's two articles written for the *Journal of Speculative Philosophy,* "Dante's Inferno" (XVIII [1884], 121 ff.), and "Dante's Purgatorio" (XIX [1885], 61 ff.), reprinted in book form with the addition of "Dante's Paradiso" under the title *A Study on Dante* (New York, 1896), represent the first attempt made by an American Dantist to analyze the structure of the *Divine Comedy* for the purpose of discovering in detail the philosophical, spiritual meaning of its allegory. The author was a follower of William Torrey Harris, who wrote the introduction to her book. The same subject was chosen as the main topic of the lectures, conversations, and discussions at the Concord School of Philosophy in the summer of 1886. There P. F. Mullany (Brother Azarias) gave a lecture on "The Spiritual Idea of Dante's Divine Comedy"; [14] Julia Ward Howe, on"Dante and Beatrice"; [15] and W. T. Harris, on "The Spiritual Sense of the Divine Comedy," published first in his *Journal of Speculative Philosophy* (XXI [1887], 349 ff.), and then in the form of a little book in 1889 and again in 1896.[16]

William Torrey Harris (1835–1909) was the foremost exponent of Hegelian philosophy in America. He founded the *Journal of Speculative Philosophy* (1867–93) and, with Bronson Alcott, the Concord Summer School of Philosophy (1879–88). In his youth Harris had read the *Inferno* "superficially in the original, using Carlyle's translation as a sort of dictionary," and the *Purgatorio* and the *Paradiso* in the versions of Cary and Wright. The horrors of the *Inferno* repelled him, and the whole poem "as a vision of the future state of any portion of mankind" appeared to him absurdly childish. Later on, however, having thought of the possibility of an inner meaning which would reconcile him to the outward form of such works of art as the "Last Judgment" of Michelangelo and the *Divine Comedy,* he began to see that there was a permanent truth in Dante's poem. The *Divine Comedy* presents a threefold view of human deeds:

First there is the deed taken with the total compass of its effects and consequences; this is the picture of the "Inferno." Secondly, there is the evil deed seen in its secondary effects by way of reaction on the doer—a process of gradual revelation to the doer that his deed is not salutary

14. See above, note 11. On the Concord school of philosophy: T. W. Brown, *Alcott and the Concord School of Philosophy* (Concord, 1926); also Austin Warren, "The Concord School of Philosophy," *New England Quarterly,* II (1929), 199–233; and Schlesinger, *op. cit.,* p. 239.

15. The substance of these lectures was first given in a series of reports by Harriett Shattuck to the *Boston Evening Transcript* and to the *Springfield Republican,* and later reprinted with additions in the *Library Magazine,* II (January 22 and 29, 1887), 303–308; 313–318. Julia Ward Howe's lecture was published in her book *Is Society Polite? and Other Essays* (Boston, 1895), pp. 181–202.

16. During the winter of 1883–84, Harris gave a series of ten lectures on Dante to a St. Louis audience. The Concord lecture was a summary of them. His book *The Spiritual Sense of the Divina Commedia* (New York, 1889) contained an expanded form of the Concord lecture, in which he had incorporated the marginal notes of his previous lectures.

either for himself or for others. . . . This is a purifying process . . . in which the doer becomes enlightened by the wisdom of his experience. . . . Hence a third aspect of human deeds becomes manifest, the purified action which emits only such deeds as build up the social whole affirmatively, and consequently return upon the doer to bless him continually.[17]

Up to that time, American Dantists had been primarily men of letters who had little or no interest in philosophy. In their approach to Dante, the allegorical and symbolical content of the *Divine Comedy* had been considered as having only a relative importance. The notion that the structure of the poem reflected broadly the human experience of sin and its punishment, of repentance and purification, and finally of repose in moral goodness, was a commonplace. Had Harris been familiar with Dante literature, he would have discovered it at the beginning of his acquaintance with Dante. This moral content of the *Divine Comedy* had appealed very much to the American spirit of the Romantic period, when the moral element in literature was considered a matter of primary importance and often the decisive element in judging the value of a work of art.

In fact, however, the structure of the *Divine Comedy* has a much deeper implication. It is closely bound to the dogma of the Church and its interpretation in medieval theology, wherein Hell and its sufferings, Purgatory and its expiations, and Paradise and its joys are not mere symbols or allegories of a moral experience in this life, but realities existing in the after life. Dante's philosophy and theology were medieval and Catholic; the *Divine Comedy* is his poetic visualization of those realities in which the earthly moral experience of sin, repentance, and purification found its consummation and eternal fulfillment. A Catholic reader like Brother Azarias had no difficulty in identifying human experience and theological realism as one and the same process in the spiritual world. But others, men like Harris, on the one hand considered Dante's theological realism as a mere poetical myth, a more developed form of the fables of antiquity, and on the other hand wished at all costs to ex-

17. *Idem*, pp. 7–8, and the entire Introduction.

tract from the *Divine Comedy* a philosophical content which could fit in with their own concept of life and its spiritual processes. They achieved their purpose by discarding the whole theological background of the poem as if it had never been in Dante's mind, and then made Dante express himself in the vaporous language of a nineteenth-century German professor of philosophy.

Harris' *Spiritual Sense of the Divina Commedia* is a thoroughly Hegelian interpretation of Dante's moral and spiritual world,[18] by which, for instance, the doctrine of Hell "is the first appearance in a conceptive form of the deepest of all comprehensions of Personality," that comprehension which makes "the citizen completely universal by the laws of the state as in modern times." Out of this comprehension of Personality "have grown our modern humanitarian doctrines, however paradoxical this may seem." [19] Whatever all this may mean, we may be sure that Dante was not thinking in such terms while writing the *Divine Comedy*.

Harris' book, the conflicting opinions of its reviewers concerning its merits and faults, together with the publication of an English translation of Scartazzini's essay "On the Congruence of Sins and Punishments in Dante's Divine Comedy" by Thekla Bernays (*Journal of Speculative Philosophy*, XXII [1888], 21–82)—all served to awaken a new interest in the subject and in the philosophical and religious allegorism of the poem.[20]

18. *Idem*, p. 12. Harris was not unaware that the theory of the world and of the world order which he attributed to Dante is not completely obvious to readers, and that it might not have been obvious to Dante himself. In his opinion, however, "a poet may introduce a theory of the world into his poem which is not so deep and comprehensive as that implied in the spiritual sense of his poem. This is often true in the case of Dante—that his poetic vision has glimpses of a higher world-view than is contained in his interpretation of the philosophy of the Schoolmen; and his poetic discrimination of the states of the soul under mortal sin is deeper and truer than the ethical scheme which he borrowed from that philosophy" (p. 31).

19. "The fundamental idea of Dante's Purgatory has formed the chief thought of Protestant humanitarian works of art. The thought that the sinful and wretched live a life of reaction against the effects of their deed is the basis of most of our novels. Most notable are the works of Hawthorne in this respect. . . . Thus if Protestantism has omitted Purgatory from its Religion, certainly Protestant literature has taken it up and absorbed it entire." (*Idem*, pp. 20–21.)

20. Theodore Pease, "Dante's Vision of Sin and Judgment," in his volume, *The Christian Ministry* (Boston, 1894); Philip Schaff, who had written on Dante as early as 1846, in the chapter on Dante in *Literature and Poetry* (New York, 1890); J. E. C. Sawyer, "The

As Harris had found in Dante his Hegelianism, so Frank Sewall in an essay (*New Jerusalem,* XVII [1893], 114 ff.), reprinted with additions in his book *Dante and Swedenborg and Other Essays* (London, 1893), claimed Dante as the forerunner of Swedenborg's teaching on sin and purification. Going still further, Katherine Hillard, an American who lived in London and translated Dante's *Convivio* into English, discovered in Dante elements of Theosophic ideas and cults ("The Beatrice of Dante from a Theosophic Point of View," *Lucifer,* VIII [London, 1893], 459 ff.), as did Caroline Cust in "After Death States in Dante's Divine Comedy" (*Theosophical Review,* XXX [1902], 149–157). The same subject was treated on a larger scale by L. Schram in his book *Theosophical Analogies in the Divine Comedy* (New York, 1903).

Other American women contributed to this philosophical-religious Dante literature, but along more orthodox lines. Mrs. Rebecca N. Hazard, in a lecture given in 1887 and reprinted with another under the title *Two Views on Dante* (Kirkwood, Mo., 1891), commented on the system of penalties in the *Inferno*. Mrs. Ellen M. Mitchell preferred to dwell upon the joys of Paradise (*The Paradise of Dante* [Syracuse, 1898]; and *The Beatific Vision, A Study of Dante* [Syracuse, 1905]). Soaring even higher, Mrs. Caroline K. Sherman tried to force the doors of the empyrean (*Dante's Vision of God, A Critical Analysis* [Chicago, 1897]). Miss Vida Scudder kept closer to earth in her suggestive book *Life of the Spirit in Modern English Poets* (Boston, 1898), in the long chapter which she dedicated to the "Ideals of Redemption, Medi-aeval and Modern: Dante, Spenser, and Shelley."

To Harris, his Hegelianism notwithstanding, much credit must be given for this extraordinary popularity of Dante, especially among women writers, during the last two decades of the century. As an original writer on education he enjoyed a national reputation and had considerable influence both in the West and in the East. As we have seen, he was co-founder with Alcott of the Concord School of Philosophy, where he faithfully lectured until the time of his ap-

Spiritual Significance of the Divine Comedy," *The Methodist Review,* LXXIII (1901), 232–243; R. J. Wyckoff, "Dante's Message to the Preacher," *The Methodist Review,* LXXXVII (1905), 75–87; and others. List of reviews of Harris' book in Koch, *DA,* p. 122, and Roberts' *Supplement,* p. 14.

pointment to the newly established office of Commissioner of Education in Washington. In St. Louis, where he lived and taught for many years, Harris not only explained Dante to his students but created a sort of Dante furore in the intellectual circles of the city. Upon his urging, the Public Library there acquired a modest collection of books on Dante and published a *Reference List for Dante Studies* in 1890. In 1893, a "Dante School" was held in the city (February 18–25) at which he lectured on "Dante's Inferno and Purgatorio: The Essential Difference of Their Punishments" (published by the St. Louis Froebel Society, 1893). In addition, George P. Brown lectured on "The Relation of the Divine Comedy to Education"; [21] William M. Bryant, on the "Historical Presuppositions and Foreshadowing of Dante's Divine Comedy"; [22] Mrs. J. C. Learned, on "The Symbolism of Dante"; and Denton J. Snider, on "Dante's Purgatorio."

Denton J. Snider (1841–1925), also of St. Louis, a follower of Harris and Hegelianism, and a prolific writer on many subjects, even something of a poet, likewise joined the ranks of Dante devotees. He gave Dante courses and wrote "for the use of his classes" a bulky *Commentary of the Divine Comedy,* a hodge-podge of philosophical, historical, and encyclopedic excursions and notes which must have been as bewildering to his students as they are to modern readers.[23]

To this period belongs also the compilation of new American encyclopedias on a large scale, of biographical dictionaries, and, above all, of voluminous collections of masterpieces from all literatures, that began to fill the shelves of public and private libraries. Dante was always given a conspicuous place in them, and the articles on his life and works were contributed in some cases by competent scholars such as, for example, Lowell and Norton. To quench the irrepressible thirst for varied knowledge which was

21. George P. Brown published a study on "Dante's *Divina Commedia: An Interpretation,*" in the *Public School Journal*, X (Bloomington, Ill., 1891); XI (1892).

22. This lecture was published in the *Andover Review*, XIX (1893), 525–550. Bryant was also the author of "A Dante Study" in the *American Journal of Education*, XXIX (1896), 8 ff., in which he dealt with the Cornell Dante Collection.

23. The first volume, on the *Inferno*, was published in 1892 (St. Louis); and the second, on the *Purgatory* and *Paradise*, in 1893 (St. Louis). Snider stated that his commentary was privately printed and not for the general public.

then so keen in American society, many books, published under alluring titles, provided summaries and bird's-eye views of the highest intellectual achievements of men of all times and places. In not a few of them there are sketches or more elaborate presentations of Dante's life and works, with extensive quotations from the *Divine Comedy*.[24]

This was a period of great expansion for the Chautauqua summer gatherings and for the "star courses" or lecture series, often called "schools," which were offered in many places to people in search of knowledge.[25] Courses and lectures on Dante were common and fashionable not only at such meetings, but also in colleges and other institutions.[26] This infatuation for Dante had spread so widely, especially among women who had literary interests, that in

24. Condé B. Pallen, *Epochs in Literature* (1900); W. Roland, *Among the Great Masters of Literature* (1900); Washington Gladden, *Witnesses of the Light* (1903); Franklin H. Head, *Studies in Mediaeval and Modern History* (1899); Augustus H. Strong, *Great Poets and Their Theology* (1897). Other books dealt with Italy or more directly with Dante: Levi O. Kuhns, *The Great Poets of Italy* (1903); E. Schuyler, *Italian Influences* (1901); E. L. Rivaud, *Views on Dante* (1904); Walter L. Sheldon, *The Study of the Divine Comedy* (1907); Nathan E. Dole, *A Teacher of Dante and Other Studies in Italian Literature* (1903). Several Dante anthologies were also published: *Selections from Divina Commedia*, chosen, translated and annotated by R. J. Cross, Italian and English (New York, 1901); *Ad Astra, being Selections from the Divine Comedy of Dante* [in Longfellow's translation], with illustrations by Margaret and Helen Maitland Armstrong (New York, 1902); and others.

25. Schlesinger, *op. cit.*, pp. 172–174. These Dante Schools were praised and encouraged by the Dante Society in its Report for the year 1886: "The Council learned with pleasure of the formation in several Western cities of large classes for the study of Dante. The course and scheme of work appears to have been arranged with much care and judgment and should produce excellent results. The Society is interested in the success of these classes and desirous of promoting it in any way that shall suggest itself."

26. In a "Goethe School" held in Milwaukee in 1886, Mrs. Caroline K. Sherman lectured on "The Divine Comedy and Faust." This lecture was published in the volume *Poetry and Philosophy of Goethe*, edited by Maurice V. Dudley (Chicago, 1887). A "Dante School" was held in Chicago in April, 1892, at which Thomas Davidson lectured on "The Paradise of Dante" (published in the *Parthenon*, I [Chicago, 1892]). E. W. Evans lectured at the Princeton Philosophical Club on "The Ethics of the Divine Comedy" (*Princeton College Bulletin*, IV [May, 1892], 60 ff.); A. H. Strong, at Vassar, on "Dante and the Divine Comedy" (February, 1888; published in his book *Philosophy and Religion* [New York, 1888]): Theodore W. Koch lectured at Cornell "(Revival of Literature: Dante" [1898]); and Genevieve Tucker, at the Chautauqua meetings, on "A Study of Dante" (*Chautauqua Magazine*, XIX [June, 1894]). Edward H. Griggs published *A Syllabus of Six Lectures on the Divine Comedy* (Philadelphia, 1899), and later on expanded it into a kind of guide for lecturers on Dante (*The Divine Comedy of Dante Alighieri: A Handbook of Lectures* [New York, 1905]); Cecil F. Lavell, another *Syllabus* of a course of six lectures (1903); and so on.

such far-away places as Denver, Colorado, guidance was provided for them in special books, such as Mrs. Ellen M. Mitchell's *Twelve Lessons on Dante's Divine Comedy; A Syllabus* (1892). Even libraries in eastern and western towns published *Reading Lists on Dante.*[27]

The romantic story of Dante's love was not overlooked by popular writers such as Elbert Hubbard (*Little Journeys to the Homes of Great Lovers* [1906], "Dante and Beatrice," pp. 51–76) and Clara E. Laughlin (*Stories of Authors' Loves* [1902], "Dante and His Beatrice," I, 225–229). Dante was even pressed into service for instructing and entertaining children, as witnessed by Elizabeth Harrison's *The Vision of Dante, A Story for Little Children and a Talk to Their Mothers* (Chicago,1892). Last but not least, enterprising publishers tried to exploit this Dante furore by issuing elegant Dante calendars [28] to adorn the boudoirs of wealthy intellectual ladies, as well as the modest parlors of the equally intellectual women of the bourgeoisie. Noteworthy indeed was the achievement of the *Ladies' Home Journal,* which got a "scoop" by obtaining an excellent article on Dante by no less a celebrity than William Dean Howells (December, 1894).

In 1881, the same year in which the Dante Society of Cambridge was organized, another Dante Society was formed in Philadelphia, but the only activity of which there is mention was a first annual dinner on May 14, where a menu enlivened by quotations from Dante was produced. A more ambitious American Dante Society was organized in New York in 1890. It published its first *Year Book* in 1891, which contained an address by Marvin Vincent, the translator of the *Inferno,* and papers on "The Teachers of Dante" by Thomas Davidson and on "Dante's Doctrine of Sin" by Harris. No other issues of the *Year Book* were published, however, and the Society shortly became extinct.

27. San Francisco, 1898; Lowell, Mass., 1899; Cincinnati, 1903; Fitchburg, Mass., 1904; Helena, Mont., 1905; Decatur, Ill., 1905.

28. Dante Calendar for 1901; Being certain excerpts from the writings of Dante (Translated by E. Wilson) with decorations and picturings by Blanche McManus, New York, 1900; Dante Calendar, 1906, designed by Marion C. Bridgman, Springfield, Mass.; Daily Thoughts from Dante Alighieri. Selected and arranged for each day in the year by J. B., New York, 1905.

Besides the new version of the *Divine Comedy* by John A. Wilstach (Boston, 1888) and Norton's prose translation of the poem
(1891–92), numerous translations of passages from it and of sonnets
from the *Vita Nuova* and of other Dante lyrics, and even of his
Latin works, appeared in the periodicals of that time.[29] In addition,
Dante became a favorite subject for original poetical composition.
Longfellow's sonnets and Parsons' ode on Dante, often ranked with
the more choice bits of American lyric poetry, are only two items
in a long list of poetical homages paid by Americans to the immortal Florentine. In this list, too, women hold a conspicuous
place.[30]

29. Among the translators were Charles T. Brooks, "A Canzone of Dante" (the second
in the *Convivio*), published in the *Crayon*, February, 1858; John W. de Peyster, "Francesca
da Rimini" (1885); Titus M. Coan, the sonnet "Negli occhi porta la mia donna amore,"
Lippincott's Magazine, October, 1874; Minot J. Savage, the sonnet "Tanto gentile e tanto
onesta pare" (1885); the same sonnet by Richard W. Gilder in the *Catholic World*, XLVI
(October, 1887); Louise Imogen Guiney, four sonnets from the *Vita Nuova* (1887); and
Samuel Byrne, "The Vision of Beatrice" (from Canto XXXI of the *Purgatorio*), *Catholic
World*, February, 1889.

30. William Cullen Bryant paid tribute to Dante in a poem written for his six hundredth anniversary and later published in the *Atl. Mo.*, XXIII (January, 1869), 81;
Oliver Wendell Holmes also published some verses in the *Atl. Mo.*, XLVII (March,
1881); Julia Ward Howe had a poem "Dante" in her first collection of verses, *Words for
the Hour* (Boston, 1885), and another, "The Price of the Divine Comedy," in her volume
Later Lyrics (Boston, 1886); James Russell Lowell, "Paolo to Francesca," sonnet, *Hearts-
ease and Rue* (Boston, 1888); Frances Anna Keble, "On the Picture of Paolo and Francesca," *Poems* (Boston, 1869); Frederick G. Tuckerman, "Paolo to Francesca," *Poems*
(Boston, 1860); George H. Calvert, "To Dante," sonnet, *Anyta and Other Poems* (Boston,
1866); Richard W. Gilder, "Francesca and Paolo," sonnet, *The New Day, Poems* (New
York, 1876); Charles T. Turner, "Dante and Beatrice," sonnet, *International Review*,
1876; Arthur S. Hardy, "Francesca da Rimini, a Poem" (Philadelphia, 1878); Marion
Muir, "Dante," *Ave Maria*, August, 1881; Heloise Durant, "Dante's Masks," sonnet, *Pine
Needles* (New York, 1884); Julie K. Wetherill, "Francesca to Paolo," *Atl. Mo.*, November,
1884; William H. Vamble, "After Reading the Paradiso," sonnet, *Melodies* (Cincinnati,
1885); Oscar F. Adams, "Francesca to Paolo," *Post-laureate Idyls* (Boston, 1886); Helen
Gray, "Madonna Pia," *Atl. Mo.*, December, 1886; Caroline W. Fellowes, "A Volume of
Dante," sonnet, *Atl. Mo.*, August, 1886; W. A. Leahy, "Dante e Francesca," *Harvard
Monthly*, April, 1887; Walter Kelly, "Dante e Beatrice," *Atl. Mo.*, November, 1888; Sarah
I. D. Stevens, "Dante," *Poets of Maine*, G. D. Griffith, ed. (Portland, 1888); Frank Sewall,
"Dante," sonnet, *New Jerusalem*, March, 1889; Celia Thaxter, "And His Will Is Our
Peace," *Century Magazine*, April, 1890; Edith M. Thomas, "Beatrice," *The Critic*, Septem-
ber 13, 1890; E. Wilson, "Dante," sonnet, *The Critic*, June 7, 1890; Anne R. Aldrich,
"Francesca and Paolo," *Songs About Life, Love and Death* (New York, 1892); E. Faw-
cett, "To Dante," sonnet, *Cosmopolitan*, October, 1892; Ralph A. Cram, "Dante in Exile,"
sonnet, *New England Magazine*, June, 1893; Katrina Trask, "Paolo to Francesca," sonnet,
Sonnets and Lyrics (New York, 1894); W. F. Barnard, "Dante," sonnet, *Donahoe's Magazine*, July, 1895; Edith Bigelow, "Francesca," poem, *Cosmopolitan*, XX (January, 1896),
316; William V. Byars, "Francesca-Beatrice," *Glory of the Garden and Other Odes* (1896);

G. W. Featherstonhaugh's attempt to dramatize the episode of Francesca da Rimini was followed in 1855 by a more sucessful play on the same subject by the poet and playwright George Henry Bocker (1823–90). This play, which has been said to be the best written in America during the nineteenth century, made a second tour of American theaters in 1882 and a third in 1901.[31] Less sucessful was the new play *Dante; A Drama* (Philadelphia, 1904), by John F. X. O'Connor. Finally, several outstanding works on Dante by European scholars were translated into English during that period, among them Scartazzini's *Handbook to Dante* by Thomas Davidson (Boston, 1887).

With the turn of the century, the great fervor of the general American public for more knowledge of Dante's works, especially of the *Divine Comedy,* began to decline. Thenceforth, articles on Dante appeared less frequently and finally ceased, except for occasional brief revivals of interest suggested by special events such as the sixth centenary of Dante's death in 1921. At the same time, however, the results of scholarly research on Dante and his works began to be published by new learned periodicals.

Parsons and others of the "sacred band" of Boston could sneer as much as they liked at the "newly sprung and pretentious" colleges and universities of the Middle and Far West; they marked a great step forward in the cultural history of America. Several of them, provided with large means, by recruiting their teaching staffs from the eastern schools and occasionally importing European scholars,

---

Mary S. Daniels, "Beatrice Portinari," poem, *Wellesley Lyrics* by C. Nevers (1896); Robert D. Dripps, "Dante," sonnet, *Cornell Magazine,* IX (April, 1897), 307; May Martin, "Beatrice," poem, *Buff and Blue,* V (May, 1897), 248–249; William M. Payne, "Dante," sonnet, *The Dial,* XXII (1897), 325; Charles S. Omsted, "Dante," sonnet, *Musing and Other Poems* (New York, 1898); James H. West, "Dante's Spirals," sonnet, *New Unity,* XII (1898), 489; Russell H. Loines, "In a copy of the Vita Nuova," poem, *Harvard Monthly,* November, 1895; Margaret S. Anderson, "Dante's Beatrice," poem, *Poet-lore,* XV (1904), 45; Helen G. Smith, "Gemma to Dante," poem, *Atl. Mo.,* XCV (1905), 610; George Cabot Lodge, "Dante," sonnet, *Song of the Wave and Other Poems* (Boston, 1898), p. 112.

31. Published in the first volume of Bocker's *Plays and Poems* (Boston, 1856). See article on Bocker by K. McKenzie in *Enciclopedia italiana,* VII (1930). Arthur Foote, a Boston musician who had studied in Germany, composed a Symphonic Prologue "Francesca da Rimini," published in Leipzig and Boston under the German title "Symphonischer Prolog," *Francesca da Rimini,* C minor. Für grosses Orchester. Op. 24 (1892). It was performed at the Boston Symphony concerts of January 23, 1891, and March 2, 1895.

started local traditions of sound scholarship which were to bear fruit in the following generation. Meanwhile, the older institutions of higher learning in the East were blooming into great modern universities.

New forces were at work in the colleges and universities as well as in the wider reaches of popular education. Not only did institutions of higher learning grow in number, endowment and quality of instruction, but for the first time they began to take seriously their obligation to enrich the world's store of knowledge. "Nothing more strikes a stranger who visits the American universities," declared an English scholar familiar with Oxford and Cambridge, "than the ardour with which the younger generation has thrown itself into study, even kinds of study which will never win the applause of the multitude." By way of historical parallel observers were reminded of the brilliant days of the Italian Renaissance.[32]

In some of the older universities and colleges of the East, courses in the Italian language and literature and courses on Dante had been included in the curriculum for some time. The method of approach to foreign literatures in general and to Dante in particular had been of the literary-romantic sort, leading easily to vague generalizations in essays and outlines in which imagination and literary brilliancy had free play, often at the expense of historical accuracy and critical discrimination. Now, however, under the influence of European scholarship, brought to this country not only through the medium of books and publications, but much more by hundreds of young American scholars who had completed their training in German and French universities, the historical and philological method of studying literature began to gain ground in America:

Postgraduate instruction represented the culmination of the Teutonic influence in higher education. The graduate school was the American counterpart of the *philosophische Facultät*. Its quick and firm rooting in the national soil attested the missionary zeal of hundreds of young scholars who, returning home with German doctorates, resolved to replace American superficiality with the Teutonic ideal of patient thor-

32. Schlesinger, *op. cit.*, p. 202.

oughness. During the 1880's over two thousand Americans were studying in German universities, twice as many as the preceding ten years and considerably more than in the next decades.[33]

German Dantists contributed greatly to the methodical exploration of historical and literary sources of Dante's life and works and to the analysis of textual problems. K. Witte's researches in the manuscript tradition of Dante's works and his first critical edition of the *Divine Comedy* (1862) opened a new path and marked the beginning of the long and painstaking labors of a generation of German, English, and Italian scholars to whom we owe the modern critical editions of Dante's extant writings. At the end of the century, the Swiss Dantist of Italian descent, G. A. Scartazzini, an indefatigable and prolific scholar, was one of the most prominent figures in Dantean scholarship.

In England, which had a glorious tradition in this field, the period of the brilliant essays of Coleridge, Carlyle, Macaulay, and Dean Church was coming to an end, and interest had shifted to the more exacting task of the new scholarship, which produced the works of such outstanding Dantists as Edward Moore, Edmund G. Gardner, and Paget Toynbee. The *Oxford Dante,* a new critical edition of all Dante's works edited by Edward Moore (1894), which was a revision of Witte's text incorporating the best results of researches on textual criticism made by many other individual scholars as well as Moore's own findings, became for the time being the generally accepted text.

During the Risorgimento, Italian literature, Dante studies included, had been dominated by the political and patriotic aspirations of the time. In the following period, however, under the new regime of national independence and political liberty, old schools, institutions of higher learning, and libraries began to be reorganized and revitalized. Historical and literary studies took on new life. The history of medieval Florence, especially that period in which Dante lived, was newly explored by men like Isidoro Del Lungo, R. Davidsohn, Pasquale Villari, and their disciples who continued in their footsteps. The brilliant essays on Dante by Francesco

33. *Idem*, p. 211.

De Sanctis, who introduced an exacting method of literary criticism into Italy,[34] and the studies on Dante by that eloquent interpreter of early Italian poetry, Giosuè Carducci, were soon followed by the substantial scholarly researches of A. Bartoli. A. D'Ancona, Pio Raina, F. Torraca, F. Flamini, F. D'Ovidio, T. Casini, and then by those of G. Vandelli, M. Scherillo, N. Zingarelli, M. Barbi, G. Busnelli, and many others whose works gained for Italian scholarship a most prominent place in modern Dante studies. The new critical edition of all Dante's works known as the *Testo critico della Società Dantesca Italiana* (1921) has now superseded the Oxford and other editions as containing the best and most accurate restoration of the original texts.[35]

The European influence on American Dante scholarship, which had begun with Ticknor, became an important factor in Norton's time. Through his own personal experiences while translating Dante and through his controversies with Longfellow's critics, Norton had come to realize more and more how important it was that a Dante scholar be well trained in textual criticism and philological inquiries as well as in historical and philosophical research. He struggled valiantly against the handicap of not having had a sufficient early training in the use of these tools; and, though it cannot be said that he mastered the method, he made his students at Harvard fully aware of the advantages of implementing the aesthetic approach to Dante's works by the skillful use of the historical and philological method.

The influence of English Dante scholarship had been from the beginning and continued to be a strong factor. Modern Italian literature on Dante, on the contrary, had been almost ignored by the Americans with the exception of the commentaries on the

34. F. De Sanctis' *History of Italian Literature,* the most original work of literary history and criticism of that period, was far in advance of the ideas and traditions then dominant. It was not sufficiently appreciated in Italy and remained unknown elsewhere for some time. Another generation had to pass before De Sanctis came into his own. An English translation of his book made by Joan Redfern was published in New York in 1931.

35. Revised editions of the *Testo critico* of the *Divine Comedy* were subsequently published by M. Casella (Bologna, 1923) and by G. Vandelli (Firenze, 1927); of the *Vita Nuova* by M. Barbi (Firenze, 1932); of the *Convivio* by G. Vandelli and G. Busnelli (Firenze, 1934). On these critical editions of Dante's works see K. McKenzie's "Observations on Dante's Lyrical Poems" in *Rep. Dante Soc.,* 1934, pp. 2–28.

Divine Comedy by Biagioli and Fraticelli, the old essays of Foscolo, the works of Gabriel Rossetti, and Cesare Balbo's *Vita di Dante*. Although all the commentaries appended to English and American texts and translations of the *Comedy* were much indebted to the works of the old Italian Dantists, it had been long maintained both in England and in America that Italian commentators on Dante, whether early or modern, had created more problems than they had solved and had made Dante's thought appear more involved and obscure than it is. By the end of the nineteenth century, however, American students of Italian history and literature had begun to go to Italy, where they not only visited the places still haunted by Dante's memories, but established closer connections and worked with Italian scholars whose books came thus to be better known and better appreciated in America.[36]

Yielding to these various influences and to the general trend in scholarship, the departments of modern languages and literatures in both the old and the new American universities and colleges introduced more study of modern languages into the curriculum, Italian among them. Furthermore, they gave more room to philological studies in their graduate schools, raised to a higher level their methods of research in literary history, and increased the range of courses and seminars in all these fields.

One prerequisite for the advance of Dante studies was that American libraries—university libraries in particular—acquire extensive collections of books and other publications on Italian literature, and specifically on Dante. The formation of a Dante collection at Harvard had been from the very beginning one of the main objectives of the Dante Society in Cambridge. Norton's books and other gifts, to which a few volumes from George Ticknor's library were later added, made an excellent starting point.[37] Under the direction of W. C. Lane, then assistant librarian of the Harvard

36. The publication of new Italian periodicals of Dante studies such as the *Bullettino della Società Dantesca Italiana* (from 1890), and the *Giornale dantesco* (from 1893), with their extensive bibliographies in which the contributions of Italian Dantists are conspicuous for quantity and quality, soon became the best source of information on current Dante studies for all scholars the world over.

37. Ticknor's collection of books and manuscripts was bequeathed to the Boston Public Library, of which he was one of the founders and promoters.

Library, and from 1887 a member of the Society, the collection grew rapidly, aided by annual contributions from the Society itself and by other gifts.[38]

Gradually, similar collections were formed in other libraries. In addition to the constant acquisition of new publications, books were frequently obtained from old private European collections, thus giving American students the necessary tools for their work. The Cornell University Library came in this way to possess the largest and most complete Dante collection to be found outside of Italy. It was made by Willard Fiske, professor of northern European languages at Cornell, a man of considerable means, a good scholar, and a discriminating collector of books.[39] Having resigned his professorship, Fiske made his home in Florence, where between 1893 and 1896 he acquired at great expense several thousand volumes and items of Dante literature, including an almost complete set of all the editions of the *Divine Comedy* made in the fifteenth and sixteenth centuries, as well as many other rare volumes. These he presented to Cornell as a gift. Theodore W. Koch, already known for his study on *Dante in America,* accepted the invitation to make a catalogue of this unique collection, and fulfilled the task with great competence and accuracy.[40]

In 1887 the Dante Society of Cambridge established a prize to

38. A catalogue of the collection compiled by Lane and issued by the Harvard Library ("The Dante Collection in the Harvard College Library and Boston Public Library," *Bibliographical Contributions,* XXIV, 1890) listed 1,218 volumes at Harvard, among them 302 different editions of the *Divine Comedy* (including translations), 94 editions of Dante's other works, over 800 books on Dante, and 570 articles or essays. Among the books marked "gift of the author" is a copy of Carducci's *L'Opera di Dante* (2d ed., 1888). Lane's catalogue ended with a long note on the portraits of Dante.

39. A visit to the Engadine Valley in the summer of 1891 led to his forming a Rhaeto-Romanic collection of over one thousand volumes; this he gave to Cornell. The Petrarch Collection, Fiske's most cherished possession, he kept with him in Florence. In 1904 he contributed to the celebration of the six hundredth anniversary of Petrarch's birth and offered anonymously a prize of twenty-five hundred lire to be awarded by a committee of Italian scholars for the best research on "Francesco Petrarca e la Toscana." He attended the festivities at Arezzo in July; then he went to Switzerland on a summer trip and died there in September. The Petrarch Collection of almost four thousand volumes was bequeathed to Cornell University, together with his great Icelandic Collection.

40. T. W. Koch, *Catalogue of the Dante Collection Presented to Cornell University by Willard Fiske* (2 vols. Ithaca, N. Y., 1898-1900). *Additions* (1898-1920), compiled by Mary Fowler (Ithaca, N. Y., 1921). Also T. W. Koch, "A List of Danteiana in American Libraries," *Rep. Dante Soc.,* 1900.

be granted every year "to students or recent graduates of Harvard College for the best essay on specified subjects relating to Dante." The prize was a modest one; the essays of the students were not expected to be original contributions or worthy of publication.[41] The *Annual Report* published by the Society usually contained one or two essays or studies on Dantean subjects, and this tradition has been kept to the present time.[42]

One of the Society's most important services to the stimulation of Dante studies in America was the preparation and publication of general works on Dante. Having failed in its plan to edit the Latin *Comment* of Benvenuto da Imola (which task was left, in deference to Lord Vernon's memory, to his sons), the Society decided to prepare a concordance of the *Divine Comedy*. The work was entrusted to E. A. Fay, then a professor in the National Deaf and Mute College in Washington, D. C. An announcement of the project was made in the *Annual Report* of 1884, and the time stipulated for completion was three years. It was published by the Society in 1888.[43]

A few years later, E. S. Sheldon compiled, with the collaboration of A. C. White, the *Concordanza delle opere minori italiane in prosa e del Canzoniere di Dante Alighieri* (Oxford, 1905) as a companion volume to Fay's *Concordance of the Divine Comedy*. In a *Supplementary Concordance to the Minor Italian Works of Dante* (Harvard Univ. Press, 1936), L. H. Gordon covered the additional lyrics now accepted as genuine, with the new readings in both the

41. The fund for this prize was provided in 1886 by George A. Armour of Chicago, a member of the Society. The opening of the first competition was announced at the May meeting of the following year. In 1890 the Society voted to broaden the scope of the prize by admitting to the competition students and recent graduates of all American universities and colleges.

42. Italian scholars followed the development of the Dante Society in Cambridge with interest. In 1890 Bartoli and Carducci were made honorary members. R. Bonghi wrote on the subject of the Dante Society and its reports in *La Cultura* (VIII [June, 1889], 346 ff.) and *L'Alighieri* (I [October, 1889], 214 ff.).

43. Some slight defects in Fay's *Concordance* were noted by G. R. Carpenter in the *Nation* (XLVII [1888], 338). It was very favorably reviewed by Paget Toynbee in the *Academy* (XXXV [1889], 124 ff.), and by the Italian Dantists in the *Giornale storico della letteratura italiana* (XII [1888], 482) and in *L'Alighieri* (I [1889], 60). E. Moore, the eminent English Dantist, wrote: "I have often thought that the most generally useful commentary on the Divine Comedy in existence is the invaluable Concordance of Dr. Fay." (*Studies on Dante*, I, [1896], 45.)

lyrics and the Italian prose works according to the latest critical editions of them.

To complete the series of Dante concordances, which were all provided by American scholars, Edward Kennard Rand of Harvard and Ernest H. Wilkins of the University of Chicago compiled the *Dantis Alighierii operum latinorum concordantiae* (Oxford, 1912), to which they later added a supplement, *A Concordance to the Battifolle Letters* (Dante Society, Cambridge, 1926). In connection with the publication of these works, the questions of concordances in general and of Dante concordances in particular, and of the best method to be adopted in their compilation in view of the manifold practical ends to be attained, were discussed by K. McKenzie and E. H. Wilkins. In his essay "Means and Ends in Making a Concordance, with Special Reference to Dante and Petrarch" *(Rep. Dante Soc.,* 1906, pp. 19–48), McKenzie traced the history and exact meaning of the term "concordance," the proper function of a concordance as distinguished from other works of reference, such as an index or dictionary, and the different methods of adapting means to end in such books. Above all, McKenzie passed in review all the *rimari,* alphabetical indexes, concordances, and dictionaries of proper names and subjects of the *Divine Comedy* and other works of Dante published from the sixteenth century to modern times. E. H. Wilkins' "Methods in Making a Concordance" *(Rep. Dante Soc.,* 1910, pp. 1–5) gave practical suggestions for organizing the work in collaboration, and Edward K. Rand, in "The Latin Concordance of Dante and the Genuineness of Certain of His Latin Works" *(Rep. Dante Soc.,* 1910, pp. 7–38), contributed an elaborate philological discussion of the evidence furnished by the *Concordance* of Dante's Latin works on the question of their genuineness and their chronology. These concordances made a substantial addition to Dante literature; they have performed and will continue to perform great services to scholars. Scartazzini's statement concerning Fay's *Concordance* may well be extended to all of them: "Their value can only be recognized and estimated after a lengthened use of them. It is certain that these at any rate will never grow dusty in the library of a student of Dante." [44]

44. Koch, *DA*, p. 62.

Obviously the readers of reviews and magazines catering to the general public had little interest in the specialized articles and papers on philological and historical subjects which now came forth from the ranks of scholars throughout the country. New periodicals were needed which would address themselves to a specialized audience and would be able to publish learned papers and partial results of researches without causing financial worry to their editors and without the necessity of regarding the whims of their readers. During the last two decades of the century, such periodicals began to blossom forth. Among the oldest is the *Modern Language Notes,* founded in 1885. This was followed in 1890 by the *Publications of the Modern Language Association of America,* and later on by the *Romanic Review, Modern Philology,* and other learned journals.

Meanwhile, "just as American life was being channeled by science and scholarship, so amidst the turmoil of everyday living significant changes were occurring in literature and in fine arts." [45] The literary taste was changing under the impact of new trends, the most active of which was American realism. In this new phase of American intellectual development, Dante, the hero of Romanticism, seemed to be inevitably bound to lose his former wide appeal to the rank and file of American readers guided more by fashion than by reflection and discrimination. As a compensation, however, the study of Dante's works gained in intensity and depth in scholarly circles and institutions of learning throughout the country. New general books on Dante, written no longer by mere dilettanti, but by scholars of high standing, found a large and appreciative public among the intellectual classes. In spite of all changes in taste and ideas, Dante remained on his high American pedestal so laboriously built up primarily by the Cantabrigian triad and their immediate successors. As Scartazzini, the great Swiss-Italian Dantist had said, America was already "the new Ravenna of the great poet."

45. Schlesinger, *op. cit.,* p. 247.

CHAPTER VIII

AMERICAN TRANSLATIONS
OF THE *DIVINE COMEDY* IN THE
TWENTIETH CENTURY

In the preface to his translation of the *Divine Comedy,* the eminent English Dantist E. H. Plumptre recalls a remark by Sainte-Beuve to the effect that in the study of a work like the *Divine Comedy* one is led to feel "that the great poem has not hitherto been adequately translated—to the wish, if it be possible, to meet the deficiency by yet another translation, which, whatever may be its defects, may at least be more adequate than its predecessors." [1] This irresistible urge spurred English students and lovers of Dante on to attempt translation after translation of the *Divine Comedy* during the nineteenth century. In the last two decades of that period as many as fifteen translations, either of the whole poem or of one of its three parts, were published in England, besides a few others which, according to Paget Toynbee, were made but not published. Fifteen translations in twenty years was certainly a high record. [2]

Doubtless the most successful of all these efforts was that of Plumptre (1886–87). In his preface Plumptre says that when he began his work in the 'sixties he believed himself to be the first to undertake the task of making an English version of Dante in *terza*

1. E. H. Plumptre, *The Commedia and Canzoniere of Dante Alighieri* (2 vols. London, 1886–87). We quote from 3d ed. (London, 1896), I, ix.

2. Some of them were severely judged by American critics who were no longer novices in matter of Dante translations. Edward Sullivan's *Inferno* (1893), in prose, was said to be fluent and readable enough but much inferior to the versions of Carlyle and Norton. George Musgrave's *Inferno* (1893–96), in Spenserian stanza, was judged "neither a good translation, nor a good English poem" (*The Nation,* LXII [February, 1896], 160). C. L. Shadwell's *Dante's Purgatory* (1893), an experiment in literal verse translation with an introduction by Walter Pater, was compared to an attempt to interpret "a Beethoven symphony by a single player with flute or ocarine." Of Pater's introduction the same critic remarked: "We need only to say that it presents in his usual whipped-cream style a dilettante's appreciation of Dante." (*The Nation,* LVII [November, 1893], 393.)

rima, for he was unaware of the existence of the translations which had been made by John Dayman (1843–65), C. B. Cayley (1851–55), and Mrs. C. H. Ramsay (1862–63). Before Plumptre had finished his own, more versions in *terza rima* appeared by the following: James Ford (1870), E. R. Ellaby (1874), C. Tomlinson (1877), Warburton Pike (1881), J. R. Sibbald (1884), and J. T. Minchin (1885).

Although Plumptre could not claim the distinction of being an innovator, he produced a better translation in triple rhyme than most of his predecessors.[3] In addition he translated all Dante's minor poems into English, keeping as much as possible the metrical and rhyme form of the originals. Thus, he states, he was able "to read the *Commedia* in the light thrown upon it by the Minor Poems, and the Minor Poems in the light thrown upon them by the *Commedia*" and was helped in his effort to identify himself with his author.[4]

The idea that Dante is his own best interpreter, or that every part or aspect of his thought and art must be explained and understood in the light of his works as a whole, was not original with Plumptre. It went back to the exegetical method of internal concordance, which was familiar in the Middle Ages to commentators of books having an allegorical content. It was not unknown to the old commentators of the *Divine Comedy*. But the slogan "interpret Dante with Dante" had never been so common and had never been taken

3. The American reviewer of Plumptre's translation in the *Nation* (XLIV [1887], 102–104) was convinced that only a prose translation could be faithful to the original, and found Plumptre's version unsuccessful: "The concise straightforward diction of Dante has vanished . . . It is with a sense of the vain effort and wasted ingenuity that one recalls the original." The "Life of Dante" and the "Comments" added by Plumptre to his version were praised for the diligence and learning which they showed, but the reviewer denounced the author's "tendency to suggest fanciful hypotheses in regard to matters concerning which nothing is known." In conclusion, the reviewer remarked that it was fashionable to read Dante just then; hence, "Dr. Plumptre's work falls in very well with the occasion. But the serious student of the poet will revert to sounder methods of interpretation and less ambitious performance." Among the essays at the end of the second volume of Plumptre's version, there was a survey of Dante studies in various European countries and in America. Speaking of the latter country, Plumptre limited his remarks to a perfunctory mention of Longfellow, Lowell, and Norton, and a few rather patronizing general words. Later on, however, Plumptre's translations were highly recommended by Charles H. Grandgent in the bibliography to his edition of the *Divine Comedy*. Grandgent often used them in preference to other versions when quoting passages from Dante's poem.

4. Plumptre, *op. cit.,* I, xvi.

so literally as with the students of Dante of the late nineteenth century.

After the versions of Parsons, Longfellow, and Norton, only one attempt was made in America before the end of the century to translate anew the *Divine Comedy*. John A. Wilstach had already published a translation of the *Æneid* and of other works of Virgil, disclosing thereby a rather defective knowledge of Latin. Nor did he receive any laurels for his translation of the *Divine Comedy,* an offhand rendering in a complex metrical form of rhymed couplets alternated with an unrhymed verse and gathered into stanzas of nine verses.[5] George Rice Carpenter (*The Nation,* XLVIII [February 21, 1889], 163–164) dismissed this version as "so distinctly commonplace, or worse, that it would not be worth while to speak of it at any length, had not certain reviews of it which have appeared as advertisements taken pains to praise it highly." Wilstach dealt in such a cavalier manner with the original, adding, omitting, and paraphrasing according to whim, that the translation "bears sometimes so little resemblance to the original that one wonders if the author had ever read Dante in Italian." His notes were taken mostly from Longfellow and Butler. To their comments he added what Carpenter calls "a sort of cheap American wit, the wit that tries to be smart." In conclusion, Wilstach's translation was "neither faithful, nor accurate, nor intelligible." [6]

During the first forty years of the present century, English translations of Dante continued to flow from the press. Eighteen new translations, either of the whole or of one or two of the three parts of the *Comedy,* made in England in the twentieth century have brought the total number of English versions to a high figure, exceeding the number of translations made of the poem in any other language. American students of Dante, yielding to the urge so well described by Sainte-Beuve, have also made a good record.[7]

5. John A. Wilstach, *The Divine Comedy of Dante* (2 vols. Boston and New York, 1888).

6. This bad taste was also deplored by an English reviewer in the *Athenaeum,* London (February 23, 1889, pp. 241–242), who wondered how the translator could have thought of drawing a parallel between Camillus and the Indian Chief "Sitting Bull."

7. From 1865 to the present, nine translations of the entire *Divine Comedy* have been made in America, five of the *Inferno,* and one of the *Purgatorio* almost complete (Par-

The earliest of these American translations made in the twentieth century was Marvin Richardson Vincent's *Inferno* (New York, 1904). Vincent (1834–1922) was a clergyman first of the Methodist, then of the Presbyterian, faith. Trained in classics at Columbia College, he taught Latin for several years in a Methodist school. Later he became pastor of a Presbyterian church in New York, and in 1887 was appointed Professor of Sacred Literature at the Union Theological Seminary, where he lectured on the New Testament until his retirement in 1916. Mellowed by his classical training, and perhaps not so rigid a theologian as Presbyterians were said to be, Vincent through his experience as a teacher had come to the conclusion that "the study of Dante ought to form a part of the curriculum of every theological institution." It was no longer possible to ignore the Middle Ages:

The department of Church history is compelled to deal largely with the Mediaeval Church; and the history of Theology cannot pass over Aristotle and the company of the great Scholastic Divines whose methods he inspired, and whose works played so important a part in Dante's literary training. No well-equipped clergyman can afford to be ignorant of these; but in order to know the Middle Ages, it is indispensable to know Dante, who is the exponent not only of their society and their politics, but equally of their ethics, their theology, and their ecclesiasticism.[8]

This remark about the curriculum of Protestant theological schools is very significant. The realization was dawning that the thousand years between the closing of the ancient period of the Church and the beginning of the Protestant Reformation were not to be skipped lightly over.

In his blank-verse translation of the *Inferno* Vincent proposed to follow closely the letter of the original without attempting "to produce a smooth and elegant English poem," because the spell of the original, which cannot be conveyed by any translation, "will not be restored by rhetorical amplifications . . . or by emasculating Dante's vigorous diction to meet the demand of conventional pro-

---

sons'). Besides these, many cantos and large fragments from the three parts of the *Comedy* have been rendered in English by various American Dantists.

8. Vincent, *Inferno*, Preface, pp. viii–ix.

priety." He therefore warned his readers not to be startled by "occasionally disagreeable forms of expression." For these "Dante and not the translator must be held responsible." In actual practice, however, Vincent borrows so freely from Longfellow's version that his work at times seems to be a revision of his predecessor's rather than a new translation. This impression is strengthened by the fact that Vincent has very often substituted words of Anglo-Saxon origin for those with Romanic roots, which were so prized by Longfellow and so distasteful to his critics. Now and then the changes introduced by Vincent represent an improvement upon his model. He, moreover, is addicted even more than Longfellow to inversions and transpositions. Above all, no trace is left in Vincent's translation of that measure of poetical feeling which permeates Longfellow's version. A glance at the opening verses of the *Inferno* (I, 1–7) in both versions will illustrate more clearly these points:

Longfellow:

> Midway upon the journey of our life
>   I found myself within a forest dark,
>   For the straightforward pathway had been lost.
> Ah me! how hard a thing it is to say
>   What was this forest savage, rough, and stern,
>   Which in the very thought renews the fear.
> So bitter is, death is little more.

Vincent:

> Midway upon the journey of our life,
>   I found myself within a forest dark,
>   For the right road was lost. Ah! what it was—
> That savage wood, bristling and obstinate,
>   Which in the very thought renews the fear,—
>   How hard a thing it is to tell! so great
> The bitterness, that death is little more.

Although Vincent had announced in his preface to the *Inferno* that the *Purgatorio* was "about ready for the press," he did not publish his renderings of the other parts of the poem. Since he lived many years after the publication of the *Inferno*, it may be that the indifferent reception of his first effort discouraged him from further attempts.

Henry Adams, whose *Mont-Saint-Michel and Chartres* (Boston, 1905) contributed so much toward increasing the interest of American readers in medieval studies, branded as criminal all attempts to translate Dante: "The whole Trinity with the Virgin Mary to aid, has not the power to pardon him who should translate Dante or Petrarch" (p. 251). But the fear of eternal damnation decreed by the inexorable Adams did not disturb the consciences of American Dantists.

In 1915 a complete translation of the *Divine Comedy* (Yale Univ. Press) was published by Henry Johnson (1853–1918), at that time the incumbent of Longfellow's chair of modern languages at Bowdoin College. Johnson's version was hailed with great delight by American lovers of Dante as "an event of real significance for scholarship and literature," and as "the best in blank verse" ever made in English.[9] Johnson felt that a good translation of the *Comedy* "in modern English and line for line" was sorely needed, and that it was impossible to make such a translation in any rhyme system without altering and spoiling both the thought and the poetry of the original. Longfellow's blank verse with its grouping of lines in *terzine* seemed to him the best method to adopt; but at the same time Johnson was eager to avoid being influenced by Longfellow's or by other poetical versions:

Since a metrical translation is a work of art as well as a work of science, the translator must avoid, when he is at his task, consultation of previous poetical solutions of the problem. Given the Italian text and sound commentaries, it has seemed merely honorable to rely solely on one's control of the English medium, unaided. That the result should prove the same as another's in very many cases has not caused discouragement. Translation of the Divine Comedy is progressive, yet the time seems not yet come for a *variorum*, composite version. . . . Experiments in imitating foreign excellences have their own interest; yet . . . the day of mock-Miltonic lines or like solecisms is past.[10]

9. Review of Johnson's version by K. McKenzie, *Yale Review,* V (April, 1916), 637–639. The first printing of 750 copies of Johnson's version was sold out quickly, and in January, 1916, a second printing of one thousand copies was made.

10. Johnson, *Divine Comedy*, Preface, pp. vii–viii.

In fact, many of Johnson's lines are identical with corresponding lines in Longfellow's, although he did not consult the work of earlier translators while writing his own. This is not to be wondered at, for, as McKenzie remarks, "Dante's expression is so direct that the same rendering of a line or a phrase frequently suggests itself to different interpreters." Furthermore, a comparison of the two versions of Longfellow and Johnson where the rendering is different shows that "Johnson's is usually the better," because "Johnson is more flexible in his English, and does not follow rigidly the line-for-line principle; at times he even makes the sentence overlap Dante's normal unit, the terzina. But in changing the order of the words he does not add ideas of his own, nor modify those of Dante." [11]

Shortly afterward there appeared another translation of the *Comedy* (Harvard Univ. Press, 1918–21), also in blank verse, by Courtney Langdon, Professor of Romance Languages in Brown University. Both Johnson's and Langdon's works were highly praised by Charles H. Grandgent as upholding the fine tradition of Cary and Longfellow. But unlike Cary, whose "majestic and sonorous" blank verse was "more reminiscent of the eighteenth century than of the fourteenth," Johnson and Langdon "keep much closer touch with old Florence." As for the relative merits of the two new versions, Grandgent stated that both are scholarly "and both are so good that a comparsion seems ungracious. One may perhaps say that Johnson's inspiration glows with a somewhat more even light, while Langdon's flashes brighter at its brightest and burns duller at its dullest." [12]

Johnson's and Langdon's versions marked the end, at least for the time being, of the American predilection for blank verse and for Longfellow's method in translating the *Divine Comedy*. Looking back at the results obtained by the use of that method, Grandgent summed up his impressions as follows:

If a translation is so close and so intelligible as to assist the tyro, word for word, in his approach to an understanding of the original, it serves

11. McKenzie, *op. cit.*, p. 638.
12. C. H. Grandgent, "New Renderings of Dante," *Italica*, III (May, 1926), 22.

a useful purpose. For the *Divine Comedy* this aid has been furnished so well, in verse and in prose, by Longfellow and by Norton, that little chance is left for improvement; and, in fact, no rival of any consequence has appeared. Both of these versions, moreover, are works of art, exquisite in diction, precise in correspondence. Norton's is a shade nearer to absolute literalness, Longfellow's is a bit easier to follow because of its division into verses. Neither can give genuine satisfaction without the Italian, the prose version being scarcely comprehensible alone, while the poetic one is metrically too rough for unalloyed pleasure.

One may disagree with Grandgent's sweeping statement and hold that the later American translations of the *Comedy* in blank verse, especially Johnson's, mark a considerable improvement over Longfellow's method and its results. His remarks concerning the usefulness of the old translations, their claim to be works of art, and their failure to give complete satisfaction remain true. As Shelley said, an adequate translation of the *Divine Comedy* can be only one in *Terza rima* because it is "an essential justice to an author to render him in the same form." [13] Prose, even at its best, cannot give the same impression as verse: "The nearer the structure of the verse to the author's structure," says Grandgent, "the nearer is the possibility of catching some of the author's effects."

John Pyne published under the title *An English Dante, A Translation in the Original Rhythm and Rhymes* (New York, 1914) the first canto of the *Inferno,* two small fragments from the second and third, and the episode of Francesca da Rimini from the fifth. It is said that Pyne translated the whole *Inferno,* but published only this much. His version is unique in that he not only used *terza rima,* but made each line end in an unaccented syllable and made the accented rhyme-syllable have the same vowel sound as in Italian. He succeeded in doing this chiefly by the monotonous repetition of

13. Quoted by Grandgent, *ibid*. In 1932 Grandgent did not select Norton's version for a new American edition of the most valuable prose version of Dante. *The Divine Comedy of Dante Alighieri. The Carlyle-Wicksteed Translation. Introduction by Grandgent. Illustrated by George Grosz.* (New York, The Illustrated Modern Library, 1932.) Reprinted in 1944. This is a reprint of Carlyle's Inferno revised by H. Oelsner, and with some borrowings from Norton's and Butler's versions, of Thomas Okey's Purgatorio, and Oelsner-Wicksteed's Paradiso, from the British edition in The Temple Classics. The choice of this translation, says Grandgent in his introduction, "was made after careful consideration. It is clear, dignified, and accurate, in simple idiomatic prose. It can be readily followed without any reference to the original Italian text."

rhymes in -*ing*—there are sixty-eight of them in one hundred thirty-five lines of the first canto—and at the price of many distortions of meaning.[14]

The cause of the *terza rima* was also taken up by Eleanor Prescott Hammond (*Dante in English: A Terza Rima Translation and Critique of Terza Rima Translations of the Inferno of Dante, Cantos I–VII* [Chicago, 1919]). This book passed almost unnoticed, perhaps because it was privately printed and sparingly distributed. In a diffuse introductory essay the author rejects in general prose translations and also those in blank verse (which she considers equivalent to prose). The versions of Longfellow and Johnson she finds particularly distasteful because "the dry monotone of the translations . . . gives no impression of the forte and soave of Dante's epic chant. Accuracy the reader has, freedom from the substitutions and additions to which the verse-translator is driven; but the armour of accuracy has crushed the spirit of poetry."

The chief concern of the author is to discover why the *terza rima* has never been successfully used in English renderings of the *Divine Comedy,* in spite of its being the most desirable poetic form for a good translation of the poem. She believes that the fault lies not in the English language, although it is rhyme poor, so much as in "the effect which the task produces upon some minds . . . the belief of partnership in poetic dignity which leads an insufficiently disciplined taste into a lamentable display of its own misapprehensions."

Thus, for instance, Dante's characterization of Pope Celestinus:

> Che fece per viltà lo gran rifiuto,
> (*Inferno,* III, 60)

14. The opening *terzine* of the first canto read as follows:

> Midway the pilgrimage of life completing
>   Come to myself, I saw a wood obscuring
>   Which rendered vague, advancing or retreating.
> To tell of that abode of gloom enduring
>   Back to that savage wood my mind transporting
>   Recalls the terror of my dark immuring.
> No doom but death so bitter were, supporting,
>   But, in the effort, Will with Pain is vying
>   Good to reveal, the evil, too, reporting.

becomes in James Ford's metrical translation:

> who declined
> Bright honour's post, and meanly sought the shade.

The terseness of Dante's line has been diluted by a "swaggering wordiness." Another cause of failure is the fact that indolent minds will accept "the nearest word which may occur to them as a possible third rhyme when the other two of the tercet have been found."

Neither amplifications nor substitutions are admissible. One must remember, however, that "fidelity in translation is, of course, rather fidelity to the poet's intention in choosing words than literal conformity to their outward shells." Longfellow, in his pursuit of words derived from Latin, often overlooked the fact that the Anglo-Saxon word had the connotation which he was seeking.

The translator may also fall into error when dealing with imagery. In his attempt to transfer an image from one language to another, he must "reproduce the amount and kind of sense-suggestion characteristic of the original." Thus, if the line "Che è, che i ben del mondo ha sì tra branche?" (*Inferno,* VII, 69) is rendered: "What is she, of such earthly power possessed?" the translator "loses Dante's visual image of the clutching hands of Fortune; the line is abstract and general instead of concrete and imaginative."

There is also another problem in handling the tercet. It often seems as if Dante himself had been forced to obtain one of his three lines by a circumlocution or by an unnatural selection of words. Shall the translator "reproduce the jar which the original gives him . . . or . . . smooth it out?" In spite of the passage in the *Ottimo Commento* which "cites Dante as declaring 'that never a rhyme had led him to say other than he would . . . ,' " he, too, felt the difficulties of the *terza rima.* It must be remembered, however, that many of the rhymes which seem to us to have been achieved by some violence are in reality quite normal, for "a minute study of the verse and prose of Dante's forerunners . . ." will show us that expressions which appear forced to us were then an accepted part of the *dolce stil nuovo.*

But, as the author herself remarks, "It is a relatively simple matter to discourse of the translator's duty, and something very different to fulfill that duty." The translation of the first seven cantos of the *Inferno,* which Eleanor Hammond gives as an attempt to realize the idea of a perfect, or at least less imperfect, version of the *Divine Comedy,* is remarkable only for the felicity of the rendering of a few passages. Although she tries to keep closely to the rhythm, imagery, and meaning of the original, she, like those translators whose shortcomings she had denounced, frequently adds epithets and includes amplifications which dilute or destroy entirely the condensed vigor of the original. In the first canto (13–24), for example, she adds "dark" to the simple "valley" of the text, and, having translated *colle* by "steep," she adds to its "shoulder" the adjective "broad." Dante's lines:

> Uscito fuor del pelago alla riva,
> Si volge all' acqua perigliosa e guata,

become:

> emerge
> From out the sea, and having gained the shore,
> Turns him to look upon the perilous surge:

The additions "having gained" and "him" are of the kind which the author herself deplored in her introduction. Although she intended to translate the entire *Divine Comedy,* no final publication of these seven cantos and no translation of others have appeared up to the present. Perhaps Miss Hammond dropped her task, not so much on account of the "pained bewilderment" of which she spoke as attacking the translator, but because of the publication of a new version of the *Divine Comedy* by Melville Best Anderson in 1921.[15]

Before we go on to Anderson, however, mention must be made of a translation by another American woman, Eleanor Vinton Murray, under the title *The Inferno of Dante* (Boston, privately printed, 1920). This version, in *terza rima,* is neither better nor worse than the many others from which the translator borrowed passages and

---

15. Melville B. Anderson, *The Divina Commedia of Dante Alighieri* (3 vols. San Francisco, 1921). A second de luxe edition ("For the Honor of California") in four volumes was published in 1929. In the first volume of this edition Anderson included a series of essays on Dante. A new edition with the Italian text (Oxford Text) was published in England in the "World's Classics" series (3 vols. Oxford Press, 1932), and also an edition in one volume without the Italian text. For this edition Anderson revised several hundred lines of his version.

phrases with only slight modifications of her own. Following Grandgent's text and interpretation, she strove to be accurate, but as a whole her translation lacks poetical inspiration and smoothness of rhythm.

Among the translators who had "accomplished the tremendous task of turning the whole *Comedy* into English tercets" Grandgent thought for a while that Plumptre was the most successful. But now "Anderson, the Californian (1921), deserves to supersede him, excelling as he does in ease, smoothness and happy phrasing. And, in spite of the great stress of rimes, one rarely catches him taking greater liberties with the sense than do the recent users of blank verse." [16]

In the preface to his version Anderson states that he labored over his translation for twenty-one years. Norton, he adds, advised him against attempting triple rhyme, but he felt that the fact that previous attempts had not been successful was no reason for his avoiding the *terza rima*. It is fair to say that the result of this long labor of love was a version which is, for the most part, superior to all previous ones of the same kind in the English language. In spite of inevitable additions to the text and of the occasional use of words chosen for rhyme rather than for their exact connotation, Anderson's version is as literal as possible. Furthermore, it is poetical and conveys in good measure the unbroken rhythm of the original. He could state with reason that his choice of the *terza rima* had not been a mistake. "There were moments," he writes, "when I felt near the Master, when he seemed to take the pen out of my hand and show me how the lines should read in English. Moments of happy stimulating illusion, such as come to the translator as the supreme reward of fidelity."

Anderson's translation was highly praised by the English Dantist Edmund G. Gardner:

His rendering is generally accurate, readable, and not monotonous in movement (his occasional use of the English equivalent of the *rima sdrucciola* is happy), though there are halting lines here and there. Taken as a whole, his work is a highly creditable achievement, and

16. Grandgent, *loc. cit.*

needs only a little revision in places to make it perhaps the best translation of its kind that we have in English.[17]

No less appreciative was the Italian review of Eugenio Masucci,[18]
who pointed out, however, several passages in which Anderson had
not been entirely successful. He called attention to Anderson's too
frequent rendering of Dante's positive expressions by sometimes
weak negatives, as in these verses from the Francesca da Rimini
and Conte Ugolino episodes: "Ma solo un punto fu quel che ci
vinse" (*Inferno,* V, 132), translated as "But only one point we resisted not"; and "Poscia più che il dolor potè il digiuno" (*Inferno,*
XXXIII, 75), translated as "The hunger did what sorrow could not
do." Anderson's negatives ("resisted not," "could not do"), according to Masucci, weakened the strong descriptive phrases of
Dante (*ci vinse, potè il digiuno*). Lacy Lockert remarked that
Anderson's version seems to be affected by "a certain coldness of
temper, which it possesses in sharp contrast with the burning intensity of the original." [19] This coldness of temper Lockert attributed to the fact that Anderson did not allow himself enough freedom in rhyme.

That the burning intensity of the original sometimes falls by
several degrees in Anderson's as well as in all good translations is
perhaps inevitable. The tyranny of the triple rhyme in English may
be partly responsible for the loss of intensity. Whatever its shortcomings, however, the reader of Anderson's version will find that
it gives a larger measure of that "genuine satisfaction" which
Grandgent required of a good translation than most of the others.
It contains more passages wherein absolute fidelity to the original
and exquisite English poetical form go hand in hand with no apparent effort and no distortions. Note, for instance, the perfect
rendering of this passage:

> D'anime nude vidi molte gregge,
>   Che piangean tutte assai miseramente,
>   E parean posta lor diversa legge.

17. *Mod. Lang. Rev.,* XVIII (July, 1923), 354–357.

18. *Giornale dantesco,* XXVI (Florence, 1923), 176–182. Cf. also K. McKenzie, "Recent
Dante Publications," *Literary Review,* III (October 14, 1932), 105.

19. Lockert, *Mod. Lang. N.,* XLVII (November, 1932), 481 ff. Cf. also Preface to his
own translation of the *Divine Comedy* (Princeton Univ. Press, 1931).

Supin giaceva in terra alcuna gente;
  Alcuna si sedea tutta raccolta,
  Ed altra andava continuamente.
Quella che giva intorno, era più molta;
  E quella men che giaceva al tormento,
  Ma più al duolo avea la lingua sciolta.
                              (*Inferno*, XIV, 19–27)

Manifold flocks of naked souls I saw
  Who all did woeful lamentations pour,
  And they seemed subject unto diverse law,
Supine were lying some upon the floor,
  And some were sitting all together bent,
  And others went about for evermore.
The more were those, who round about there went,
  And fewer those who lay in torment low,
  But had their tongues more loosened to lament.

The expectation voiced by some of Anderson's admirers that his version was destined to discourage further attempts was short-lived. The quest continued for an English translation so perfect that there was no possibility of a better one being made. Jefferson Butler Fletcher, a former student of Norton, at one time an assistant professor at Harvard, and later professor of comparative literature at Columbia University, published a new version in 1931.[20] Previously he had published some specimens of the metrical system which he thought best fitted to render Dante in English.[21] In the introduction to his translation Fletcher states that no translator has so far reproduced in English the special quality of Dante's verse. From a certain point of view a prose translation of the *Comedy* would be preferable. The prose translators at least achieve their purpose of giving accurately the substance of the poem. On the other hand, a prose translation cannot even attempt to reproduce the beauty of form of the original. In order to capture the spirit of Dante's art it is necessary to keep the tercet intact, "pivot as that is

20. Jefferson Butler Fletcher, *The Divine Comedy of Dante Alighieri* (New York, 1931).
21. "An Experiment in Metre Translation from the *Divine Comedy* in English; Inferno, I, II, V, XXVI, XXXIII," *Rom. Rev.*, XVIII (July–September, 1927), 199–219.

no less of Dante's rhetoric than of his metrics." Longfellow's method of using "unrhymed English tercets, meanwhile breaking the flat monotony of the measure by frequent redundance of syllables" cannot be considered successful. Indeed Saintsbury, in his *History of English Prosody,* dismisses this device as "one of the most abominable measures ever invented." [22] According to Fletcher, the reasons which militate against the successful use of the *terza rima* in English are: first, that English is poor in rhymes; second, that the rhymed interlocked tercet does not lend itself to the language; third, that the English verse does not adapt itself to a constantly occurring rhyme form: "it is like a kettle-drum going all the time." A compromise must be effected. The *terza rima* can be saved only by not linking the tercets: "by one step we cut all but one pair of rhymes." [23]

Fletchers version was praised by McKenzie as one "which takes high rank among those already published." [24] Lacy Lockert thought it "comparable among the translations of the entire *Comedy* only with that of Anderson." In his judgment: "Fletcher's *Inferno* is a little the better of the two, though less well done than the subsequent sections of either; in the *Purgatorio* the honors are doubtful; Anderson's *Paradiso* is distinctly the better. . . . Anderson's *terza rima,* read in larger units, reveals a lyric quality, and his finest passages attain a poetic height, which Fletcher never quite achieves." [25]

Although the mutilated *terza rima* used by Fletcher did not receive an enthusiastic response, the version had the merit of being, in considerable measure, really new. In his introduction Fletcher mentions his indebtedness to Longfellow, Johnson, Norton, and Grandgent "for occasional phrases adopted" from their versions. As a rule, however, he departs from the phraseology adopted by pre-

22. Quoted by Fletcher from George Saintsbury, *Hist. of Eng. Prosody,* III, 107.

23. Fletcher's idea was not entirely new; both Ichabod C. Wright (London, 1833–40) and S. Farley Wright (*Inferno* [London, 1928]) had used a similar though not identical form in their translations of Dante.

24. *Saturday Review of Literature,* November 7, 1931, p. 262. McKenzie takes issue with Fletcher on the latter's assumption that a prose translation of the *Comedy* cannot reproduce its beauty of form. In his opinion, "the beauty of form depends not only upon rhyme and metre, but also upon the choice and arrangement of words, so that a masterly rendering like Norton's certainly does suggest at least some of the elements of Dante's style as his substance."

25. Lockert, *Mod. Lang. N.,* XLVII (November, 1932), 481 ff.

vious translators and expresses the meaning of the original in a new English form.

Another and perhaps more important merit of Fletcher's version is that it contains a minimum of the additions, substitutions, and transpositions which detract from previous rhymed translations, Anderson's included. To the reader who is familiar with the original, a comparison between Fletcher's version of the beginning of St. Bernard's prayer to the Virgin Mary in the last canto of the *Paradiso* and Anderson's rendering of the same lines will serve as an excellent example of Fletcher's method and its results.

Fletcher:

> Thou Maid and Mother, daughter of Thy Son,
>   Thou humble and high over every creature
>   Bourn by eternal counsel fixed upon,
> Verily thou art she who, by partaking,
>   Did even so ennoble human nature
>   Its Maker scorned not to be of its making.
> Within thy womb rekindled was the love
>   Under whose warmth in the eternal peace
>   This flower had its burgeoning. Here above
> Unto ourselves meridian torch thou art
>   Of charity, and thou art there below
>   The living spring of hope in mortal heart.
> Lady, thou so prevailest in all things
>   That whose would have grace, and seeks not thee,
>   Would have his wish fly upward without wings.

Anderson:

> Daughter of thine own Son, thou Virgin Mother,
>   of the eternal counsel issue fated,
>   lowlier and loftier than any other,
> To such nobility hast thou translated
>   man's nature that its Maker did not spurn
>   to make Himself the thing that He created.
> Beneath thy heart was made again to burn
>   the Love by virtue of whose warmth withal
>   this Flower has blossomed in the peace eterne.

> A living torch here art thou to us all
>   to kindle love, and down where mortals sigh
>   thou art a fount of hope perennial.
> Thou art so prevailing, Lady, and so high
>   that who wants grace and will to thee not run
>   would have his longing without pinions fly.
>   (*Paradiso*, XXXIII, 1-15)

Not discouraged by Anderson's success, Albert R. Bandini, an Italian Catholic priest, decided to try his hand at translating Dante once more in *terza rima*.[26] Bandini was a Florentine who had taken up residence in the United States, and since English was not his native tongue, the task he had taken upon himself was a considerable one. Bandini states frankly in his preface that he was moved to publish his translation because he felt that it "is a little better than others of the same kind." Still, he was aware that such a conviction "might be only induced by presumption," and that his work was not without its defects. The *Inferno* was done in less than two years, "amidst many other occupations." He foresaw that critics and reviewers would find awkward constructions, defects of rhyme, and infidelity to the original in his work, as they did. Instances of faulty language and a "constant tendency to overload his line with many syllables" were noted by several reviewers.[27]

Bandini gained the distinction of being the first Italian-American to attempt such a task. Although he had, as a Florentine, the advantage of being in closer contact with Dante through his language than any of his American and English competitors, he likewise had the serious difficulty of translating Dante into a language not his own. This was a veritable *tour de force,* rather uncommon in American literary history.

Also in *terza rima* was Lacy Lockert's translation of the *Inferno*.[28] Lockert shared with Anderson and others the view that "the metrical form of the *Divine Comedy* is too distinctive, and too striking in aesthetic effect, to be properly separable from it." On the other

26. Albert R. Bandini, *A Lineal and Rhymed Translation of the Divina Commedia; With a Biographical Sketch of Dante* by Matthew J. Dooley (San Francisco; *Inferno*, 1928; *Purgatorio*, 1930; *Paradiso*, 1931).

27. Frederick Anderson, *Italica*, VI (March, 1929), 32.

28. *The Inferno of Dante, Translated into English Terza Rima Verse with Introduction and Notes* by Lacy Lockert (Princeton Univ. Press, 1931).

hand, he agreed with Fletcher that the preservation of the rigid scheme of Dante's *terza rima* in an English translation would inevitably lead to unsatisfactory results. As we have already mentioned, he attributed the coldness of temper of Anderson's translation to the strictness of the *terzina*. But the compromise suggested by Lockert differs from Fletcher's total abolition of the middle rhyme of the tercet. Lockert advocates "a greater license, at times the most extreme," in the matter of rhymes, so that "the employment of half rhymes, of bare suggestions of rhyme, or even occasionally of mere assonances" be permitted to the translator. He held that the use of such substitutes does not destroy the reader's impression of a continuity of medium, while the additional latitude of phrasing thus gained opens hitherto unexplored possibilities of rendering. Translations, he says, are dependent upon "stratagems." As in the matter of precise rhyme, so in matter of literalness he wandered about at will: "At times I have boldly paraphrased the letter of the original; at other times I have spared no effort to render Dante exactly. Here I have put abstruse Italian into plain English; there I have been careful to preserve the dubiety of an obscure or doubtful text." Finally, Lockert acknowledges having made free use of translations in prose and blank verse to the extent of adopting from them whole lines. He did not, however, make use of any rhymed versions, with the remarkable exception of Rossetti's last thirty-five lines of the Francesca da Rimini episode, which he transplanted bodily into his own rendering. A certain latitude in matter of English rhymes, often made more for the eye than for the ear, is common to all translators of Dante, even the best ones: but with Lockert, the exception became almost the rule. He was confident that by this method it was possible to produce a new version which would in every line be better than any ever made in blank verse, and have in addition "a fair percentage of individual lines and passages, not infrequently, even superior to all previous renderings of them." Unfortunately his theory is not supported by the results of his version.[29]

29. Note the simile of the cranes (*Inferno*, V, 46–52) as treated by Lockert, Longfellow, and Fletcher:

Lockert: And as the cranes go chanting their sad lay,
                Making in air a long line of themselves,
                Thus by that steep commotion on their way

The most recent American translation of the *Divine Comedy* by Louis How [30] presents some novel features, which are described by him as follows in his preface to the *Inferno:*

> I call mine an American version, but have made no effort to tie myself to the colloquial usage which may be termed American. I have used an eclectic language. Like my great original, I have not eschewed either obsolete words, neologisms, coinings, dialect, foreign phrases, or slang. . . . I have made the metre of some lines depend on elisions left to the shrewd and amiable reader; and have been forced by certain proper means to throw the rhythm of other lines on my reader's charity.

The author, who lived long in Italy and has a remarkable command of Italian, is well acquainted with the large Italian literature on Dante. In addition, he had the opportunity of discussing some of the problems of translation with several prominent Italian Dantists, especially with Francesco Torraca, whom he considers "tremendously clever but audacious," and to whom he owes "some of his possibly surprising interpretations."

After reading How's blithe confession of numerous literary sins, one expects the worst. In reality, however, the *Divine Comedy* in its new American dress is less shocking than one would suppose. The use of colloquialisms is not so general as to verge on caricature. In

---

	I saw the shades borne, uttering their wails;
	Wherefore I said: "Master, who are these folk
	Whom the dark tempest so doth scourge with ills?"
Longfellow:	And as the cranes go chanting forth their lays,
	Making in air a long line of themselves,
	So saw I coming, uttering lamentations,
	Shadows borne onward by the aforesaid stress.
	Whereupon said I: "Master who are those
	People, whom the black air so castigates?"
Fletcher:	And as the cranes go singing their sad lay,
	Making themselves in air a long-drawn line,
	So I saw coming carried on that fray,
	The host of shades, all uttering long wails.
	Wherefore I said: "Master, what folk are those
	Whom the black air so bitterly assails?"

30. *Here Beginneth the Comedy of Dante Alighieri, Florentine by Birth but Not in Conduct,* Part I, *Hell,* American Translation by Louis How (New York, 1934); *The Comedy of Dante Alighieri,* Part II, *Purgatory* (1938); Part III, *Heaven* (1940).

some passages, colloquial phrases adapt themselves better to the original than does the dignified, Victorian phraseology of older translations. He does not employ them everywhere. As one of his reviewers stated, colloquialisms "do not occur in the finer passages which he translates with striking grace and fidelity." [31]

How claimed that he used colloquialisms and slang when Dante himself employed them, and that by so doing he could remain closer to the original in spirit if not in letter. Thus, in his translation of the *Inferno*, Canto XXI, where the swindlers are plunged into a pond of boiling pitch and hooked by the devils, How tried to match colorful English colloquialisms with the Tuscan of Dante. A devil brings a newcomer in on his shoulders:

> From our bridge we heard him cry:
> "O Wicked Talons, look what I have ta'en,
>   Another of the Ancients of Saint Zita.
>   Just pop him in. I'll go back there again . . ."
> He throws him in, and turns his rapid feet
>   Back o'er the bridge; and never a mastiff reared
>   Was loose upon a robber's track more fleet.
> The victim sank; rose, doubled and besmeared;
>   The fiends beneath the bridge cried out to him:
>   "Down here the Holy Face is not revered!
> The Serchio is a different place to swim!
>   If thou art shy of scratches, 'ware the cooks,
>   Keep down below, and don't come up and skim."
> They grappled him with over a hundred hooks,
>   And said: "The dancing here is forced to plumb;
>   The filching's underhand, befitting crooks."
> Not otherwise the scullions' rule of thumb,
>   Which makes them fork the meat inside the pot
>   To hinder it from floating with the scum.
>
> (*Inferno*, XXI, 36–57)

In Anderson's version, which is always closer to the original than How's, this passage reads as follows:

> "Maltalons," he cried, as on our bridge he strode,
>   "look ye, one Elder of Saint Zita—dash
>   him under, while I get another load . . ."

31. *Rom. Rev.*, XXVII (December, 1936), 307.

Flinging him down, upon the flinty cliff
   he wheeled, and never gave so hot a chase
   an unleashed mastiff running down a thief.
That sinner plunged, and aired his back apace;
   but demons, lurking there the bridge below,
   cried: "No invoking here the Holy Face!
Here swim ye not as in the Serchio:
   therefore take heed, unless you mean to try
   our grapples, not above the pitch to show."
Then, pricking him with hundred prongs, did cry
   "Here must thou dance about in covert guise,
   that, if thou can, thou swindle on the sly!"
Cooks make their scullions do not otherwise,
   when with their hooks they plunge the carcass clean
   down in the caldron, that it may not rise.

Anderson has taken no liberties with Dante's text. In this passage
he does not omit or add material as How does. Now and then, as
in some of these lines, Anderson's rendering may sound less smooth
than How's, but Anderson always gives the visual image of the
original faithfully and in detail. For instance, contrast his line,
"Flinging him down, upon the flinty cliff," with How's nonde-
script, colloquial: "He throws him in." How takes it upon himself
to add to Dante's words and to Dante's meaning more often, perhaps, than any other American translator except Parsons. In the
passage quoted above, Dante's line, "sì che, se puoi, nascostamente
accaffi," rendered faithfully and forcefully by Anderson: "that, if
thou can, thou swindle on the sly!" is unnecessarily padded in
How's version: "The filching's underhand, *befitting crooks,*" omitting at the same time the sarcastic *se puoi* of the text.

   How does not mention his indebtedness to his predecessors. With
so many English translations of the poem in the field, this matter
is taken now for granted. His indebtedness is more conspicuous in
the "finer passages," where colloquialisms and slang were out of
place. His reviewer, quoted above, gives as an example of the "grace
and fidelity" of How's version the last lines of the famous episode of

Ulysses where his indebtedness to Grandgent and Anderson is obvious:

Grandgent:

> Three times it made the boat and waters spin,
> And, at the fourth, lifted our stern amain;
> At Someone's beck, our stem went plunging in,
> Till over us the ocean closed again.
> (*Inferno*, XXVI, 139–142)

Anderson:

> Thrice with the waters all, it whirled her fast;
> the fourth upheaved the stern and sunk amain
> the prow, as pleased Another, till at last
> The ocean had above us closed again.

How:

> Three times it whirled us and the waters round;
> The fourth it lifted up our stern amain,
> The stem went down,—for so was Someone bound—
> And then the sea closed over us again.

In general, however, it must be said of How's American and in part Americanized version that it is easy and pleasant to read and may be considered a valuable addition to the Danteana of this country.

Although he never published a complete version of any of the three parts of the *Divine Comedy,* Grandgent must be included among American translators of Dante, for in his various books and articles Grandgent, always eager to have Dante "speak for himself," quoted extensively from the *Divine Comedy* and other works of the poet in English translation. Sometimes he borrowed from Cary, Longfellow, Plumptre, and Rossetti; more often he used his own renderings, of which he said simply that he had tried "to copy the metrical forms of the original as closely as the habits of our tongue permit." [32]

32. C. H. Grandgent, *Dante* (New York, 1916), Preface.

In Grandgent's opinion, a translation of the *Divine Comedy* intended to be not merely a crib to aid students, but "a thing of loveliness" made to convey "independently" the meaning and charm of the original, should be judged by the test of whether or not "it can be read by a non-Italian with the same joy which the original awakens in the Italian." To attain this end "a prime requisite is that it be clearer than Dante's text; for while a reader may be glad to burrow laboriously into the sweet primal Italian, nobody will gracefully submit to a like imposition on the part of a mere counterfeit." A happy medium must be struck between terseness and too great elaboration. Last but not least, a beautiful and poetical translation of the *Divine Comedy* "must run trippingly—which, in English, means polysyllabically; for the English poetic ear is averse to congestions of monosyllables, enemies of the assurance of regular rhythm which we crave. It must avoid translators' jargon. After all, it takes a poet to translate a poet." [33]

By following these principles and at the same time adhering as much as possible to the verbal expressions of the original, Grandgent avoided the rigid and often awkward literalness of Longfellow. The tyranny of the *terza rima* forced him inevitably into transpositions and verbal additions, but he skirted the pitfalls of too obvious paraphrasing and modernization. Above all, he strove to attain transparent clearness in rendering Dante's thought and images in flawless English poetical form, and with this end in view he did not hesitate to sacrifice literalness to the exacting demands of an impeccable English style. One may well doubt whether Grandgent could have attained the same high level of excellence throughout, had he made a complete version of the *Divine Comedy*.[34] At any rate, a collection of all the passages translated by him and scattered throughout the pages of his books would make a very valuable anthology of Dante's poetry in the English language.

John Jay Chapman (1862–1933) must also be ranked among American translators of Dante. Selections of considerable length

---

33. Grandgent, "New Renderings of Dante," *Italica*, III (May, 1926), 22.
34. "C. H. Grandgent, in some passages scattered among his various essays, has gone far towards achieving the impossible. But I doubt if even he could carry such a *tour de force* through the whole poem." (Fletcher, *op. cit.*, Introduction, p. ix.)

from the *Divine Comedy* translated in *terza rima* are included in his book *Dante* (Boston, 1927). Chapman had some ideas of his own about translations in general and translations of Dante in particular. "The reason that translators are slashed, maimed, and borne bleeding from the field after a duel with Dante, is that they accept the conditions which the judges lay down—the judges being certain large-wigged antiquarians whose minds are as much encumbered with the paraphernalia of learning as was the sanctum of Don Quixote" (p. 1). Dante is privileged to be obscure, to invent his own language, to fashion his own rhymes, to coin new words, while the translator "must use his own idiom in a conventional, flat-footed way." This, says Chapman, is absurd. The translator should be allowed as much freedom as Dante. It should be granted to him "to wander freely in the reserve and to sketch in water-colors or write original verses there" (p. 3).

From these words the reader gets the impression that, in Chapman's opinion, all translations should be paraphrases. On the other hand, he states that the paraphraser and the translator belong to different categories, and that his own renderings of Dante are paraphrases rather than translations. The question which he seems to be toying with is whether a paraphrase is better than a translation. He seems to have had no doubts on this point: Translations made according to the rules laid down by the "large-wigged antiquarians" are misfits; the only good translations are those which deal freely with the original.

When one dares it, new side-lights of meaning and fresh little dramatic vistas appear in the background of Dante's scenes and episodes—sights that remain hidden to the reverent eye, but reveal themselves to the impudent. . . . the vitality of a translation depends somewhat on the consciousness of these shadowy underplots . . . [pp. 36–37].

In spite of his clamorings for freedom, Chapman felt obliged to keep the most difficult feature of the original, the *terza rima*. His renderings of Dante, sometimes literal, more often not, are smooth and terse. Actually he made much less use of his freedom than one would expect from his protestations. His translation of the fourth canto of the *Inferno,* an early effort made before he had begun to look so scornfully upon the rules of the Dantists, is almost literal. In his later renderings he dealt more freely with his text, omitting now and then whole tercets, condensing two lines into one, or expanding one into two or three. Even so, Chapman's paraphrases have an unmistakably Dantean ring (something which one cannot say of Parsons' work), although a recurring irregularity in rhyme and rhythm makes the reader miss often what Fletcher called "the drum beat" of Dante's *terzina*. He is at his best in rendering such striking descriptive passages as this:

> or son venuto
> là dove molto pianto mi percote.
> Io venni in loco d'ogni luce muto,
>   che mugghia come fa mar per tempesta,
>   se da contrari venti è combattuto.
> La bufera infernal che mai non resta,
>   mena gli spirti con la sua rapina;
>   voltando e percotendo li molesta.
> Quando giungon davanti alla ruina,
>   quivi le strida, il compianto e il lamento;
>   bestemmian quivi la virtù divina.
>
>   (*Inferno,* V, 26–36)

> We now had come
> where many a plaint for sorrow waked my own;
> And where the air—although the light was dumb,—
>   was bellowing like a tempest, or a sea
>   with giant winds at battle o'er the foam.
> The infernal drench and bluster carelessly
>   beats down, lifts up, and sweeps the spirits on;
>   whirls, smites, torments. In their extremity
> Before its onrush, many a shriek and groan
>   goes up, with blasphemy of heavenly things.

It would be hard to maintain that by his free method of rendering this passage Chapman discovered in Dante's text "new sidelights of meaning and fresh little dramatic vistas." On the other hand, Norton could not have said of Chapman's version as he had said of Parsons', that its poetical language and imagery were Chapman's, not Dante's.

Chapman's selection of certain passages of the *Divine Comedy* in preference to others was dictated by his theory of poetry in general and of Dante's poetry in particular, with which we shall deal later. As a translator or paraphraser of Dante, he deserves recognition, if for nothing else, for his rendering of Cantos VII and VIII of the *Inferno,* which in Grandgent's judgment is "a thing of beauty."

Any attempt to assign a proper place in the general history of Dante literature to the American translations of the *Divine Comedy* must take into account the many translations made in the English language on the other side of the ocean. A comparative analysis, however brief, of the merits and shortcomings of even a few selected versions made in England and America is bound to become too detailed and to lead us, moreover, into a field in which individual opinions and tastes play a very important part. In general, anyone who has some familiarity with this extensive English and American literature of Dante translations will agree that the good American versions of the *Divine Comedy* easily stand a comparison with the good ones made in England.

The Americans, though later comers in the field, did not lag behind in experimenting with all possible methods of translating Dante. Parsons' free version of the *Inferno* remains still, perhaps, the best "English lyrical poem" paraphrasing Dante. In the class of blank-verse translations, Longfellow's new literal line-for-line version still commands respect, as do Johnson's and Langdon's versions in a less rigid literal method. Norton's prose version, though less used now than Carlyle's *Inferno* revised by H. Oelsner, T. Okey's *Purgatorio,* and P. W. Wicksteed's *Paradiso,* has not lost its literary value. Among the poetical versions which have compromised with Dante's *terzina,* Fletcher's is one of the best, and, of the many *terza rima* translations which exist, that of Anderson was judged by the English critics to be the best of its kind up to that time.[35] Very recently another version of the *Divine Comedy* in

35. This chapter was already written when a new translation of the first five cantos of the *Inferno* by Wendell P. Stafford came into my hands (*Dante's Inferno, Cantos I–V in English Verse* [Privately printed; no place or date of publication given, but issued in 1945]). The author in his long and honorable career as a magistrate has not forsaken the Muses which inspired him in his native Vermont and in his Dartmouth days. Side by side

terza rima, by Laurence Binyon, has appeared in England.[36] Many
critics think that Binyon's excellent work, as a whole, is preferable
to Anderson's translation. A close comparison of the two leaves
little doubt that Binyon's version is more evenly accurate in rendering clearly the meaning of the text, and more evenly successful in
the choice of rhymes, thus securing a steadier flow of the *terzina*
than does any other version of the *Divine Comedy.* Yet, while admitting that the new English translation taken as a whole gives
more "genuine satisfaction" than the American one, the reader is
forced to admit also that Anderson's version again and again
"flashes brighter at its brightest." [37]

---

with a *Handbook of Equity,* he has published various volumes of poetry. His translation
of the first cantos of the *Inferno* in rhymed couplets, to be read only by his friends, is a
sentimental homage to the aspirations and tastes of his youth, the time of the great "Dante
furore" of the 'nineties.

36. Laurence Binyon, *Dante's Inferno, With a Translation into English Triple Rhyme*
(London, 1933); *Dante's Purgatorio* (London, 1938); *Dante's Paradiso,* (London, 1943).

37. Compare Binyon's version of the beginning of St. Bernard's prayer with Anderson's
and Fletcher's, given above:

Binyon: Maiden and Mother, daughter of thine own Son,
        Beyond all creatures lowly and lifted high,
        Of the Eternal Design the corner-stone!
    Thou art she who did man's substance glorify
        So that its own Maker did not eschew
        Even to be made of its mortality.
    Within thy womb the Love was kindled new
        By generation of whose warmth supreme
        This flower to bloom in peace eternal grew.
    Here thou to us art the full noonday beam
        Of love revealed: below, to mortal sight,
        Hope, that for ever springs in living stream.
    Lady, thou art so great and hast such might
        That whoso crave grace, not to thee repair
        Their longing even without wing seeketh flight.

Also his version of *Inferno,* V, 26–36 to Chapman's, quoted above:

Binyon: I am come
    Where thronging lamentations hold me chilled.
  I came into a place of all light dumb
        That bellows like a storm in the sea-deep
        When the thwart winds that strike it roar and hum.
  The abysmal tempest that can never sleep
        Snatches the spirits and headlong hurries them
        Beats and besets them with its whirling sweep,
  When they arrive before the ruin, stream
        The cries up; there the wail is and the moan,
        There the divine perfection they blaspheme.

The admirable record which America has made in translating the *Divine Comedy* is a most significant witness to the place that Dante has gained in American intellectual life. Pointing at those translations, the great Florentine could well say to American youth in search of wisdom and beauty:

> Del lume che per tutto il ciel si spazia
> noi semo accesi; e però se disii
> di noi chiarirti, a tuo piacer ti sazia.[38]
>
> *(Paradiso, V, 118–120)*

38. The light that through all heaven is spread abroad
    Enkindles us; and so, if thou desirest
    Enlightenment of us, sate thee at will.
                    (Fletcher's version)

CHAPTER IX

DANTE'S AMERICAN BIOGRAPHERS

By the end of the nineteenth century, it seemed very difficult for a scholar of any nation to find something new to say about Dante. There were already so many extensive biographies of Dante, so many detailed pictures of his times and environment, of his political and intellectual background, so many analyses and commentaries of the *Divine Comedy,* that it appeared that there was little left for the Americans to do—last comers to this carefully harvested field—beyond gleaning what might have been overlooked by previous reapers. Indeed, it might seem as if the only task left to American Dantists was the modest one of absorbing the material already gathered and reworking it into books and essays for the American public. This they did and did well, but they did much more and are still continuing their good work.

Like all other great figures in the history of human intellectual achievements, Dante will always appeal to the searching minds of every new generation. Not only are there problems in the study of his personality and in the interpretation of his works which call for more satisfactory solutions, but new approaches from new angles to his thought and art are constantly being provided by the advances made in the knowledge and understanding of the Middle Ages and by the changes which take place in the intellectual outlook and in the taste and aesthetic appreciation in any new period of the cultural history of mankind.

Down to the end of the nineteenth century, the attitude of European scholars toward American learning tended to be rather supercilious. Although the old notion that American soil could produce dollars and dollar-worship, but only dilettantism in cultural pursuits, was no longer so widespread as at the time of Lowell's essay "On a Certain Condescension in Foreigners," and of his caustic remarks in his "Fable for Critics"; still, the tendency either to ignore or to treat American scholarship as unimportant was not uncommon in learned European circles.

English scholars, who had done so much for Dante, were often very severe with American books on and translations of Dante, not excepting those of Longfellow and Norton, though both of them had been taken by the British to their hearts. The Germans occasionally took note of the fact that a tradition of Dante studies was growing across the Atlantic, but they were accustomed to seeing American students and young scholars worshiping at the German shrine and were inclined to regard their works as little more than the exercises of willing but immature pupils.

The Italians were torn between pleasure at seeing Dante, their greatest Italian genius, become an important figure in American culture, and skepticism about the ability of the American mind to understand his thought and appreciate his art. Italian Dantists well knew how greatly they were indebted to British and German Dantists, but, after all, British and German scholarship sprang from the humanistic tradition engendered in Italy. The Americans, on the contrary, seemed to have no roots in the past and no appreciation for anything save the present.

The emphasis with which the Italians affirmed the universality of Dante—of his being, as Carducci said, not a national poet in the sense that Shakespeare was English and Goethe German, but a poet for the whole world and for all times—kept them from claiming a monopoly on interpreting Dante. On the other hand, they could not help feeling that they were in a privileged position where he was concerned, for they had a closer familiarity with the language in which Dante wrote, and with the history, the institutions, and the psychology of the nation to which he belonged. The new American literature on Dante was greeted, therefore, with a kind of big brother's condescension. Even in cases of adverse criticism of American works, Italian reviewers seldom failed to add a word of praise and encouragement.

It is only in recent times that an Italian, Giovanni Papini, who started his literary career as a wild, iconoclastic debunker and then became a reactionary academician, decreed the expulsion of all foreigners from Dante's inner temple, and indeed of anyone who was not, like him, "a Catholic, an artist and a Florentine." [1] Only such a one is able to understand Dante. Papini warns his startled reader not to regard his statement as "a capricious and distorted fantasy, or the fruit of a foolish delusion." He knew whereof he spoke, because in his younger days, when he was afflicted with the disease of "bibliophagy," he had made a collection of the most important opinions expressed by men of every nation on Dante and his writings, and had found out that "very few, especially among foreigners, have understood Dante."

When Papini's book was being translated into English for an American edition, however, the author had a change of heart and made a notable exception to his decree of expulsion:

Outside of Italy no other country has so greatly loved and studied the creator of the Divine Comedy as have England and America. Not only have they produced accomplished Dante scholars—like the English Lord Vernon, H. C. Barlow, Edward Moore, Paget Toynbee, and the American Longfellow, C. E. Norton, J. R. Lowell—worthy to stand on an equality with the Italian and the German; but the first-hand knowledge of Dante's work, even among those of moderate culture, is more widespread than elsewhere. The English-speaking peoples not only know Dante, but they admire him, appreciate him, understand him and love him. [2]

American readers could not fail to appreciate the compliment. Papini's knowledge of American Dantists did not go beyond the names of the old Cantabrigian triad. Of their successors he knew nothing; or perhaps he herded them with the "professional Dantists, Dantologists and Dantomaniacs," who are but "fanatical adulators and pedants with extravagant imagination." [3] Had not

1. Giovanni Papini, *Dante vivo* (Florence, 1933). Eng. trans. by H. E. Broadus and A. Benedetti (New York, 1935), Introduction, pp. 9–11.

2. *Idem,* Foreword. Karl Vossler claimed for the Germans the privilege of understanding Dante as well as the Italians and better than other nationalities, because "only we Germans have a thoroughly personal, naive, and equally eminent poet to set beside the great Italian. And since *Faust* has come to be our loftiest and most cherished creation, and because we flatter ourselves that we are moderately familiar with it, we have a right to hope that we may approach the *Divine Comedy* with a prepared mind." (Eng. trans., *Mediaeval Culture, An Introduction to Dante and His Times,* by William C. Lawton [New York, 1929], I, 16.) See Grandgent in *Speculum,* V (1930), 238–239.

3. Papini, *op. cit.,* Introduction, pp. 5–6.

John Jay Chapman, himself an American, denounced those pedants with much vituperation in his *Dante* (1927), years before the publication either in Italian (1933) or in English (1935) of Papini's *Dante Vivo?* [4]

American literature on Dante of the last fifty years may be broadly grouped around three main points: first, the biographical reconstruction of Dante's personality in its historical setting and a comprehensive description and analysis of his works; second, the study of the allegorical and symbolic elements of Dante's poetry as an integral part of Dante's conception of the universe and an essential instrument of his art; third, the problem of Dante criticism, or the analysis of those elements in his works which are still living forces acting upon the mind and the sense of beauty of contemporary readers.

For convenience, all miscellaneous publications—chiefly short monographs, articles, and notes dealing with minute details of philological or historical import, or with interpretations of individual passages, phrases, and words of Dante's works—have been gathered together as a sort of appendix to the other three groups.

Among the many books which may be broadly classified as belonging to the biographical section, there are not a few, especially of those written during the second and third decades of this century, which, in spite of their author's devotion to Dante, have nothing new to say nor an original method of presentation. These books were designed for the numerous American readers who were not prepared to cope with more scholarly works. Although several of them possess charm and sound information, they have no special merit to justify a detailed consideration of them, as might have been the case, had they been written earlier when Dante studies in America were still in their infancy.

The oldest sources of Dante biography, such as the brief sketch of his life in the *Chronicles* of Giovanni Villani, Boccaccio's *Life*

---

4. There seems to be no doubt that Papini had read and utilized Chapman's book, though he never mentioned it. But Papini was eager to claim priority in time as the "debunker" of Dantists, and thus in a note he stated: "Since 1905 I have been denouncing, perhaps with too summary a judgment, the spiritual insufficiency of the professional Dantist." (See Papini, "Per Dante contro il dantismo," republished in *Eresie Letterarie* [Florence, 1932].)

of Dante, the little that Filippo Villani says about him, the somewhat later *Life of Dante* by Leonardo Bruni Aretino, as well as sundry information given by the early commentators of the *Divine Comedy*—these have been explored, studied, and analyzed from all points of view in the light of recent, more detailed knowledge of the Florence of that period, which the patient searchings and findings in the archives of Florence and other Italian cities on the part of modern scholars and historians have revealed. Although the historical value of some of these early sources, especially of Boccaccio's *Life of Dante,* the most important among them, is still disputed, and although modern Dantists prefer to rely more upon what can be learned by deduction from Dante's own words and works; there is, nevertheless, no Dante scholar who has not made a special study of, or at least read the early sources of, his biography.

The first scholarly survey of these sources in English was made by Edward Moore (*The Early Lives of Dante* [London, 1890]). There was, however, no English translation of Boccaccio's *Life* until Philip H. Wicksteed published his version (London, 1898), omitting several chapters. The first complete translation in English and first in any language, was made and published in America by George R. Carpenter (*Boccaccio's Life of Dante* [New York, Grolier Club, 1900]). In dealing with the question of the two extant redactions of Boccaccio's text, the long one and the compendium, Carpenter followed the conclusions reached by Edward Moore and used the long text edited by Macri-Leone (Florence, 1888). Another translation of Boccaccio's *Life,* with the addition of Bruni's biography and the passage from Filippo Villani's *Chronicles,* was made soon afterward by James Robinson Smith (*The Earlier Lives of Dante,* "Yale Studies in English," X [New York, 1901]). A useful selection of passages from these early sources in Smith's translation was included by Charles A. Dinsmore in his *Aids to the Study of Dante* (Boston, 1903).

One of the outstanding American Dantists of recent times was Charles Hall Grandgent (1862–1939), professor of Romance languages at Harvard (1896–1932) and president of the Dante Society of Cambridge. When he took over Norton's Dante course, Grandgent continued Norton's method of reading the entire *Comedy*, the *Vita Nuova*, and summaries of other minor works of Dante in the classroom. He made the course more exacting than it had been before, however, and raised the tradition of Dante studies established by his predecessors to a high level. He had the advantage over those who had given the course previously of being a learned philologist and an accomplished scholar in the wide field of Romance languages and literatures.[5] The Italian Dantist E. G. Parodi, for many years editor of the *Bullettino della Società Dantesca Italiana,* introduced Grandgent to his Italian readers as follows:

As a professor of Romance languages and literatures, he has to keep many strings to his bow, and he knows how to pass firmly and with ease from the preparation of a very good manual of Old Provençal to the writing of a more exacting and more creditable book on the so-called Vulgar Latin; but he always dedicates to the study of Dante his best talent and his loving care.[6]

Grandgent's first publication on Dante was an article entitled "Dante and St. Paul," [7] soon followed by another, "Cato and Elijah." [8] But he was already engaged in the more important labor of preparing an American edition of the Italian text of the *Divine*

5. While still an instructor at Harvard, he published his *Italian Grammar* (1887). This was followed by his *Italian Composition* (1891). These books have been widely used in colleges for half a century. They are, however, a better guide to literary and academic Italian than to the more flexible language and style of modern Italian writers. His earlier contributions to philological science were his *Outline of the Phonology and Morphology of Old Provençal* (1905) and his *Introduction to Vulgar Latin* (1907). The latter, translated into Italian by B. Maccarone and published with an introduction by E. G. Parodi in the collection *Manuali Hoepli* (Milan, 1914), became a familiar textbook to students of philology in Italian universities. His most important work in this field, *From Latin to Italian,* a historical survey of the phonology and morphology of the Italian language, was published in 1927, when he had reached the full maturity of his scholarship. With his usual modesty, Grandgent presented the book in these words: "This work, the result of over thirty years' collecting, classifying, and speculation, after many reconstructions is at last offered to fellow-scholars in the hope that it may render service, in America and perhaps England, to the study of Romance Philology."

6. *BSDI*, XXIV (1917), 121.

7. *Romania*, V (1902), 14–27.

8. *PMLA*, XVII (1902), 71–90.

Comedy with explanatory notes in English.[9] In his preface he states his purpose clearly:

This work, the first annotated edition of the Italian text of the *Divine Comedy* published in America, is intended primarily for the general literary public, though adapted also to academic use. I have aimed to make it so complete that readers will need, for the comprehension of the poem, no other book save their dictionary; but to those (may they be many!) who may be led to push their inquiry further, a great abundance of bibliographical suggestion has been offered. Remembering how often the *Commedia* is read and enjoyed by persons whose Italian equipment is scanty, I have explained in the notes many words and forms that present no difficulty to the experienced student. On the other hand, I have endeavored, by discarding a vast accumulation of interesting but unnecessary erudition, so to curtail the annotation that the reader's attention shall not be constantly distracted from the text. This allevia- tion has been facilitated by the relegation of all lengthy discussions and involved explanations to the arguments that precede the several cantos. . . . I have tried to give the "allegorical and true meaning," as Dante calls it, the place it deserves, but seldom receives, beside the literal.

The text adopted by Grandgent was basically that of the Oxford Dante of Edward Moore (latest edition), although he took note of more recent investigations by other scholars and readily accepted sound textual suggestions. But in the second revised edition of 1932 Grandgent used the *Testo critico della Società Dantesca Italiana*.[10]

In an introduction of about forty pages, Grandgent drew a clear picture of what the reader of Dante should know about his life, his character, his times, his connection with political events. In addi- tion, he sketched the main features of the literary tradition which formed the background of Dante's poetry. He also gave some space to a consideration of the various problems connected with the man-

9. *Inferno* (Boston, 1909); *Purgatorio* (1911); *Paradiso* (1913). *Divina Commedia* in one volume (1913); 2d ed. revised (1932). The first American edition of the Italian text was published in 1867: La Divina Commedia di Dante Alighieri; testo comune colle variazioni dei codici publicati da Carlo Witte. Prima edizione americana arricchita del ritratto di Dante per Gustavo Dorè. Boston, 1867. It was printed at the University Press in Cambridge. A reimpression from the same plates was issued in 1894.

10. Grandgent acknowledged his indebtedness to English and Italian Dantists, especially to Torraca and Flamini, whose readings and interpretations he followed sometimes too readily.

uscript tradition of the *Divine Comedy,* of its various editions, a brief survey of Dante's early and later commentators, and a selected bibliography.

An outstanding feature of Grandgent's edition is the argument which precedes each canto, outlining the content, explaining allegorical or doctrinal meanings, and, when necessary, discussing briefly controversial problems. The notes, which are very brief, consist in concise explanations of terms, phrases, historical allusions, and doctrinal statements.[11]

Grandgent's four books on Dante, together with his many articles and essays, form what is perhaps the largest, certainly one of the most notable, contributions made by American scholarship to Dante studies. Although they appeared as separate works, they may be considered as a series in which the various aspects of Dante's personality, thought, and art are analyzed from different angles, but with continuity and completeness.

In his *Dante,*[12] Grandgent portrays the figure of the poet and his work in the medieval world of which he was the immortal voice. In the *Power of Dante*[13] the poet's individual features stand out in relief, marking him as one above his contemporaries, a power whose influence and irresistible attraction have grown with the passing centuries. In *The Ladies of Dante's Lyrics,*[14] Grandgent

11. Paget Toynbee, reviewing this first American edition of the *Divine Comedy* in the *Modern Language Review* (V [1910], 124–126 [*Inferno*]; VII [1912], 421–422 [*Purgatorio*]; IX [1914], 134–135 [*Paradiso*]), did not seem very pleased. His main objection, however, was that the American edition was too expensive, for new English or Italian editions could be bought at a much lower price. As for the notes in English added to the text, Toynbee remarked that those who read Dante in the original should be able to read notes in Italian. He admitted, nevertheless, that the book was well done. Evidently Toynbee did not see the purpose of Grandgent, whose teaching experience had shown him that the average student could not read Dante in Italian well enough to dispense with the aid of notes and explanations in English.

12. In the series *Master Spirits of Literature,* G. B. Noyes and W. M. Hart, eds. (New York, 1916 [2d ed., 1921]).

13. Boston, 1918. Eight lectures delivered at the Lowell Institute in Boston, in the autumn of 1917. "They are here presented substantially as they were pronounced; but I have reinforced them, in some of the thinner places, with material drawn from a course on the *Artistry of Dante* given by me in the early months of 1918 at Yale University. The translations are my own; while most of them are new, some are borrowed from works already in print" (Preface).

14. Cambridge, Harvard Univ. Press, 1917. Lectures delivered in February, 1917, at Western Reserve University.

pries delicately into the poet's emotional life, unveiling the literary sources of his poetical mannerisms and symbolism, and the process of development of his original artistic technique. The *Discourses on Dante* [15] and his articles and essays scattered through many learned periodicals are partly subtle searches into special aspects of Dante's personality, and partly interpretation of passages, phrases, and words from his works, or brief psychological and historical explorations into the background of episodes, comparisons, and allusions from the *Divine Comedy* and other works of Dante.[16]

Grandgent does not claim in these writings to have discovered anything strikingly new about Dante. In submitting old problems to a new analysis, however; in searching with loving care and great skill Dante's thought, emotions, and art; and, above all, in making Dante his own interpreter, Grandgent successfully achieved his aim of presenting the poet and the significance of his work in full perspective. A life-long study of Dante's poetry and an intimate familiarity with the poet's way of thinking and modes of expression enabled him to fulfill his task convincingly.

In the preface to his *Dante,* he explains his purpose and method as follows:

It has been my purpose to present my hero, not as an independent figure, but as the mouthpiece of a great period of the world's history. I have attempted to trace a portrait of the Middle Ages with Dante's features showing through. At length or in brief according to the degree in which

15. Harvard Univ. Press, 1925. Addresses, articles, and two poems written on the occasion of Dante's centennial in 1921.

16. "Dante's Verse," *Studies in Philology* (Univ. of North Carolina), XVII (1920), 1–18; "Dante in Italy," *Columbus,* XV (1920), XVI (1921) (this was translated into Italian by V. Campora); "Illumination," *Studies in Philology,* XVIII (1921), 377–391; "The Centre of the Circle" (an address on Dante), *Harvard Alumni Bulletin,* XXIV (1922), 308–319; "New Renderings of Dante," *Italica,* III (May, 1926), 21–23; "Lo Bello Stilo," *Todd Memorial Volumes,* I (New York, Columbia Univ. Press, 1930), 171–184; "Islam and Dante," extract from *Studi medioevali,* III (1930); "Confessio Dantis," in *Prunes and Prisms, With Other Odds and Ends* (Harvard Univ. Press, 1928), pp. 161–182; "Rime and Rhetoric in the Divine Comedy," extract from *Mediaeval Studies in Memory of Gertrude S. Loomis* (Columbia Univ. Press, 1927); "Quid Ploras?" *Rep. Dante Soc.,* 1926; "Vele di Mar," *Rep. Dante Soc.,* 1928, pp. 1–10; "The Pentateuch and the Divine Comedy," *Rep. Dante Soc.,* 1930, pp. 1–17; "A Prototype of the Convivio," *Rep. Dante Soc.,* 1934, pp. 29–30. For a complete bibliography of Grandgent, see *PMLA,* XLVII (1932), 911–914. See also the biographical sketches in *Italica,* XVI (1939), 159–161; and *Speculum,* XV (1940), 379–381.

they wore his likeness, various phases of medieval life have been first discust and then illustrated by copious citations from the mighty spokesman. Thus I have hoped to differentiate my study from the many volumes already devoted to the Florentine poet, and, at the same time, to contribute somewhat to the diffusion of knowledge of the interesting but still generally unfamiliar epoch which he represents. For he does represent his time as no other age has ever been represented by any one man.

Grandgent's claim that his Dante was different from the many other biographies of the poet may appear at first sight the paternal over-fondness of the author for the child of his brain. Other biographers of Dante had studied and reconstructed his life and the significance of his works in the light of the historical background of his time. That Dante was the mouthpiece of his age and that his work was the synthesis of medieval culture and life was a commonplace. In fact, however, there is a real difference between Grandgent's book and other biographies of Dante.

The novelty lies in the approach and in the method of exposition. In general, Dante biographers begin by drawing a picture of the Middle Ages and then proceed to superimpose Dante upon it and try to discover wherein he was not medieval. Grandgent, on the contrary, starts with Dante and tries to see the picture of the Middle Ages through his eyes. It is Dante himself who describes the Middle Ages to us, illustrating his description from episodes of medieval life in all its aspects. He unfolds before our eyes maps of terrestrial and supermundane geography, and guides us through a long gallery of portraits of people from all classes, nations, and times, whose features reveal the tragedy and the comedy, the depravity and the heroic virtues, the barbarity and the spiritual refinement, the rude realism and the noble dreams, of the manifold medieval soul. Medieval society, politics, feudalism, culture, courtesy, fiction and romance, Guelfs and Ghibellines, Papacy and Empire, Church and State, philosophy and theology, learning and schools, classical survivals and new artistic ideals and literary forms, allegory and symbolism—all these constitutive elements of the medieval world are shown to us not as static pictures in a historical album, but in action in Dante's great drama of heaven and earth.

"The Medieval Temper" (chap. xii), for example, is a composite picture made chiefly from Dante's own words, of the medieval ways of thinking and feeling, of the medieval man's reaction to nature and beauty, to religious traditions and social habits, to literature and art. In drawing this picture, which to a great extent is Dante's self-portrait, "we must make allowance for medieval reticence" as against "modern volubility." "Our ancestors probably felt more than they exprest, while we, no doubt, express a good deal more than we feel" (p. 292). On the other hand, we must not overlook the fact that "Dante was taller than the tradition he followed and could not hide behind it. In his negation of progress, in his worship of authority, he was unreservedly a citizen of his own commonwealth; but the concealment of his towering self was beyond his power" (p. 283).

Grandgent's *Dante* was favorably reviewed both in America and in Europe.[17] The Italian Dantist E. G. Parodi, after complimenting the author on his mastery of the subject and his brilliancy of presentation, remarked that there was in the book "much which was obvious to Dantists." Furthermore, Grandgent had failed to note "what distinguished Dante from other men of the Middle Ages," what made him "a powerful individual having sentiments and religious and political ideas and an art of his own." It was a shortcoming to emphasize "what Dante had in common with all others."[18] Parodi's criticism that Grandgent emphasized what Dante had in common with other men, rather than what distinguished him from them, shows that the Italian critic missed the author's intention, which was to do precisely that, but without forgetting or overlooking the qualities peculiar to Dante alone. Throughout the book the reader is reminded of the originality of Dante and of his "towering" above others. It is especially stressed in the chapter on "The Medieval Temper." On this quality of

17. "Grandgent introduces no controversy on disputed points and gives information which will be generally accepted as orthodox. Though he still inclines to Flamini's system of interpretation, he does not present the disputed theories as facts. The most interesting chapter is on Allegory. . . . The explanation of Dante's definition of the *Dolce Stil Nuovo* is quite inadequate. The dictation of *Amore* does not show itself merely in direct and sincere expression of feeling; that is too simple a statement of a very complicated matter." (K. McKenzie in *Mod. Phil.*, XIV [1917], 88–90.)

18. *BSDI*, XXIV (1917), 123.

Dante's personality Grandgent was then writing another book, his *Power of Dante,* in which he set himself to discover in detail the secret of Dante's enduring power, why today "dwellers in lands far remote from Italy, many of them nearly ignorant even of Dante's tongue, still find in his writings a spell which binds them ever closer, a solace which comforts when all other consolation fails" (p. 2).

In his own time and long afterward, Dante's works were most admired as an inexhaustible mine of philosophical and theological learning. Today his speculations have lost for us their immediate utility and seem to be out of tune with present modes of thought. Dante was an allegorist and as such was highly esteemed. His early commentators read into his works all sorts of minute secondary meanings which perhaps were not there. Now, generally speaking, we care little for allegory, and few readers are really interested in his symbolism except in its broadest outlines. Thus the two attributes which fascinated Dante's contemporaries have lost much of their attraction. But there are enough left, some of them more effective today than they were six hundred years ago. In Grandgent's opinion, these elements of Dante's power are his "Faith, Morality, Temperament, Experience, Vision, Conception, Workmanship, Diction."

In a sense, Grandgent presents Dante's own spiritual and artistic autobiography. Dante's faith, the outward shell of which was his intellectualistic theology derived from Aquinas, filled his heart and stirred his emotion. His high moral ideals were the solid foundation upon which he built his conception of man and of the spiritual universe. The chief feature of his temperament, says Grandgent, seems to have been his intensity. "He applied himself more unreservedly than other men to all he did, thought harder, felt more keenly; and that is why, after all these years, his thoughts and feelings affect us so sharply" (p. 67). Dante's strongest emotion was not aroused by his hatred of his enemies, but by gratitude. For ingratitude is reserved the worst punishment in hell. "It was Dante's thankfulness to God that made him so unsparingly vehement in his denunciation of the wicked" (p. 89).

In the same analytical manner Grandgent traces Dante's experiences as revealed through his works. Finally, in the last chapters, he deals with Dante's workmanship, his love of symmetry, his *bello stile,* the magic of his words, and what Dante himself calls *il fren dell'arte,* "the check of art." This last is "a significant phrase. In Dante are united two qualities very seldom mated in one person: spontaneity and discipline. Surely no poet was ever more exuberantly original; yet no other great poet on a large scale has equaled him in severity of restraint, in strict adherence to a preconceived artistic plan" (p. 186).

Obviously this scheme of eight elements which make up Dante's power is arbitrary, and, as J. E. Shaw remarked, it is almost "geometrical" and makes the work seem "forced." [19] One cannot help feeling that the number eight was suggested by the fact that the chapters of this book were first given in a course of eight lectures. Had the course consisted of seven or nine lectures, very likely Grandgent would have accordingly subtracted or added to his list of elements and perhaps might have indulged in a little symbolism of his own with these sacred numbers so dear to Dante. The book was judged to be one of the best written in America on Dante. The chapters dealing with Dante's art ("Workmanship," vii; "Diction," viii) were praised especially as being "models of clarity and economy in choosing the essential and neglecting the unessential." Grandgent, said Shaw, had "a talent for sobriety."

Grandgent was at his best when dealing with Dante's literary background and art, his superb skill as a poet, his gift of imagery, and as the unrivaled master who forged a rude language into an instrument of immortal beauty. He had already dealt with this subject in the chapters on "Mediaeval Song" and "Language and Poetry" in his *Dante,* as well as in the two chapters just mentioned in the *Power of Dante.* In *The Ladies of Dante's Lyrics* Grandgent's analysis of this aspect of Dante's art is concerned primarily with his lyrics, the *Rime,* including the poems of the *Vita Nuova* and of the *Convivio.* Of the many problems arising out of Dante's lyrics,

---

19. *Mod. Lang. N.* XXXV (1920), 101–107. Shaw and other reviewers (*Giornale dantesco,* October–December, 1923, p. 376; and *BSDI* XXVII [1920], 104) pointed out several inaccurate statements in Grandgent's book and disagreed with him in his "bold" interpretation of certain passages in Dante.

Grandgent chose as the main subject of his inquiry those concerning the period in which they were written, the women to whom they were addressed, and hence their primary literal meaning. As for the involved question of their genuineness, he accepted the more recent conclusions of Dante scholars, with one or two exceptions in which he overlooked some special modern publications.[20]

Grandgent's plan was that of grouping most of those lyrics around the names of the five ladies to whom Dante addressed praises of love: Violetta, Matelda, Pietra, Beatrice, and Lisetta.[21] But who were these ladies and what part did they really play in Dante's emotional and intellectual life? To find an answer to this question, Grandgent had to approach also the problem of Dante's allegorism and symbolism. The ballad to Violetta:

> Ah! Violet, which once didst meet mine eyes
> Shadowed by Love, appearing suddenly,
> Pity the heart which wounded was by thee,
> Which hopes in thee, and yearning for thee dies,

is used as an opening to Grandgent's discussion of the character of the *dolce stil nuovo,* in which the esoteric elegance and the immorality of the poetry of the troubadours were abandoned for a poetry "simpler, clearer, prettier, fresher in form, and deeper in

20. E. G. Gardner (*Mod. Lang. Rev.,* XIII [1918], 508–509) noticed Grandgent's slip in attributing the canzone "Morte poich' io non trovo" to Dante, although Michele Scherillo had shown that it belonged to Jacopo Cambi, and in claiming for Dante the sonnet "Io son si vago," which M. Barbi had restored to its real author, Cino da Pistoia.

21. In assigning special poems to one lady or another Grandgent now and then relied only upon his feeling and not on any definite evidence. Thus he finds it "pleasant to think" that Violet was the Lady of the Screen of the *Vita Nuova* and that Matelda was the "beauteous lady" whose death led Dante to write "Morte villana": "On taking leave of this maiden so full of 'joyous youth' and of 'loving charm,' let us venture, for once to call her Matelda" (p. 66). (See K. McKenzie, *Yale Review,* VIII [1919], 141–143.) The reviewer for the *Giornale dantesco* (XXV [1922], 83) remarked: "Apart from a rhetorical breeze, the book is not lacking in excellent observations and shows a remarkable mastery of the subject. . . . In spite of some inaccuracies and repetitions of things known, it contains some notable observations and, above all, appears clothed in an intimate sense of poetry in the reconstruction of the Florentine environment and in the psychological analysis of Dante's loves. This makes me forgive the author the boldness of some conclusions." The reviewer complained, however, that in dealing with Lisetta and Matelda the author had not mentioned the studies of Graf, Torraca, and Monaci. The problem of Lisetta was taken up again by C. G. Concetto ("La questione della Lisetta," *Giornale dantesco,* XXV [1922], 211–228), and later on by M. Barbi ("La questione della Lisetta," *Studi danteschi* [1930]).

thought" (p. 15). In this poetry the adored one, while keeping her reality, became also "a symbol of something unquestionably venerable: to wit, the heavenly intelligence, which is another name for the angels, readers of God's mind and executors of his design. Both woman and angel she now was, an object of love and reverence" (p. 16).

Dante's women were symbols based on reality. But "do they refer to shifting but real affections . . . or to social attentions politely tinged with tenderness; or to purely literary attachments?" (p. 9.) The story of Dante's loves, the veil of mystery that surrounds his women—partially lifted in the case of Beatrice—together with descriptions of their characters as they appear in Dante's verses, and the various theories advanced by Dante scholars concerning them, are weighed by Grandgent in the balance of exacting scholarship. But his delightful narrative manner, sprinkled with charming translations of many lyrics from Dante and other poets of the *dolce stil nuovo,* disguise the weight of erudition which makes so many books on Dante cumbersome and difficult to read.

To discover where history and self-revelation end and where allegory begins in Dante's love songs is not an easy task. The narrative of the *Vita Nuova* does not suggest any symbolic meaning and not a few of his love songs have no symbolic content at all. Some of the so-called "Pietra" poems, an inexhaustible source of controversy among Dante commentators and biographers, are especially to be noted as having no "allegorical content." The canzone "Così nel mio parlar voglio esser aspro" is a "weird, uncomfortable poem with a note of desperate wickedness, such as one might expect from a middle-aged man violently in love with a very young girl."

> If I could seize those golden locks and pull
> —Those curls, for me a scourge, my heart to flay—
> From early in the day
> I'd hold thee tight till vespers and the dark;
> And I should not be kind or pitiful,
> But rather like a bear, when he's at play.
> A thousand should repay
> Love's lashings, which on me have left their mark.
>
> (P. 96)

"There is nothing of mystic significance in the verses themselves: in fact, their tenor makes a symbolic purpose seem uncongrous." Also the episode of the Lady of the Window in the *Vita Nuova* "contains nothing to suggest an allegorical personage: on the contrary, one would say that this is the most realistic part of the *New Life*" (p. 157). Dante's guilt, in the eyes of Beatrice (*Purgatorio,* XXX, 118 ff.; XXXI, 1 ff.), consists precisely in his having yielded to love for other women, "real love, such as the love of the *pargoletta,* the little maid of flesh and blood." How does Grandgent explain then the passage of the *Convivio* in which Dante wishes us to believe that his loves were mere allegories and his ladies mere symbols?

Substantially, Grandgent sides with the realists. In the scene in the Earthly Paradise on the top of the mountain of Purgatory, Beatrice, according to Grandgent, rebukes Dante not only for his infidelity to her love, but also for "harboring a mundane spirit, a worldly pride that attempts to hide a shortcoming under the cloak of allegory." In other words Dante himself has confessed that his allegorical interpretation of his love for the *donna pietosa* in the *Convivio* was only an afterthought. But is there any way of extenuating Dante's guilt? Grandgent's view on this point is similar to that once held by Norton. The side loves of Dante followed the same course as his love for Beatrice; they conform to a pattern which appears to have been in accord with Dante's natural bent:

First Dante's fancy is stirred by a real person; then, having come to regard this person as a symbol of something abstract, he little by little loses consciousness of the reality and consecrates himself to the cult of the symbol. Having reached this stage, he believes, or tries to persuade himself, that his whole experience has been an allegory [pp. 173 ff.].[22]

In expounding Dante, Grandgent acceded to the opinion of those who believed, "Better too much symbolism than none at all." He was not, however, in sympathy with the practice of applying the

22. "We may conclude, then, that the author of the *Banquet* was right in attributing to the odes in that work an allegorical sense, and that his friends were equally justified in believing in the reality of the emotion which had inspired the sonnets in the *New Life*. The friends were mistaken, however, in extending the realistic meaning to the whole series; and Dante, perhaps, was deceiving himself when he carried back the allegory to the episode described in the *New Life*." (Grandgent, *The Ladies of Dante's Lyrics*, p. 174.)

medieval method of Biblical exegesis with its multiple symbolism to the exposition of the *Divine Comedy*. Dante, as is evident in the *Convivio,* "seems quite satisfied with two interpretations, the literal and the allegorical. Dante was, above everything else, a poet." [23]

Grandgent did not leave as his heritage to Dante studies any ponderous book bristling with notes and critical apparatus. His books on Dante, as well as his essays, have almost no notes and, save for summary indications of literary works used and short bibliographies appended at the end, they bear no external sign of his great erudition as an accomplished Dante scholar.[24] As with all those who have fallen under Dante's spell, Grandgent's love for the great poet became almost a cult. But this American of Huguenot descent, a Unitarian in his religious associations, an exacting philologist, and an indulgent humanist, was at the same time a man with a great sense of humor and a writer of exquisite English prose. His Dante worship was neither blind nor absolute. His critical sense, his balanced judgment, and, more important, the long years he had spent in familiarizing himself with Dante's ideas, modes of expression, and techniques, enabled him to grasp so intimately what he called Dante's temper as to discern clearly the shadows as well as the light in the great poet whom he loved.

For thirty years Grandgent labored at Harvard to raise Dante studies to the high level of an exacting scholarship and to free them from dilettantism and the vague, romantic aestheticism of former times. He demanded from his graduate students a thorough philological training and a close familiarity with the historical, critical method of research. How fruitful his labors were is witnessed by the teaching and the publications of many former students of his, who as teachers and scholars have carried on the sound tradition of his method.

Charles Allen Dinsmore (1860–1941) was primarily interested in

23. Grandgent's review of H. F. Dunbar's *Symbolism in Mediaeval Thought and Its Consummation in the Divine Comedy* (Yale Univ. Press, 1929), in *Speculum,* V (1930), 108–109.

24. Grandgent's translations which keep the original meter of many lyrics of Dante, as well as of other Italian and Provençal poets contemporary with or earlier than Dante, are admirable for their fidelity to the text and their smooth English style.

the moral and religious aspect of life, and his approach to Dante was mainly from this angle.[25] His first book, *The Teaching of Dante,*[26] was a detailed, conventional exposition of Dante's conception of man as a part of the moral order of the universe. His subsequent volume, *Aids to the Study of Dante,* was a useful compilation in which an analysis of Dante's life and works was presented in a series of essays, two by him, the others selected from the writings of various Dante scholars.[27] Although far from sharing Dante's theology and philosophy, which to him, a Congregational minister in Boston, appeared as an artificial structure of sophisticated minds, Dinsmore considered the *Divine Comedy* a poetic masterpiece which revealed effectively the fundamental notion of the spiritual and moral law that rules the universe. He was irresistibly attracted by literature and beauty of form, but to his way of thinking the enchanting world of poetry and of the imagination would lose its charm and real beauty—indeed, its right to exist—unless it carried a true spiritual message. Great poets, like the prophets of old, were the vehicles of a kind of revelation and the mouthpieces of the universal spirit which speaks in myths and visions, according to the temper and the cultural and religious level of each age. This is the secret of their greatness. As lecturer and then professor at Yale, Dinsmore dealt extensively with Dante and the *Divine Comedy* in his courses. No other great work of literature, except the Bible, was to him so rich in spiritual meaning, and no other poet had revealed the universal moral law of life clothed in the overpowering beauty of an immortal art.

Dinsmore's *Life of Dante Alighieri* (Boston, 1919) was the work of his maturity, after long study of the *Divine Comedy.* In his

25. A graduate of Dartmouth College and the Yale Divinity School; held pastorates in the Congregational Church in Boston and in Connecticut; lectured at Yale Divinity School, where he became professor of Spiritual Content in Literature, in 1920.

26. C. A. Dinsmore, *The Teaching of Dante* (Boston, 1901), in four chapters: i, "The Burden of the Message"; ii, "The Vision of Sin"; iii, "The Quest of Liberty"; iv, "The Ascent of God."

27. Boston, 1903. It contains excerpts from the lives of Dante by Boccaccio and Bruni; essays by Longfellow, Lowell, and Norton; by Bryce, Saintsbury, Church, Gardner, Wicksteed, Gaspary and Witte; one by Scartazzini; and one from the Italian by D. Comparetti on "The Nature of Virgil in the *Divine Comedy.*" In Dinsmore's later volume, *The Great Poets and the Meaning of Life* (1937), there are also many pages dedicated to Dante.

Teaching of Dante he extracted from the poem what appeared to him to be its moral content, but he paid little or no attention to the personality of the poet or to the historical climate of which his work was a product. He had followed the old homiletic tradition by which, in a sermon, a moral lesson can be extracted from any passage in the Bible, regardless of its historical context. Now Dinsmore turned to the problem of Dante's personality and moral and religious experience, of which the *Divine Comedy* is the poetical history. In his preface Dinsmore states that he had to "overcome a certain reluctance." Was it because he was conscious of his unilateral approach to Dante? Whatever the cause of his reluctance, he was persuaded by two considerations:

First, no exhaustive Life of Dante has been written on this side of the Atlantic. . . . Secondly, Dante's true life is not to be learned from any facts which the documents record; it is to be found in his own self-revealing books. The personality there made manifest presents a most interesting psychological problem: What forces changed the gentle dreamer of the Vita Nuova into the stern prophet of the Divina Commedia? [28]

Although he followed the usual pattern of all Dante biographies, describing first the age in which the poet lived and then what is known of his life, Dinsmore's book was essentially concerned with Dante's character and was an attempt to lift the veil in order to discover by what processes, psychological or otherwise, Dante "became Dante." This process began when "Dante's sense of mission overshadowed his selfish ambition; he was saved by regarding himself only the servant of the larger truth" (p. 230). But the change in Dante's life which lifted him so high in the realm of spiritual things was due to "the influence of the Divine Comedy upon Dante himself" (p. 245): "The concentration of all his powers on a stupendous and congenial task not only released undiscovered energies of his mind . . . but enhanced Dante's sense of personal worth" (p. 247). Thus he was confirmed in "the conviction of having a special mis-

28. These two reasons given by Dinsmore were in reality one and the same, because, in his opinion, no life of Dante was "exhaustive" which did not solve Dante's "psychological problem."

sion from the Almighty to man." [29] Finally: "His imagination could not walk in the steep and arduous way of life without his heart and will following. Naturally he would become more austere both in morals and temper and his quick wrath flame the more intensely against unrighteousness" (p. 251).

Notwithstanding this growth toward a higher level of spirituality, not all the defects in Dante's character were entirely uprooted. Dinsmore professes to have felt always a strong urge to find excuses for Dante's foibles, but he found it impossible to deny that he had been "proud, censorious and scornful," and that he was fiercely intolerant of individual liberty in religious thinking: "Proud as Lucifer, sensitive in the extreme, volcanic in passional energy, this poet of the justice of God was at times guilty of an untempered speech which seems to spring from personal vindictiveness" (p. 277). Yet, "whatever his blemishes, they were not small or mean in their nature. Neither were they shameful . . . Dante was magnificent even in his faults" (p. 281).

Like Grandgent and most American Dantists before and after him, Dinsmore was much concerned with the question of Dante's universal appeal. A few years before, he had heard Lord Bryce say in one of his Lowell Lectures in Boston that the great interest in Dante was an outstanding "literary phenomenon of England and America." "Why is it," Dinsmore asks, "that groups of eager students of the Florentine poet were appearing in the most unexpected places?" Grandgent had approached the problem from a comprehensive point of view and traced the power of Dante to the multiple sources which he catalogued in a rather scholastic fashion. Jefferson B. Fletcher, in his *Dante,* found the sources of the universal appeal of the *Divine Comedy* in its artistic beauty, its ripe worldly wisdom, and its revelation of Dante's unique personality. Dinsmore considers these answers utterly inadequate:

It is like praising Hamlet, with Hamlet left out. Is Aeschylus read to-day for the beauty and wisdom of his quotable sentences? Is not the hiding of Dante's power in the profound and ineffaceable impression he makes

29. This idea of Dante's special mission had been much stressed by J. B. Fletcher (*Dante,* [New York, 1916]), to whom Dinsmore was greatly indebted. On Fletcher, see the next chapter, "Realists and Symbolists."

upon the reader of an august and unvarying law which presides over human destinies, a sense of the Mystery which is in the background of life? [p. 241.]

The supreme importance of the *Divine Comedy* is to be found "in the fact that it told men the way of life in a manner that would persuade them to walk therein." [30] Throughout the poem there is "a pervading spiritual atmosphere." There is also "moral truth stated with unforgettable energy." Dante "called his poem a Comedy; his readers soon added the adjective 'Divine,' because its pages were vital with the strength and glory of spiritual realities. It is this divineness which will charm men for unnumbered generations" (p. 241).

Even in his last chapter, "Dante the Artist"—a series of commonplace considerations—Dinsmore's aesthetic appreciation of Dante's poetry is wholly subordinated to the moral element.[31] Dante was a great artist; he could so master language and style not only because of his knowledge of classical Latin, but, above all, because of "the rare nobility of his own nature." Emerson had said: "When there is depravity, there is a slaughter-house style of thinking" (p. 284).

Grandgent's Dante is the Divine Poet as seen and loved by a philologist and humanist, a scholar steeped in the severe mental discipline of the history of languages and literature and at the same time endowed with bold imagination and keen poetical sensitiveness, an elegant and thoughtful writer brushed lightly with a reticent Victorianism. His Dante is the Florentine poet of the late thirteenth and early fourteenth centuries, sharing the ideas of his

30. "Men in every age will turn to this miracle of song for the emotional elevation which comes from reading it. By a most fortunate provision our minds are clothed with the character of the objects which engage their attention. The reader may repudiate every dogma that Dante loved, and be a consistent agnostic concerning all his supreme affirmations, yet he cannot live in the great poet's world and think his thoughts without having created in his mind those exalted and productive moods which make life worth living and all things seem possible. One catches the solemn elevation of mind of the ancient prophets, and the ecstasy of the mediaeval saint, without the intellectual necessity of believing their creeds" (p. 238).

31. "The superlative fascination of the 'Inferno' . . . does not lie in the charm of its episodes, nor in those vivid lines which delineate a character by a word or a gesture, nor in the revelation of the author's tremendous personality, but in its envisagement of a sovereign and inexorable law of retributive Justice" (p. 240).

time and environment, but rising by force of genius and nobility of character far above his background to reach a greatness that will endure as long as men cherish beauty in poetry and lofty ideals in life.

Dinsmore's Dante is a stern moralist as seen by a preacher who felt the attraction of poetry and beauty, but looked at life with pessimistic eyes and saw in it only the thorny path that leads to salvation through moral righteousness. The historical Dante—no matter how many pages of his book deal with the times and events of the poet's life—is only a shadow. What counted to Dinsmore was Dante's spiritual and moral experience as reflected in his poem and projected against the screen of life at all periods and in all places. Only this element in Dante's life and works is "eternal"; the rest is "ephemeral."

Henry D. Sedgwick's *Dante* ("An Elementary Book for Those Who Seek in the Great Poet the Teacher of Spiritual Life") [32] is also primarily concerned with Dante as a source of moral and spiritual power, especially in the present time, because "the comfort that depends upon supernatural virtue has lost its soothing, and the precepts of Stoicism are not enough to give us the courage to look upon the world as we see it." [33] Likewise John Slattery's *Dante, The Central Man of All the World* [34] stresses the moral, social, and

32. New Haven, Yale Univ. Press, 1918. This book "is a primer which leaves learning one side and busies itself with Dante as a poet and a believer in eternal righteousness" (Preface).

33. A. M. Brooks, *Dante: How To Know Him* (Indianapolis, 1916), a collection of representative passages from Dante's works, part translated but mostly paraphrased or condensed, offering to the readers "the complete unfolding of the story, together with its moral and philosophical significance."

34. New York, 1929. A series of lectures given at the Teachers' College in Albany, N. Y. Other books also for the general public: Frances F. Sanborn, *About Dante and His Beloved Florence* (San Francisco, 1901); J. H. Leigh Hunt, *Dante's Divine Comedy: The Book and Its Story* (New York, 1903); Eugene L. Rivaud, *Views on Dante* (Chicago, 1904); Walter L. Sheldon, *The Divine Comedy of Dante* (Philadelphia, 1905) ("Four Lectures intended especially for those who have never read the poem, but would like to know something about it"), and *The Study of the Divine Comedy of Dante* (Philadelphia, 1907). More elaborate is the work of T. N. Page, *Dante and His Influence* (New York, 1923). Well written and well informed is M. B. Whiting's *Dante the Man and the Poet* (New York, 1903). The concluding chapter in the third edition of Henry Osborn Taylor's *The Mediaeval Mind* (New York, 1919) must be mentioned for its suggestive sketch of Dante's character and of his works. Taylor's book, its gaps and limitations notwithstanding, has been for years on the reading lists of courses on medieval history given in American colleges, and as such has had considerable influence on American medieval studies.

religious significance of Dante's life and works for the modern world.

To Ernest H. Wilkins (*Dante, Poet and Apostle*),[35] Dante, rather than a stern teacher, an uncompromising judge, and an irascible mentor in the path of righteousness, is "the Apostle of temporal and eternal joy," which forms the purpose of human life. The temporal joy is twofold, the joy of the active life and the joy of the contemplative life, and is symbolized by the Terrestrial Paradise. The eternal joy consists in the contemplation of God in heaven, a contemplation which is in no sense material and is symbolized by the Celestial Paradise (pp. 16–17). Dante's life and his works, both in verse and in prose, are described and interpreted in the light of his apostleship of joy: *"The Divine Comedy* conveys the message of an Apostle rapt to exaltation by the noblest of all themes; and it conveys that message in the power of a poetry worthy of such apostleship" (p. 83).

M. B. Anderson's essays in the introductory volume (de luxe edition) of his translation of the *Divine Comedy* form a concise but effective biography of Dante. In the first chapters ("The Florence of Dante's Time") a fictitious thirteenth-century English traveler, Roger Purbeck—whose name the Florentines italianized as Perbacco—tells of his long visit to Florence where he met Dante and all other Florentine worthies of that period. Though fictionized, the early life of Dante is presented in action, in vivid colors, and with essentially historical accuracy. From the third chapter on, the fiction is abandoned and Dante's life, his exile and his wanderings through Italy are described in historical fashion. Then follows a brief analysis of the *Vita Nuova* and of the lyrics, especially of the canzone of "The Three Ladies," which is "the chief poetic link between the early poems and the Divine Comedy." A survey of Dante's allegory and of the *Divine Comedy,* and a comparison of Dante with Milton and Shakespeare, bring this short but charming biography to a close.

35. Chicago, 1921. Lectures given first at Columbia University and then in Chicago. E. H. Wilkins, a pupil of Norton, professor of Romance languages in the University of Chicago, and then president of Oberlin College, has contributed many valuable articles, notes, and book reviews to Dante studies.

In Anderson's intention this book had the double purpose of "supplementing the notes" of his translation of the *Divine Comedy* and of adding, "if possible, a few fresh observations to the sum of Dante criticism in our language." The author fulfilled well his task of providing a comprehensive introduction to the study of the *Divine Comedy;* but as a contribution to Dante criticism his book contains little or nothing that is really new or very impressive.[36]

The *Catholic World* dedicated its entire issue of September, 1921, to Dante, publishing eleven articles by various writers, each dealing with a special topic. The article "Il Dolce Stil Nuovo," a contemplation of Dante as a poet, by Margaret Munsterberg, is a conventional treatment of the subject and has nothing new to say about the real problem of the *dolce stil nuovo,* or about the essential qualities of Dante's poetry. Learned and well written is the article on "Dante as a Philosopher" by W. Turner, Bishop of Buffalo, who stresses Dante's Platonism, even though he was so steeped in Aristotelian philosophy. The essay on "Dante the Theologian" by H. Moynihan once more vindicates Dante's orthodoxy. It is regrettable, however, that the author could not refrain from repeating the absurd phrase that "the *Divine Comedy* is the *Summa* of Aquinas in verse," which belittles Dante's work and suggests not a great poetic masterpiece but a doctrinal versification like the *Tesoretto* of Brunetto Latini. The last article, on "Dante the Monarchist," by Hilaire Belloc, maintains that Dante was wrong from beginning to end in upholding the monarchical form of government as being the pure and normal regime for men and the nearest form of God's government of the universe. Suspecting that his readers would think that he has "wasted a good deal of time in examining a curious political phase of the later Middle Ages which is of no practical value in modern debate," Belloc expresses his opinion that this question is "of high immediate interest" in view of the "changes which are passing before our eyes to-day" (p. 865).[37]

36. Reviewed by Bontempo and Gerig, *Rom. Rev.,* XXI (1930), 150–152. The very high cost of Anderson's de luxe volume caused it to pass almost unnoticed, since only few libraries and fewer private individuals could afford to buy it.

37. J. T. Slattery (mentioned above) also published *My Favorite Passage from Dante: Chosen and Explained by the Most Distinguished Dante Lovers of the World Today* (New York, 1928). The compiler invited some four hundred men and women from various

The papers read before the Chicago Literary Club by E. H. Wilkins, K. McKenzie and T. W. Koch were among the best given on the occasion of the sixth centennial of Dante's death in many colleges, universities and cultural societies.[38] More significant, perhaps, was a series of seven lectures delivered at the Rice Institute in Texas by members of the faculty and then collected in a volume.[39] The significance of this series lies primarily in the fact that none of the lecturers was a specialist in Dante or in Italian literature, and yet, as McKenzie remarked, "all of them show an admirable knowledge of Dante, at least in relation to their several fields of history, philosophy, mathematics or general literature."[40]

It will not be amiss at this point to compare this new American Dante literature with that of the last decades of the preceding century. The most striking difference between the two lies in their tonal quality. The cultural level of the new is far above that of the old one. At the turn of the century, as we have seen, an amazing collection of writings on Dante came into existence almost overnight; but in general it lacked substance, was mostly devoid of critical discrimination and of sense of proportion. Dante appeared everywhere: in popular magazines, Chautauqua lectures, schools for Dante, Dante calendars, and even in books for children. At the same time, philosophical and pseudo-philosophical speculations made Dante the precursor of Hegel, of Swedenborg, or even of Mrs.

countries, especially from Italy (represented by more than one hundred) and America, to send him their favorite passage from Dante, together with comments and the reasons for their choice. The contributors were selected without much discrimination.

38. *Dante Six Hundred Years After*. A Symposium: With an Introduction by M. Starr (Chicago, 1921).

39. *Dante Sexcentenary Lectures, The Rice Institute Pamphlet*, VIII (April, 1921), No. 2: "University Extension Lectures on Dante in Observance of the Six Hundredth Anniversary of His Death—A Series of Lay Lectures Delivered at the Rice Institute in the Spring of 1921." I. "Historical Background of Dante," by Curtis H. Walker; II. "The Physical Universe of Dante," by Griffith C. Evans; III. "The Aesthetic of Dante," by Henry E. Conklin; IV. "Dante's Idea of Immortality," by Radoslav A. Tsanoff; V. "The Political Writings of Dante," by Robert G. Caldwell; VI. "Dante and the Renaissance," by Albert L. Guerard; VII. "Dante and English Literature," by Stockton Axson.

40. *The Literary Review*, III (October 14, 1922). G. C. Evans' lecture gives a careful, thoroughly scientific exposition of the physical universe of Dante's time, and compares medieval with modern astronomical science. The paper, illustrated with diagrams, is an important contribution to one phase of Dante studies that is usually neglected because technical and difficult. From the literary point of view the lectures of A. L. Guerard and Stockton Axson are the most attractive of the series.

Besant's Theosophy. Meanwhile only a few competent scholars in some institutions of higher learning were training a younger generation of Dantists in the severe critical method of Dantean research.

The new American Dante literature is the product of this training. The leading figures in this new phase of Dante studies came primarily from Norton's school: Charles H. Grandgent, Jefferson Fletcher, Kenneth McKenzie, Ernest Wilkins, and others whose names occur so frequently in the more recent bibliography of Dante studies in America. From their schools came in turn many American Dante scholars of today.

The "Dante furore," in part naïve, in part extravagant, which had its heyday at the turn of the century, has been superseded by a sober, critical, and scholarly appreciation of Dante's thought and art even in books written for the general public and not merely for specialists. They are addressed to a new audience which is better prepared and is more discriminating in historical sense and literary taste.

CHAPTER X

REALISTS AND SYMBOLISTS

ALL the theories advanced by the numerous interpreters of the allegory of the *Divine Comedy* may be reduced to four main tendencies or schools. The old commentators who considered the poem as being primarily a doctrinal treatise stressed in their voluminous and learned notes the moral, philosophical, and theological allegorism of the poem. That the *Divine Comedy* had a political content and significance was not ignored, but the theory that its allegorism was primarily political and strongly colored by anticlericalism began to prevail about the end of the eighteenth century and held the field, especially among the Italian Dantists and patriots, during the period of the Risorgimento. The more obvious interpretation of the poem as a moral-spiritual allegory of redemption and salvation through suffering, purification, and spiritual enlightenment won more general recognition in modern times. More recently a mystical interpretation, according to which a complex, even esoteric, symbolism runs through the whole poem, has found not a few followers among Dante scholars, especially in Italy.[1]

Since, however, by common admission, the *Divine Comedy* is the record of Dante's own moral and spiritual experience, the allegory and symbolism of the poem must have some relation to the events of his life. The problem is to find out the facts behind the allegory, and to discover where allegory ends and history begins. The *Vita Nuova* is ostensibly the story of Dante's youth; but is it the real story of his youthful loves, and therefore strictly autobiographical in character; or is it partly a real story and partly an idealization of events which gradually were transformed into symbols in Dante's mind; or, finally, is it a wholly fictitious story, allegorical from beginning to end?

1. On these variations in Dantean exegesis see Zingarelli, *La Vita, i Tempi e le Opere di Dante*, II, 884.

Up to recent times American Dante students had raised no doubts about the historical reality of Beatrice, of Dante's love for her, and of her transformation into a symbol in the *Divine Comedy*. The *Vita Nuova* was considered as being essentially a record of real experiences embellished by poetical fictions. Norton shared this view in the first and second editions of his *New Life*. Dante's statement in the *Convivio* that the *donna pietosa* of the *Vita Nuova* was to be interpreted allegorically was taken as being an afterthought, not really a denial of the reality of the lady and his love for her, but a mere superimposition of the allegorical upon the real.

In his later and final edition of the *New Life,* Norton admitted the wholly allegorical character of the *donna pietosa*. Lowell also, after some wavering, seems to have accepted her as a symbol of intellectual speculation. The strictly allegorical character of this episode of the *Vita Nuova* was defended by George Rice Carpenter in his elaborate essay "The Episode of the Donna Pietosa,"[2] a detailed discussion of the dates of the *Vita Nuova* and of the three canzoni of the *Convivio*. The element of time is for Carpenter the most important factor in reaching his conclusion in favor of the allegorical interpretation stated by Dante in the *Convivio*. It seems that Carpenter's essay had some influence upon Norton in his final conversion to the allegorical theory.[3]

On this point, however, Norton was not followed by his most

2. "Being an Attempt to Reconcile the Statements in the Vita Nuova and the Convito Concerning Dante's Life in the Years After the Death of Beatrice," *Rep. Dante Soc.,* 1889. George Carpenter (1863–1909), a pupil of Norton and translator of Boccaccio's *Life of Dante,* also edited for the Dante Society the "Documents Concerning Dante's Public Life" (*Reports* 10–11, 1891–92) and Latham's translation of Dante's Latin Letters (*Report* 1891). In the winter of 1892–93 Carpenter gave a series of lectures at the Lowell Institute in Boston on the "Early Italian Poets." Later he taught at Columbia University.

3. The problems of the *Vita Nuova* were also discussed during those years from various angles by L. C. Kuhns, "Dante Alighieri and the New Life," *Methodist Review,* 1894, pp. 269 ff.; Lewis Mott, *Dante and Beatrice, An Essay in Interpretation* (New York, 1892); A. G. H. Spiers, "Vita Nuova" (chaps. xxiv–xxviii), *Haverford Essays* (1909), pp. 43 ff.; "Vita Nuova and Dolce Stil Nuovo, *Mod. Lang. N.,* XXV (1910), 37–39; "Dolce Stil Nuovo, The Case of the Opposition," *PMLA,* XXV (1910), 657; A. A. Livingston, "The Meaning of the Vita Nuova," *Rom. Rev.,* I (1910), 89–93. Apart from Emerson's version, which was not published and not intended for publication, Norton's is still the only complete translation of the *Vita Nuova* made in America. Many of the poems have been translated by Grandgent and others, and all of them by Henry Johnson and published posthumously (*Rep. Dante Soc.,* 1924), though death prevented him from submitting his versions to a thorough revision.

distinguished pupils such as C. H. Grandgent, K. McKenzie, E. H. Wilkins, and others who remained faithful to the realistic interpretation of the *Vita Nuova* and to the theory that there had been in Dante's mind a gradual transformation of a real emotional experience into allegories and symbols.

Kenneth McKenzie's main contribution to Dantean literature is the first American edition of the *Vita Nuova,* a companion volume to Grandgent's *Divine Comedy.*[4] But as a teacher and writer of essays and articles on Dante and on other aspects of Italian literature, McKenzie has done much to raise and keep high the standards of Dante and Italian studies in America. For years he has followed closely the new publications on Dante both in Europe and in America, and his critical reviews of them, occasionally and rightly severe, have had a wholesome influence upon the younger generation of American Dante scholars.[5]

His edition of the *Vita Nuova* is a work of thorough and discriminating scholarship.[6] Since the *Vita Nuova* is ostensibly the autobiography of Dante's youth, the most essential task is to study first its literal meaning, because "whether or not there is symbolism and allegory in addition to the obvious idealization, to proceed to the hidden meaning without first comprehending the literal meaning would be, as Dante declares in the *Convivio,* irrational." [7] The explanation of this literal sense is the main purpose of the extensive notes, added to the text and containing an exhaustive commentary—grammatical, philological, and exegetical—with abundant references to old and new commentaries and to modern Dante literature. The problem of the allegorical and symbolic content of

4. *La Vita Nuova di Dante Alighieri,* ed. with Introduction, Notes and Vocabulary by K. McKenzie (New York, 1922). The text used is that of Barbi as contained in *Le Opere di Dante, Testo critico della Soc. Dantesca Ital.* (Florence, 1921). See reviews by E. H. Wilkins, *Mod. Lang. J.,* VII (1923), 445–446; J. E. Shaw, *Mod. Lang. N.,* XXXVIII (1923), 432–440; G. Mombelli in his book *Le traduzioni della Divina Commedia e delle opere minori* (Florence, 1926), p. 38.

5. K. McKenzie taught Romance languages and literatures first at Yale, then at the University of Illinois, and finally at Princeton. See a complete bibliography of his publications to 1938, including his book reviews, in *Italica,* XV (September, 1938), 93–102, a special issue dedicated to him.

6. Wilkins remarked (*op. cit.,* p. 445): "His own [McKenzie's] opinions, so far he gives judgment, are conservative. Those who disagree with him in one point or another will recognize that in any case, or nearly every case, there is weighty reason on his side."

7. McKenzie, ed., *Vita Nuova,* Preface.

the *Vita Nuova,* though not discussed in detail, is briefly outlined
in the introduction and then comes up again and again in its various
aspects in the notes concerned with the interpretation of individual
passages of the text.

Grandgent frankly characterized Dante's endeavor in the *Convivio* to deny the reality of the Lady of the Window and his love for
her as a conscious self-deception which left in him a sense of guilt,
as shown by the reproaches flung at him by Beatrice in the well-
known passage of the *Purgatory*.[8] McKenzie followed the more
lenient exegetical school which finds the solution of the problem in
Dante's typical medieval mental attitude toward allegory as containing a higher truth than reality. Dante, some years after he had
written the *Vita Nuova,* "hit upon the idea of making of the Lady
of the Window the symbol of his philosophical studies—the idea
being suggested by Boethius who in his *De Consolatione* personifies
Philosophy as a sympathizing lady." In Dante's method of ascribing
to real events an allegorical meaning, it is not necessary to make the
allegory correspond in every detail to the original facts. "The
method of Dante is to start with a literal meaning and proceed
thence to the allegorical; the latter being more 'true' because in
accord with permanent underlying principles. Understood in this
way, the two accounts of the episode do not contradict each other."[9]

McKenzie shared fully Norton's views concerning the symmetrical arrangement of the poems of the *Vita Nuova*. As early as 1903
he had crossed swords with the Italian Dantist Michele Scherillo,
who held that such vague correspondence as was to be found between one part and another of the *Vita Nuova* was the result of
chance and not of design.[10] In his reply[11] McKenzie traced the
history of Norton's discovery[12] and refuted Scherillo's arguments
not without success.[13] That there is a certain symmetrical structure

---

8. Grandgent, *Dante,* pp. 285 ff.

9. McKenzie, ed., *Vita Nuova,* p. 128.

10. "La forma architettonica della *Vita Nuova,*" *Giornale dantesco,* IX (1902), 34 ff.;
reproduced with slight changes in his book *La Vita Nuova e il Canzoniere di Dante* (Milan,
1921), pp. 467 ff.

11 "The Symmetrical Structure of the *Vita Nuova,*" *PMLA,* XXVIII, (1903), 341–355.

12. See above, p. 120.

13. The symmetrical grouping of the shorter poems around the canzoni was accepted
as a fact by Witte, D'Ancona, Scartazzini, Mazzoni, Moore, and others.

in the poems of the *Vita Nuova* is now commonly admitted, even by those who do not fully accept the Norton–McKenzie scheme.[14]

To the realistic school belongs also James E. Shaw, who in his collection of *Essays on the Vita Nuova* [15] discussed anew the fundamental questions of the date, meaning, and character of the book, as well as several problems of detail, such as the meaning of some phrases and passages. To the many suggestions, hypotheses, and guesses that have grown thick around the *Vita Nuova* and which are most reliably surveyed in his book, Shaw has added new ones of his own, "undismayed by the unending array of contrasting arguments which he himself has masterfully reviewed." [16]

Shaw brings some new evidence in favor of the date of the *Vita Nuova* now commonly accepted and dispels any doubt that by *Nuova* Dante meant "renewed" life—an interpretation already advanced by Norton and others—and not "youthful" life, as had been formerly believed. In his explanation of the apparent discord between the narrative of the *Vita Nuova* concerning the Lady of the Window and Dante's statement in the *Convivio,* Shaw adopts emphatically and tries to strengthen the opinion that the solution of the problem is to be sought in the difference in time of the two books. *Distingue tempora et conciliabis iura,* as the old jurists used to say. The fundamental mistake of the allegorists is that they ignore the considerable lapse of time which occurred between the composition of the *Vita Nuova* and the *Convivio,* and, still more, between the *Vita Nuova* and the *Divine Comedy.* On this point Shaw quotes M. Scherillo's remark that in general, the allegorists

14. McKenzie, ed., *Vita Nuova,* Introduction.

15. Princeton Univ. Press, 1929. Also: "Dante's Gentile Donna," *Mod. Lang. Rev.,* X (1915), 129–149, 320–337; "The Donna Angelicata in the Ring and the Book," *PMLA,* XLI (1926), 55–81; " 'Per l'altre,' Convivio III, XV, if.," *Mod. Lang. N.,* LVII (1942), 581–584. Shaw taught Romance languages at the University of Toronto. From the beginning of *Italica* to 1940 he contributed to this periodical very useful quarterly bibliographies of Italian studies in America. (See *Italica,* XVIII [1941], dedicated to him.)

16. Dino Bigongiari, *Speculum,* VII (1932), 296–302. Reviewed also by G. T. Wilkinson, *Phil. Quart.,* IX (1930), 409 ff.; E. H. Wilkins, *Mod. Phil.,* XXVIII, 367–368. Shaw's far-fetched interpretation of Dante's nightmare ("Morràti, Morràti") and some of his astronomical calculations concerning the date of the *Vita Nuova* and of the canzone of the *Convivio* "Voi che intendendo il terzo ciel movete" were not favorably received by his reviewers.

wrongly considered the complex work of Dante as having bloomed all at once, in the same moment, from the brain of the poet. . . . To mix together the Beatrice of the *Divina Commedia* with the Beatrice of the *Vita Nuova* is tantamount to being incapable of understanding the wonderful psychological and artistic genesis of the phantom that fascinated Dante and gave a soul to his whole poetical work.[17]

The allegorists read into the *Vita Nuova* the ideas of the later *Convivio* and the *Comedy;* and only by this uncritical and arbitrary method can allegory be found in a book which, taken at its face value and set against the background of Dante's youth and environment, contains no elements that might be connected with the complex allegorism of his later works. There is no contradiction between the narrative of the *Vita Nuova* concerning the Lady of the Window and the statement in the *Convivio*. In view of Dante's unawareness of any contradiction, the apparent difference between the two books is to be attributed primarily to the fact that they represent two different stages in his intellectual and moral life. Dante's statement in the *Convivio* that the literal sense is "a beautiful lie" (*parole fittizie*) is to be interpreted also in the light of the theories about allegory which were held by Dante and his contemporaries especially in connection with the literary works of antiquity. These theories did not imply a denial of the historical reality of facts stated, but rather superimposed a nobler and truer meaning upon the literal sense.[18] His detailed analysis of the *Vita Nuova* leads Shaw to the conclusion that

The Vita Nuova is the story of how Dante, the poet of Love, singled out by an inscrutable Providence, was led by Beatrice, a lady endowed for his sake with miraculous powers for good, to free himself first from the conventional superficiality of other poets of love, and then from the

17. Shaw, *Essays on the Vita Nuova,* p. 213. M. Scherillo, in his book *Le Origini e lo svolgimento della letteratura italiana* (I, *Le Origini* [Milan, 1919], 134 ff.), gives a concise but impressive summary of his views on this question already expounded in his previous publications.

18. Bigongiari's criticism of Shaw's evidence and conclusions ended on a note of skepticism of ever finding a satisfactory solution of the problem: "The question of allegorical interpretation, owing to its importance and to our incomprehension, can often be effectively played as a joker."

serious naturalism of still other poets, and to experience a finer because holier kind of sexual love than had hitherto been dreamt of [p. 203].

Shaw's explanation did not convince either the out-and-out symbolists or those realists who preferred to solve the question by denying that the Lady of the canzone "Voi che intendendo" of the *Convivio*, represented by Dante as Lady Philosophy, is identical with the Lady of the Window of the *Vita Nuova*. Shaw attacked this view held by M. Barbi and his Italian colleagues, Busnelli and Vandelli,[19] in a new essay on "The Lady Philosophy in the Convivio," [20] which was also implicitly an answer to the critics of his earlier essays. Though convinced that he had proved his point, Shaw concluded his discussion with the wise remark: "I am well aware that self-delusion is always a human possibility, and one who contends for an unpopular opinion in a matter which is not without its importance, cannot but be aware of the weight of opinion against him." [21]

Among the younger generation of Dante students, the symbolist school has recently made headway in America. Neither deterred by the seemingly hopeless task of finding a solution which would draw followers of other theories into the fold, nor baffled by the large literature on the subject, which seems to have already explored every possibility,[22] several American Dantists have tried to find a new thread to guide them safely through the labyrinth of Dante's symbolism. The way was shown by Jefferson Butler Fletcher (1865–1946), a Dantist of the older generation trained in Norton's circle.

In Fletcher's symbolical interpretation of all Dante's poetry, the historical reality of Beatrice and of the episodes of the *Vita Nuova*

19. Barbi, Introduction to *Il Convivio: Ridotto a migliore lezione e commentato da G. Busnelli e G. Vandelli* (2 vols. Florence, 1934, 1937).

20. *Publications Dante Soc.*, 1938.

21. Recently Professor C. S. Singleton of Johns Hopkins University has begun to publish studies on the *Vita Nuova*: "Vita Nuova, XII, Love's obscure words," *Rom. Rev.*, XXV (1945), 89–102; "The Use of Latin in the Vita Nuova," *Mod. Lang. N.*, 1946, pp. 108–112, in which he takes up the problem of the *centrum circuli* and proposes a different solution from Shaw's.

22. E. Moore, *Studies in Dante*, II (Oxford, 1899). For a more recent bibliographical list of symbolistic Dante literature, see N. Zingarelli, *op. cit.*, I, 307.

often seems to have vanished altogether. In fact, however, he does not deny the historical reality of either. He considers the question to have no importance at all, because only as symbols do they have meaning in Dante's works. As often happens in intellectual adventures, some of Fletcher's disciples went farther and crossed the bridge into the realm of out-and-out symbolism.

Fletcher, professor of comparative literature at Columbia University, worked in several contiguous fields of learning, but, like Grandgent, made the study of Dante his primary interest.[23] The main results of his life-long explorations in Dante's thought and art are condensed in his two short books, *Dante* (New York, 1916) and *The Symbolism of the Divine Comedy* (New York, 1921).

Fletcher's *Dante* is not a biography in the strict sense of the word, but a subtle search of the poet's mind and intentions as revealed in his works, for the purpose of identifying the central point of his inner experience which may be the key to his symbolism. Fletcher firmly believes that Dante wrote according to a prearranged scheme that stretched from the first sentence of the *Vita Nuova* to the last line of the *Comedy*. It was in the elaboration of this scheme that Dante created his symbolism and superimposed it upon the literal sense of his words.

Symbolism as understood and applied in the Middle Ages was, by its very nature, multiform and accommodating, but in a work of art such as the *Divine Comedy* it must have a central structural point. To discover this central point was Fletcher's aim in the first two chapters of his *Dante* (i, "Dante's Personal Confession"; ii,

---

23. "Dante and Beatrice: A Variety of Religious Experience," *Atl. Mo.,* CV (1910), 268–278 (This article was part of a larger study, *The Religion of Beauty in Women* [New York, 1911]); "The Modernness of Dante," *Anniversary Papers by Colleagues and Pupils of George Kittredge* (Boston, 1913); "The Allegory of the *Vita Nuova,*" *Mod. Phil.,* XI (1913–14), 19–38; "Dante's Second Love," *Mod. Phil.,* XIII (1915), 129–142; "The True Meaning of Dante's *Vita Nuova,*" *Rom. Rev.,* XI (1920), 95–146; "The Comedy of Dante," *Studies in Philology,* XVIII (Univ. of North Carolina, 1921), 392–411; "The Crux of Dante's *Comedy,*" *Rom. Rev.,* XVL (1925), 1–42; "Dante, Aeneas, and St. Paul," *Todd Memorial Volumes,* I (New York, 1926), 153–170; "The Daughter of the Sun: A Study on Dante's Symbolism," *Rom. Rev.,* XVI (1926), 330–340; "Dante's School of the Eagle," *Rom. Rev.,* XXII (1931), 191–209; "Left and Right Turns in the Divine Comedy," *Rom. Rev.,* XXIII (1932), 236–237; "Dante's Image in the Sun," *Rom. Rev.,* XXIV (1933), 99–128; "Dante's La Pietra," *PMLA,* LIII (1938), 971–989; "The Serpent in the anti-Purgatory," *Italica,* XII (1935), 45–50; "Dante's Own Comedy," *The American Scholar,* XIV (Winter, 1944–45), 60–71.

"Dante's Teaching"). Dante's confessions are not collected in one book like those of St. Augustine; they are scattered through his various works, and are to be found primarily in the *Vita Nuova,* the *Convivio,* and the *Divine Comedy.* Following St. Augustine, Dante traces "his own progress from bad to good, and from good to better, and from better to best." He describes these successive stages of his spiritual experience not for purposes of self-glorification, as if he had progressed by his own power, but only to assert the power of God: "Dante is not his own hero in his writings . . . his true hero, his real protagonist is God. The action of his drama is how God drew him to himself by the agency of Beatrice." This being Dante's purpose, he disclosed of his own life only what was strictly necessary to his plan. Hence, "for us to pry further into his privacy . . . would, I suspect, have appeared to him as both irrelevant and impertinent" (p. 15).

Starting from these premises and from the idea that to Dante "all reality is symbolic," that "the higher allegory is only the inner truth of reality" (p. 32), Fletcher sees in the *Vita Nuova* "a carefully thought out attempt to render dramatically the gradual process of his own spiritual enlightenment under the guidance of love" (p. 33). Whether or not Dante was "reading back" a symbolical interpretation of his youthful poetry in the *Vita Nuova* and the *Convivio* is immaterial; that poetry was merged with the symbol in the poet's mind, and it does not matter whether the external circumstances which gave occasion to the poetry were real or fictitious.

The purpose of the *Vita Nuova* is to show how love—the spiritualized love of the *dolce stil nuovo,* in which the lady loved becomes a mirror reflecting somewhat of God's wisdom and beauty—got hold of Dante's heart first in a transitory way, inhibited by the blind impulses of his unregenerate nature, and finally by the grace of God became permanent.

In other words, the inner truth of which his experience was but a running symbol or allegory written by God's hand, reached his sense-darkened mind at first only confusedly, then as veil after veil is lifted, with perfect clarity [p. 33].

There is no contradiction between the *Vita Nuova* and the *Convivio* concerning his love for the Lady of the Window, because what Dante means to say is that his wooing of the Compassionate Lady was as much at the dictation of true love as his wooing of Beatrice, and should have involved no disloyalty to Beatrice. If temporarily he had been in act disloyal, it was no fault of the love that moved him, but of his own incapacity to understand its dictates (p. 42). The Compassionate Lady was the providential agency by which God had won him to return to his appointed task in life, when desperate for loss of Beatrice. This is why Dante makes her the symbol of Philosophy in the *Convivio*.

Dante then does not mean—as has been too often assumed—to get rid of his question-raising second love by dissolving her away into a mere allegorical abstraction. She is Philosophy only as, in the Divine Comedy, Beatrice is Theology. She was actually, like Beatrice, a human being whose influence had providentially set him in that path of felicity which is charted for all by philosophy and theology. Whether at the time he realized this, or whether either lady was ever conscious of her saving mission, is another story, and in the present connection unimportant [pp. 44-45].

The idea of the Divine Comedy already existed in that part of the personal confession of the *Vita Nuova* which follows Beatrice's death. In his great poem, however, Dante's confession assumed a cosmic significance, because he projected his own personal experience against the screen of universal human life and made of it an experience of universal value: "A subjective state of mind is magnified into one objective and universal" (p. 51). Fletcher's elaborate interpretation of the symbolism of the *Divine Comedy* is built upon these foundations and rises layer by layer, maintaining a degree of consistency in line and design.

It must not be forgotten, however, that the *Divine Comedy* is primarily a work of art which gives the full measure of Dante's genius, and that the symbolic element permeating the whole poem becomes poetry, vivified by his inexhaustible imagination, yet checked by the *fren dell' arte*—that exquisite sense of harmony, balance, and proportion—and, above all, by the unity and finality

of the poem as Dante planned it. A survey of the characteristics of
Dante's art (chap. iii, "The Art of Dante") shows, for instance, how
keen he was to adapt "his mood and style, and to a certain extent
even his personal sympathy, to each otherworld kingdom in turn"
(p. 201). His poetic art, images, style, and language are so handled
as to conform to the philosophical doctrine of the correlation between grades of intelligence and grades of reward. In the *Inferno*
Dante writes as if for a lower intelligence than he demands for the
Purgatorio, and he warns away all but the intellectually elect from
the *Paradiso.*

Surely, understanding of evil is no easier than understanding of good;
but Dante seems to be applying his doctrine of "accommodation" to
aesthetic ends. "In church with saints, and with guzzlers in the tavern,"
he exclaims with half humorous deprecation of the diabolic escort provided for Virgil and himself in the circle of the barrators [p. 201].

Fletcher's interpretation of Dante's symbolism is developed
further in his second book, *The Symbolism of the Divine Comedy.*
In two long chapters (i, "Ariadne's Crown"; ii, "The Three Blessed
Ladies of the Divine Comedy") the author shows how the many
threads are drawn together in the *Paradiso,* in the culmination of
his spiritual uplift through the power of God and the agency of
Beatrice's love to the state of a revealer and a prophet. This point is
forcefully presented in the last chapter (iii, "The Comedy of
Dante") in the form of an exegetical commentary on Dante's
epistle to the lord of Verona, Can Grande della Scala. As he stated
in this epistle, his mission was "to bring men living in this life out
of a state of misery, and to lead them into a state of felicity." This
inner consciousness of being vested by God with a special mission
for the salvation of men, like the prophets of old and St. Paul, is
the key to the inner meaning and to the symbolism of the *Divine
Comedy:*

He stands alone with St. Paul in God's favor. . . . No wonder that
Beatrice declares that the Church Militant has no son of greater hope
than he (Parad. XXV, 55–57); No wonder the spirits met in Purgatory
and Paradise, amazed at his mortal presence among them, reverently

felicitate this special friend of God (Purg. XX, 41 ff.; XIV, 10–15; Parad. XXIV, 1–8). . . . Demons and angels, sinners and saints, are diverted from their eternal occupations to his aid [pp. 228–230].

Yet nothing was farther from Dante's mind and intention than to exalt himself in a spirit of pride and self-aggrandizement. Like St. Paul and St. Augustine, he was moved only by his desire to glorify God, His mercy and power, by telling the marvelous things that the Divine Grace had accomplished in him, in spite of his weakness and sins.[24]

It is not possible here to follow the meandering way of Fletcher's detailed exposition. It is important to note, however, that he finds the main key to Dante's symbolism primarily in the *Paradiso*, which stands, therefore, not only as the crown but also as the foundation of the structure of the *Comedy*, and, though the last in execution, was the first in Dante's mind from the very beginning of his poetical creation. To the realists, like Scherillo and Shaw, who protest against extending the symbolism of the *Comedy* to the early rhymes and consider those who attempt to do so as men incapable of entering the sacred portals of Dante's world, Fletcher replies by asking in his turn a simple but very important question: Is it not a fact that Dante himself, at any rate, wished his readers to believe in the unbroken continuity and the unity of his symbolism?[25] Fletcher is so fascinated by his reconstruction of the psychological process which culminated in Dante's claim to be vested with so high a mission, that he considers seriously the possibility that Dante—not the protagonist of the *Comedy*, but the actual Dante Alighieri who wrote the *Comedy*—did derive his inspiration from

24. Fletcher's interpretation of the Dantean symbolism was not altogether original and he was heavily indebted to his predecessors of the moderate symbolistic school. But as a colorful and coherent presentation of the inner spirit and purposes of Dante's poetry, his books—apart from some inaccuracies in matter of detail and some unwarranted generalizations noted by the critics—hold a respectable place in Dante literature.

25. Not a few Dante scholars who are not extreme symbolists, but who, like Fletcher, admit the historical reality of the *Vita Nuova*, believe in the continuity and unity of Dante's symbolism. Among them is N. Zingarelli: "Dante made of Beatrice not merely a symbol, because she remained always bound to her terrestrial existence and to her love for him, but the idea of Divine Wisdom . . . There is always one and the same Beatrice from the *Vita Nuova* to the *Comedy*, or if you like, one and the same symbol, splendor of living eternal light." (*Op. cit.*, II, 878.)

an actual mystical vision of God, or thought that he did (p. 241).[26]

To be sure, Dante never claimed, as did St. Paul, that he had been raised bodily to the third heaven in a mystic trance. None of his contemporaries ever mentions that Dante had such a mystical experience. Dante's son Pietro says frankly that the literal story of the *Divine Comedy* was "a poetic fiction." Even so, Fletcher is inclined to maintain his point of view and offers this explanation:

Feeling himself moved by a strong spirit of charity actualized by the influence of Beatrice, Dante would have theological justification for believing himself given in consequence the gift of the Holy Spirit . . . intelligence and wisdom, possessing which, man "by a certain connaturalness" has cognition of divine things, not by discursive reason merely, but by a 'divine instinct' above reason and participant in the intuitive faculty of separate, or angelic intelligences [p. 242].

The goal of this intuitive cognition of divine things "is the beatific vision." Hence, Dante, through Beatrice, who is Divine Charity, must have thought that, possessing the gift of the spirit, he had also experienced the high blessing of intuitive cognition.

In the concluding chapter of his *Dante Vivo*, Giovanni Papini seriously discussed the question, "Where is Dante now?" Certainly he is not in Hell, because his sins, however grievous, were not such as to condemn him to dwell among those who have lost all hope. But is he in Heaven? Perhaps; but he was not a saint, and "according to the absolute standard of the Gospel, he was not even a perfect Christian." Therefore, it is "entirely probable" that he was sent to Purgatory. Possibly he is still there, purging his soul. Papini then would like to know what Dante thinks of the *Divine Comedy* at present, whether it appears to him to be a work worthy of acclaim, or a cause for remorse and shame.

Fletcher's inquiry whether Dante experienced a mystical rapture which inspired him to write the *Divine Comedy* may be far-fetched. Papini's question, however, is not only futile but may be taken as a bad joke at Dante's expense. It is rather amusing that such a question should have been raised—a question which beats all the records

---

26. L. Pietrobono (*Il Poema Sacro* [Bologna, 1925], I, 55) compares Dante's dreams and visions to those of the saints, and he too suggests that they might not have been mere inventions of the poet, but real experiences in his mystical apprehension.

of the Dantomaniacs for impertinent and absurd queries—by the very man who was so eager to condemn all pedantic Dantists to the frozen hole of the traitors in Dante's Hell.

The irrepressible urge which descends upon all Dante enthusiasts to explain the obscurer shades of Dante's personality, to reconstruct his intellectual and psychological life and penetrate the secret of his overwhelming artistic power, has always led to new conjectures—often extreme, and fanciful as some of those set forth by the modern school of symbolism in American Dante studies.

Lisette A. Fisher's *The Mystic Vision in the Grail Legend and in the Divine Comedy* (New York, 1917) purported to be a new discovery in Dante symbolism that had hitherto escaped the keen, searching eyes of Dante commentators. In the first part of her book, which deals with the ritual of the Eucharist and the doctrine of transubstantiation as supplying the background of the Grail Legend, the author, following a well-trodden path in explored regions, is less original but more convincing in her reconstruction of the constitutive elements of the Mystic Vision. In the second part, in which she tries to find in the *Divine Comedy* a similar Eucharistic symbolism as an integral part of Dante's mystic vision, she walks on less solid, and even treacherous, ground.

To all appearances, the Eucharistic ritual and doctrine play a very inconspicuous role in the poem, and no commentator has ever discovered in it any extensive Eucharistic symbolism. In Miss Fisher's opinion, the commentators are wrong. The famous picturesque pageant which unfolds before Dante's eyes in the Terrestrial Paradise (*Purg.,* XXIX) and which is usually interpreted as symbolizing the triumph of the Church is, in fact, a graphic description of the great procession of the *Corpus Domini* as it was celebrated in Florence and throughout the whole western Church in Dante's time and afterward. This similarity between the external features of the pageant and the procession suggests a similarity in content and meaning. Hence it seems obvious to Miss Fisher that the pageant symbolizes the Eucharistic rite and its doctrinal and spiritual implications.

Thus the central mystery of the Christian cult, which, strangely enough, was supposed to have been ignored almost entirely by

Dante in his poem, holds a prominent place in the culminating scene of the Terrestrial Paradise. It is there that the poet finally meets Beatrice again. After his confession of sins and his final purification in the waters of Lethe—symbols of the sacrament of penance—he looks into the eyes of Beatrice and sees reflected in them as in a mirror the wonderful transformation of the "Griffin." He then concludes:

> Mentre che piena di stupore e lieta
> l'anima mia gustava di quel cibo,
> che saziando di se, di se asseta.
> (*Purgatorio,* XXXI, 127–129)

> While filled with amazement and delight,
> my soul feasted on that food,
> which both satisfies and quickens hunger.

Since the Griffin is, by common admission, Christ in his two natures, and since Dante sees his transformation not directly, but through the eyes of Beatrice, the symbol of guiding faith, it seems evident to Miss Fisher that these lines are a symbolic description of the transubstantiation and that the food *che saziando di se, di se asseta* is the Eucharistic communion.

The notion that there may be also an allusion to the Eucharist in this passage had been suggested before by some commentators. But the focal point of the whole scene is the apparition of Beatrice, whom Dante recognizes by the great love which stirs his heart. The obvious explanation of the symbolic *cibo* which both satisfies and renews hunger is then taken to be Dante's contemplation of the beloved one, who stands high "with cloak of green, above a garment red as living flame" in a cloud of flowers raining from angelic fingers; while the three symbolic figures dancing around her implore her to turn her eyes toward her faithful servant *che per vederti ha mosso passi tanti,* and bless him with a smile. Ingenious as Miss Fisher's suggestion may be, it has not overcome the legitimate skepticism of American and European critics.[27]

27. Reviews by E. G. Gardner (*Mod. Lang. Rev.,* XIII [London, 1918], 508–509) and J. L. Gerig (*Rom. Rev.,* XI [1920], 87–92). On this procession and its probable liturgical

The modern Italian symbolist school has not been widely discussed in America. Pascoli's works have been almost totally ignored,[28] and little attention was paid to Luigi Valli's first volumes, *Il Segreto della Croce e dell'Aquila nella Divina Commedia* (1922), and *La Chiave della Divina Commedia* (1925). But his last and most daring interpretation of Dante's symbolism, *Il Linguaggio segreto di Dante e dei Fedeli d'Amore* (1928), did not pass altogether unnoticed by American Dantists. According to Valli, Dante was a member and the great voice of a secret political-religious and heretical sect which went under the name of *Fedeli d'Amore,* and whose esoteric doctrines were clothed in a conventional poetical language, understood by them, but incomprehensible to those not initiated into the mysteries of the association. With a wealth of learning and a most subtle method of interpretation, Valli lifts the veil which for him hides the real meaning of that language and, therefore, the real meaning and content of the *Divine Comedy.* It cannot be said that Valli made many converts to his theory in America, but, on the other hand, his book seems to have had a certain influence in encouraging the tendency toward an all-symbolistic interpretation of Dante.[29]

Gratia E. Baldwin's *The New Beatrice and the Virtue That Counsels* (New York, 1928) seems to have been the first American book advocating this extreme symbolism. "Recoiling from any idea of love, of even the memory of a woman of flesh and blood" having ever possessed Dante's mind and heart, the author rejects the historical reality of Beatrice and of all other women mentioned in the *Vita Nuova* and the *Canzoniere.* The literal meaning is altogether "a fiction" as Dante said in the *Convivio;* the truth lies only in the allegory. Beatrice was never a woman but the symbol of the Virtue

---

connections see the suggestive article by J. S. P. Tatlock, "The Last Three Cantos of the Purgatorio" (*Mod. Phil.,* XXXII, 113–123).

28. Giovanni Pascoli, *Minerva oscura* (Livorno, 1898); *Sotto il velame* (Bologna, 1923); *La Mirabile Visione* (Bologna, 1923). On Pascoli's interpretation see Valli, *L'Allegoria di Dante secondo G. Pascoli* (Bologna, 1922).

29. While on a visit to the United States in 1928, the late Carlo Formichi of the University of Rome tried to gain adherents to Valli's theories, but with no appreciable results. (See "Il Simbolismo nella Vita Nuova e nel Canzoniere di Dante," *Italica,* V [1928], 81 ff.) Valli's books, in spite of his extreme theories, deserve much more recognition than they have received from American students of Dante.

that counsels, or, in a larger aspect, the Word of God. All the old, time-worn arguments are marshaled together once more in this book, about which the discerning reader feels, with McKenzie, that the author was "trusting too much to intuition and often ignoring the results of previous investigations." The novelty of proposing a new name, that of the "Virtue that counsels," in place of other personifications used for Beatrice as a symbol was of little importance, because, apart from the question of its fitness as connoting the essential characteristic of Dante's Beatrice, it is not unlike the usual "Revealed Truth," "Divine Guidance," or even Luigi Valli's *Sapienza Santa.*[30]

A more comprehensive and more exacting task was undertaken by Helen Flanders Dunbar in her large book *Symbolism in Mediaeval Thought and Its Consummation in the Divine Comedy* (Yale Univ. Press, 1929). The author reminds students of Dante of what the poet wrote in his epistle to Can Grande della Scala concerning the meaning of his *Comedy:*

> Be it known that the sense of this work is not simple, but, on the contrary, it may be called polysensous, of more senses than one. . . . It should be known that writings may be taken and should be understood chiefly in four senses.

It seems, however, that many students of medieval thought and of Dante either have never read these words, or think that Dante "was not in full possession of his senses" when he wrote them and that therefore they merit no attention. And see what confusion reigns among Dante commentators and interpreters. To some the *Divine Comedy* is an aesthetic and imaginative masterpiece, and for them its symbolism has no importance whatever. To others the poem is a revelation of the poet's private life. Still others see in it the work of a patriot and a social reformer. Many more take it to be a prolonged tractate on ethics, having solely a philosophical and mystical interest. And each one of them thinks that he is right and

---

30. K. McKenzie, *Italica,* VI [1929], 61 ff.) remarked also that the author was not exactly a follower of Valli's theories as she seemed to suggest: "There is little use in trying to make Valli speak the same language with those who disagree with him; he certainly would not approve of Baldwin's definition of the *Fedeli d'Amore* as 'a group of elect souls whose motive for being was to pose figurative enigmas to one another.'" (See also E. Underhill, *Spectator,* February, 1930.)

all others are wrong. The truth is, says Miss Dunbar, that all of them are wrong and all of them are right:

No Dante critic need feel himself without justification since Dante said "more senses than one." Hence the full comprehension alike of Dante and of the Middle Ages can be attained only as critics cease to insist that the true solution must be a question of "either-or," and to ignore both the possibility and Dante's assertion of "both-and" [Introduction, p. xiii].

A good knowledge of medieval symbolism is a prerequisite to the understanding of the *Divine Comedy*. Miss Dunbar does not presume, however, to give an exhaustive exposition either of medieval symbolism or of the *Divine Comedy*, but only "a basis for a thorough and detailed interpretation of the poem, a pattern into which detailed studies may be fitted" (Introduction, p. xii). Her method of exposition is rather unusual: A chapter dealing with some aspect of medieval symbolism is followed by a chapter in which the conclusions are applied to the specific symbolism of the *Divine Comedy*, and so on, alternately, to the end. As Grandgent remarked of this work:

It is really two books in one, not in sequence, but intertwined, for the sake of bringing as far as possible, every part of each into juxtaposition with every part of the other, like the Primum Mobile and the Empyrean.[31]

Drawing upon the large storehouse of knowledge of primitive and ancient religions which anthropologists, historians of religion, and art historians have accumulated, Miss Dunbar has found that sun-worship held a central place in a tradition of symbolism which continued unbroken down to the Middle Ages in Christian liturgy, theology, poetry, and art. Dante's symbolism derives from the same general source and can be explained only if set against this background of sun-worship and solar symbolism.

Very strong is Dr. Dunbar's sense of continuity: heathen cults persist conspicuously in our own. It is a bit startling to encounter in Dante's universe our Deity designated as a sun god, even as a wolf god, with

31. *Speculum*, V (1930), 107 ff.

their several attributes. Throughout the work runs insistence on sun worship and sex worship, inseparable in pre-historic belief, and still recognizable in Christian imagery.[32]

In the light of this symbolism, "the cross indicates essential union of the principles of sun and sex." It did not occur to Dr. Dunbar that the readers might ask her whether Dante knew all these things. Were the medieval theologians and Dante himself aware that their doctrine of the Trinity and other Christian doctrines, as well as liturgical invocations and ceremonies, were all directly connected with, and derived their symbolic meaning from, the sun-worship of primitive religions, or at least from the religious solar syncretism of the Hellenistic and Roman periods?

There is no doubt that the symbol of the sun irradiating life, heat, and light often occurs in Christian theological and liturgical language to express Christian religious thoughts and emotions. Yet, even granting that this figurative language went back to pagan cults and had been borrowed by Christianity, it is no less true that in Christian usage it no longer had any conscious reference to the old solar mythology and symbolism. After all, the sun was still shining in the sky in medieval times, and its power of suggesting images and symbols to the Christian imagination was still strong.

To quote Grandgent once more, whose review of this book is appreciative of the effort made by its author and at the same time wittily skeptical of its results, this scheme of symbolism with an amazing abundance of detail attributed to Dante, "showing all possible associations that may have been intended by the poet, or may have lurked hidden but potent in his mind, may not have been there at all, because with all his wealth of knowledge Dante's store was surely less than Dr. Dunbar's." [33]

As interpreted by Dr. Dunbar and some other lovers of Dante, the whole symbolic scheme of the *Divine Comedy* lies in the struc-

32. *Idem*, p. 109.

33. *Idem*, p. 107. Grandgent was far from convinced of the soundness of Miss Dunbar's interpretation, but he recognized the fact that, in so far as the object of her book was to stress the symbolic temper of Dante's time and to recreate the atmosphere in which he lived and wrote, the author had "admirably performed this important task." Other reviews: H. H. Vaughan, *University of California Chronicle*, XXXII (1930), 143 ff.; E. Underhill, *Spectator*, February, 1930.

ture of the *Paradiso,* which must have been the first part to take shape in Dante's mind when planning his poem, although last in execution. In fact, however, Miss Dunbar finds it very difficult to trace with consistency the same symbolism in the other two parts of the *Comedy.* In Fletcher's case, the essential content of the symbol was Dante's inner experience, which gave him the consciousness of having been called to perform the mission of prophet and revealer. Although this symbolism fits primarily the *Paradiso,* it was not inapplicable to or inconsistent with the other parts of the poem. In Dunbar's interpretation, however, the whole symbolism comes from exernal esoteric sources and does not find equal confirmation in all three parts of the *Comedy.*

One can hardly take seriously Miss Dunbar's statement that "for centuries, modern mediaevalists, ignorant of the philosophy and method of mediaeval symbolism, have labored in a confusion even worse than that of Babel" (p. 450); and that, "in ignorance not only of the philosophy and method of mediaeval symbolism, but even of the great scripture in which it centered, even more astonishing mistakes are made." On the other hand, she is right when she says that "the only salvation for the student of the *Divine Comedy* lies in the visualization of Dante in his setting amid the thought currents of his time, and against the background that produced them" (p. 451). This has been precisely the purpose and aim of all good modern Dante scholars in all countries, America included. Whether Dr. Dunbar's involved and often misty projections of a bewildering symbolism upon the *Divine Comedy* will help students attain a clear visualization of Dante in his historical and philosophical setting may well be doubted.[34]

34. One of the boldest attempts to discover the hidden meaning of Dante's allegory was made by an Englishwoman, Gertrude Leigh, in her *New Light on the Youth of Dante,* "The Course of Dante's Life Prior to 1290. Traced in the Inferno, Cantos 3–13" (London and Boston, 1930). The author maintains that Dante set out to teach his generation the profound religious philosophy developed by the Spiritual Franciscans—by Peter Olivi in particular—but, being unable to do so openly for fear of the Inquisition, he used the allegorical method. The *Divine Comedy* is a disguised autobiography of Dante himself and contains a minute account of his struggle against the antispiritual teaching and practices of the Church. Having found the key to the mystery, the author ingeniously builds up a concordance, at times striking, between her allegorical interpretation of the text and the events of Dante's life to 1290. Thus Minos is the venal confessor to whom Dante confessed his sins before his first communion; Cerberus is the tyrannical power of ecclesiastical dis-

Directly related to Dante studies is Angelo Lipari's *The Dolce Stil Novo According to Lorenzo de' Medici* (Yale Univ. Press, 1936). We are told by the author in his preface that his quest started from the usual problem of the apparent contradiction between the literal meaning of the *Vita Nuova* supported by the passage in the *Purgatorio* in which Beatrice rebukes Dante for his unfaithfulness to her, and the passage in the *Convivio* wherein Dante states that the *donna gentile* was but Lady Philosophy. Lipari says that as long as he had no doubts about the reality of Beatrice Portinari, he could not find any satisfactory solution to his problem. Then it occurred to him that the key to the mystery might be found in a fundamental principle in Croce's *Aesthetics*. Croce distinguishes between the intuitive faculty which is productive of artistic images and the rational faculty which is productive of philosophic concepts. The two are akin; yet they are opposed, because the genuine artistic images produced by the intuitive faculty are generally altered by the intervention of the rational faculty. It seemed, then, that the Beatrice of the *Vita Nuova* stands for the intuitive faculty, while the Beatrice of the *Purgatorio* stands for the rational faculty. Of course Lipari was aware that "to admit this point of view means to pre-suppose unwarrantably Dante's anticipation of the modern science of aesthetics, and yet such a conflict in the poet between the artist and the philosopher might have existed." The serious objection to this interpretation is the fact that it is the same Beatrice of the *Vita Nuova,* the intuitive faculty, who becomes in the *Purgatorio* and *Paradiso* the personification of Philosophy, or, better, of Christian Revelation. The antithesis between the two should have required two different persons. The author then came to the conclusion that

cipline; Pluto the figure of the simoniacal conclave which elected Pope Nicholas III; Flegyas figures the monastic authorities; the boat in which Dante travels safely is the ascetic rule of the Spirituals. The three Furies are a satirical personification of ecclesiastical courts, and the Gorgon's head is a caricature of excommunication. The Celestial Ambassador is Peter Olivi and the Minotaur is the Guelph League, and so on to the end. K. McKenzie pointedly remarked that if Dante's purpose was to avoid trouble with the Inquisition "we must admit that he was singularly unsuccessful in avoiding persecution and too successful in concealing his meaning" (*Speculum,* VI [1930], 153). A. De Salvio also championed the theory of Dante's heretical intentions in his doctrinal expositions (*Dante and Heresy* [Boston, 1936]). The Joachite influence on Dante was studied by A. Donini ("Appunti per una storia del pensiero di Dante in rapporto al movimento Gioachimita," *Rep. Dante Soc.,* 1930).

the Beatrice of the *Paradiso* was "no longer the Beatrice of the *Vita Nuova*, but a combination and fusion of her previous self with the nature of the *donna pietosa*."

Lipari had gone quite a way with his theory when it occurred to him that he never could "convince any one on those grounds," and that at best he "might be stamped as another symbolist, which would not be flattering." Hence he laid aside his original project and began to inquire into the nature of the *donna gentile*, or *donna angelicata*, of the primitive Italian poets. At last, in the *Commento* of Lorenzo de' Medici upon some of his own sonnets, Lipari found "the very critic and the very evidence" he had sought so long.

His book, however, is only an introduction to the whole subject. It contains a minute, subtle analysis of the *Proemio* and the *Principio*, a small portion of Lorenzo's treatise, but a very important one, because it discloses the fundamental characteristics of what may be considered as the *Ars Poetica* of the *dolce stil nuovo*. The reader is warned that, "owing to the philosophical nature of the subject matter, the reading will be hard at times." As a matter of fact, it is not always easy to follow the author in his subtle interpretation of Lorenzo's often obscure language and thought.

Being only a preliminary survey, the final conclusions concerning the problem of Dante are not reached in the book. Lipari established, however, the main points which will serve as the basis upon which the final structure will be erected, as follows: First, that Lorenzo's *Commento* is a Dantean and Neoplatonic treatise. Neoplatonism provides the philosophical foundations of the *dolce stil nuovo*, but this *stil nuovo* "is the translation of the Neoplatonic principle into a complete *Ars Poetica*, which may be called *stilnovistic*." Its elaboration was not the work of Dante alone, but also of Guinizelli, Cavalcanti, Petrarch, Boccaccio. A great deal is an original contribution by Lorenzo himself. Second, that the spirit of this Stilnovistic *Ars Poetica* is primarily revealed in the notion of *gentilezza*, which has an esoteric, aesthetic, and comprehensive meaning and content in the whole Italian literature down to the Rinascimento. Third, that the various features and episodes of the life of the "Lady" celebrated in Stilnovistic poetry—her age, her apparitions, her death, and so on—have special meaning in the light of this mystic, esoteric notion of *gentilezza*. As yet, however, the core of the problem has not been reached. "The real key" will be provided in "the continuation of the *Principio* in Lorenzo's following *Nuova Vita*" (p. 332). As the Italians say: *"Se son rose fioriranno."* [35]

Broadly speaking, we may say that the tendency toward an absolute, symbolic interpretation of Dante's poetry has not gained much ground in America, and that the historical reality of Beatrice and of the other women in the *Vita Nuova* is firmly maintained by most Dante students here.[36] The theories which American Dantists have followed reconciling the discordant statements of the *Vita Nuova* and the *Convivio* did not originate with them; nevertheless their contributions to the discussion of the problem have been valuable and have received recognition from abroad. More original have been the contributions of the symbolists, but unfortunately this originality has been attained only by the advancing of arbitrary and hypothetical assumptions which, however alluring to the imagination, fall far short of conviction. Perhaps Dante would say: *"State contente umane genti al quia."*

35. In several articles appearing after the publication of his book, Lipari summarized the results of his further researches on the same general problem: "Donne e Muse," *Italica*, XV (1938), 3; "The Structure and Real Significance of the Decameron," *Yale Romance Studies*, XXII (1943), 43–82; and his debate with Charles S. Singleton "On Meaning in the Decameron," *Italica*, XXI (1944) and XXII (1945). Also: "Dante e la nuova concezione dell'arte nel primo Rinascimento," *Italica*, XXI (1944).

36. Other articles dealing with Dante's multiple allegory and symbolism: H. N. Fairchild, "Matelda, A Study in Multiple Allegory," *Rom. Rev.*, XVI (1925), 136 ff.; H. D. Austin, "Multiple Meanings and Their Bearing on the Understanding of Dante's Metaphors," *Mod. Phil.*, XXX (1932), 129–140; G. G. Walsh, "Dante's Matelda," *Thought*, XII, 78 ff.

CHAPTER XI

ON DANTE CRITICISM .

DANTE's right to be honored as one of the great poets of all time has not been challenged seriously since the beginning of the nineteenth century, but opinions are sharply divided concerning the poetic and artistic value of the *Divine Comedy* as a whole. That there are passages and episodes in it of immortal poetic beauty all agree; that the entire poem in its structural form and significance is a literary masterpiece has often been questioned, however, even denied by many. G. A. Borgese summarizes the problem effectively in these words: "The main issue is between the *beauty* and the *beauties;* whether the *Divine Comedy* is a masterpiece in its totality, or only in some of its elements: a crown of one piece, or a necklace in which some pearls are oriental and some are not." [1]

Early lovers and students of Dante in America, such as John Chipman Gray, believed that they could follow the "narrative structure" of the *Divine Comedy* without difficulty and enjoy to the full "its greatness as poetry" without bothering with "its mystical and doctrinal" aspects. According to Gray, in his essay of 1819, the reader who did not share Dante's beliefs, or had no interest in the medieval dogma and theology which formed the background of his poem, could derive from it a general moral lesson and even find in it "an escape from the vexations of life in moments of sober contemplation." Contrary to the opinion of Italian commentators, the *Divine Comedy* was "easy reading"; its architectural design, even when considered mythological, had both poetical value and moral significance. As a poet, however, Dante was at his best and reached his greatest poetic heights in the episodes and in the descriptive passages of his poem. [2]

The following generation, to which Longfellow, Lowell, and

1. Borgese, "On Dante Criticism," *Rep. Dante Soc.,* 1936, p. 20.
2. See above, p. 32.

Norton belonged, had a better knowledge of Dante's world and a fuller appreciation of the wide range of his artistic creation. To these men the beauty of the *Comedy* in its entirety was almost a dogma beyond discussion, an act of faith toward the noblest of all poems in its lofty conception and artistic execution. For years the Cambridge triad had pondered over each line and each word of the poem, weighing meanings and rhythmical qualities with great care in an effort to find the nearest English equivalent for their translations, made either as classroom exercises or for publication.

Longfellow, a poet of smooth surfaces and romantic pathos, bowed reverently before Dante's superb descriptive power and was content to stop at the literal meaning and structural narrative of the poem. He was struck with awe before the eruptions of the burning passions of Dante's soul:

> Ah! from what agonies of heart and brain,
>   What exultations trampling on despair
>   What tenderness, what tears, what hate of wrong,
> What passionate outcry of a soul in pain,
>   Uprose this poem of the earth and air,
>   This mediaeval miracle of song!

Within the portals of the temple of Dante, Longfellow,

> Kneeling to pray and not ashamed to pray,

felt no urge to wander into the adyton of Dante's allegory: even there he could sense how

> The tumult of the time disconsolate
>   To inarticulate murmurs dies away,
>   While the eternal ages watch and wait.[3]

Norton and Lowell were not so indifferent to the allegorical and symbolical aspects of the *Divine Comedy;* they were willing and eager to explore "the crowd of statues" and strange sculptures that adorned the towers of the temple, the parvis "canopied with leaves" and the "dragons and the gargoiled eaves" at which Longfellow looked only from afar.

3. From Longfellow's six sonnets, "Divina Commedia."

W. T. Harris and his Hegelian followers in St. Louis started
with the question of whether a poem must possess a spiritual sense
as well as poetical structure:

It is essential that a poem should be built out of tropes and personifications. Its real poetic substance, in fact, is an insight into the correspondence that exists between external events and situations on the
one hand, and internal ideas and movements of the soul on the other.
Rhyme and rhythm are less essential than this.[4]

But if the poet thinks philosophic ideas in philosophic form, he
will be likely to spoil his poem by attempting to introduce them
into its texture. Allegory is not in itself poetical, and therefore,
"neither philosophy as such nor allegory can be the best feature of
a genuine poem." How, then, can a poem have a spiritual sense and
still be a good poem? How is it that the *Divine Comedy* is a great
poem, when philosophical and allegorical elements have such a
large share in it? According to Harris:

There are certain great poems which owe their supreme pre-eminence
to the circumstance that they treat themes of such universal significance
that they reflect the operation of a supreme principle and its consequences
in the affairs of the world, and hence, exhibit a philosophy realized, or
incarnated, as it were. Their events and situations, too, being universal
types, may be interpreted into many series of events within the world
order, and hence, stand for so many allegories. Such poems may be said
to have a spiritual sense. Homer's *Iliad,* and more especially his *Odyssey,*
contain a philosophy and many allegories. Goethe's *Faust* contains likewise a philosophy, and its poetic types are all allegoric, without detriment
to their genuine poetic value. But of all the great world poems, unquestionably Dante's *Divina Commedia* may be justly claimed to have
a spiritual sense, for it possesses a philosophic system and admits of
allegorical interpretation. It is *par excellence* the religious poem of the
world.[5]

Whatever we think of the consistency of Harris' explanation, it is
clear that the Hegelian philosopher of St. Louis was convinced that
the *Divine Comedy,* although bristling with philosophy and alle-

4. Harris, *The Spiritual Sense of Dante's Divina Commedia,* p. 27.
5. *Idem,* pp. 28–29.

gory, was great poetry of universal value and not a collection of poetic fragments lost in a sea of versified moral and dogmatic theology.

A few decades later another American philosopher, George Santayana (*Three Philosophical Poets, Lucretius, Dante, Goethe* [Harvard Univ. Press, 1910]), holding the view that Lucretius, Dante, and Goethe sum up the chief phases of European philosophy—naturalism, supernaturalism, and romanticism—asked the following questions:

Can it be an accident that the most adequate and probably the most lasting exposition of these three schools of philosophy should have been made by poets? Are poets, at heart, in search of a philosophy? Or is philosophy, in the end, nothing but poetry? [Introduction, p. 8.]

At first sight, it seems that philosophy and poetry have little in common. Philosophy as investigation of truth, or reasoning upon truth, is "a leafless forest"; it is something reasoned and heavy, while poetry is something winged, flashing, inspired. "The poet has his worst moments when he tries to be a philosopher, or rather, when he succeeds in being one." But philosophy is not merely investigation and reasoning. These are only means to an end, which is the sublime vision of philosophy:

The order it reveals in the world is something beautiful, tragic, sympathetic to the mind, and just what every poet is always trying to catch . . . a steady contemplation of all things in their order and worth. Such contemplation is imaginative . . . A philosopher who attains it is, for the moment, a poet; and a poet who turns his practised and passionate imagination on the order of all things, or on anything in the light of the whole, is for that moment a philosopher [pp. 10–11].

The more scope and the more depth the philosopher gives to his vision of the world, the more highly imaginative and supremely poetical it will become:

For a philosophic poet the whole world of man is gathered together; and he is never so much a poet as when, in a single cry, he summons all that has affinity to him in the universe, and salutes his ultimate destiny. It is the acme of life to understand life. The height of poetry is to speak the language of the gods [p. 14].

Lucretius sees the world as one great machine, all its parts re-acting upon one another in obedience to a general pervasive process of life. His poem describes the nature, birth, and composition of all things made of atoms in perpetual motion, so that old things perish and new things arise. Under such conditions, human life can be, at its best, an aspiration toward freedom and quietness of spirit. Materialism in natural science, and humanism in ethics—this was the gist of Greek philosophy before Socrates. Lucretius is the unrivaled poet of this naturalism.

In Dante's world, on the contrary, all minds, all institutions, are dominated by a religion that represents the soul as a pilgrim upon earth. The world is fallen and subject to the devil; pain and poverty are considered normal; happiness, impossible here and to be hoped for in a future life. The sources of this view of the universe and of life are "in the solitude of the spirit and in the disparity or the opposition between what the spirit feels it is fitted to do, and what, in this world it is condemned to waste itself upon. The unmatched poet of this supernaturalism is Dante."

Goethe's world is that of the Teutonic races that have begun to understand themselves. They turned against the Roman world in their restless search for a new outlet to their energies:

They have turned successively to the Bible, to learning, to patriotism, to industry, for new objects to love and fresh worlds to conquer; but they have too much vitality or too little maturity to rest in any of these things. . . . This is romanticism, and the greatest monument to this romanticism is Goethe's *Faust*. Goethe presents experience in its immediacy, variety, and apparent groundlessness . . . he presents it as an episode, before and after which other episodes may be conceived to come. There is no possible totality in this [p. 203].

Dante's vision of the world and of life is more universal than that of the other two poets. It is a vision of Christian theology which derived its concept of a providential history and of a great task to be performed in this world from the Hebrew tradition, and its natural and moral philosophy from the Greek Platonic tradition:

Although this theology was the guide to Dante's imagination, and his general theme, yet it was not his only interest: or rather, he put into the framework of orthodox theology theories and visions of his own, fusing all into one moral unity and one poetical enthusiasm. The fusion was perfect between the personal and the traditional elements. He threw politics and love into the melting-pot, and they, too, lost their impurities and were refined into a philosophic religion. Theology became, to his mind, the guardian of patriotism, and, in a strangely literal sense, the angel of love [p. 85].

Yet this universal vision of life, although it may seem more complete than Lucretius' massive materialism or Goethe's episodic looseness, is itself an illusion: "Dante's idea of nature is not genuine; it is not sincerely put together out of reasoned observation. It is a view of nature intercepted by myths and worked out by dialectic" (p. 208).

To Dante, however, this mirage was a reality, and to his mind, which lived in this fictitious reality, everything appeared to be a symbol. In other words: "The science and philosophy of Dante did not have to be put in verse in order to become poetry: they were poetry fundamentally and in their essence." In the future, "Dante's vision of the universe, where all is love, magic and symbolism, may charm mankind exclusively as poetry." Then "no one will think of reproaching Dante with his bad science, and bad history and minute theology. These will not seem blemishes in his poetry, but an integral part of it" (p. 103).

The *Divine Comedy,* according to Santayana, "is not poetry where the parts are better than the whole." Here, as in a great symphony, "everything is cumulative: the movements conspire, the tension grows, the volume redoubles, the keen melody soars higher and higher . . . It remains by us in its totality, a revelation and a resource for ever" [p. 133]. At the same time, however, Santayana feels that Dante's art was somehow handicapped by the fact that his intellect was "hypnotized by a legendary and verbal philosophy." As a consequence:

there is an attenuated texture and imagery in the *Divine Comedy.* The voice that sings it, from beginning to end, is a thin boy-treble, all wonder and naïveté. This art does not smack of life, but of somnambulism [p. 208].

Santayana's judgment on Dante, setting him higher than Lucretius and Goethe on the one hand, and emptying his work of all objective value on the other, certainly could not find favor with those who either shared Dante's philosophy or were sure that it was possible to reinterpret it in the light of more modern ways of thinking. Much less could his conclusions and his description of Dante's poetic voice as "a thin boy-treble," and his art as smacking of "somnambulism," fail to stir the wrath of all Dante lovers. Jefferson B. Fletcher was sure that Santayana's criticism of Dante's idea of life was the consequence of his reading the *Divine Comedy* "too exclusively as a system, whether of natural or moral philosophy," and overlooking all that reveals Dante's deep knowledge of men and life and Dante's personality. "Out of the depth and breadth of his living, out of his loves and hates, his hopes and despairs, his laughters and tears, was built up his personality—a personality that spoke no thin boy-treble." If this was the voice Santayana heard in the *Divine Comedy*, "we may feel reasonably sure that there is something wrong with the philosopher's hearing." [6]

From the heights of Santayana's subtle thinking and elegant prose we must descend to a low level and mention a book by Albert Mordell (*Dante and Other Waning Classics* [Philadelphia, 1915]).[7] This book was soon forgotten, and it would be advisable to let it lie undisturbed in its grave were it not for the fact that notice of it was taken abroad, even by men like Croce, and that it was considered by some Europeans as representing a widespread current of American thought, or, as the Italians would say, as being a genuine *Americanata*.

A few years before, Mordell had published a booklet (*The Shifting of Literary Values*) upholding the theory that books must not be judged according to the ideas and literary standards of the time

6. Fletcher, *Dante*, pp. 234–235.
7. Samuel D. Davis, an obscure predecessor of Mordell, in an article, "Dante's Claim to Poetic Preeminence" (*Poet Lore*, IV [1892], 490 ff.), held that "Dante's claim to a place as a great poet which he now holds in popular esteem will not bear investigation." Davis could find in Dante "only tediousness and brutality," especially in many of the episodes in the *Inferno*. He did not make much of an impression, however. *The Nation* (LV [1892], 433) mentioned "an unscholarly article in *Poet Lore*," whose author was "a crank," and did not even give his name.

in which they were written, but according to the ideas and literary standards of today. Applying this principle in his new book, Mordell found out that from the modern point of view, the so-called classics of all literatures, and especially those expounding old philosophies and theologies long discarded by intelligent people of today, are most obnoxious, because they perpetuate past errors and corrupt literary taste.[8] Dante is the worst of all; in fact, any reader of the *Divine Comedy* will easily and immediately discover two things about this poet: "The first is that Dante delighted in contriving horrible and imaginary tortures in the next world for those who have sinned here. The stern and vindictive Florentine heaps up the most revolting and nauseating horrors upon horrors. . . . He fails in the first function a poet should have, that of winning our sympathy." The second fact is that "Dante follows the scholastic philosophy and peoples his heaven chiefly with saints, theologians, crusaders, and characters who subscribed to theological absurdities. Dante was a man of great learning, but little intellect." As a result, "his power as a poet is corroded by his weakness as a thinker." The poem as a whole has no artistic value at all. In it, "we have living before us again all the bigotry and fatuity of the mediaeval ages; we have a summing up of all the speculation which rational men to-day reject; all the superstition, darkness and intolerance of a millennium are crystallized in this poem." Not enough stress can be laid "on all the ugliness, grotesqueness and cruelty" that are in it. What can be more revolting than to see the best of the world's thinkers lamenting and baking in Hell, while the insipid theologians go to Heaven? And what do they do in Heaven? Nothing but engage in idiotic theological discussions, sing Latin songs, carol with lights, stars, and angels, wheel around Beatrice and Dante, and then again sing and keep time (p. 27). The *Purgatorio* bristles with pseudoscientific and theological discussions also, but it contains more human scenes and finer pictures than either of the other two portions of the poem (p. 34).

Dante is a poet only in a few "secular" episodes and passages

---

8. Other classics besides Dante which should be discarded are Milton's *Paradise Lost,* Bunyan's *Pilgrim's Progress,* À Kempis' *Imitation of Christ,* St. Augustine's *Confessions,* and Pascal's *Thoughts.*

scattered through the poem. But "as a poem with a purpose, the *Divine Comedy* is a failure not only because of its inability of conviction, but because of its perverted viewpoint and its emphasis on the trivial" (p. 37). After discarding all the trash that fills the poem, we have left a residuum which "will still give Dante a place in literature, although not among the greatest of the world's poets." In conclusion, Mordell remarks, "It will be salutary to humanity if his fame declines and the Dante worship ceases" (pp. 11, 45).

Most of this disparaging criticism was neither new nor original with the American writer. It can be traced back to the Renaissance period, and more directly to the late eighteenth-century polemics.[9] These adverse views on the poet, and the acid remarks of Voltaire, Walpole, and other famous men, were not unknown to the early American essayists on Dante. They mention the accusations of cruelty and vindictiveness leveled against him, but to them the fact that he condemns to Hell kings, popes, poets, peoples of all conditions and times, and among them not only his enemies but also some of his best friends, seemed to be evidence, not of cruelty and lack of human feeling, but of the unflinching nobility of Dante's sense of justice. Needless to say, the theory that, in judging books, no consideration should be given to the age in which they were written, and that they should be wrested from their historical en-

9. In an appendix (pp. 124–125) Mordell gives the "adverse views on Dante" of famous writers, Oliver Goldsmith, Voltaire, Goethe, Lamartine, Horace Walpole ("Dante was extravagant, absurd, disgusting; in short, a Methodist parson in Bedlam"), Nietzsche, and others. On this point, see the last chapter, "Survey of Dantean Criticism," in Croce's *The Poetry of Dante* (Eng. trans., 256 ff.). Of Goethe Croce remarks that "although he never attained a profound knowledge of Dante, he came to understand and consider him in a way very different from that he had adopted in 1788. . . . Dante was now placed [by Goethe] among new and lofty companions" (p. 272). Mordell lists Emerson among those who had but contempt for Dante: "Emerson's biographer, Cabot, reports the opinion of the sage of Concord on the Florentine poet as follows: 'A man to put in a museum, but not in your house: another Zorah Colburn; a prodigy of imaginative function, executive rather than contemplative or wise.' Zorah Colburn was a mathematical prodigy" (p. 123). Even if this oral report collected by Emerson's biographer is exact, Mordell should have given more weight to what Emerson said in writing about Dante after he—like Goethe— became more acquainted with his works. In the chapter mentioned above (p. 268), Croce says of Mordell: "An American critic also returns to the charge—against Dante—declaring that in the confused mass of extravagance and disorder he can discern nothing save 'several literary jewels, a very small residuum.' Answers to such criticisms were often dictated by simple good sense in the eighteenth century, as, for example, when . . . Gaspare Gozzi taught that the way to understand Dante was to study the times in which he had lived and the other books he had written."

vironment and judged in a vacuum, because "historical criticism often becomes an apology for past errors," is so patently absurd as to preclude any possibility of understanding any work of art and of literature.

More consistent and weighty, because it came from a gifted writer, was the attack against both Dante's character and his poetical work by John Jay Chapman (*Dante* [Boston, 1927]), who stated his intentions and purposes clearly in the preface:

This volume has resulted from an impulse to bring together thoughts and impressions that have accumulated in my mind during many years as a reader of Dante. . . . In battling my way through the "Divine Comedy" and its commentaries I gained what appeared to me to be a clear view of Dante as a human character; and this I here offer for what it is worth, in a few essays and remarks. . . . A glance at the table of contents will tell the theme of the book: Disparagement of Dante as a Character, praise of him as a Poet, and a kind of amazed wonder about him as a force.

In the American tradition, Dante's character had always been exalted as the inner spring of his greatness as a man and a poet. In Chapman's picture, Dante appears as a typical *Solitary Egoist,* whose moral sense is warped by his intolerably self-centered pride. Thus, for instance:

Dante's attitude toward the Empire and the Papacy was that of a super-autocrat who is above both of them, and holds a commission from on high to regulate the affairs of each. He is the Czar of religion . . . Dante represents the spirit that was at the bottom of Protestantism, the impulse of a man to decide the religious question for himself [p. 84] . . . The artistic blemishes in Dante are always due to an intrusion of the Personal and often to an exhibition of bad temper . . . Dante stages and organizes his venom [p. 92] . . . Dante's attempts at humor are lamentable [p. 94].

Santayana, who seems to have been Chapman's source on this point, had called Dante an "egotist" who "talked too much about himself." Dante's egotism" extended so far that he cast the shadow of his person not only over the terraces of Purgatory, but over the whole of Italy and of Europe which he saw and judged under the

evident influence of private passions and resentments" [p. 130].
Nonetheless, Dante is a universal poet, because "his imagination
dominated and focused the whole world," and "his poetry covers
the whole field from which poetry may be fetched, and to which
poetry may be applied, from the inmost recesses of the heart to the
uttermost bounds of nature and of destiny."

According to Chapman, on the contrary, the whole *Divine
Comedy* is nothing more than an almost incredible work of self-
apotheosis; it is Dante's political testament and personal justification.

Whatever experience he had woven into the expanding spider-web of
his conceptions, became to Dante a part of the Cosmos; and whoever
laid hands on it was an enemy to Truth [p. 74]. . . . Dante's personal
history so dominates his philosophy that one comes to look askance at
even his most abstract ideas [p. 75]. . . . This very self-centered quality
is one source of Dante's popularity. He is the archetype of the Intro-
spective writer and his works are a *journal intime* [p. 76].

This personal quality of the poem is at times so obvious as to
obscure its poetic meaning. Its purpose "was to show that, if on
earth the poet has had many enemies and few friends, nevertheless
there were friends waiting to welcome him on the other side of the
grave." And what friends! "The great saints, great intellects, and
great rulers of history": The Virgin Mary had sent Saint Lucy to
Beatrice, who had sent Virgil to guide him out of the dark forest;
in Hell, demons and doomed souls are at his service; Lucifer serves
to him as a climbing pole to reach Purgatory. But "the introduction
of the author's friends to the public begins seriously as soon as
Dante and Beatrice arrive in Paradise. Every one there has heard
of Dante." The Emperor Justinian, kings and empresses, and, above
all, the great theologians do him honor and develop his views on
many a question:

The support for his own views which Dante sought to draw from the
Celestials was more personal than a writer on theology is apt to claim
from the Church Fathers. It is not merely for his thought that Dante
claims approval, but for his passions, his rancors, and his fancies [chap.
xii, "Dante's Obsession," pp. 77-79].

Obviously Chapman had read Fletcher's book and derived from it this description of Dante's glorification in Paradise. But while, according to Fletcher, Dante was thus walking in the footsteps of St. Paul and St. Augustine and celebrating the grace of God which lifts the sinner to the mystical joy of God's possession; to Chapman, on the contrary, all this was merely the manifestation of Dante's irrepressible vainglory, of his presumptuous reaction against the sad vicissitudes of his life, and of a morbid self-exhibitionism.

Chapman praised Dante as a great poet, but not because the *Divine Comedy* is a great poem as a whole, which it is not, but because it reveals, here and there, Dante's poetic genius: "The merits of the Divine Comedy are essentially lyrical." Although Dante had "a greater talent for exposition than any man ever possessed," yet the largest part of the *Divine Comedy,* which is filled with doctrinal, moral, or pseudoscientific expositions, is not poetry at all.

The happiest touches in the Divine Comedy are descriptive, whether of natural scenery, of sky and air, dawn, dusk or moonlight, or else of monsters and myths. . . . The intellectuals of the world are spellbound by his exposition, and the populace by the pictures which he throws upon his screen [p. 72] . . . but even those parian bits in Dante, which recall the Greek spirit, are often surrounded by gargoyles, and his sublimities followed by a grimace [p. 54].

Among these "parian bits" are the passages which Chapman collected and translated in his book as being representative of Dante's lyric genius at its best, and also as being almost all that is alive and worth reading in the *Divine Comedy;* the rest is mostly dead wood. How, then, can one explain the fact that the *Divine Comedy* as a whole "has found enough readers to keep it alive in each century since Dante's death in 1321"? (p. 95.) In the early part of his book Chapman suggested that one of the reasons for Dante's popularity may lie in the fact that the *Divine Comedy* is a work written by a typical solitary egoist. Santayana had remarked that "there is a sense in which Dante's egotism is a merit, or at least a ground of interest for us moderns; for egotism is the distinctive attitude of modern philosophy and of romantic sentiment. In being egotistical Dante was ahead of his time" [p. 130]. But to

Chapman Dante's egotism was an extreme pathological case, a kind of disease which still retains its virulence and affects the morbid minds of modern readers. In his last pages, however, Chapman offers other explanations of the cult of Dante in modern times.

From the very beginning and for some time afterward, the *Divine Comedy* was regarded with great veneration, almost as being next to the Bible, because Dante was taken seriously as a philosopher, and the *Comedy* was considered a kind of encyclopedia of all human and divine sciences. Early commentators were firm in this belief. With the rise of modern philosophy, however, the interest in Dante began to wane. The seventeenth and eighteenth centuries barely knew him. Since the nineteenth century, we have been living "in a sort of *furore* about Dante, in a kind of Dante-whirl so strangely at variance with the apparent preoccupations and temper of our own age that it must bear some organic relation to them or it could not exist" (p. 95).

According to Chapman, this organic relation is to be found in the fact that since the early nineteenth century we have been living in an Age of Science, and "as the enthusiasm for Science increased, the spirit of research chilled the genial currents of the soul, and Dante became a refuge. He was an indestructible reservoir of Mediterranean heat" (p. 96). At bottom, it was the archaeological, quasi-scientific, and documentary character of the nineteenth-century culture that brought Dante back. It was the great illusion that anything could be discovered by a scientific method of research, and "in the meantime we have all but forgotten the languages of Art, Poetry, and Religion, which alone can express the passion for truth with which we burn" (p. 99). Fortunately, however, this period is now passing, and "it seems possible that Dante's lack of humor and of kindliness may shorten the skirts of his fame as time goes on and as that passionate interest in the Middle Ages which marked the nineteenth century begins to decline" (pp. 70–71).

Chapman's unorthodox treatment of Dante made little impression upon American literary circles, although it met with the approval of literary radicals and professional "debunkers." Most Dante-lovers regarded it as one of the usual explosions of a writer who, in spite of his fine literary taste, was temperamentally a crank.[10] The task of commenting upon this disparagement of Dante's character was undertaken by Dinsmore:

Such criticisms are hoary with age. Yet one reads them again with interest because Chapman discovers them with such cheerful zest. Nevertheless, the portrait he draws of Dante is altogether distorted. He forgets that this man of wrath is one of the world's greatest lovers. A lofty idealism, not vindictiveness, habitually governed his actions. First the love of a pure woman, then the love of philosophy, then love of divine truth, inspired his poetry, and his final judgment on life was that the soiled leaves of human experience are bound together by an all-encompassing love. . . . Dante wrote a great poem because he was a great man. His passion for truth was more ardent than his desire for fame. His self-valuation was, indeed, exceedingly high, but posterity has ranked him higher than he dared to dream.[11]

That Chapman's criticism of Dante was not altogether new is obvious; on the other hand, it cannot be denied that he brought old indictments up to date and presented his case forcibly and with a wealth of detail. Dinsmore's sentimental and rather vague rebuttal did not penetrate to the roots of the fallacy upon which Chapman had hung his principles of literary criticism. This task was performed later by Giuseppe A. Borgese in his essay "On Dante Criticism," the best contribution to this aspect of Dante studies that has appeared in America during recent years.[12]

The old theory—common to all adverse critics of Dante—that the

10. Owen Wister, writing on Chapman after his death (*Atl. Mo.*, May, 1934, pp. 524 ff.), said of his friend: "Chapman was inclined to run tilt against any current opinion or established reputation. Goethe was now a mere dilettante, Plato a clever literateur, Shakespeare would bear watching, and many other extravagances of the sort." Even so, apart from its general theory, Chapman's Dante is a stimulating book not lacking fine analytical power and suggestive remarks; not, however, enough to justify the opinion of a discriminating critic like J. E. Spingarn that "the casual wisdom of J. J. Chapman's brief *Dante* is more illuminating than a bushel of handbooks and essays by most professional Dante scholars." (Bibliographical Note to *Mediaeval Culture*, English translation by W. C. Lawton of K. Vossler's *Die göttliche Komödie* [New York, 1929], II, 428). Borgese (*op. cit.*, p. 40) suggests that G. Papini was influenced by Chapman: "Now and then Papini echoes almost verbatim Chapman's sentences about Dante's ambition and harshness."
11. *The Yale Review*, XVIII (1928), 818 ff.
12. *Rep. Dante Soc.*, 1936, pp. 19–70. Review by J. E. Shaw, *Italica*, XIII (1936), 82–83.

Divine Comedy has no poetical value as a whole and may be "safely left to the commentators" after the bits of lyric and descriptive poetry it contains have been extracted, was given systematic form by the school of aesthetics primarily represented by Croce.[13] The method of literary criticism of this school is based on the theory that "pure art and pure poetry" are entirely distinct from philosophy and the rational processes. Pure poetry is the genuine product of intuitive creative imagination unmixed and unspoiled by reflection and rational elaboration. Borgese surveys concisely but clearly the history of this theory and of its variations, and shows how it was applied to Dante with different results by Francesco De Sanctis, Karl Vossler, Giovanni Gentile, and then by Benedetto Croce and his followers.[14] By analyzing its fundamental premises, Borgese reaches the conclusion that "pure poetry" is but a figment of the mind, without reality either in the creative processes of the artist and the poet, or in literary and artistic history.

Dante has been made a test case by the theorists of pure poetry. Thus, on the one hand, the *Divine Comedy,* its structural poetical unity disregarded, is torn into bits of poetry and nonpoetry; and, on the other hand, Dante's character is pictured in dark colors to show that his poem is an artificial and not a genuine expression of his personality:

The philosophers of the Neapolitan school wanted to separate Dante's poetry from Dante's structure, his genius from his mind, the lyricism of the *Divine Comedy* from its architecture. Some biographers, in their turn, want to separate Dante's poetry from Dante's personality. . . . In fact, their purpose subconsciously is the same: namely, to disintegrate the unity of the poet and the poem, to strip the *Divine Comedy* of Dante's moral will, as the others did of his rational knowledge and structural intentions, to reach the evidence that there is such a thing as

---

13. Chapman "most probably had read and liked Croce's book, although he never quotes it. But he enjoyed besides, being a foreigner, the privilege of not taking into account the taboo of the Dante worship, practically inexorable for Italians. Thus he could go straight at Dante's personality, without any fear of penalty." (Borgese, *op. cit.*, p. 40.)

14. A more complete exposition of Borgese's views and his divergencies from and criticism of Croce's aesthetic theories is found in his book *La Poetica dell'unità* (Milano, 1934). The fifth essay of this book is a condensed but suggestive summary of the history of literary criticism.

pure poetry, pure of knowledge and will, and to hold it in their hands, the bluebird of poetry, all throat and feathers.[15]

The search for this elusive bird is nonsensical. The fallacy of the whole theory lies in its assumption that because we can distinguish theoretically between the faculties of the human mind, we can and must also find this distinction in the products of these faculties, as if the human mind and the human personality did not constitute a unit and did not work as a unit:

Thence the search after the pure poet, the pure poem thoroughly destitute of reason and morals: that grasping the air, or trampling the shadow, which, more strikingly in cases like Dante's is so desperately futile as to become almost humorous.[16]

Every work of art, the *Divine Comedy* included, is a unity, but its inherent qualities differ. The *Divine Comedy* has the unity and diversity of Dante, the light and the shadow of his character; it has the excellence and the faults of its author: "The *Comedy* is a unity; Dante's structure and poetry, Dante's personality and work are a unity, and his personality and work are organically united to his society and his age." It is true that there are passages in the *Divine Comedy* wherein the lyrical quality soars higher than in others; such passages are the "beauties," which serve as "beams" to support the "beauty" of the whole structure.[17]

Croce's theory also failed to find any support in T. S. Eliot's "Dante," an essay published in the series *The Poets on Poets* (London, 1929). According to the plan of the series, Eliot's task was only "to give a faithful account of his acquaintance with Dante." He disclaimed being a Dante scholar, or even of having an extensive knowledge of Italian. His progress in reading Dante had been slow:

15. Borgese, *op. cit.*, p. 39.
16. *Idem*, p. 47.
17. Borgese reminds us that "the tradition about Dante's beauties and the Comedy as a tormenting alternation of failures and successes" is essentially "an inheritance from neo-classic criticism, which lay, still very much alive, under the laurel wreaths of Dante enthusiasm increasingly heaped by many modern critics in the pious and unconscious hope of concealing the permanence of some rhetorical habits of discrimination from themselves and from their audience." (*Idem*, p. 28.)

I began with passages which I could understand, passed on to the Purgatorio in the same way, and only after years of experience I began to appreciate the Paradiso; from which I reverted to the other parts of the poem and slowly realized the unity of the whole.[18]

As a result of his reading and meditation, Eliot became convinced of three things. First, the poetry of Dante is the one universal school of style for the writing of poetry in any language: "There is no poet in any tongue, not even in Latin or Greek, who stands so firmly as a model of poetry." Second, Dante's allegorical method has great advantages in the writing of poetry; it simplifies diction and makes the images clear and precise: "In good allegory like Dante's, it is not necessary to understand the meaning first to enjoy the poetry, but our enjoyment of the poetry makes us want to understand the meaning." Third, the *Divine Comedy* is a complete scale of the *depths* and *heights* of human emotions; the *Purgatory* and *Paradise* are to be read as extensions of the ordinarily very limited human range: "Every degree of the feeling of humanity, from lowest to highest, has, moreover, an intimate relation to the next above and below, and all fit together according to the logic of sensibility" (p. 56).

Eliot wished to avoid the two extremes of Dante criticism: on the one hand, the belief that the "understanding of the scheme, the philosophy, the concealed meanings of Dante's verse was essential to appreciation"; and on the other hand, the opinion that "these things were quite irrelevant, that the poetry in his poems was one thing, which could be enjoyed by itself without studying a framework which had served the author in producing the poetry, but could not serve the reader in enjoying it" (p. 16). According to Eliot, it is possible to begin to enjoy the poetry of the *Divine Comedy* without giving any attention to the general framework and the philosophy of the poem; but full enjoyment and understanding of its poetic intensity can be had only from the study of the poem as a unity. As a consequence, "you cannot afford to ignore Dante's philosophical and theological beliefs, or to skip the passages

18. Preface, p. 12. Eliot believes that it is better to read the *Vita Nuova* after the *Divine Comedy* instead of before, because "an English reader who reads the *Vita Nuova* too soon is in danger of reading it under pre-Raphaelite influence."

which express them most clearly." Of course, it is not necessary that you believe them.

It is wrong to think that there are parts of the *Divine Comedy* which are of interest only to Catholics or to mediaevalists. For there is a difference between philosophical *belief* and *poetic assent.* . . . I will not deny that it may be in practice easier for a Catholic to grasp the meaning, in many places, than for the ordinary agnostic; but that is not because the Catholic believes, but because he has been instructed. It is a matter of knowledge and ignorance, not of belief or skepticism. The vital matter is that Dante's poem is a whole; that you must in the end come to understand every part in order to understand any part [pp. 42–43].

Out of his own experience, Eliot found also that "the poetry of Dante is extremely easy to read." He does not mean by this to imply "that Dante writes simple Italian, for he does not; or that his content is simple or always simply expressed." Eliot means that Dante is "the most *universal* of poets in the modern languages" (p. 17). Dante's style has a peculiar poetic lucidity; "the thought may be obscure, but the word is lucid or rather translucent." The allegorical method—though this may seem a paradoxical statement—"makes for simplicity and intelligibility," because in Dante "allegory means *clear visual images,* and Dante's is a visual imagination" (pp. 22–23). Finally, Dante is easy to read, "even for a foreigner who does not know Italian very well," because in "Dante's time Europe, with all its dissentions and dirtiness, was mentally more united than we can now conceive." Hence we may speak of the universality of Dante, "which is not solely a personal matter" (p. 18).

Most readers will agree with Borgese that Eliot was too optimistic in so minimizing the difficulty of Dante's work:

That there is in Dante no obscurity at all, save for our ignorance, is flattery to Dante; to presume, as T. S. Eliot does, that we can easily understand him all the way through, even with a featherlight historical and philological apparatus, if we only use our individual power of simply understanding poetry, is flattery to ourselves.[19]

19. Borgese, *op. cit.,* p. 59. "Eliot's essay on Dante may seem at times rather vague, with some details of questionable information. But it has a touch of plainness and humility which comes near to truth where more ambitious methods fail. It seems as if he had in

T. S. Eliot's empirical approach to Dante and his notion that Dante is easy reading remind us of J. C. Gray's essay of 1819. But while Gray, after enjoying Dante's poetry undisturbed by allegorism and theological subtleties, went no further than to extract from it a moral lesson or a subject for contemplation in the sober moments of life, Eliot considers this kind of enjoyment of Dante's poetry only as the first step toward a higher goal:

> The enjoyment of the *Divine Comedy* is a continuous process. If you get nothing out of it at first, you probably never will; but if from your first deciphering of it there comes now and then some direct shock of poetic intensity, nothing but laziness can deaden the desire for fuller and fuller knowledge [p. 16].

Henry E. Conklin's "The Aesthetic of Dante," one of the seven "lay" lectures given at the Rice Institute (Texas) in 1921,[20] approaches the subject from the notion that beauty is realized intuitively, but that aesthetic judgment comes only from synthesizing emotional analysis with intellectual analysis. He illustrates his theory by contrasting Keats and Dante. The comparison between the two is one "of pleasant vagueness with pleasant incisiveness," and hence it is necessary "to derive the aesthetic value of this Dante's precision." The lecture then deals with the aesthetic ideas inherited by the Middle Ages and Dante from classical antiquity. Art is the impression left in the wax into which the stamp has been pressed; it is twice removed from the image formed by God. Such is the Aristotelian tradition which derives art from nature, and nature from God, expressed in Dante's famous line, *L'arte che a Dio è nepote.*

The essay on Dante in Charles G. Osgood's *Poetry as Means of Grace,*[21] though primarily concerned with the spiritual values connected with religion, deals also with literary forms and artistic beauty as vehicles of spirituality. Being a churchman and address-

mind the method of Poe and Poe's epigoni and wished purposely to contradict it. In the main problem of the beauties or beauty of Dante he hits the mark." (*Idem,* p. 54.) See also: Mario Praz, "T. S. Eliot and Dante," *The Southern Review,* December, 1936.

20. See above, p. 212.

21. Princeton Univ. Press, 1941. The five chapters of this book (i, "Your Poet"; ii, "Dante"; iii, "Spenser"; iv, "Milton"; v, "Johnson") were lectures given at the Princeton Theological Seminary in 1940.

ing primarily a clerical audience, Osgood pleads for the study and meditation of the *Divine Comedy,* because Dante in this poem fulfills all the requirements that we expect in the ideal poet. Such a poet must be "focal"; that is, he must gather within himself in highly intensified form as many as possible of the cultural influences of previous civilizations; he must be "encyclopaedic" and include within his scope all things that man is capable of considering; he must be "inexhaustible," and a man "of deep, passionate, and reasoned humanism"; last but not least, he must be a "singer, a master of the most beautiful of all music, the music of poetry." Dante has all these qualifications. A close association with him "will bring us into close intimacy with the rich tradition of Christian worship and experience"; it will affect the quality of our style of expression, in matter of "order, clarity, beauty and even music of utterance"; but, above all, Dante will lead us to acquire in the midst of our active life the habit of contemplation, because Dante, "beyond all other poets, throws all things into true spiritual perspective." [22] We are very far here from Croce's world of separate compartments and opposition of rational and poetical faculties. To Osgood "the briar of dialectic is indispensable to the rose of poetry." But after all, as Borgese remarked, Croce himself, perhaps to forestall obvious objections, granted that there is a unity of some sort in the *Divine Comedy,* such as "the dialectical unity of a theological romance," or of "the poetical spirit of Dante," of "the tonality of his poetry," or the unity of "a view of the world founded on firm faith and steady judgment, and inspired by a strong will." Going still further, Croce, while denying that this structural unity of the

22. Don Luigi Sturzo, an Italian Catholic priest, while in America as a political refugee, has also taken up the cudgel against Croce's aesthetic devaluation of the *Divine Comedy* as a whole. In his article "Modern Aesthetics and the Poetry of the *Divine Comedy"* (*Thought,* XVII [1942], 412–432), Don Sturzo debates the question whether the *Divine Comedy* "is a single poetical reality, a living whole, with a synthetic value as a work of art." After a refutation of the various objections raised by Croce and his followers, Sturzo concludes that "the Divine Comedy is one poem, and it is—with rare exceptions—all poetry. . . . In general, the Inferno is dramatic and the Purgatorio is idyllic; by contrast, the Paradiso is lyrical . . . It is theology and poetry . . . Theology is something that can be transmuted into inmost living and therefore into the poetry of sublime song. . . . Poetry is, and must be, light and love, a reflected beam of Light and Love, an intuition of the mysterious Reality which is in us, in nature and in God; else it is simply no poetry at all. . . . The Divine Comedy will remain a work of art—perhaps the very greatest of all human works of art."

Comedy is poetical, grants that it is not devoid of poetry; nay, that it is submerged in Dante's irresistible poetical flow, and that this structure, just because it was not poetical, forced Dante to overcome its resistance by raising higher his poetical powers.[23] Dante could not help being a poet; automatically, by the power of his intuitive imagination, even when he was thinking of being a theologian or a scientist:

Scheme and poetry, theological and lyrical romance, are not separable in the work of Dante, any more than the parts of his soul are separate from one another. One conditions the other and flows into it. In this dialectical sense, the Comedy is certainly a unity.[24]

Yet what is not separable must be separated to distinguish what is structural and what is poetical. The structure itself is neither poetry nor poetical, and to speak of the architectonic beauty of the *Comedy* is sheer rhetorical nonsense. Croce prefers to compare it to a massive building almost covered by a tropical vegetation of climbing vines and blooming flowers, which leave only here and there some bare corners and some harsh lines of the structure to be seen. Borgese observes pointedly that this metaphor, supposing that it fits the *Comedy,* implies much more than Croce is willing to grant, "since even the deadest masonry has its vital efficiency and influence on the directions and opportunities of the vegetation that grow upon it." [25]

Chapman enjoyed Dante only as a poet who could throw on his

23. "The poetry of Dante assumes a sort of necessary character, bursting its way through barriers and rendered more vigorous by the opposition. It tops all obstructions in such a way that one could not offer a better case to the unbelievers in the real, autonomous existence of poetry, who look upon it as something artificial and unessential. We would have them reflect on this poetic fury of Dante, the theologian and politician, this torrent that flows in so lofty a vein, opening its way between the boulders and tearing impetuously along. Such is its force, such its richness, that as it penetrates into all the hollows of the rocks and covers the mountain landscapes with spray and foam, it often leaves nothing to the sight but the motion of its own waters. The poetry of Dante, when it can do nothing else, vivifies the argumentative and informative and technical parts of the narrative, even the not infrequently laboured conceits of the erudite historian, and invests all with its own accent, emotional and sublime." (B. Croce, *The Poetry of Dante,* trans. Douglas Ainslie [New York, 1922], pp. 95–96.)

24. *Idem,* p. 96.

25. Borgese, *op. cit.,* p. 36. Croce's theories on poetry and on Dante are restated in popular form in Isaac Goldberg's *Dante, An Aesthetic View* ("Little Blue Books," Pocket Series No. 423, Edited by E. Haldeman-Julius, Girard, Kan., 1923).

screen beautiful descriptive pictures. Likewise, according to Croce, we should read Dante "paying little heed to the other world, very little to the moral divisions, none at all to the allegories, and enjoying the representations in which all the poet's multiform passion is condensed, purified and expressed."

At the end of his canzone "Voi che intendendo il terzo ciel movete," Dante, doubting whether most of its readers would be able to understand its true meaning, took leave of his song with the exhortation,

> I pray thee, beloved new song of mine
> Have comfort in thyself and say to them:
> Take heed at least, how beautiful I am.[26]

Croce's directions to the readers of the *Divine Comedy* follow the same line of thought, but they are addressed to all and not only to the unlearned readers of the poem. Furthermore, they introduce into Dante's line a variant which would have filled him with a sense of utter frustration: "Take heed *only* how beautiful I am."

26. Translation by C. E. Norton.

CHAPTER XII

DANTEANA MINORA

THE many-sided character of Dante; the dramatic events of his life; the wide range of his learning as a philosopher, theologian, and scientist; his political ideas; his greatness as a poet; the importance of his works in literary history and in philological studies—all have been and continue to be subjects for minute historical explorations and erudite researches. Every year new monographs, articles, and notes appear in various modern languages, increasing the already extensive Dante bibliographies. American contributions to these diversified and specialized studies on Dante's life, on less obvious aspects of his thought, and on passages of his works have been considerable and stand well the comparison with parallel scholarly productions in other countries. Although a few monographs on more important or more extensive topics have been issued in book form, most of these contributions have appeared as articles or notes in learned journals, especially in those on literature and philology, and were often merely the partial results of research undertaken in the preparation of more extensive and elaborate publications. Not all of them are valuable, to be sure, nor are their conclusions always acceptable. Nonetheless, they bear witness to the lively interest of American scholars in Dante and his work during the present century.

For convenience, these *Danteana Minora* may be surveyed in the following order: writings on the minor works of Dante other than the *Vita Nuova;* studies on special aspects of the *Divine Comedy* or parts of it; studies of Dante's influence on the literature of various countries; interpretations of and comments upon special passages of the *Divine Comedy;* and grammatical, philological, and metrical investigations of passages from his works.

By the end of the nineteenth century the task of restoring the original texts, especially of Dante's minor works which had suffered greatly both in the manuscript tradition and later in modernized printed editions, was already well advanced, but it was not completed until the first decades of this century. Translations of those works made earlier, therefore became in part obsolete and had to be supplanted by new ones based on more reliable texts.

We have already mentioned the translation of several of Dante's lyrics from the *Rime* made by Brooks, Norton, Grandgent and others; but no complete translation of all of them has appeared in America to the present time.[1] Neither has the *Convivio* ever been translated here, unless the English version of it made by Katharine Hillard (1889), who lived in England and published it in London, should be counted as American.[2]

For a while Norton seems to have been very anxious to have translations of the Latin works of Dante produced in America. He urged some of his more advanced students or former students to undertake this task. One of them, Charles S. Latham, translated Dante's *Epistles,* but death (1890) prevented him from revising his work before publication. It was edited the following year by George R. Carpenter.[3] Latham's version, a creditable performance, was highly praised by American reviewers; but, as Paget Toynbee remarked, Latham has based his translation upon the text of Fraticelli, which was more defective than the one edited by Giuliani. In any case, said the British critic, a translation of Dante's *Epistles* was premature, as long as the text had not been made available in

1. For English translations of Dante's *Rime* see above, pp. 116, 202. The last complete verse translation of the *Rime* made in England (including the lyrics of the *Vita Nuova* and the *Convivio*) by Lorna de Lucchi (Oxford, 1926) has the merit of being more literal than its predecessors. On the other hand, "Lorna de Lucchi borrowed from Rossetti's vocabulary," but she "lacks his grand manner and, on the whole, she is more nearly literal than he is. . . . There are times when Rossetti is closer, or when his paraphrase is more effective than her literality. . . . Signora De Lucchi is often labored and stiff and there are few of her translations which bespeak the beauty of the original. Notable exceptions are the Canzone *Donna Pietosa* and the *Pietra Poems.*" (A. E. Tromby, *Italica,* IV [1927], 73–75).

2. K. Hillard, *The Banquet of Dante Alighieri* (London, 1889). The first English translation of the *Convivio* was made by Elizabeth P. Sayer, *Il Convito—The Banquet of Dante Alighieri* (London, 1887). A new version by Philip H. Wicksteed appeared in 1903 (Oxford); the last and the best was made by W. W. Jackson, *The Convivio of Dante Alighieri* (Oxford, 1909).

3. *A Translation of Dante's Eleven Letters:* "With Explanatory Notes and Historical Comment by Charles Sterret Latham," G. R. Carpenter, ed., preface by C. E. Norton (Boston, 1891). Also a Memorial Edition (Cambridge, Mass., 1891). On Latham, see *Rep. Dante Soc.,* 1891, p. 10. See list of reviews of Latham's book in Koch, *DA,* p. 126.

a scholarly critical edition. Yet, considering the difficulties of the original and the crabbed Latin language and style of Dante, Latham's version was "at once faithful and readable." [4]

Alain Campbell White translated the *Quaestio de Aqua et Terra* (*Report Dante Soc.,* 1902) from the text of the Oxford Dante edited by Moore. White wrote also an introduction in which he discussed briefly the question of the authenticity of the work, and added many notes on the text and concerning the sources of Dante's scientific beliefs. The edition found little favor with Toynbee and was even more severely reviewed by an Italian critic, who noticed several misinterpretations and serious lacunae in White's work. [5] To Aurelia Henry of Yale University we owe the first and only complete American translation of the *De Monarchia*. It was made also from the Oxford Text, but with variants from other editions. [6]

Wilmon Brewer's translation of *Dante's Eclogues* [7] made for those "who read Dante as literature," may be called a modernized paraphrase of the text. Brewer's blank verse runs more smoothly than the often stilted hexameter of Dante and conveys a meaning more clearly than the Latin text which is often so obscure. Whether the translator by departing so much from the letter of the text has preserved, as he thinks he has, the spirit of the original may be open to question.

American Dantists have made no contribution—except in the matter of some small details—in the long, painstaking work of

4. *The Academy,* April 2, 1892.

5. Toynbee in *Romania,* XXXIII (1904), 103–104; *GSLI,* XLIII (1904), 128–131.

6. The *De Monarchia* of D. A. Edited with Translation and Notes (Boston and New York, 1904). The Latin Text was not given. The *De Monarchia* had already been translated into English by F. J. Church (London, 1879) and the first book of this version had been reprinted in Boston in the series *Old South Pamphlets* in 1888. The new translation made by P. H. Wicksteed (London, 1896) was later revised and included in the two-volume *Translation of the Latin Works of Dante Alighieri* (London, 1904), which contained also the *Epistolae, Eclogae,* and the *Quaestio de Aqua et Terra* in English, translated by Wicksteed, and the *De Vulgari Eloquentia* by A G. F. Howell (revised after the first edition of 1890). A new translation with a critical edition of the Latin text of the *Epistolae* was made more recently by Paget Toynbee, *Dantes Alighieri Epistolae,* Oxford, 1920, with notes and an appendix on the cursus.

7. *Dante's Eclogues* (*The Poetical Correspondence between Dante and Giovanni del Virgilio*), Translated from the Latin into English Blank Verse (Boston, 1927). The translation is followed by an essay on "The Literary Importance of Dante's Eclogues." See *Italica,* IV (1927), 18.

establishing the texts of Dante's writings.[8] Neither did they take part in the minute analysis of the manuscript tradition and in the historical and philological scrutiny of the collections of Dante's *Rime,* which led to the elimination of lyrics hitherto attributed to him. Obviously such work could be done more conveniently in Europe by European scholars.

Dante's lyrics are of great importance for the reconstruction of his sentimental and intellectual history as well as for the history of the *dolce stil nuovo,* and they have been analyzed and interpreted from this point of view in the American biographies of Dante and in works dealing with the *Vita Nuova.*[9] Grandgent's *The Ladies of Dante's Lyrics* is especially to be noted as a detailed analysis of these poems grouped according to Grandgent's own scheme and re-interpreted in the light of it. As we have already seen, American biographers of Dante have also given careful attention to the content of the *Convivio* and its relation to the other works of Dante, especially when dealing with Dante's allegory and symbolism. Passages from the *Convivio* occur often in comments on the *Divine Comedy* by Longfellow, Norton, and Grandgent, and in those on the *Vita Nuova* in McKenzie's edition. Though no special work dealing entirely with the *Convivio* has been published in America, this book, which holds a central position between the *Vita Nuova* and the *Divine Comedy,* has been thoroughly studied by American Dantists and some of its problems have been discussed in special articles.[10]

Dante's political theories as expounded in *De Monarchia* and the bitter denunciations of the political conditions of his times which he expressed in the *Divine Comedy* and in some of his letters were familiar subjects with the early American essayists, who never

8. Dino Bigongiari, "Notes of the Critical Text of Dante's Epistles," *Mod. Lang. Rev.,* XVIII, 476–479; "The Text of Dante's Monarchia," *Speculum,* II, 457–462.

9. Grandgent, *Dante,* chap. iv, "Mediaeval Song." See also McKenzie's notes to the *Vita Nuova* and his article "Observations on Dante's Lyrical Poems," *Rep. Dante Soc.,* 1934.

10. Theodore H. Silverstein, "Two Notes on Dante's *Convivio*," *Speculum,* VII (1932), 542–551; G. G. Walsh, "The Doctrine of Thomas Aquinas in the *Convivio* of Dante," *Gregorianum,* XVI (1935), 504–530. H. D. Austin, "Roma, Maria, Lucia, a Dante Study, *Convivio,* III, v," *Grad. Studies Univ. Calif.* (1936), pp. 11–28. J. E. Shaw, "Per l'altre, Conv. III, xv, 15," *Mod. Lang. N.,* LVII (1942), 581–584.

failed to dedicate to them at least a section of their sketches on Dante's life and works. The first extensive exposition of these theories, which appeared in Botta's book, was highly colored by the patriotic Ghibellinism of the author. In later American biographies of Dante the analysis of his political ideas still holds a conspicuous place.

Grandgent's chapter on "Church and State" (*Dante,* chap. iii, pp. 59–89) is a concise but clear survey of Dante's political thought as set forth in *De Monarchia,* the *Convivio,* the *Divine Comedy,* and the *Epistles,* with many quotations from Dante himself. "Of course," says Grandgent, "Dante's political scheme was not practical, but it was in keeping with his temper." To those who have given up "the idea of discipline to make way for self-development, self-realization, self-assertion, in our democratic day and country, Dante's *Monarchy* seems so strangely antiquated and unreal." [11]

Dinsmore, following the conclusion reached by Edward Moore in his *Dante and Aristotle,* discussed the question of the date of *De Monarchia.* This he follows with a dry summary of the content of the work, ending with the observation that Dante misunderstood the spirit of the times, because "the hope of Italy was in the rising strength of the free cities, not in the benevolent despotism of the German monarch." [12]

Fletcher does not find Dante so antiquated: "Dante postulated for his international tribunal a world emperor at Rome; we, a world parliament at the Hague." And Dante, though he belonged to a world of caste and social hierarchy, "in the true sense of the word, does not seem to be so undemocratic, after all." [13] As a matter of fact, "what a richly democratic ideal is implied in the single line that, fully understood, contains Dante's whole philosophy of love: 'Love and the gentle heart are all the same.' " Hitherto it had not occurred to anyone to attribute a political and democratic content to this line of Dante which summarizes the notion of love of the poets of the *dolce stil nuovo,* as defined by Guido Guinizelli. In his latest article, "Dante's Own Comedy," [14] Fletcher goes even farther

11. Grandgent, *Dante,* p. 60.
12. Dinsmore, *Dante,* p. 162.
13. Fletcher, *Dante,* p. 238.
14. *American Scholar,* XIV (1945), 60–71.

in assuming that the *Divine Comedy* tells by means of allegory and symbols the whole story of Dante's political sins and experiences; it is *his own Comedy*. At the end of this essay, Fletcher states again, more forcibly, that Dante's conception of a universal empire, or a world superstate essential to world peace, may be taken as an anticipation of modern ideas, if we eliminate from Dante's system the medieval element of its connection with Rome.

J. J. Kolbiecki's *The Political Philosophy of Dante Alighieri* [15] traces the classical and Christian sources of Dante's concept of the state, a subject which has been treated more than once not only in Dante literature, but also in histories of medieval political thought and medieval philosophy. Special questions reflecting Dante's political ideas and judgments raised either by the *De Monarchia* or by passages in the *Divine Comedy* have been discussed by several American Dantists. [16]

Dante's *De Vulgari Eloquentia* and his queer notion of the origin of the Italian language were first briefly summarized by Longfellow in his early essay on the subject. Dante's theories about the nature of the *volgare* and his distinctions of styles according to different purposes which he had previously expounded in the *Con-*

15. Doctoral dissertation (Catholic Univ. of America, Washington, D. C., 1921).

16. J. J. Kolbiecki, "Dante's Views on the Sovereignty of the State," *Catholic Historical Review*, III (1923), 91–102; Theodore Silverstein, "On the Genesis of De Monarchia," *Speculum*, XIII, 326–348; "The Throne of the Emperor in Dante's Paradiso and the Mediaeval Conception of Christian Kingship," *Harvard Theological Review*, XXXII, 115–129; A. Gilbert, "Had Dante Read the Politics of Aristotle?" *PMLA*, XLIII, 602 ff.; R. F. Egan, "Dante's Letter to Morsello Malaspina," *Rom. Rev.*, XI (1920), 149–169 (a new interpretation); B. B. Carter, "Dante's Political Ideas," *Review of Politics*, V (1943), 339–355. Following in the footsteps of E. Anitchkof (*Joachim de Flore et les milieux courtois* [Paris, 1931]) and going much farther, the author holds that Joachim's doctrine of the three ages of revelation provides the background for Dante's political thought. There is no doubt that Dante venerated the Calabrian prophet and that the Joachite ideal of spiritual perfection, so strong among the Spiritual Franciscans, had some influence on his general concept of the mission of Christianity. It is, however, preposterous to assume that there is any direct connection between a political system based—as was Dante's—on a universal Empire and a universal Papacy, and Joachim's age of the Spirit, in which men were expected to live according to the rules of monastic perfection, and the Church of Christ was to disappear in order to make room for the free association of the Spirit. Anitchkof, who made of Joachim a Montanist, and who found Joachite influences in Mazzini, Georges Sand, Marx, and Bakounine, used his imagination too much. On Joachim's idea of a "spiritual society" see E. Buonaiuti, *Gioacchino da Fiore, I Tempi, la vita, il messaggio* (Rome, 1931), and A. Donini, "Appunti per una storia del pensiero di Dante in rapporto al movimento gioachimita," *Rep. Dante Soc.*, 1930, pp. 48 ff. On Anitchkof's book see G. La Piana, "Joachim of Flora, A Critical Survey," *Speculum*, VII (1932), 257–282.

vivio have not been overlooked in American Dante biographies [17] and in the commentaries to the *Comedy* and the *Vita Nuova,* but no special comprehensive work on this unfinished treatise has been published here.

Both in his *Life of Dante* and in his *Comment* on the *Inferno,* Boccaccio stated that Dante wrote the first seven cantos of the *Inferno* before his exile in 1302; and that about five years later the manuscript was discovered among his papers and sent to Moroello Malaspina, with whom he was staying at the time. Dante then took up the work again, beginning the eighth canto with the words *Io dico seguitando.* Boccaccio was puzzled, however, by the apparent reference to Dante's banishment from Florence in the prophecy of Ciacco (Canto VI, 64–69), and suggested that perhaps this reference may have been added by Dante to the text at a later date. The meaning of this passage and the date of these early cantos of the *Inferno* have been the cause of much debate and disagreement among Dantists. In general, however, it is agreed that there is a marked difference between these cantos and the rest of the poem, and that there must have been a lapse of time between them. The history of the controversy and of the different solutions reached by scholars has been neatly summarized by Kenneth McKenzie, who seems to favor the explanation offered, on sound circumstantial evidence, by Giovanni Ferretti.[18] The Italian Dantist maintains that Ciacco's prophecy-after-the-event does not refer to Dante's exile, as usually stated, but rather to the oppression of Dante's White party by the Blacks between November, 1301, when Charles de Valois entered Florence, and the following January. Boccaccio's statement may then be accepted as true.

This view is not agreeable, however, to Giuseppe A. Borgese, who in his essay "The Wrath of Dante," [19] gives first a suggestive and keen analysis of the elements that mark the difference between the first seven cantos and the rest of the *Divine Comedy,* and then states his own theory as to the dating of their composition. Borgese emphasizes the point that the explosion of Dante's revengeful

17. See especially Grandgent's *Dante,* chap. v, "Language and Poetry," pp. 138–144.

18. K. McKenzie, *"Tal che testè piaggia," Italica,* XVIII (1941), 87–96; G. Ferretti, *I due tempi della composizione della Divina Commedia* (Bari, 1935).

19. *Speculum,* XIII (1938), 183–193.

passion in the episode of Filippo Argenti (*Inferno,* VIII) introduces
a new feature in his poem. Commentators and interpreters of the
Divine Comedy have tried to explain Dante's almost sadistic rage
against his old Florentine enemy by making use of the theories of
Aristotle or Thomas Aquinas concerning just wrath. To Borgese
this approach to the question is of no great importance. Whether
Dante's wrath and his cruelty against Argenti are or are not justi-
fiable matters little; the essential point is that this episode marks a
turning point in the *Divine Comedy*.

   In the whole poetical work of Dante previous to the eighth canto
of the *Inferno,* pity, fear, and humility are the dominant sentiments of his psychological attitude; but from the eighth canto on,
"pride and anger are unmistakably present, to remain, however
ably the latter may be surnamed disdain, and together with them,
most probably, is revengefulness, of the most personal and passionate kind." At the same time, the Argenti episode marks the appearance of a structural novelty in Dante's technique:

Dante proves able for the first time to handle three persons at once:
Argenti, Virgil and himself. Thus far he had not surpassed the flat of
Byzantine technique of straight dialogue between himself and Virgil,
or between himself and a shade, or between Virgil and an official of the
underworld. . . . Now in the eighth canto, it is as if he at one stroke
had achieved in his dramatic technique a transition like that from the
two-actor to the three-actor performance in Greek tragedy. Together
with the other enrichments in landscape, movement, language and
rhythm, this change implies a profound allotropy in the poet's imagination.

   According to Borgese, this psychic change was due to the release
of anger, by which "the pre-Raphaelite poet of the sweet new style,
was superseded by the master of the grand and not seldom violent
style." It is not surprising that,

together with the inner proportion of feelings, his poetic taste and
technique of expression also underwent a metamorphosis; the primitive
draftsman yielded to the Renaissance painter, with a stupendous increase
of realistic color and dramatic power.

This cleavage between the eighth and the preceding cantos suggests not only a lapse of time between their composition sufficient to allow for the poet's "conversion," but also a decisive crisis in Dante's life and moral experience causing this conversion. Borgese suggests that this crisis came in 1313 at the death of the Emperor Henry VII, an occurrence which marked the end of all Dante's hopes and dreams for the restoration of the empire and for his own return to Florence. The extinction of his hopes released his anger. And then

all earthly hopes and earthly love spent, with old age and death at his heels, and on the other hand sheltered in more comfortable hospitalities, he could ply his work in the concentration and continuity without which the intensity of the result would be nearly unthinkable.

Borgese then thinks that the first seven cantos of the *Inferno,* though planned and even sketched by Dante as early as his Florentine period, were actually written much later, more precisely at the beginning of Henry's expedition in Italy, when Dante's hopes and expectations were running high. The rest, from the eighth canto of the *Inferno* to the end of the poem, was written after Henry's death in 1313, when all Dante's hopes had vanished. At any rate, it was "the allotropy in pride and anger that lifted Dante to the height of his power."

From the very beginning, Dante's concrete presentation of the punishment of sin and the reward of virtue has been amply discussed and analyzed by commentators and interpreters of the *Divine Comedy*. It was, in fact, a favorite subject with American writers and lecturers on Dante during the last decades of the nineteenth century. In general, commentators have emphasized the fitness of the punishments and rewards which Dante assigned to each sin and each virtue, thereby revealing his deep psychological insight as well as the power of his imagination in utilizing historical and mythological elements in his picture of final retributive justice. Behind the picturesque concreteness of his descriptions there was a definite notion of this justice, a notion based on philosophical and theological premises.

Allan Gilbert's *Dante's Conception of Justice* (New York, 1925) traces the sources of Dante's concept of justice in the classical, patristic, and scholastic tradition, especially in Aquinas' commentary on the fifth book of Aristotle's *Ethics;* and then analyzes its application in the three parts of the *Comedy.* This analysis leads the author to the conclusion that, whatever else there is in the poem, or "in whatever way Dante's personal experience appears in it, God's justice is still its theme."

Gilbert's oversimplification of the complex structure of the *Divine Comedy* did not meet with the approval of various reviewers of his book. In the opinion of Kenneth McKenzie, Gilbert exaggerated the significance of justice and ignored some valuable studies on the subject. Moreover, his interpretation of several passages appeared questionable:

The author perhaps makes plainer than it had been made before that Dante has the ideal of justice constantly in mind; but he [the author] has a tendency to confuse the abstract philosophical idea as it existed in the poet's mind, with the purely poetic or literary criterion which guided the composition of the poem—not of course to the exclusion of the philosophic purpose, but equally important with it.[20]

Vincenzo Cioffari traced the history of the ideas of *Fortune and Fate from Democritus to Thomas Aquinas*[21] and then continued his inquiry with an analysis of "The Conception of Fortune and Fate in the Works of Dante"[22] and an essay on "Fortune in Dante's Fourteenth Century Commentators."[23] A summary of the teaching of Aristotle and of its reinterpretation in the light of Christian theology provides the background for the analysis of the similarities and dissimilarities of Dante's concept of Fortune and Fate, first in his minor works and then in the *Comedy,* with his sources both

20. McKenzie, *Speculum,* II (1927), 348. McKenzie agrees with Gilbert's valuable suggestion that "this material concerning justice gathered from the *Divine Comedy* is essential for the understanding of Dante's *De Monarchia* and many passages of his other writings." Other reviews by C. H. Grandgent, *Mod. Lang. N.,* XLI, 268–270; Dino Bigongiari, *Rom. Rev.,* XIII (1926); C. E. Young, *Italica,* V (1928), 19–21. In connection with this subject see also Lane Cooper, *Evolution and Repentance: Mixed Essays on Aristotle, Plato and Dante* (Cornell Univ. Press, 1936).

21. New York, privately printed, 1935.

22. *Publications Dante Soc.,* 1940.

23. *Publications Dante Soc.,* 1944.

classical and medieval. Although this subject had been treated many times before, as the author is well aware, Cioffari's study has the merit of presenting with clarity and consistency Dante's thoughts on a subject very much mishandled by the early commentators of the *Divine Comedy*. The traditional connection of Fortune and Fate with theological or astrological determinism caused some of the early commentators to assume a defensive attitude in order "to ward off charges of heresy leveled at Dante for his supposed suppression of free will." [24] Their approach to the problem was polemical; and hence their comments, instead of explaining Dante's ideas, discuss the commentators' notions in the light of their theological preoccupations.

A much wider field for research is offered by Dante's concept of the physical universe, of nature, by his scientific theories about life in all its forms, and by the great variety of natural phenomena which he describes so often in the form of similes. Systematic exploration of the vast expanse of medieval science has been intensified in the present century, giving rise to a new branch of history to which American scholarship has made valuable contributions.[25] In monographs and special studies dealing with medieval science, the name of Dante occurs often, but American studies concerned directly with Dante's scientific learning are few. Botta's chapter on Dante as a scientist—the first outline of the subject written in America—was inadequate and biased by the author's belief in Dante's omniscience.[26] The Cambridge triad relied on previous commentators and interpreters in all matters concerning Dante's scientific theories and their application. Among American biographers of Dante, Grandgent gave his readers a brief but sufficiently clear outline of the medieval world of science in which Dante

24. Review by Paul H. Harris of Cioffari's essay of 1944 in *Italica*, XXIII (1945), 53–55. On this special problem see also Thomas L. Collins' "Freedom and Necessity in the *Divine Comedy*," *The Personalist*, XXIII, 62–70.

25. C. H. Haskins, *Studies in the History of Mediaeval Science* (Cambridge, Harvard Univ. Press, 1927); G. Sarton, *History of Science*, II, Carnegie Institution of Washington (Baltimore, 1931); Lynn Thorndike, *History of Magic and Experimental Science*, I–VI (New York, 1929–41); Lynn White, "Technology and Inventions in the Middle Ages," *Speculum*, XV (1940), 141–159 (with copious bibliography in notes and in the final "Note to the Sources").

26. See above, p. 136.

lived.[27] Oskar L. Kuhns's *Treatment of Nature in Dante's Divina Commedia,* a series of articles published first in various American periodicals (1896–97) [28] and later collected in one volume (London, 1897), was little more than a survey of the conventional representation of nature which the Middle Ages inherited from classical poetry.

Richard T. Holbrook, in his *Dante and the Animal Kingdom* (New York, 1902),[29] planned to set forth "Dante's whole philosophy of the animal kingdom, to show from what sources he derived his knowledge, and to what end his knowledge is employed" (Preface). He collected and commented minutely upon all passages in the *Comedy* (chiefly similes) in which animals are described or mentioned—man, angels, and demons appearing in visible form included. These passages reveal Dante's familiarity with the sources of zoölogical learning of his time, with Aristotle and his commentators, with some of the bestiaries and special treatises, such as that of Frederick II on falconry; and, what is more important, they bear witness to his habit of direct observation and to his great descriptive power. Holbrook's analysis of the animals which appear in the *Comedy* leads him to the conclusion that, in general, the existence of lower animals interests Dante "only in so far as it furnishes him imagery to make us comprehend the actions of men, of devils and of angels, or in so far as the animals furnish lessons for the guidance of men. He neither loves nor portrays them wholly for their sake."

Holbrook's work was limited in range, being chiefly concerned with external descriptions and legendary animal lore, and therefore overlooked or failed to give satisfactory explanations of the significance and the function that animal lore assumed in the poem according to the medieval vision of the physical as a mirror of the

27. Grandgent, *Dante,* chap. vii, "Mediaeval Learning" (alchemy, magic, astrology, cosmography); chap. ix, "Man and His World" (anatomy, geography, the Antipodes, vapors, ocean, bestiaries, nature of heavenly bodies); chap. x, "Man and His Works." Specific problems are discussed in the "Argument" that precedes each canto in his edition of the *Divine Comedy.* On Griffith C. Evans' lecture "The Physical Universe of Dante" at the Rice Institute, Texas, in 1921, see above.

28. E. D. Roberts, "American Dante Bibliography," May 1896–May 1908, *Rep. Dante Soc.,* 1909, p. 32.

29. Originally a doctoral dissertation, Columbia University. After three years of study in Europe, Holbrook (1870–1934) taught successively at Yale, Columbia, Bryn Mawr, and the University of California at Berkeley. (See *Italica,* XI [1934], 96.)

spiritual world. Furthermore, in his use of sources—only the printed sources then available—Holbrook overlooked important material and did not always give an exact interpretation of that which he used.[30] Since the appearance of his book, more works of the considerable medieval literature of bestiaries and treatises on zoölogy, natural and symbolical, have been studied, providing new material for the illustration of Dante's treatment of the animal kingdom.

Although no other extensive work on Dante's scientific learning has been published in America, interest in this subject is not lacking, as we may see by the appearance of occasional articles and notes, some of which seem to be preliminary explorations gathering material for more substantial works.[31]

During the Renaissance and post-Renaissance period, Italian commentators of the *Divine Comedy* were greatly concerned with the descriptive and mythological elements of the poem, which were clearly of classical derivation, and they filled their notes with parallels and reminiscences from passages of Virgil, Ovid, and other Latin poets. Modern commentators continue to employ, though more sparingly, these references to the Latin classics, and Dante scholars find occasionally something new to glean in this well-harvested field.[32]

30. A thorough review of Holbrook's book pointing out gaps and deficiencies of the work and questioning the validity of its conclusion was published by Kenneth McKenzie in *Mod. Lang. N.*, XVIII (1903), 118–122. Holbrook replied to McKenzie's criticism in the same review: "The Understanding and Misunderstanding of Dante's Animal Lore," *Mod. Lang. N.*, XVIII (1903), 156–159. See also review by J. E. Spingarn, *Bookman*, XVII (1903), 82–83.

31. H. D. Austin, "Numbers Definite and Indefinite in the *Divine Comedy*," *PMLA*, XLVII, 915 ff.; "Number and Geometrical Design in the *Divine Comedy*," *The Personalist*, XVI, 310 ff.; "Heavenly Gold: A Study of the Use of Color in the *Divine Comedy*," *Phil. Quart.*, XII (1933), 44 ff.; "Dante and Mirrors," *Italica*, XXI (1944), 13–19; "Dante's Metals," *Phil. Quart.*, XXIV (1945), 83–85; "Dante's Precious Stones and Those of the Heavenly City," *Italica*, XXII (1945), 62–68; "*Mola* in Dante's Usage," *Speculum*, XIX (1944), 127–129 (a proposal to amend the text of *Convivio*, III, v, 18, based on a study of Dante's use of the word *mola* and its astronomical context); V. Cioffari, "A Dante Note: *Smeraldo*," *Speculum*, XIX (1944), 360–363; G. F. Lloyd, "The Landscape of the *Divine Comedy*," *Willinson's Monthly*, IV (Toronto), 173 ff.; L. A. Fisher, "Dante's Idea of the Sensible Appearance of the Spirits Beyond the Grave," *Rom. Rev.*, V (1914), 238 ff.

32. K. McKenzie, "Dante's References to Aesop," *Rep. Dante Soc.*, 1898, pp. 1–14; K. McKenzie and G. R. Silber, "Troia and Ilion in Virgil and Dante," *Studi medievali*, new series, V, 206 ff.; O. M. Johnston, "Similarities of Thought in Dante and Ovid," *Phil. Quart.*, XIII, 84 ff.; E. K. Rand, *Ovid and His Influence* (Boston, 1925), pp. 143 ff.;

With the progress which has been made in medieval studies and with the increasing knowledge of medieval literature, the question of Dante's Christian and medieval sources has assumed great importance and has given rise to an extensive, often controversial, literature. This is a field, however, in which, compared to their British, Italian and German colleagues, American Dantists are scantily represented.[33] To their search for classical and medieval influences on Dante, nineteenth-century commentators, reversing the process, added a new quest: they sought to determine the influence which Dante has in his turn exercised over the thought and literature of various nations. The English Dantists, and Longfellow too, filled their notes on the *Divine Comedy* with passages from Bunyan, Shakespeare, Milton, and other great English writers which seemed reminiscent or imitative of Dante, or which suggested chance parallelisms with Dante's thought or images. Italian commentators quoted passages from Ariosto, Tasso, and lesser stars of their poetic firmament, while commentators of other nations sought Dante's influence in their own literatures.

This search for Dantean influences, a tempting field of investigation in comparative literature, has not been overlooked in America; indeed, it has been often extended even to minor lights of literature as a convenient subject for erudite research. As might be expected, this search has been more extensive in English than in any other literature and has been the work not only of Dante

---

Founders of the Middle Ages (Harvard Univ. Press, 1928), chap. viii, "St. Augustine and Dante"; A. E. Carter, "An Unrecognized Virgilian Passage in Dante," *Italica*, XXI (1944), 149–153.

33. E. Becker, *Mediaeval Visions of Heaven and Hell* (Baltimore, 1899); A. Steiner, "St. Jerome and the First Terzina of the *Divine Comedy*," *Mod. Lang. N.*, LII, 259–260; Theodore Silverstein, "Did Dante Know the Vision of St. Paul?" *Harvard Studies and Notes in Philology and Literature*, XIX (1937), 231–247; "Inferno, XII, 100–126; and the *Visio Karoli Crassi*," *Mod. Lang. N.*, LI, 449–452; Martha D. Gnudi, "Might Dante Have Used a Map of Orosius?" *Italica*, XV (1938), 112–119; H. D. Austin, "What Form of Uguccione da Pisa's Lexicon Did Dante Use?" *Rom. Rev.*, XXVIII (1937). Dante's indebtedness to Provençal poetry is dealt with in Grandgent's *Dante* (chaps. iv and vi), and in more detail in *The Ladies of Dante's Lyrics, passim;* and by McKenzie in his notes to the *Vita Nuova* and his essay "Observations on Dante's Lyrical Poems," already mentioned. See also H. Boyers, "The Cleavage in Bertran de Born and Dante," *Mod. Phil.*, XXIV, 1–3. Asin Palacios' theory (*Islam and the Divine Comedy*, Eng. trans. [London, 1926]) that Dante knew and took over from Arabic sources the plan of his ultramundane voyage does not seem to have appealed to American Dantists.

scholars but also of specialists in the field of English letters. In his two large volumes, *Dante in English Literature,* Paget Toynbee reproduced from the works of English writers hundreds of passages which quoted or mentioned Dante, from Chaucer to the nineteenth century, and made a list of all English authors who dealt with Dante and his works. He did not, however, attempt to analyze Dante's influence on the works of these writers or on English literature as a whole. The two volumes mentioned above, his *Chronological List of English Translations from Dante from Chaucer to the Present Day,* and his *Dante in English Art* provide the starting point and the documentation for the study of what Dante has contributed to English literature and art.

The two great English authors whose connections with Dante's works have been most often investigated and written about are, of course, Chaucer and Milton. In the nineteenth century studies appeared in the form of parallels, especially between Dante and Milton; such was the famous essay of Macaulay. The general character of their poetry, the measure of their power of description and representation, and the scope of their creative imagination were compared according to the principles and ideals of Romantic criticism. Modern essays, on the contrary, written by men trained in the philological method, are more concerned with the borrowings made by one poet from another. As a result, much time is spent in tracing in detail the processes by which these transmissions occurred and in weighing the results thus obtained. The American bibliography on this subject is not large, but it contains several very valuable contributions by well-known scholars.[34] There are also some short studies and notes concerning the influence of Dante on

34. E. Benson, "Dante and Shakespeare," *Appleton Journal,* VII, 468 ff.; H. P. V. Bogue, *Paradise Lost and the Divine Comedy,* (New York, 1895); A. S. Cook, "Literary Genealogy of Tennyson's Ulysses," *Poet Lore,* III, 449–504; G. W. Cooke, "Browning's Interpretation of Romantic Love as Compared with That of Plato, Dante and Petrarch," *Poet Lore,* VI, 225 ff.; M. Hamilton, "Chaucer's Marcia Catoun," *Mod. Phil.,* XXX, 361 ff.; T. R. Lounsbury, "Chaucer's Obligation to Dante," *Studies in Chaucer,* II (New York, 1892), 236 ff.; J. L. Lowes, "Chaucer and Dante's *Convivio,*" *Mod. Phil.,* XIII, 19 ff.; XIV, 705 ff.; T. Spencer, "The Story of Ugolino in Dante and Chaucer," *Speculum,* IX, 295 ff.; K. McKenzie, "Echoes of Dante in Milton's Lycidas," *Italica,* XX (1943), 121–126; H. Matson, "Dante and Milton," *References for Literary Workers* (Chicago, 1892), pp. 273 ff.; F. N. Robinson, "Chaucer and Dante," *Journal of Comparative Literature,* I (1909), 192–247.

works or passages from works in Italian, French, Spanish, and German literatures.[35]

As yet, there has not been any work investigating the influence of Dante's thought and art on American literary development. This interesting problem has not been entirely ignored, however. There are already several essays, mostly by J. C. Mathews, on the attention given to Dante's works by such American poets and thinkers as Irving, Bryant, Poe, Whitman, Emerson, Hawthorne, and Longfellow, which seem to be preliminary explorations for a comprehensive work on this subject.[36]

Although there has been no American edition of the *Divine Comedy* published since Grandgent's, and therefore no general commentaries of the poem in this country, nevertheless many American Dantists have concerned themselves with the minute and detailed work of reinterpreting difficult passages of the *Divine Comedy* and solving minor problems of exegesis.

Last but not least, American Dantists have contributed not a few articles and notes dealing with grammatical, philological, and metrical questions in the *Divine Comedy* and other works of Dante. H. D. Austin has been the largest contributor to discussions of lesser problems of form and meaning of verbal terms and phrases

35. L. O. Kuhns, "Some Verbal Resemblances in the *Orlando Furioso* and the *Divine Comedy*," *Mod. Lang. N.*, X, 170–174; C. P. Merlino, "Equicola's Knowledge of Dante," *PMLA*, XLIII, 642–647; E. Schuyler, "Carducci and Dante," *The Nation*, XLVI, 133–134; R. J. Clements, "Marguerite de Navarre and Dante," *Italica*, XVIII, 37–50; A. S. Cook, "Comparisons: Dante, Inferno I, 80; Petrarch, Montaigne . . . ," *Rom. Rev.*, XII, 185–186; M. E. Temple, "Paraphrasing in *Livre de Paix* of Christine de Pisan of the Paradiso, III–V," *PMLA*, XXXVII, 182–186; G. H. Gerould, "The Gawain Poet and Dante," *PMLA*, LI, 31–36; H. J. Harvitt, "A Parallel Between *Le Roman de Flamenco* (vv. 2357–2383) and Dante's Purgatorio," *Rom. Rev.*, I, 57–63; J. D. M. Ford, "Dante's Influence upon Spanish Literature During the Fifteenth and Sixteenth Centuries," *Rep. Dante Soc.*, 1895 (prize essay); Chandler R. Post, "The Beginnings of the Influence of Dante in Castilian and Catalan Literature," *Rep. Dante Soc.*, 1907, pp. 1–59; Obershoff, "Bodmer Indebted to Dante," *Mod. Lang. N.*, XXXIX, 247–248; A. Steiner, "A Trace of Dante in Goethe's Ilmenau," *Mod. Lang. N.*, XLVIII, 86–87.

36. E. Goggio, "The Sources of Longfellow's Michelangelo," *Rom. Rev.*, XXV, 314–324; "Italian Influences on Longfellow's Works," *Rom. Rev.*, XVI, 204–222; "Emerson's Interest in Italy and in Italian Literature," *Italica*, XVII, 97–103; J. C. Mathews, "Washington Irving's Knowledge of Dante," *American Literature*, X (1939); "Bryant's Knowledge of Dante," *Italica*, XVI, 115 ff.; "Walt Whitman's Reading of Dante," *Univ. of Texas Studies in English*, 1939; "Emerson's Knowledge of Dante," *Univ. of Texas Studies in English*, 1942, pp. 171–192; "Hawthorne's Knowledge of Dante," *Univ. of Texas Studies in English*, 1940, pp. 157–175.

peculiar to Dante. A collection of his "Notes to the Divine Comedy" to 1940 [37] shows how valuable and important is this work of minute research when its results are put together. Some of his notes are grammatical or historical investigations; many more contain appropriate quotations from works used by old poets or by Dante himself, compiled as an aid in finding the exact meaning of words, phrases, or allusions in the *Divine Comedy;* others try to explain certain passages or allusions and ideas which are obscure, by following very sensitively the mental associations of Dante as he was writing.[38] No less important are many of the articles and notes of American scholars and Dante students, published during these last decades in American periodicals dedicated to the study of modern languages, literatures, and philology. This fragmentary literature of short notes and brief articles on Dante may seem unimpressive when one looks at single items. Its usefulness and value can be gauged only when it is considered in its entirety, as a constantly growing supplement to the existing commentaries on Dante's works, and thus providing new material for a better understanding of his thought, of the working of his mind, of his linguistic qualities and innovations, and indirectly for a fuller appreciation of his art.[39]

37. *PMLA,* LV (1940), 660–713.
38. *Italica,* XVIII (1941), 15.
39. R. Altrocchi, "The Story of Dante's Gianni Schicchi and Reynard's Legataire Universel," *PMLA,* XXII (1914), 200–224; "Dante and Tufail," *Italica,* XV, 125–128; "Three Coincidences in the *Divine Comedy,*" *Rep. Dante Soc.,* 1934, pp. 31–35; G. Altrocchi, "Dante and the Three Guidi Castles," *Thought,* 1931, pp. 370–398; E. Armstrong, "Dante in Relation to the Sports and Pastimes of His Age," *Mod. Lang. Rev.,* I (1906), 173 ff., 303 ff.; E. Auerbach, "St. Francis of Assisi in Dante's Comedia," *Italica,* XXII, 166–179; H. D. Austin, Notes on Dante published subsequently to his collection of 1941 (*PMLA,* LV, 660–713): "Dante's Guides in the Divine Comedy," *Rom. Rev.,* XXXIV, 71–74; "Beatrice's Eyes," *Mod. Lang. N.,* LIX, 466–468; "An Inheritance of Magic?" *Mod. Lang. N.,* LX, 324–325; "Dante Notes," *Rom. Rev.,* XXXVI, 257–265; A. R. Benham, "Two Notes on Dante," *Mod. Lang. N.,* XXII, 46; Angela L. Bianchini, "Ancora della Stella nell'uso dantesco," *Italica,* XIX, 56–60; G. Bonfante, "Ancora le tre fiere," *Italica,* XXII, 69–72; "Lucevan gli occhi suoi piu che la stella," *Italica,* XXI, 116; M. A. Buchanan, "Notes on Dante," *Transactions Royal Society* (Canada, 3d series), XXXVIII, 71–78; A. Camilli, "La Concubina di Titone antico, *Purg.* IX, 1–9; and Pia dei Tolomei, Purg. V, 135–136," *Italica,* XIV, 126; V. Cioffari, "A Dante Note: Heliotropium," *Rom. Rev.,* XXVIII, 59–62; A. S. Cook, "Dante, Purg. XXII, 67–69," *Rom. Rev.,* VII, 463; A. K. Coomaraswamy, "Two Passages in Dante's *Paradiso,*" *Speculum,* XI, 327–328; W. G. Curry, "The Bottom of Hell," *Mod. Lang. N.,* XXXVIII, 253; E. D. Ancona, "Dante and His American Friends in Florence," *Wellesley Magazine,* XXV, 192–195;

A. De Salvio, *The Rhyme Words in the Divina Commedia* (Paris, 1929); W. C. De Vane, "Sordello's Story Retold," *Stud. in Phil.*, XXVII, 1–24; J. S. Diekhoff, "The Milder Shades of Purgatory," *Mod. Lang. N.*, LIII, 409–410; W. L. Edward, "Dante's *Paradiso*, XXIV–XXVI," *PMLA*, IV, 24–40; J. D. M. Ford, "Dante: *Purgatorio*, XIII, 49 ff.," *Rom. Rev.*, I, 208–209; A. H. Gilbert, "The Paradox of Paradise," *Personalist*, IX, 100–112; "Can Dante's Inferno Be Charted?" *PMLA*, LX, 287–306; B. I. Gilman, "Dante's Choice of Terza Rima," *Rom. Rev.*, XX, 326 ff.; "On a Disputed Terzetto in the *Paradiso*," *Mod. Lang. N.*, XXVII, 148–149; C. Grimm, "A Note on the XX Canto of the *Inferno*," *Italica*, XIV, 87–89; George Hamilton, "The Pedigree of a Phrase in Dante," *Rom. Rev.*, XII, 84–89; G. B. Heberden, "Dante's Lyrical Metres: His Theory and Practice," *Mod. Lang. Rev.*, III; E. G. Hills, "Dante's Versification," *Rom. Rev.*, III, 301–308; V. F. Hooper, "Geryon and the Knotted Cord, Inf. XVI, XVII," *Mod. Lang. N.*, LI, 445–449; D. Internoscia, "Purgatory: A Note to Canto XII, 94–96," *Phil. Quart.*, XV, 384–390; O. M. Johnston, "Interpretation of the First Canto of Dante's *Divine Comedy*," *Phil. Quart.*, V, 35–43; "The Ugolino Episode," *Rom. Rev.*, XIX, 328–331; "Dante's Comparison Between the Seven Planets and the Seven Liberal Arts," *Rom. Rev.*, XXI, 34–35; "Amount of Knowledge Attributed to the Spirits in Dante's *Inferno*," *Rom. Rev.*, XXV, 223–225; "Repetition of Words and Phrases at the Beginning of Consecutive Tercets in Dante's *Divine Comedy*," *PMLA*, XXIX, 427 ff.; Krappe, "Notes on Dante's *Inferno*," *Archivum Romanicum*, XI, 592–603; K. McKenzie, "The Problem of the Lonza, with an Unpublished Text," *Rom. Rev.*, I, 18–30; A. L. Mezzacappa, "Why God Resides in Heaven: A New Interpretation of *Purg.* XI, 2–3," *Italica*, XXI, 49–60; "The Preposition *A—Ab* and Its Use in the *Divine Comedy*," *PMLA*, LVII, 327–342; O. H. Moore, "The Infernal Council," *Mod. Phil.*, XVI, 169–194; H. L. Norman, "Cupid and Psyche: A Dantean Episode," *Italica*, XV, 120–124; L. Olschki, "Dante and Peter de Vinea," *Rom. Rev.*, XVII, 113–115; H. R. Patch, "The Last Line of the Commedia," *Speculum*, XIV, 56–65; "Three Mediaeval Ideas," *Smith College Studies in Modern Languages*, XXI, 159–173; J. L. Perrier, "Bertran de Born, Patriot and His Place in Dante's *Inferno*," *Rom. Rev.*, XI, 223–238; XII, 21–43; R. S. Phelps, "The Running Cue in Dante," *Mod. Lang. N.*, XXXVI, 144 ff.; J. S. P. Tatlock, "Another Parallel to the First Canto of the Inferno," *Rom. Rev.*, V, 90–93; "*Purgatorio* XI, 2–3, and *Paradiso* XIV, 30," *Rom. Review*, X, 274–276; "Mohammed and His Followers in Dante," *Mod. Lang. Rev.*, XXVII, 186–195; "Dante's Terza Rima," *PMLA*, LI, 895 ff.; K. E. Tilton, "Bibliography of the *De Vulgari Eloquentia*," *Italica*, XI, 117–121; Sister Rose, S.S.J., "Realistic Elements in Dante's *Vita Nuova*," *Mod. Lang. J.*, XXVIII, 413–421; Vera Sandomirski, "The New Russian Dante," *Italica*, XVIII, 117–119; I. J. Semper, *In the Steps of Dante and Other Papers* (Dubuque, 1941); A. H. Schutz, *"Re, Ri* in the *Divina Commedia*," *Mod. Phil.*, XXII, 379 ff.; K. C. M. Sills, "Another Word on Dante's Cato," *Mod. Lang. N.*, XX, 162–164; T. Silverstein, "The Passage of the Souls to Purgatory in the *Divine Comedy*," *Harvard Theological Review*, XXI, 53–63; "*Inferno*, XII, 100–126," *Mod. Lang. N.*, LI, 449–452; "The Weeping Statue and Dante's Gran Veglio," *Harvard Studies and Notes in Phil. and Lit.*, XIII, 165–184; "Il giusto Mardocio, *Purg.* XVIII, 29," *Mod. Lang. N.*, 188–190; D. L. Simons, "The Individual Human Dramatis Personae of the Divine Comedy," *Mod. Phil.*, XVI 1918), 371–380; C. S. Singleton, "Dante in the Divine Comedy," *Italica*, XVIII, 109–116; L. Spitzer, "Two Dante Notes," *Rom. Rev.*, XXXIV, 247–262; "Speech and Language in *Inferno*, XIII," *Italica*, XIX, 81–104; "The Farcical Elements in *Inferno*, XXI–XXIII," *Mod. Lang. N.*, LIX, 83–88; G. G. Walsh, "Dante's Matelda," *Thought*, XII, 76–101; L. Ulrich, "Dante in Germany," *Italica*, XVIII, 97–106; D. Vittorini, "Dante e Francesca da Rimini," *Italica*, X, 67–76; "La Corte del Cielo; Interpretazione del Canto II dell'Inferno," *Italica*, XX, 57–64; E. H. Wilkins, "The Living Dante," *Italica*, XXII, 40–58; "Dante's Scheme of Human Life," *Studies in Philology*, XVIII (Chapel Hill, 1921), 412–416; "The Invention of the Sonnet," *Mod. Phil.*, XIII, 463–494; "The Prologue of the *Divine Comedy*," *Rep. Dante Soc.*, 1926; "The Literal

Meaning of the Unveiling of Beatrice," *Italica*, XV, 110–111; "Dante and the Mosaics of His Bel San Giovanni," *Speculum*, II, 1–10; H. Wieruszowski, *"Ars Dictaminis* in the Time of Dante," *Mediaevalia et Humanistica*, Fasc. I, 95–108; "Art and Commune at the Time of Dante," *Speculum*, XIX, 14–33; C. Wright, "An Approach to Dante," *The Virginia Quarterly*, 1936, 523–567.

CHAPTER XIII

DANTE'S PORTRAITS AND ILLUSTRATIONS
OF THE *DIVINE COMEDY*

THE rediscovery in 1840 of Giotto's portrait of Dante in the Bargello of Florence, in which the American Richard H. Wilde had an active part,[1] was hailed as a great event by all Dante lovers. Once again Dante's real features were revealed to the world after having been hidden for almost three centuries under a heavy coat of whitewash in the former Chapel of St. Mary Magdalene in the Palazzo del Podesta.[2] According to an old tradition, Giotto had been a close friend of Dante; hence there was no doubt that the youthful profile of the portrait was that of Dante as he must have looked about the time of the *Vita Nuova*.

Unfortunately the Florentine painter Antonio Marini, who was given the task of removing the whitewash and restoring the picture, first ruined Dante's eye by the unskillful extraction of a nail, and then repainted the whole portrait, altering the lines and changing the expression of the face as well as the color of Dante's garments. By a stroke of fortune, however, an English artist Seymour Kirkup was able to trace the head on thin paper before it was damaged by the restorer, thus preserving the lines and proportions of the face. Kirkup also made a sketch in water color of the whole portrait as it had appeared originally. Another artist, the Florentine sculptor Fantoni, also made a sketch which, in the main, agrees with Kirkup's. When art historians speak of Giotto's portrait, they mean the likeness known through these sketches and not the actual figure in the Bargello which Marini ruined.

Many other pictures portray Dante in his maturer years with a

1. See above, p. 60.
2. The Palazzo del Podestà became in 1574 the headquarters of the Bargello (Police), and part of it was remodeled to serve as a prison. The chapel was divided horizontally by flooring and its walls were whitewashed.

grim face, lined by sorrow and toil. Some of them made by various artists of the fifteenth and sixteenth centuries were believed to be more or less faithful reproductions of the features of the poet in the last years of his life, preserved also in some death masks supposedly made in Ravenna before Dante's body was laid to rest in the little burying ground of the Church of San Francesco. At first no doubts were raised about the genuineness of the newly rediscovered Giotto's fresco and of its early date, but the authentic character of the death masks was occasionally challenged by some skeptics. New investigations of these and many other widely divergent portraits of Dante in paintings, sculptures, and illustrated manuscripts of his works made it clear that most of them were copied one from another or, more often, were imaginary portraits expressing the artist's idea of how Dante should have looked, but having no connection with any reliable tradition. Giotto's portrait itself was suspected and the death masks were denounced by many as late forgeries.[3] Was it possible to trace back through this maze of portraits or pseudo-portraits an original or originals which could be relied upon to have preserved for posterity the true likeness of Dante?

Charles E. Norton, in his essay "On the Original Portraits of Dante," [4] was firm in his belief that Giotto had painted the portrait of his friend from life between 1290 and 1300, and that the death masks, or rather the original mask from which others were modeled, was "taken from nature," because "the countenance and expression" of the face were "worthy of Dante." Norton's authority not only as a Dantist but also as art historian had so much weight in America that his conclusions were then accepted as final, and served as a guide to the writers of some articles on the subject which ap-

3. Giotto's authorship was denied by G. Milanesi and L. Passerini in "Del ritratto di Dante nella Cappella del Podestà in Firenze attribuito a Giotto," an official report of the Commission appointed by the Italian government to search for the most authentic portrait of Dante, published in the *Giornale del centenario,* 1864–65, Nos. 17, 37, 38. As late as 1900, the British Dantist E. Gardner was still of the same opinion and stated that it was "absolutely certain that the Bargello fresco was not a contemporary portrait nor painted by Giotto" (*The Story of Florence* [London, 1900], p. 222).

4. Privately printed in 1865 and then appended to the "Illustrations" to Longfellow's translation of the *Inferno* (1865) and to the translation of the whole *Divine Comedy* (1867).

peared in the American periodicals during the last decades of the century.[5]

Meanwhile, in Italy, Germany, and England the problem continued to be discussed and investigated from various angles. Many studies were published throwing much light especially on the dating of the most significant portraits or types of portraits of Dante.[6] But the first methodical survey of the problem as a whole, submitting all the evidence at hand to a detailed and exacting analysis, was the work of an American scholar, Richard Thayer Holbrook (1870–1934), in his book *Portraits of Dante*.[7]

Holbrook began by remarking that, though the problem of Dante iconography had been discussed for a long time, "the evidence has never before been completely presented by one author, nor by all together, and it has often been presented with so many errors and omissions as to befog what otherwise might have been clear and convincing." [8] The case, in his judgment, "was to be treated as a purely historical problem"; the aim was to discover "what the oldest authorities actually said and what they really meant by their statements about Dante's looks." The task of the author, then, was to make a minute study "of the oldest portraits from Giotto's to Raffael's, with the one main purpose of showing to what extent they can be trusted and what place they properly hold in Dante iconography." [9]

This task Holbrook fulfilled so well that his work superseded

5. Sarah F. Clark, "The Portrait of Dante," *Century Monthly Magazine,* XXVII (1884), 574–581 (mostly quotations from Norton's essay); W. F. Parsons, "The Portrait of Dante," *Catholic World,* LXXVIII (1904), 749–766. See M. Fowler's *Supplement to the Catalogue of the Cornell Dante Collection,* under "Iconography."

6. The most important were F. X. Kraus's *Dante: sein Leben und sein Werk* (Berlin, 1897), the most valuable contribution to the subject of Dante iconography made to that date; L. Volkmann's *Iconografia dantesca* (Leipzig, 1897) dealt briefly with about 115 illuminated manuscripts of Dante's works in 27 European libraries. From his research it was learned that there are some 800 manuscripts of Dante ranging from a few years after his death to the end of the Renaissance, many of which contain illustrations and miniature portraits of Dante. Also: A. Venturi, *Storia dell'arte italiana,* V (Milan, 1907).

7. R. T. Holbrook, *The Portraits of Dante, From Giotto to Raffael: A Critical Study, with a Concise Iconography; Illustrated After the Original Portraits* (London, Boston, and New York, 1911).

8. *Idem,* p. 4.

9. *Idem,* p. 5.

those of all his predecessors. His approach by the strictly historical method was highly praised by all the reviewers of his book, even by those who did not accept all his conclusions: "It is the first time within my knowledge that a genuine scientific method has been applied to the genealogy of a portrait," remarked Frank J. Mather.[10] Grandgent, who gave a compact synopsis of Holbrook's book, was no less outspoken in his appreciation of its method:

With persistent industry he has gathered together all the material that can throw light on the subject; he discusses fully and intelligently all the important likenesses down to 1512; and in a field where nearly everything is uncertain, and fancy is continually betraying critics into unwarranted conclusions, he habitually maintains a cautiously judicial attitude.[11]

Some of the conclusions reached by Holbrook at the end of the long trail which he had cleared so well of many thorny spots, in part confirmed old theories and traditions; others were new, based on new material, or on new interpretations of material already investigated. The final and most important result of the whole inquiry—the establishing of a genealogy of Dante portraits through a new classification of their various types—was Holbrook's own finding.

Giotto's authorship of the Bargello portrait was confirmed by historical evidence much stronger than any objection already raised,[12] but its date was finally assigned to the last years of Giotto's life, more precisely to a date between 1334 and 1336, after the fire of

10. F. J. Mather, Jr., "Dante Portraits," *Rom. Rev.,* III (1912), 117–122.

11. C. H. Grandgent, review of Holbrook's book, *Rom. Rev.,* III, (1912), 123–125. The book was also reviewed at length by the Italian Dantist E. G. Parodi (*BSDI*, New Series, XIX [1912], 89–106), who submitted to a careful scrutiny all the evidence on which Holbrook based his conclusions, and added some documents which Holbrook had missed. On the whole, Parodi agreed with Holbrook, except for some points in his reclassification of the portraits.

12. Especially the sonnet of Antonio Pucci, who, referring to the Bargello portrait, says, "This man clad in crimson dress . . . Giotto painted in the form of Dante." Pucci, born about 1300, was the town crier of Florence in the following 'thirties and probably had seen Giotto at work in the Chapel, and certainly could not have made a mistake in mentioning Giotto as the painter of the fresco. Holbrook, following A. D'Ancona (*In Lode di Dante, capitolo e sonetto di Antonio Pucci* [Pisa, 1868]), who first published the sonnet, gave much importance to this witness. There is a more faithful text of the sonnet in K. McKenzie, *Antonio Pucci, Le Noie* (Princeton, 1931), p. 59.

1332 which destroyed part of the building.[13] Since by this time Dante had been dead thirteen or more years, the portrait must have been made from memory, from description, or possibly from a previous sketch. Giotto had certainly met Dante in his youth, but there is no evidence that the two were bound by such a close friendship as many commonly thought. The only other portrait of Dante known to have been painted by an artist who may have known the poet in life, was that made by Taddeo Gaddi, a disciple and assistant of Giotto for many years. Unfortunately this portrait, which stood in the Church of Santa Croce in Florence, was destroyed in 1566 and we know nothing of it save that it was regarded as lifelike.

According to Holbrook's classification, next in line comes Dante's portrait, also in profile, in the Palatine manuscript,[14] which, he believes, is a copy, direct or indirect, of Giotto's fresco, although it makes Dante's face older. The resemblance of the two portraits, in Holbrook's judgment, is striking in spite of the differences, especially in the size of the eye, which is larger in the Palatine and smaller in Giotto's picture.[15] The Palatine portrait, or some unknown picture of the same type, was in its turn the source or model for the grim and tragic Dante of many other likenesses, most notably the famous bust of the poet in the Museum of Naples.

To the so-called death masks Holbrook dedicated a minute study strengthening the evidence against their genuineness already provided by previous inquirers. To this he added a historical survey of the art of making death masks, an art known in ancient times in

13. This late date had already been suggested on good evidence by F. X. Kraus (*op. cit.,* p. 171), by A. Venturi (*op. cit.,* V, 448), and by others.

14. Codex Palatinus 320, National Library of Florence, of unknown origin, but certainly of the fifteenth century (*ca.* 1450). The portrait, done with a quill in water color, covers the whole page.

15. Boccaccio, in his *Life of Dante,* written about 1363 or 1364, described him as follows: "His face was long, his nose aquiline, and his eyes rather big than small. His jaws were large; and his lower lip protruded. His complexion was dark, his hair and beard thick, black and curly and his expression ever melancholy and thoughtful" (Holbrook's translation, p. 16). But in Giotto's profile-portrait, as seen in Kirkup's tracing, the eye is small. This fact seems to contradict the derivation from Giotto of the Palatine portrait which agrees with Boccaccio's description. This discrepancy between the latter and Giotto's fresco is difficult to explain away. (Cf. Holbrook, pp. 18 ff.) The question of Dante's beard mentioned by Boccaccio, while all his portraits are beardless, and of the color of his hair, which according to Boccaccio was black, while Dante in one of his Latin Eclogues seems to say that it was tan (*flaventia*), are not easily solved either.

Egypt and Greece and mentioned by Pliny in his *Natural History,* but one which seems to have been lost or to have ceased to be practiced long before Dante's death. It was later revived by Andrea del Verrocchio (1435–88), who, according to Vasari, knew how to make plaster (*gesso*) out of a soft stone found near Volterra. Later in his time, says Vasari, "they began to model the heads of dead persons, at little cost; so that now (about 1545) one may see in every house in Florence no end of such portraits." There is no evidence that this art was either understood or practiced in Dante's time. Following the conclusions reached by C. Ricci,[16] Holbrook held that the Torrigiani death mask, the best of all of them, has the same type of face which we find more delicately executed and in a slightly different pose in the bust of Naples. There seems to be some evidence suggesting that the Torrigiani mask, or the model of it, and of all other masks, was made by Tullio Lombardi at the time Dante's tomb in Ravenna was rebuilt and embellished in 1483.

The Naples bust of Dante, a real artistic masterpiece, was the work of a great but unknown fifteenth-century sculptor of the school of Donatello, and is in part an imaginary portrait, in part inspired by the same type of face as in the Palatine portrait. It also relies somewhat upon Boccaccio's description of Dante's features. All other supposed Dante portraits are either composite derivations and alterations of this type—as, for example, those painted by Raphael in the Vatican—or, more often, fanciful portraits of no value to the study of Dante iconography.

Holbrook's handsome book, copiously and beautifully illustrated, also contains a "Descriptive Catalogue" of all portraits of Dante, ancient and modern, whether paintings and sculptures, or drawings found in manuscripts and books down to the nineteenth century, and gives at the end the most complete bibliography of the subject up to that time.

Though all reviewers of Holbrook's book recognized that it was and would remain a fundamental work for further studies of the subject, objections to some of his conclusions, especially to his genealogical tree of the portraits, were raised by several scholars and art historians. The most cogent criticism came from another

16. Corrado Ricci, *L'Ultimo Rifugio* (Milano, 1891), pp. 280 ff.

American who was a humanist as well as an art historian, Frank Jewett Mather of Princeton University.[17] Holbrook's main contention that there was "a single root for all Dante's likenesses, namely Giotto's portrait of the Bargello," and hence that this is our only real evidence of how Dante looked, and that this is the only source from which all other portraits, excluding fanciful ones, are derivative, was thought by Mather to be wholly unsound. Between Giotto's youthful and serene portrait and the later gaunt and grim Dante of the Naples bust there is a gap which cannot be explained by a gradual aging process evolved from Giotto's picture.

Mather's fundamental criticism of Holbrook's work is that in dealing with iconography and works of art the historical method, though excellent and indispensable as far as it goes, is not altogether sufficient. To the evidence obtained by this method must be added the evidence provided by the analysis of the art historian, which is based on style and other elements of art criticism; and the results of the two methods should check each other. "Iconography, which is really a branch of art history is, unhappily, nearly always treated as a department of biography or general history; the result is that portrait histories abound in blunders that a tyro in the history of art would avoid."

As a matter of fact, Holbrook had not merely overlooked this other source of evidence but had deliberately discarded it as a "method of clairvoyants" and "extremely delusive." Even if "the mystery called style," he said, could be brought within the scope of scientific inquiry, " our primary sources of knowledge as to the age and authorship of ancient works of art, must still be written evidence." [18] This knowledge may be increased by internal evidence; but this evidence is supplied not by "style and manner," as is held by art critics who regard their personal impressions as demonstrating something about any old painter, but only by the subject and the scene, or, in general, the content of the work under study. For instance, by his analysis of some of the details of Giotto's portrait, such as the cluster of unidentified fruit which Dante holds, and by the three colors—red, white, and green—in which he is clad,

17. Article in *Rom. Rev.* quoted above.
18. Holbrook, *op. cit.*, p. 114.

Holbrook draws the conclusion that Giotto had in mind the "dolci pomi" and the tricolored garments of Beatrice described in the *Purgatorio,* and hence that Giotto must have been well acquainted with the *Divine Comedy* when he painted Dante's portrait. This would be, of course, further evidence against the early date formerly assigned to Giotto's fresco.[19]

Going still further, Mather gave in his article many reasons why Holbrook's derivation of all Dante portraits from Giotto's fresco could not be accepted. He made much of the details in which the Palatine portrait and those of the fifteenth century differ from Giotto's, remarking that "it is precisely such trifles that denote an iconographic tradition." Above all, Giotto's poet of the *Vita Nuova* did not correspond to the Florentine notion of the stern poet of the *Divine Comedy.* "In the Renaissance, as now, Dante was to the average Italian simply the poet of the Inferno. . . . the demand was for a tragic Dante and the painters properly betook themselves to an original containing tragic possibilities." This original was the now lost portrait painted by Taddeo Gaddi in a Franciscan miracle on the choir-screen of the Church of Santa Croce. Mather's problem, then, was to find evidence proving that, while Gaddi's original portrait is lost, there are in the extant Dante iconography of the fifteenth century copies or derivations from it which establish the link of connection between Gaddi's and such later portraits as the Naples bust. According to him, the portrait of the Palatine manuscript was such a connecting link.[20]

Mather, who had made at that time a special study of Taddeo

19. That Giotto, a friend of Dante, praised in the *Divine Comedy* as the foremost artist of the times, read the poem may be taken for granted, a priori, even if we did not have any other evidence. But obviously this conclusion would be far from certain if we had to depend only on this more than questionable "internal evidence" from Giotto's fresco offered by Holbrook.

20. Independently of Mather, E. G. Parodi in his review of Holbrook's book, cited above, and in an article in the *Marzocco* (Florence, July 26, 1912) had expressed, though more cautiously than Mather, the same view: "It is permissible to imagine that the Palatine miniature had, I will not say as its original, but as its point of departure, the portrait by Gaddi." Giotto's portrait, though famous until Vasari's time, was "singularly without influence." Mather attributes this strange fact "partly to the fact that the little chapel of the Podestà was not a place of public worship, or resort, and partly to the fact that people habitually thought of Dante as the austere poet of the Inferno." Gaddi's portrait, on the contrary, was in one of the most popular churches of Florence and its expression was more austere than Giotto's. (Mather, *op. cit.,* p. 119.)

Gaddi's works, based the evidence which he offered summarily in his article mostly on style, manner, and other details marking the Palatine portrait as a copy or imitation of Gaddi's. Later on, in his book *The Portraits of Dante*,[21] he took up the whole problem in detail and added other and more valuable evidence in support of his new classification of Dante portraits.

In 1865 Dante's bones, which had been hidden near his tomb at Ravenna, were rediscovered.[22] A committee of physicians was appointed to examine and measure them. These measurements, especially those of the skull, had been used by Holbrook and others primarily to disprove the genuineness of the death masks. Mather was the first to exploit these measurements scientifically and to the full in an analysis of the Dante portraits worth considering. With the assistance of men of science he reconstructed Dante's skull from the measurements and then he placed its outline over the portraits. It was thus discovered that the lines of the skull corresponded with a remarkable degree of accuracy to those of the head of Giotto's fresco, but still more closely to those of the head of the Palatine portrait, except for a rather strange curtailment of the occiput, a defect which, according to Mather, is to be found also in other heads painted by Gaddi. This evidence and others from various sources confirmed Mather's conclusions as to the derivation of the Palatine portrait. Gaddi's portrait and not Giotto's was the original from

---

21. F. J. Mather, *The Portraits of Dante, Compared with the Measurements of His Skull and Reclassified,* "Princeton Monographs in Art and Archaeology," X (Princeton Univ. Press, 1921).

22. The story is told in detail by C. Ricci, *op. cit.,* pp. 388 ff. Mather summarized it as follows: "On May 27, 1865, certain masons working in a close adjacent to the Church of San Francesco in Ravenna accidentally hit a coffin on which there was written in Latin: 'Dante's bones again inspected, 3 June, 1677.' Then Dante's tomb was opened and found empty. Indeed for nearly three hundred fifty years the shrine had been empty. What had happened was this: After negotiations repeated through the fifteenth century to recover the ashes of her exiled poet, Florence found in the election of the Medici Pope, Leo X, the necessary political support. In 1519 he ordered Ravenna to surrender the skeleton to Florence. The plan was thwarted by the friars who had the custody of the tomb. Cutting through the inside wall against which the sarcophagus stood, they removed the bones and buried them secretly. In this hurried translation, a few small bones were left in the sarcophagus and the lower jaw was lost. For a hundred and fifty years the friars seem to have had the custom of occasionally verifying their treasure. After the last inspection recorded on the coffin in 1677, the memory of the affair seems to have died out in the convent. There remained only the persistent rumor at Ravenna that Dante's tomb was empty." (Mather, *The Portraits of Dante,* p. 3).

which evolved the stern Dante of the iconographic tradition which
culminated in the bust of the Museum of Naples.

While Mather's book was on the press during the sexcentenary
year of Dante's death (1921), a new commission was appointed by
the Italian government and the city of Ravenna to reëxamine the
bones of Dante. This time the work was assigned to a competent
group of scientists under the direction of Dr. Fabio Frassetto, professor of anthropology at the University of Bologna. From the
reports published by this commission it appeared that the measurements made in 1865 were inaccurate and incomplete.[23] How was
Mather's theory affected by the new discovery? An excellent synopsis of Frassetto's report and of his conclusions concerning Dante's
iconography has been given by Rudolph Altrocchi,[24] and from it
we learn that the difference between the measurements used by
Mather and the new ones did not invalidate the essential points of
Mather's theory; indeed they provided a final confirmation of its
results concerning the Palatine portrait, or rather Gaddi's original,
as the prototype of the gaunt tragic Dante of the fifteenth century
and after. Frassetto suggested most ingeniously that the curtailed
occiput of the Palatine portrait was caused in Gaddi's original by
the fact that the back of Dante's head was covered by the face of
the figure on his left in the group picture. But, contrary to the
opinion of Holbrook, Mather, and others, Frassetto, from the remarkable correspondence of Giotto's fresco with the new measurements, inferred that it was made from life and not from memory
many years after Dante's death. Of course, since the historical evidence against the early date of the fresco is overwhelming, the
solution of this difficulty may be found in the compromise, already
suggested by art historians, that Giotto may have been guided by a
sketch of Dante taken from life years before.

In conclusion, the works of Holbrook and Mather must be given
full credit for having set the problem of Dante iconography on

---

23. "Ricognizione delle ossa di Dante (28–31 Ottobre, 1921)," *Atti della R. Accademia
dei Lincei,* Fifth Series, XVII (1923), 3–20; also *Rendiconti* of the same Academy, Fifth
Series, XXX, 364–368; and F. Frassetto, *Dantis ossa: La Forma corporea di Dante* (Uni-
versità di Bologna, 1933).

24. R. Altrocchi, "The Present Status of Dante Iconography," *Italica,* XII (1935), 106–
115.

the sound basis of the historical method and of a method of art criticism relying not merely on individual impressions of style and manner, but also on scientific evidence such as that provided by Dante's remains in his Ravenna tomb. Although much has been written already on this subject and new studies on points of detail or new discoveries may be made, the works of these two American scholars, Holbrook and Mather, will always remain fundamental for the study of Dante iconography.

R. Altrocchi is also the author of a valuable monograph on "Michelino's Dante," [25] a painting hanging in the north aisle of the Cathedral of Florence "where, in a dim light that is quasi darkness, it has been seen by everybody for four hundred years but studied by nobody." It was painted by an obscure artist, Domenico di Michelino, in 1465, and represents Dante standing at the gates of Florence looking over the city, with the three realms of after-life from the *Divine Comedy* sketched in the background. Dante's face has no character: "the expression is that of a querulously old spinster somewhat anaemic." [26] It has nothing in common with either Giotto's fresco or the Palatine portrait. Probably, as Holbrook had suggested, it is a bad imitation of the picture of Dante by Andrea del Castagno made between 1435 and 1457. Altrocchi, who had an opportunity to examine the painting closely from a scaffold, found that its main interest consists in the panorama of the city of Florence which the painter seems to have reproduced faithfully as it was at that time. Thus it is a valuable document for the study of the topography of the city and of several important monumental buildings of that period.

There are in American museums several old portraits of Dante in painting [27] and many more of them in prints and old editions of

25. *Speculum,* VI (1931), 15–59. Reprinted in a revised form under the title "Feather Duster in the Cathedral" in his book *Sleuthing in the Stacks* (Harvard Univ. Press, 1944).
26. *Idem,* p. 189.
27. These portraits are thus described by Mather (*The Portraits of Dante,* pp. 80 ff.): *Gardner Museum* in Boston: Pesellino's Dante (*ca.* 1450), in a *cassone* front representing the Triumph of Fame as described by Petrarch; Dante's face is grim and old with a protruding under lip; it is probably based on the Riccardian miniature or its original. *Harvard Dante,* Fogg Art Museum: panel painting by Giovanni dal Ponte (*ca.* 1440), with a straight nose, and toothless; this head or one like it should be the exemplar of Signorelli's portrait. *Yale Dante:* probably after Bronzino's portrait. Dante holds a book in right hand,

Dante's works in American Dante collections.[28] None of them, however, is of any great importance for the history of Dante iconography.[29] In one of them, a panel painting attributed to Giovanni dal Ponte (*ca.* 1440), now at Harvard, Dante is represented in the act of receiving a laurel crown from a genius and standing opposite another poet who wears a laurel crown on his head. Mather had identified the second poet as Virgil, but F. Mason Perkins[30] suggested that the figure was Petrarch. This suggestion was approved by Holbrook and taken up for more detailed discussion by E. K. Rand.[31] Noting that the second figure stands with a humble expression on his face before the stern and solemn Dante, and knowing from other works of dal Ponte that he was fond of allegorical subjects, Rand suggested that the painting may have also a symbolic meaning:

The look that Dante directs at Petrarch is one of dignity not untouched with reproof. In the look of Petrarch there is something like dismay—at any rate, something of doubt and self-reproach. The manner in which he is holding his book is not one of utter confidence in the permanent value of its contents. In short, the painting has a larger idea than merely the meeting of the two poets. I would suggest that the larger subject of

a direct derivation of Michelino's Dante. *Cleveland Art Museum:* oil painting on panel, a nearly contemporary copy of Vasari's Dante.

28. W. C. Lane, "Note on the Portraits of Dante in the Harvard Collection," in *The Dante Collection in the Harvard College and Boston Public Library* (Cambridge, 1890); T. W. Koch, *Hand-List of Framed Reproductions of Pictures and Portraits Belonging to the Dante Collection in Cornell University* (Ithaca, 1909). In the Library of the University of Pennsylvania there is an Album containing drawings by Kirkup (mostly relating to Dante).

29. E. H. Wilkins ("The Jackson Dante," *Italica,* XX [1943], 1–3) relates how in 1936 he received as a gift from Miss Margaret H. Jackson, formerly professor of Italian at Wellesley College, a marble bas-relief of Dante made by her father John A. Jackson, an American sculptor (1825–79), who lived for many years and died in Florence. According to Miss Jackson, her father, in 1853, while there was a staging up in the Bargello chapel, was permitted to make a tracing of the head of Dante. From it he made the bas-relief. In Wilkins' judgment "the lines of this Dante relief correspond very closely to those of the Kirkup drawing, more closely than to the lines of the Fantoni drawing, and far more closely than to the lines of the head as restored by Marini. . . . I think it fair to say that the Jackson Dante ranks with the Arundel print as being one of the most beautiful recreations of Giotto's portrait."

30. "A Florentine Double Portrait at the Fogg Museum," *Art in America,* June, 1931.

31. "Dante and Petrarch in a Painting of Giovanni dal Ponte," *Fogg Art Museum Notes,* January, 1933.

the picture is the contrast of Sacred and Profane Poetry with Dante and Petrarch as their representative exemplars.

It had been noticed that in Michelangelo's "Last Judgment" there is one figure among the saints who surround Christ done in profile and strongly reminiscent of Dante. E. H. Wilkins discussed the evidence for and against this identification and came to the conclusion that it was more than doubtful.[32] More recently, during the restorations of the Sistine Chapel undertaken during the reign of Pius XI, a closer examination of enlarged photographs of the head of the figure has strengthened the opinion that the profile and the head gear resemble those of the Dante portraits by Giotto and Vasari.[33]

From the very beginning, manuscripts of the *Divine Comedy* were adorned with miniatures reproducing figures and scenes from the poem. It was not long before great artists attempted illustrations and pictures. Then came engravers and artists who have decorated printed editions up to the present day. The history of this iconography is now well known from two monumental works of Corrado Ricci.[34]

The great popularity that Dante enjoyed in England during the nineteenth century is evidenced by the names of one hundred and eighty artists, either English or living in England, which Paget Toynbee listed in his catalogue [35] as having produced sculptures, paintings, drawings, and engravings of subjects taken from the works of Dante or in some way connected with Dante between 1745 and 1919. No similar catalogue has been made for America, and probably there is no need for one, since little has been done along this line.

Some of the early American reprints of Cary's translations reproduced a few of Flaxman's illustrations; Longfellow's first editions reproduced illustrations by Doré. A recent new edition of

32. "Supposed Portrait of Dante in Michelangelo's Last Judgment," *Rep. Dante Soc.*, 1917, pp. 32–36.

33. B. Nogara, *Rivista pontificia d'archeologia christiana*, X (1934), 3 ff.

34. C. Ricci, *La Divina Commedia illustrata nei luoghi, nelle persone e nelle cose* (3 vols. Milan, 1921); *La Divina Commedia nella figurazione artistica e nel secolare commento* (Turin, 1934).

35. "Dante in English Art," *Rep. Dante Soc.*, 1921.

Melville B. Anderson's translation of the *Divine Comedy* is illustrated by thirty-two drawings made by the English artist William Blake about 1793 and now printed for the first time.[36] But in this matter every lover of Dante would prefer some faithful reproductions of Dante's own mental pictures of the figures and scenes that he described in words. Unfortunately the artist able to perform such a task has not yet appeared.

H. D. Austin discussed the subject from the point of view of the practical and pedagogical value of illustrations reproducing Dante's mental pictures, and gave some suggestions concerning graphic elucidations of the text of the *Comedy*.[37] The subject had been approached long before this, but from the artistic point of view, by Bernard Berenson, art historian and critic, in an article written for the *Nation*.[38] Dante, says Berenson, could not have had the knowledge of ancient art which we have today, and his visual images of a scene taking place in Greece, Rome, or Judea would differ greatly from our own. A fourteenth-century illustrator makes Virgil look like a medieval scholar, and there is no reason to believe that Dante's conception of him was not the same. Dante's visual images of the virtues of the heavenly hosts, of Christ, of the Virgin, of St. Francis, could not have been different from Giotto's. In an art lover like Dante, visualization is largely determined by the works of art with which one is intimately acquainted. It is Giotto, Duccio, Simone Martini, Lorenzetti, who enable us to form a clear conception of Dante's visual images. Luca Signorelli's illustrations in Orvieto, although his visual images are more modern than medieval, are still much nearer to Dante's than our own, and they have great interest as visual images suggested by Dante. Michelangelo's attitude is quite modern, and his visual images give no clue to Dante's. As interpretations, however, they are invaluable; his genius is akin to Dante's in kind and quality. Botticelli's sketches are hardly to be considered as having any value as interpretations of

36. *The Divine Comedy of Dante Alighieri*, "Translated into English by Melville B. Anderson, with Notes and Elucidations by the Translator, an Introduction by Arthur Livingston and 32 drawings by William Blake now printed for the first time" (New York, The Heritage Press, 1944).
37. "Some Thoughts About Illustrating the Commedia," *Italica*, XVII, 104 ff.
38. "Dante's Visual Images and His Early Illustrators," *The Nation*, LVIII (1894), 82 ff.

Dante. According to Berenson, an illustrated edition of the *Divine Comedy* could best serve its purpose if it contained a judicious selection from the works of the best artists of the fourteenth and fifteenth centuries, as well as from some of the miniatures in the manuscripts of Dante's works.

In an article on "Botticelli's Illustrations of the *Divine Comedy*," [39] Berenson attributed Botticelli's failure to convey the chill despair of the *Inferno,* the hope and convalescence of the *Purgatorio,* and the sublimity of the *Paradiso* to two reasons. Botticelli failed "partly because his genius was not at all Dantesque, but chiefly because the poem of Dante does not lend itself to satisfactory illustration." Why does it not? Because Dante is not a great epic or dramatic poet. As a poet, Dante is great as a master of the lyric, or (to make a concession) of the dramatic-lyric. Berenson was living in Italy, and since that was the period in which Croce and the new school of aesthetics appeared, it is not surprising that his statement reflected in part the views on Dante criticism based on the aesthetic premises of this school. [40]

G. A. Borgese, [41] on the contrary, is of the opinion that, should there be a contest among all the commentators and illustrators of the *Divine Comedy* in these six centuries, there would be many votes cast in favor of Botticelli's drawings. The reason why so many artists have been misled is "their obduracy of subjecting the *Comedy* to patterns of style which were alien to it; chiefly to the pre-romantic and romantic pattern in the individualized portrayal of characters."

According to Borgese, any attempt to reconstruct Dante's own visual images is destined to failure as long as artists ignore certain facts. Dante is certainly nearer to Byzantine art than to the art of the Renaissance; and yet "with the antennae of his searching sensibility he was able to anticipate some of the coming trends," indeed

39. *The Nation,* LXIII (1896), 363 ff., written as a review of F. Lippman's *Drawings of Botticelli for Dante's Divine Comedy* (London and New York, 1896).

40. Zoltán Haraszti's "The Botticelli Dante and Other Fifteenth Century Books," *More Books,* XVIII, 96–121, is a detailed account of the making of the edition of the *Divine Comedy* of 1481 (with facsimile).

41. G. A. Borgese, "On Dante Criticism," *Rep. Dante Soc.,* 1936, p. 69.

"a precognition of modern taste looms over the *Inferno*." In the main, however, the *Inferno* is of another age; the *Purgatorio* is fully the contemporary of Giotto; and the *Paradiso* suggests the art of Beato Angelico in the late fifteenth century.

The merit of Botticelli's drawings consists in the fact that he did not care to illustrate outstanding episodes or to portray heroes of the *Comedy:*

Botticelli insists, as it was in the spirit of the poet and the poet's age, on collective staging and straight symmetries of attitudes. Canto after canto, canticle after canticle, the three real personages emerge from the choral throngs: Dante, Beatrice, and Virgil. The poet reaches his new *Vita Nuova,* eternal and infinite, to which he has battled his way through hardship and horror. More and more airy and elate, as his Dante climbs beside Virgil to the top of the holy mount and soars after his beloved one to the Empyrean, the painter unfolds in lines the final, unitary sweetness of the story and the feeling of the myth and the rhythm.[42]

Ideas and emotions akin to these attributed to Botticelli by Borgese seem to have flashed through the mind of Norman Bel Geddes a few years before. They assumed a concrete theatrical form in his *Project for a Theatrical Presentation of the Divine Comedy of Dante Alighieri,* Foreword by Max Reinhardt, Photography by Francis Bruguière (New York, Theatre Art Inc., 1924). On a gigantic circular stage hundreds of feet wide and deep, with towers rising seventy-five feet above, the other-worldly drama unfolds in mass movements of a chorus five hundred strong, out of which emerge the three principals, Dante, Virgil, and Beatrice. Not only in lines as in Botticelli's drawings, but in colors, lights, sounds, and motions, this dramatic visualization of the *Comedy* aims to give the feeling of the myth and the rhythm of Dante's battling through horrors and his final soaring after Beatrice in the empyrean. Light is one of the main elements of expression. In the *Inferno* it comes from the bottom of the funnel-shaped pit; in the *Purgatorio* it comes from the rear in silhouette, and then it rises until it comes from above and from all sides, flattening all relief and eliminating shadows to give a feeling of unending space:

42. *Ibid.*

It should be like looking at millions of stars on a clear night only it should not be night. At the very end, when the light reaches an apparent maximum intensity, Dante exclaims: "O abundant Grace, by the Eternal Light, let my sight be consumed!" and simultaneously the light is directed into the audience dazzling them for an instant. Then darkness. Gradually a soft glow returns. The place where the stage was is a dark void. This is the end. With the cold rigid dignity of the last few moments must come an appalling sense of vastness beyond the earth and indefinable.

Unfortunately this grandiose project was never put into execution and we are left wondering whether the flight of a robust modern artistic imagination supported by the almost limitless resources of modern scientific technique would have been able to express Dante's spirit at least better than such spectacular films of Hollywood which have tried to give a dramatic visualization of the creative spirit of modern man, of his myths and the broken rhythm of his life.

CONCLUSION

THE British critics who in the early nineteenth century denounced the lack of originality in American literature as "a feeble echo of antiquated opinions current in the old world," and who rebuked the American journals for being "as innocent of giving countenance to innovations as if Prince Metternich were their editor," were not at all pessimistic in their views concerning the future of intellectual life in America. One of those critics was credited by the *North American Review* (XXXI [1830], 22) with the emphatic statement that in time "America will produce men who appreciate the moral grandeur of her institutions and when these appear, her literature will become a fountain of light to the world." More modestly, William H. Prescott could foresee a rapid growth and wide expansion of American cultural life in all fields of knowledge, practical and theoretical, or as he put it "in every path of active and contemplative life," and "within the sphere of influences totally distinct from any in the old world."

Even a most benevolent critic might hesitate to think that American literature has now become "a fountain of light"; but no one will deny that in the growth and expansion of her cultural life America has more than fulfilled Prescott's expectation. In the brilliant and impressive pageant of American achievements in the realm of arts and sciences during the last century, the history of Dante studies holds a very modest place, but its significance as a reflection of the growth of modern American scholarship goes beyond the narrow limits of a special field of learning. In a larger connection, the introduction and growth of the study of Dante's works, the variations in the method of approaching them and in the reaction of the American mind to Dante's thought and art, reflect closely aspects and trends of the intellectual and spiritual history of American life in modern times.

The popularity of great works of literature produced in times and places remote from our own can only be sustained by dint of the sympathetic study of those times and places, and by persons who have a general background of culture and live intellectual interests. When a work of poetry like the *Divine Comedy* has gained recognition so as to be known, at least in a general way, by most persons of average culture, and when at a higher cultural level such a work is translated again and again into the current language and is made the object of special studies, of learned researches, of historical and critical inquiries, or, in other words, when it has become a part of the cultural tradition of a country, then it may be considered to have attained that degree of popularity that is consonant with its character. Within these limits, Dante has been and is still popular in America. But have we any reason to think that Dante will continue to hold his place in American cultural life in the years to come?

When Benedetto Croce's *The Poetry of Dante* appeared, some hasty American reader of the book thought that the Italian critic had condemned in their entirety, as altogether useless and even senseless exercises, all the labors of minute Dantean researches, especially those concerned with the interpretation of certain aspects or passages of the *Divine Comedy,* which form such a large part of modern literature on Dante. One of the reviewers of the book (Isaac Goldberg, "An Unconventional Tribute to Dante," *Boston Evening Transcript,* May 7, 1921) quoted Croce's denunciation of commentators and quibblers and then exclaimed gleefully:

What is to become of the Ph.D. type of mind and the Ph.D. type of instructor, when Croce sweeps away the fertile field in which they so long have delved? What is to become of such succulent theses as those that might have been entitled "An Enquiry into the Allegorical Symbols of Dante's Divine Comedy, with Special Reference to . . ."?

In reality Croce, who is himself much given to learned researches in literature, history and philosophy, states without ambiguity that all these erudite and minute inquiries into the allegory and symbolism of the *Divine Comedy,* into the topography of the three other-worldly regions, and similar questions, have their uses and at times are necessary to understand Dante's meaning, just as much as a good philological preparation is necessary for a serious study of his poem. There is no need of taking seriously the sneering remarks of the critic: the answer to his queries has been given by the impressive list of books, essays and other studies on Dante which have been published in America since 1921.

The fear that with the absolute prevalence of scientific interests and pursuits in American schools and institutions, Dante and not Dante alone, but all the great classics of literature, might in a not distant future disappear from the realm of American cultural traditions is to be greatly discounted as long as Dante and the classics have something important to contribute to, and a function to perform in, the intellectual life of the new American generations.

What their contribution and their function have been and will continue to be in our civilization has been forcefully described by George Santayana in the opening passage of his *Three Philosophical Poets,* with which we conclude our survey:

The sole advantage in possessing great works of literature lies in what they can help us to become. In themselves, as feats performed by their authors, they would have forfeited none of their truth or greatness if they had perished before our day. We can neither take away nor add to their past value or inherent dignity. It is only they, in so far as they are appropriate food and not poison for us, that can add to the present value and dignity of our minds. Foreign classics have to be retranslated and reinterpreted for each generation, to render their old naturalness in a natural way, and keep their perennial humanity living and capable of assimilation. Even native classics have to be reapprehended by every reader. It is this continual digestion of the substance supplied by the past that alone renders the insights of the past still potent in the present and for the future. Living criticism, genuine appreciation, is the interest we draw from year to year on the unrecoverable capital of human genius.

APPENDIX

Chronological List of Essays, Notes, and Bibliography Published in the
Annual Report of the Dante Society of Cambridge, Massachusetts, 1882–
1936.

The Reports of the Dante Society of Cambridge constitute the only
American periodical publication dealing exclusively with Dante.
Though it kept its original character of a modest bulletin of a small
association, it published in almost every issue essays and notes and extensive bibliographical compilations in the field of Dante studies. Since
no index of the Reports has been made up to the present, the following
chronological list of their content may be of some practical use to the
American students of Dante.

I. Annual Report, 1882: "Remarks of Mr. Norton at the Annual Meeting of
the Society, May 16, 1882" (a short commemoration of Longfellow).
II. 1883: "Le Vite di Dante e di Petrarca scritte da Leonardo Aretino (1426)"
(reprinted from the Italian edition of 1572).
III. 1884: "A List of Works Relating to Dante Printed in the United States
of America (1822–84)."
IV. 1885: C. E. Norton, ed., "Additional Notes on the *Divine Comedy* by
H. W. Longfellow."
V. 1886: James Russell Lowell, "Dante" (reprinted from *Appleton's Cyclo-
paedia*); Paget Toynbee, "Dante and the Lancelot Romance."
VI. 1887: William C. Lane, compiler, "Dante Bibliography for the Year
1886"; C. E. Norton, "Note on the First Edition of the *Comment* of
Benvenuto da Imola."
VII. 1888: William C. Lane, compiler, "Dante Bibliography for the Year
1887."
VIII. 1889: George R. Carpenter, "The Episode of the Donna Pietosa";
William C. Lane, compiler, "Dante Bibliography for the Year 1888."
IX. 1890: William C. Lane, compiler, "Dante Bibliography for the Year
1889."
X. 1891: William C. Lane, compiler, "Additions to the Dante Collection in
the Harvard College Library (1890–91)"; G. R. Carpenter, compiler,
"Documents Concerning Dante's Public Life."
XI. 1892: G. R. Carpenter, compiler, "Documents Concerning Dante's Pub-

lic Life," Part II; William C. Lane, compiler, "Additions to the Dante Collection, Harvard Library"; Lucy Allen Paton, "Dante's Personal Character."

xii. 1893: Edward Moore, "Dante's Obligations to the *De Officiis* in Regard to the Division and Order of Sins in the *Inferno";* William C. Lane, compiler, "Additions to the Dante Collection, Harvard Library."

xiii. 1894: William C. Lane, compiler, "Additions to the Dante Collection, Harvard Library"; Paget Toynbee, "Index of Proper Names in the Prose Works and *Canzoniere* of Dante."

xiv. 1895: C. E. Norton, "Illustrations of the *Divine Comedy* from the Chronicle of Fra Salimbene"; Edward Moore, "A Variant in the *Vita Nuova";* William C. Lane, compiler, "Additions to the Dante Collection, Harvard Library."

xv. 1896: Theodore W. Koch, "Dante in America."

xvi. 1897: Paget Toynbee, "Professor Rajna's Critical Text of the *De Vulgari Eloquentia";* William C. Lane, compiler, "Additions to the Dante Collection, Harvard Library."

xvii. 1898: Kenneth McKenzie, "Dante's Reference to Aesop"; William C. Lane, compiler, "Additions to the Dante Collection, Harvard Library."

xviii–xix. 1899–1900 (in one): Theodore W. Koch, "A List of Danteiana in American Libraries Supplementing the Catalogue of the Cornell Collection"; Paget Toynbee, "Index of Authors Quoted by Benvenuto da Imola in His *Commentary* of the *Divina Commedia:* A Contribution to the Study of the Sources of the *Commentary."*

xx. 1901: Theodore W. Koch, "An Anonymous Portrait of Dante"; C. E. Norton, "The Epitaph of Dietzmann, Landgrave of Thuringia, Ascribed to Dante"; G. L. Hamilton, "Notes on the Latin Translation of, and Commentary on, the *Divina Commedia,* by Giovanni da Serravalle."

xxi. 1902: Alain C. White, *"Translation of the Quaestio de Aqua et Terra,* and a Discussion of Its Authenticity"; C. H. Grandgent, "Seven Notes."

xxii. 1903: E. S. Sheldon, "The Concordance to Dante's Minor Italian Works"; J. B. Fletcher, "The Philosophy of Love of Guido Cavalcanti."

xxiii. 1904: William C. Lane, compiler, "Additions to the Dante Collection, Harvard Library."

xxiv. 1905: Paget Toynbee, "A Chronological List of English Translations from Dante, from Chaucer to the Present Day."

xxv. 1906: C. E. Norton, "Note on the Vocabulary of the *Vita Nuova";* Kenneth McKenzie, "Means and Ends in Making a Concordance, with Special Reference to Dante and Petrarch."

xxvi. 1907: Chandler R. Post, "The Beginnings of the Influence of Dante in Castilian and Catalan Literature."

xxvii. 1908: William C. Lane, compiler, "Additions to the Dante Collection, Harvard Library."

xxviii. 1909: William R. Thayer, "Professor Charles Eliot Norton"; Jefferson B. Fletcher, "George Rice Carpenter"; Ethel Dane Roberts, compiler, "American Dante Bibliography (1896–1908)."

xxix. 1910: Ernest H. Wilkins, "Methods in Making a Concordance"; Edward K. Rand, "The Latin Concordance of Dante and the Genuineness of Certain of His Latin Works"; Charles H. Grandgent, "Two Notes on the *Commedia"; Paget Toynbee, "An Unrecorded Seventeenth Century Version of the *Vita di Dante* of Leonardo Bruni."

xxx. 1911: Roger T. Lafferty, "The Philosophy of Dante."

xxxi. 1912: Ralph H. Keniston, "The Dante Tradition in the Fourteenth and Fifteenth Centuries."

xxxii. 1913: Louis Dyer, "A Letter Concerning Dante's Conception of Fortune"; Margaret Jackson, "Bibliographical Notes on the Manuscripts of Boccaccio's *Life of Dante* and the Compendium, Together with the *Canzoniere* in the Plympton Collection of the Library of Wellesley College."

xxxiii. 1914: Edward K. Rand, "Dante and Servius"; Howard R. Patch, "The Goddess Fortuna in the *Divine Comedy.*"

xxxiv. 1915: Charles E. Whitmore, "The Lyrics of Fazio degli Uberti in Their Relation to Dante"; E. H. Wilkins, "Three Dante Notes."

xxxv. 1916: William C. Lane, compiler, "Additions to the Dante Collection, Harvard Library."

xxxvi. 1917: Paget Toynbee, "History of the Letters of Dante from the Fourteenth Century to the Present Day."

xxxvii. 1918: C. H. Grandgent, "The Choice of a Theme"; E. H. Wilkins, *"Il Chi e il Quale."*

xxxviii. 1919: Paget Toynbee, "Dante in English Art."

xxxix–xli. 1920–23 (in one; published in 1924): Henry Johnson, tr., "The Lyrics of the *Vita Nuova"; Emilio Goggio, "Longfellow and Dante."

xlii–xliv. 1924–26 (in one): E. H. Wilkins, "The Prologue of the *Divine Comedy"; C. H. Grandgent, "Quid Ploras?"; Paget Toynbee, "The Oxford Dante."

xlv–xlvi. 1927–28 (in one): C. H. Grandgent, "Vele di Mar."

xlvii–xlviii. 1929–30 (in one): C. H. Grandgent, "The Pentateuch and the *Divine Comedy"; William C. Lane, "Correspondence Between Charles E. Norton and the Hon. William W. Vernon"; Ambrogio Donini, "Appunti per una Storia del Pensiero di Dante in Rapporto al Movimento Gioachimita."

XLIX–LI. 1931–33 (in one): Kenneth McKenzie, "Observations on Dante's Lyrical Poems"; C. H. Grandgent, "A Prototype of the *Convivio*"; Rudolph Altrocchi, "Three Coincidences in the *Divine Comedy*."

LII–LIV. 1934–36 (in one): J. E. Shaw, "Dante and Bonagiunta"; G. A. Borgese, "On Dante Criticism."

The publication of the Annual Report was discontinued in 1937. In its place the Society has published a series of short studies on Dante:

1938: J. E. Shaw, "The Lady Philosophy in the Convivio."

1939: J. G. Fucilla, "Forgotten Danteana. A Bibliographical Supplement."

1940: V. Cioffari, "The Conception of Fortune in the Works of Dante."

1944: V. Cioffari, "Fortune in Dante's Fourteenth Century Commentators."

INDEX OF NAMES